The Handbook of
SKIING

The Handbook of
SKIING
Karl Gamma

ALFRED A. KNOPF, NEW YORK, 1981

The Handbook of Skiing was conceived, edited and designed
by Dorling Kindersley Limited, 9 Henrietta Street, London WC2E 8PS

Editor Alan Buckingham **Art editor** Denise Brown
Assistant editor Jemima Dunne **Designer** Nick Harris

Technical editor Brigitta Haidinger
Managing editor Amy Carroll **Art director** Debbie Mackinnon
Consultant for American edition Peter Miller

First published by PELHAM BOOKS LTD 1981

THIS IS A BORZOI BOOK
PUBLISHED BY ALFRED A. KNOPF, INC.

Library of Congress Cataloging in Publication Data

Gamma, Karl.

The handbook of skiing.

Includes index.
1. Skis and skiing. 1. Title.
GV854.G28   1981   796.93   81-47486
ISBN 0-394-51827-6   AACR2

Contents

Introduction   **6**

Ski equipment   **16**

Ski clothes and accessories   18
Skis   22
Ski poles   27
Boots   28
Bindings   32

Ski techniques   **36**

Putting on skis   40
Standing on skis   42
Turning around on the flat   46
Walking on skis   48
Falling   50
Getting up from a fall   52
Walking uphill on skis   54
Kick turning   58
Skiing down the fall line   60
Snowplowing   64
Traversing   72
Side-slipping   76
Snowplow turning   82
Skating   90
Step turning   94
Stem turning   96
Parallel uphill turning   100
Parallel turning   104
Short swinging   112
Absorption-extension
techniques   120
Jump turning   130
Terrain jumping   132
Stepping techniques   136

Competition skiing   **144**

Special slalom racing   146
How slalom courses are set   148
Giant slalom racing   150
Slalom techniques   152
Downhill racing   156

Ski jumping   **160**

Freestyle skiing   **164**

Ballet   166
Freestyle mogul skiing   170
Aerials   174

Ski mechanics   **178**

How turns are initiated   182
Unweighting   184
How turns are steered   186

Cross-country skiing   **188**

Equipment   190
Basic techniques   194
Advanced techniques   198
Trails and touring   204
Cross-country racing   206

Functional skiing   **210**

Ski trails   212
Weather and snow conditions   218
Learning to adapt your
technique   222
Deep snow skiing   224
Spring snow skiing   228
Mogul skiing   230
Skiing difficult situations
on-trail   234
Off-trail skiing   236
Helicopter skiing   238
Alpine ski touring   240
Avalanches   246
First aid for skiers   249

Ski lifts   **250**

How to use nursery slope lifts   252
How to use the button lift   253
How to use the T-bar lift   254
How to use chair lifts   256

Ski instruction   **258**

Teaching children to ski   262
Short-ski teaching methods   266

Dry slope skiing   **268**

Grass skiing   **272**

Ski fitness   **274**

Warming up on the slope   278

Ski vacations   **280**

Ski gazetteer   **285**

Switzerland   286
Austria   289
France   292
Italy   294
Spain   295
Great Britain   296
Scandinavia   297
West Germany   298
Eastern Europe   298
Japan   299
North America   300
Australia   304
New Zealand   305
South America   305

Glossary   **306**

Index   **314**

Introduction

Skiing is more than just a sport; it is a way of life. Many people ski regularly throughout the winter, and, whereas others go skiing only once or twice a year, they all share the same objectives: the benefits of physical exercise in the healthy mountain air, the silence and beauty of the winter landscape, a release from the constraints of their working life, and inclusion in a special community of like-minded people.

Winter sports is now the fastest growing tourist industry in the world, and the growth of skiing during the last hundred years or so has been remarkable. It originated as a *Nordic* (cross-country skiing) discipline, then, following its introduction to central Europe, became almost exclusively an *Alpine* (downhill) sport. For a long time, Nordic skiing was relegated to Scandinavia and a small area of North America. Recently, however, it has spread. In 1962, Hans Ammann opened the first "ski wandering" school in Switzerland and, later, the "LLL" (*Langläufers* Live Longer) movement was established, emphasizing the physical benefits to be gained from cross-country skiing. Attracted by the truth of this, by a wish for greater independence and by a desire to escape from the crowds and queues of the pistes, skiers have turned back to Nordic skiing and, in recent years, it has re-established itself as a major sport in many countries.

The first skiers

Drawings and texts have survived to show that in Scandinavia, Siberia and Central Asia skis have been used for thousands of years as a means of transport, and for hunting and warfare. Archaeologists excavating in a peat bog near Høting in Sweden unearthed a short, wide ski which has been estimated to be about 4,500 years old. Known as the "Høting ski", it is now in the Swedish museum in Stockholm. Moreover, in northern Norway, rock drawings depicting hunters on skis have been found of about the same age.

Further evidence, in the form of written reports and illustrations, shows that in the sixteenth and seventeenth centuries skis were still used for hunting and by military troops, particularly in Scandinavia and in the bordering areas of Russia.

Nevertheless, it is to Norway that we must look for the real advances in skiing. It is there that we can see the transition from early forms of skiing,

The challenge of skiing ▶
High-altitude, off-trail skiing in the famous "Rocky Mountain powder" offers one of the most exciting and exhilarating experiences of all.
Inset Acrobatic freestyle ski jumping calls for courage, agility and style.

used solely for transport during the winter, to something more like the sport that exists today.

In 1733, Captain Jens Henrick Emahusen compiled the first skiing rules for the Norwegian ski troops. Skiing as a sport must have existed at this time, but it is not well documented and seems to have been somewhat neglected until General Bierch tried to revive it in 1831. His efforts led to the first civilian *langlauf* race and, later, to the development of ski jumping. In 1861, the first ski exhibition was held at Kristiansand, and skiing's evolution as a sport was firmly established by the formation of competition rules and by the growth of ski clubs all over Norway.

The spread of Nordic skiing to the rest of the world can be attributed to two major causes: the emigration of Norwegians, and the publication of Fridtjof Nansen's book describing his 1888 expedition on skis across the southern tip of Greenland. Nansen's book publicized the *idea* of skiing; the Norwegian emigrants spread their knowledge of the *equipment* and the *technique*. They travelled to Germany in 1853, to Australia in 1855 (the ski club founded at Kiandra in 1861 is said to have been the first in the world), to North America in 1856 and to New Zealand in 1857.

The first pair of skis to appear in Switzerland can be traced to a man named Giocondo Dotta. He left Switzerland for California where he picked up the art of skiing from a Norwegian he met while gold-digging. After his return to Switzerland in 1868, he asked a local carpenter to make him a pair of skis like those he had seen in California.

It soon became apparent, however, that Nordic skiing, as practiced by the Norwegians, could not be applied directly to the countries of central Europe. The terrain was too different. High passes, mountain peaks and steep-sided valleys demanded a different technique to that of the flat, open Scandinavian landscape. So, Nordic skiing was adapted to Alpine conditions, and Alpine skiing was born.

In Switzerland, this took the form of *ski touring* and *ski mountaineering*. Inspired by Nansen's book about the Greenland expedition, a Swiss named Christoph Iselin and a German named Wilhelm Paulcke organized the first major ski tours of the Swiss Alps, and, in 1897, Paulcke and his friends toured the Bernese Oberland climbing to as high as 3,750m (12,304ft) on the Jungfrau.

Throughout Europe, but particularly in Switzerland, the idea of ski mountaineering or "ski Alpinism" caught hold. Without the aid of any mountaineering equipment, men set out to climb the highest Alpine peaks on skis. Relying chiefly on diagonal side-stepping (p. 56), they made their way up through the deep snow for days – always making their attempts in mid-winter, not realizing that conditions would be easier in spring. This was how, in 1904, Mont Blanc (4,087m/13,410ft) was climbed for the first time on skis.

Alpine competition skiing

Surprisingly, it was the English who laid the foundations of Alpine competition skiing by adding downhill and slalom racing to the traditional Nordic disciplines of *langlauf* racing and ski jumping. In 1911, they organized the first downhill race, the "Roberts of Kandahar", at Montana in Switzerland, and, in 1913, Arnold Lunn published his book, *Skiing,* in which he suggested the first rules for downhill racing. Later, he drew up regulations for slalom racing, and the first timed slalom race, using his rules, was held in 1922 at Mürren in Switzerland.

It was in 1930 that F.I.S. (the *Fédération Internationale de Ski,* formed six years earlier) formally recognized Arnold Lunn's rules for downhill and slalom racing. After this, the F.I.S. annual world championships took over in importance from the English "Kandahar" races.

Many competitors at this time were still all-round skiers – that is, they excelled in both Nordic *and* the new Alpine disciplines. In fact, Norwegians won both the men's and women's downhill in the 1936 Olympics. But, as skiing became more firmly established in Europe, a split took place and Alpine techniques began to take over from Nordic skiing. Moreover, the English began to feel the disadvantages of being "lowlanders" and the Swiss, challenged strongly by the Austrians and Germans, began to dominate the major ski championships. The first world champions were in fact three Swiss racers: Walter Prager, David Zogg and Otto Furrer.

Later, out of Austria came the multiple world champion, Anton Seelos. As the innovator of parallel turning, he made ski history. He introduced two aids to turning which are still used now: a higher speed and body rotation.

Since then, techniques have changed again and again – from closed parallel turning with counter-rotation, through the "avalement" and jet techniques popularized by racers such as Jean-Claude Killy, to the functional movements used today by skiers like Sweden's Ingemar Stenmark or America's Phil Mahre (p. 153-5)

In the last fifteen or twenty years, Alpine skiing has also developed a highly specialized sub-discipline known as "freestyle skiing" (p. 164-77). This, too, deserves a place in the history of competition skiing.

Nordic competition skiing

As we have seen, Nordic or cross-country skiing is the oldest form of skiing, and its development from a practical means of winter transport to a sport or leisure activity has been more straight-forward than that of Alpine skiing.

Following General Bierch's efforts to revive Nordic skiing as a competitive sport in his native Norway, the first cross-country race for civilians took place at Tromsø in 1843. The sport grew in

Downhill racing ▶

Arguably the "purest" of the three Alpine racing disciplines, the downhill is certainly the fastest: on the steepest sections of the course, the top racers may well reach speeds of over 140kph (90mph). Pictured here, on her way to winning the women's downhill at the 1980 Lake Placid Olympics, is Annemarie Moser-Proell (Austria) – the woman who has dominated women's ski racing in recent years.

Nordic ski racing ▼

Cross-country or *langlauf* races are held over official distances of up to 50km (31 miles), and marathons are even longer. To ski these distances in a winning time requires strength and endurance, as well as a flawless technique. The effort and the concentration show on the face of this competitor in the 1978 World Championships.

popularity and in 1882 the first "Homenkollen" ski races were organized. These still occur today and are considered to be Norway's most important annual ski event.

In the development of *langlauf* racing technique, there have been no revolutionary advances nor any significant controversies. Racers have merely got faster. The basic gliding step that they use has remained essentially the same. What has happened is that improvements in equipment design and more specialized training have made higher speeds feasible. In 1909, in the fifth Swiss Ski Championship, the winner of the 18km "sprint" race took 5 minutes 36 seconds to ski one kilometre (0.6 mile). However, in the 1980 Lake Placid Olympics, the winners of the 15km, 30km and 50km races all managed to ski a distance of one kilometre in around 3 minutes.

Nordic ski jumping, which has always been one of the most attractive competition disciplines, has remained a sport which thousands watch but in which only few compete. Nevertheless, since its invention by Søndre Norheim in the 1840s and since the first competitions in the 1860s, no other ski discipline has received so much scientific attention. Nowadays, the angle at which the jumpers hold their skis and the angle at which they

Nordic ski touring ▲
An increasingly popular
alternative to the over-
crowded trails of many
Alpine resorts.

Nordic relay racing ▶
The start of the 1978
World Games 4 x 10km
relay – one of the most
exciting Nordic events.

lean forward over them are calculated in
accordance with the laws of aerodynamics. This,
together with improvements in the construction of
jumping hills, has meant that jumpers can fly
further and further, "riding" the air currents like an
airfoil and reaching the very limits of the landing
slope. On "ski flying" hills, this means jumps of up
to 180m (590ft).

The development of modern ski technique

The foundations of Alpine ski technique were laid
at the end of the nineteenth century by an Austrian
called Mathias Zdarsky. Inspired, like so many, by
Nansen's description of his expedition across
Greenland, Zdarsky, at the age of thirty four, set
about learning to ski. He wore shorter skis than the
usual Nordic ones, used only one pole, and
improved the binding system. He also adapted
Nordic techniques to his own Alpine conditions,
replacing the Nordic "telemark" turn with what
came to be called the "turning snowplow"
(p. 68) – thereby setting the scene for the first
controversy in the history of ski techniques.

In 1896, Zdarsky published a book, *Lilienfeld
Skiing Technique,* in which he set out his new
ideas on ski technique and on teaching methods.
His theories and his invention of the "ski school"

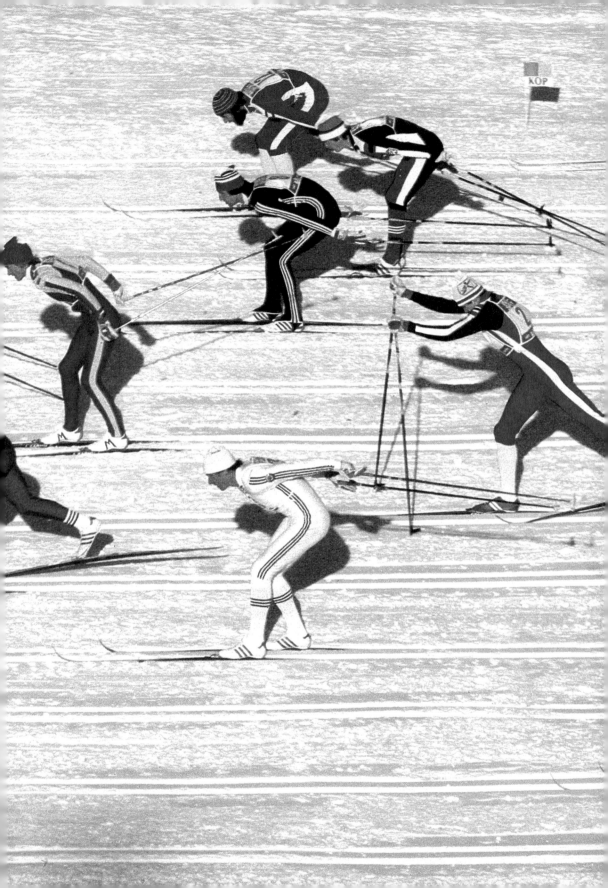

were developed further by one of his pupils, Georg Bilgeri, and by a German called Willi Rickmers.

The English, too, became involved in the arguments about ski technique. In 1910, Vivian Caulfield published his book, *How to Ski,* and established the British point of view in the controversy between the followers of Nordic skiing and the supporters of the Lilienfeld ski technique.

After the First World War, in 1920, a young Austrian called Hannes Schneider, originally a disciple of Georg Bilgeri, set up in St Anton what was known as the "Arlberg" school of ski technique. It was based on the principle of "stem turning" (p. 96) with rotation, and it was organized for the first time in the form of graded ski school classes. Hannes Schneider thus became the founder of the modern "ski school".

Probably the most influential figure to follow Hannes Schneider was another Austrian, Anton Seelos. Together with his disciple, the great French skier, Emile Allais, he invented and then popularized the theory of parallel turning with rotation. As a result, from the mid-1930s to the beginning of the 1950s, ski teaching methods throughout Europe were dominated by the principles of the Arlberg and French ski schools.

To be fair, a few experts in Switzerland and in Austria were already arguing vehemently in favour of a technique which was completely opposite to that of the Arlberg-France axis: that is, in favour of turning *without* rotation. To begin with they got no support from the racers and therefore had no success in spreading their ideas. But then, in Austria, the era of turning with "twist and heel push" began. Every middle-aged skier will remember this. *Wedeln* (p. 117) conquered the skiing world. Consequently, stylish closed parallel turning with elegant counter-rotary movements was every skier's dream. That is, until the top world racers changed to more functional techniques.

In recent years, television, with its slow action replays, has not only helped to introduce skiing into every household, but has also made ski technique – especially that of the racers – much less mysterious. In general, it is largely now recognized that the fascination of skiing lies in the ability to adapt techniques to the most varying conditions. The ideal of a "perfect style" no longer dominates ski technique, and *functional skiing,* as it is presented and advocated in this book, is on the advance.

Today, more than ever is known about ski technique. Science has been brought to bear on many aspects of the sport – in particular, on the mechanics and aerodynamics, on the training and the style of racers, and on the design of ski

◀ **Powder skiing**
Whether on the open slopes of the mountain peaks or lower down, beneath the tree line, untracked powder snow – light, feathery and beautiful to ski – is the dream of every skier.

equipment. Nevertheless, our understanding of skiing still relies chiefly on detailed analysis of the actual movements. Although film and video have transformed this process of analysis, it still results in differing personal opinions which then become differing (and sometimes conflicting) national theories of technique and instruction.

The Handbook of Skiing is based on the Swiss method. In Switzerland, we have always tried to treat the subject of skiing as objectively as possible. Since the foundation of the official Swiss Ski School in 1933, we have given 115 million hours of registered ski instruction. This, together with the fact that Switzerland has won the Team World Cup this year, speaks for the effectiveness of our approach. Our instruction methods are based on a consistent theory which really does work, for everyone from the young beginner to the experienced top skiers.

Our *Handbook* is meant to be an informative work and not a scientific one. It is designed to bring the reader closer to all forms of skiing, and it deals with many of the questions that interest the more experienced skier as well as the beginner. The ski technique which it recommends is based on the latest teaching plan of the Swiss Ski School – although it does not necessarily follow the actual curriculum in all areas. In *The Handbook of Skiing*, such basic skills as schussing, traversing and side-slipping are dealt with as self-contained topics. In the Swiss teaching plan, they are dealt with again and again in each ski class, where they are related to the ability of the pupil and adapted to increasingly difficult situations.

Special care is given to the beginner's level, since we are well aware of the difficulties many skiers experience in progressing from schussing to snowplowing or from snowplowing to snowplow turning. The learning steps for all these stages are dealt with in great detail. Often they can take days, weeks or even years to master properly – especially if the pupils' skiing holidays are short and few and far between.

In *The Handbook of Skiing,* the use of the active form in our terminology is new. For example, we no longer refer to a "snowplow turn" or a "parallel turn" but to "snowplow turning" and "parallel turning". In this way, we believe that we can better convey the "dynamic" of skiing.

The classification and naming of the turns is also new. In the past, ski technique has been plagued with an over-abundance of different names for turns – names which have often had only a symbolic character. It is our view that turns differ from each other only in the way they are initiated. Instead of half a dozen different parallel turns, for example, we now speak of *parallel turning* – and describe, as lucidly as we can, the various possible ways in which this form of turning can be initiated. The same thing applies to the basic movements in stepping techniques. Throughout

Most skiers develop along more-or-less the same lines. The discovery of new terrain in skiing is a constant challenge. As skiers improve, they will be tempted off-trail to ski deep snow and spring snow. On ski tours, many will also ski remote mountain areas or even the high peaks. Each downhill run is always something of an unknown quantity.

As far as I myself am concerned, the thing I still enjoy most about skiing is skiing itself – its many different aspects, the technical variety it offers, and the challenge of adapting my skill to the given situation. This is in spite of the fact that my profession has made me into a "ski theoretician".

I began skiing in 1931, at the time when the very first F.I.S. races were being held. My father, who was a talented skier and jumper in his own time, gave me the equipment which in those days was standard for children – boots with wooden soles, *Huitfeldt* bindings, edgeless ashwood skis and hazelwood poles. Since then I have been a ski Alpinist, a racer, a ski jumper and also, at times, a *langläufer*. For the past twenty years I have played my part in the organizations which govern Swiss ski instruction methods, and since 1971 I have been President of the International Ski Instructors Association. However, I do not pride myself; others could have done the job equally well. Ultimately, the thing that counts most is retaining my own personal relation to skiing. In this book, I wish to appear neither as a salesman of Swiss ski teaching methods, nor as an advocate of my own theories. I merely attempt to pass on my personal experience of skiing in the way that I feel it.

◀ Off-trail skiing
Away from the crowds on the prepared runs, this skier picks her own way down the mountain.

The freedom of skiing ▲
High above Verbier in Switzerland, the view is as exhilarating as the skiing itself.

our book, we have tried to make our written descriptions of the movements of skiing more precise and more objective.

Of course, there are many skiers – mostly teenagers – who ski without a great deal of conscious deliberation and who cope perfectly with any difficulties they may encounter. They seem to adopt the necessary skills instinctively.

However, most people will find that they can consciously apply the right technique only when they are able to *feel* their own movements and sense what their effects will be. In other words, to be a good skier, you must learn to ski with "feeling feet". For example, feel how, when banking, both skis tilt so that they are flat on the snow and can then be pressed into a turn, or how, when stepping, the uphill ski changes edges and takes over the steering function of the outside ski. Feel how you can deal with difficult windblown snow off-trail by using your stemmed uphill ski to "probe" the surface and to catch just the right moment for initiating your turn, or how you can find just the right amount of backward lean to keep your ski tips up in deep snow. All this holds a constant fascination and you will find that the richer your choice of techniques, the more interesting the application of them becomes.

Karl Gamma

Andermatt, Switzerland, 1981

Ski equipment

Alpine skiing is a technical sport which requires that beginners as well as more experienced skiers use expensive, sophisticated equipment. This chapter sets out the various types of equipment you will need for downhill skiing. Equipment for ski touring and cross-country skiing is dealt with in the relevant sections elsewhere.

Every skier requires certain basic equipment in order to ski. This includes a pair of *skis* fitted with *bindings*, special *ski boots* which fit into the bindings, and a pair of *ski poles*. The design of ski equipment has come a long way since the early days of skiing, and manufacturers must now produce equipment which complies with very strict safety regulations laid down by various consumer and standards organizations. The variety of equip-

ment now available is enormous and is continually changing, so you should always seek proper advice before you start.

Ski clothing must keep you warm and dry to protect you from the extremes of mountain temperature, but it should not restrict your movements in any way. Although some people do ski in jeans, they are not suitable; if you fall, they will get soaked through, and, once wet, they can freeze on you. Wear your clothes in several layers for better insulation, with long underwear when it is very cold, and buy a good hat and pair of gloves.

If you have never skied before, you may be put off by the seemingly endless list of expensive equipment and clothing. However, it is possible to rent all the most expensive parts of the equipment. In

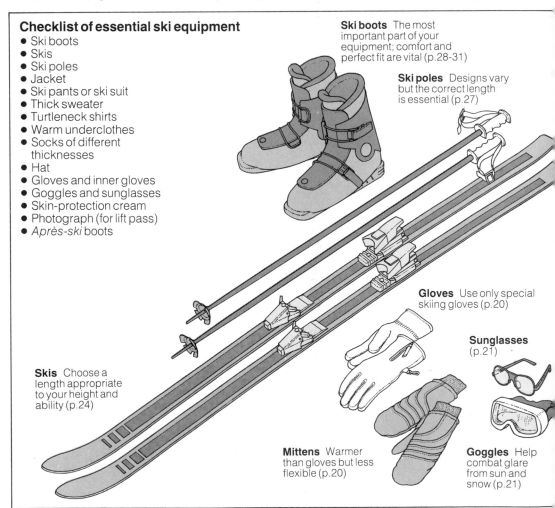

Checklist of essential ski equipment
- Ski boots
- Skis
- Ski poles
- Jacket
- Ski pants or ski suit
- Thick sweater
- Turtleneck shirts
- Warm underclothes
- Socks of different thicknesses
- Hat
- Gloves and inner gloves
- Goggles and sunglasses
- Skin-protection cream
- Photograph (for lift pass)
- *Après-ski* boots

Ski boots The most important part of your equipment; comfort and perfect fit are vital (p.28-31)

Ski poles Designs vary but the correct length is essential (p.27)

Gloves Use only special skiing gloves (p.20)

Sunglasses (p.21)

Skis Choose a length appropriate to your height and ability (p.24)

Mittens Warmer than gloves but less flexible (p.20)

Goggles Help combat glare from sun and snow (p.21)

particular, it is worth renting skis the first few times you ski; the needs of a beginner and those of a more advanced skier vary enormously, and you will probably find that you progress quite quickly to longer skis. If you decide to rent boots, rent them before you go: first, you will have more time to try them on; and, second, you avoid the danger of arriving at a resort to find that there are no boots left in your size. Skis and poles, however, are better rented at the resort because it is easier to change them and they are so awkward to transport.

If you do decide to buy your own equipment, always go to a reliable shop where you can be certain of good service. The first thing you should buy is a pair of ski boots. Whereas rented boots can be made to fit by wearing different thicknesses of socks, if you are buying your own boots, take the time and trouble to get an exact fit.

Every skier needs accessories such as sunglasses, goggles and sun-protection cream. All these are important. The mountain sun is very strong even when it is very cold. This, combined with the glare produced by the reflection of the sun on the snow, can easily damage unprotected eyes (causing temporary "snow-blindness") and can burn your skin. Use an oil-based cream with a high protection factor to protect your skin and avoid those that "aid tanning". The checklist below sets out the minimum that any skier will need, but useful extras are: a box of plasters, particularly if you are hiring boots; a penknife with a screwdriver so that you can make any necessary adjustments to your bindings (p.34); and a small backpack or fanny pack (p.21) to carry anything you may need during a day's skiing but do not want in your pocket – for example, a camera, a sun cream or a hat. Do not forget to take a couple of passport-size photographs of yourself for your lift pass (p.250).

Lastly, apart from warm après-ski clothes, you will need a pair of waterproof après-ski boots with non-slip soles to walk around on the snow when you are not actually skiing.

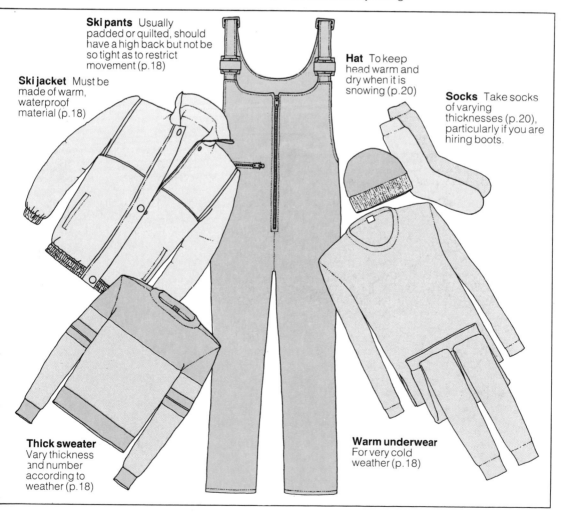

Ski pants Usually padded or quilted, should have a high back but not be so tight as to restrict movement (p.18)

Ski jacket Must be made of warm, waterproof material (p.18)

Hat To keep head warm and dry when it is snowing (p.20)

Socks Take socks of varying thicknesses (p.20), particularly if you are hiring boots.

Thick sweater Vary thickness and number according to weather (p.18)

Warm underwear For very cold weather (p.18)

Ski clothes and accessories

When you purchase ski clothes, your requirements should be as follows. They should keep you warm yet be loose enough not to restrict your movements. They should also have strong zippers, be wind-proof and water-resistant, and be made of anti-skid material. The main articles you need are a jacket and a pair of pants, or a one-piece suit. All these are now made from a variety of materials with differing thermal linings. Before you choose one, however, consider how much you want to spend, and where and at what time of the year you are going on your skiing holiday.

Clothes need to be worn in at least three layers. The first layer should be able to carry any moisture away from the skin and ought to be made from a natural fiber. The second layer should absorb this moisture, and the third, the outer layer, should protect you from the wind, yet also enable your body to "breathe". The weight of each layer will vary slightly. On a warm day, ski pants, a sweater and a down vest will probably be sufficient; on a cold day, a one-piece suit with a down vest or a thick sweater, a pair of pants and a long-sleeved jacket will be absolutely essential.

Your jacket, or parka, must be long enough to cover your kidney area, with close-fitting cuffs, neck and bottom to keep the snow out, and a high collar to keep your neck warm. It helps to have large pockets in which to carry anything you may need during the day; these should preferably be top-opening and always have a good secure fastening, such as a zipper.

The most comfortable trousers are those that look like overalls, called "over-the-boot ski pants". There are two main types: one is made of cotton or a similar fabric with a quilted thermal lining; the other is made of a thinner stretch material. Quilted ski pants are very warm, relatively inexpensive and ideal for beginners. The stretch ski pants are similar to those worn by the racers, and they often have nylon gaiters attached to the lower leg to prevent snow getting into the boots. In either case, the trousers should be fairly high, particularly at the back, and should have integral shoulder straps.

One-piece suits are very warm because they have a thermal lining throughout. A few are made in two parts, a jacket and trousers, attached by a zipper around the waist so that, on a warm day or when having lunch in the mountain restaurant, the jacket can be removed if necessary.

Finally, you will need a selection of warm socks, a hat, a good pair of gloves, and goggles or sun glasses. These items, together with other accessories, are covered on p.20-21.

Vests
These are ideal over a sweater on a warm day or over a one-piece suit on a cold day. One with a "fold-over" front fastening will be warmer.

Ski jackets
Make sure your jacket has a good thermal lining and that it is made of non-skid material to stop you sliding uncontrollably if you fall. One with "zip-out" sleeves can be useful on a warm day.

One-piece suits
If you choose to wear one of these it is very important to make sure it is comfortable in all the "maximum-stretch" positions.

◀ Ski clothes and fashion
Colors, patterns and designs vary from season to season – but the primary function of all ski clothes should be to keep you warm. Most people wear bright colors such as these so that they can be seen from a distance against the snow.

Quilted ski pants
These are often made of a lightweight material. You may find that they tend to get torn at the bottoms by your ski edges when you fall. If so, buy a pair with leather patches or sew some on yourself.

Stretch ski pants
More "sporty" than quilted ski pants, these are better suited to younger skiers. However, they are not as warm, particularly around the knees, and you may find you need to wear more underclothes on cold days.

Ski gloves and headgear

Adequate protection for both head and hands is essential because these are the parts of the body from which most heat is lost. Never be tempted to go out without a hat, if only in your pocket, because mountain temperatures can change very quickly. There are many different styles of hat available: woollen ones, quilted peaked caps, fur hats or even headbands. The basic requirement of any hat is that it should be large enough to cover the forehead, ears and neck. A peaked cap can be an extra advantage when it is snowing.

A good pair of ski gloves or mittens is important because, not only do they keep your hands warm and dry, but they also protect them when you fall. It is up to you whether you choose to wear gloves or mittens. Mittens are much warmer – and therefore children may prefer them – but you have more freedom of movement when wearing gloves. Both gloves and mittens are made from a variety of materials, but leather is the best and the most expensive. Both types must be water-resistant and designed for skiing; ordinary gloves will not do. If you are skiing in very cold temperatures, it is also worth buying silk glove liners for extra warmth.

Ski gloves and mittens
Always make certain there is a long, close-fitting cuff. The glove itself should not be too tight, or it will stop circulation in your fingers, and it is advisable to wear silk glove liners.

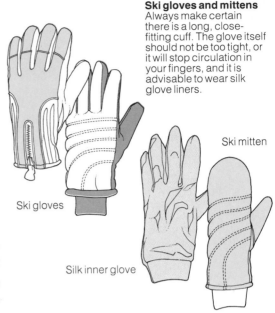

Ski mitten

Ski gloves

Silk inner glove

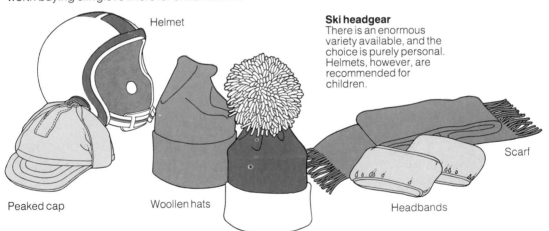

Helmet

Ski headgear
There is an enormous variety available, and the choice is purely personal. Helmets, however, are recommended for children.

Scarf

Peaked cap

Woollen hats

Headbands

Ski socks and gaiters

You will need to take at least two pairs of warm, comfortable socks with you. The best type are wool with a cotton-loop lining. Remember that your ski boots must fit exactly and that the wrong socks can make them very uncomfortable. Wear a silk inner sock if your feet get cold easily.

Nylon gaiters keep the bottom of your ski trousers dry and keep snow out of your boots. They are either slipped on over your foot or fastened by means of a zipper.

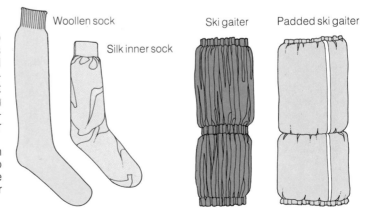

Woollen sock

Silk inner sock

Ski gaiter

Padded ski gaiter

Ski goggles and sunglasses

These are worn for two reasons: first, to protect your eyes from the intense glare produced by the reflection of the sun on the snow; second, to improve the definition on overcast days. Sunglasses, which are normally worn on fine days, need to be very dark and must cover the whole eye. Goggles are normally worn in bad light or when racing, both to help you to see and to protect your face and eyes from the cold. They are available with various different colored lenses: yellow rose-colored for bad light, dark for bright light, and brown-gold or green universal lenses.

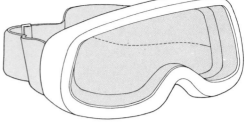

Ski goggles
Choose goggles with good ventilation; those with sealed double lenses or lenses coated with an anti-fog chemical are less likely to steam up in the cold.

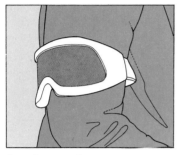

Carrying goggles
If you are not wearing your goggles, carry them on your arm as shown above to avoid losing them.

Sunglasses
These must have plastic and, preferably, polarized lenses large enough not to let light in at the sides. You may be better off buying them at the resort.

Ski bags

Skis and ski boots are very awkward things to carry about and need protection when you are travelling. It therefore helps if you have bags for both items. Ski bags need to be tough and waterproof, particularly if you are going to carry them on a car roof-rack.

Rather than fill their pockets, some people prefer to use "fanny packs" or small "day backpacks" to carry any items with them on a day's skiing. If you do use one of these, check that it is waterproof.

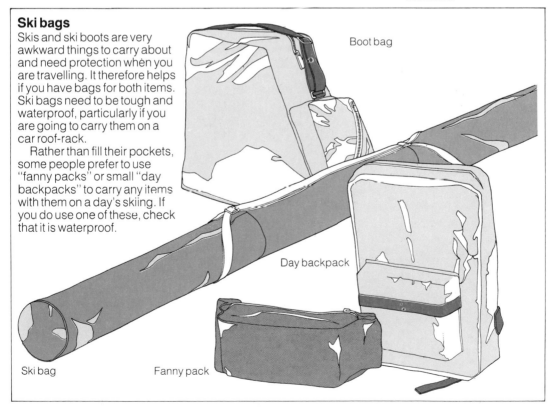

Boot bag

Day backpack

Ski bag   Fanny pack

Skis

The basic shape of a ski has not changed very much since the first "waisted" ski, the *Telemark* ski, was produced in Norway in the mid-nineteenth century. The construction, however, has changed dramatically with the advent of modern technology. Early skis were first made of solid, then of laminated, wood. The arch along the ski and the up-turned tip and tail had to be built into the ski by heating the wood in clamps; the main object of the manufacturer then was simply to produce a strong, long-lasting ski. Nowadays, modern skis are compound structures made from a variety of plastics combined with metal, fiberglass or wood, and are highly durable. Manufacturers can now concentrate on making skis for different skiers by varying such characteristics as the length, weight, flexibility and resistance to twisting or torsion. Choosing a ski to suit your purpose is dealt with on p.24-5.

All skis, whatever their purpose, have the same basic geometry. The widest point of a ski is at the front and is called the "shoulder". It forms part of the tip or shovel. The second widest point is the "heel". It is just before the tail, which is cut back to prevent the ski catching on bumps. The narrowest point of the ski, called the "waist", is near the center and is also the point over which the boot will be centered in the binding. The curve along the side of the ski, which is determined by the width at these three points, is known as the "side-cut" or "side-camber" and it defines the turning arc of the ski. On p.187, in the chapter on "Ski mechanics", we describe how this shape helps a ski to turn.

Skis also have a built-in arch known as the "camber". When laid flat on the ground, the ski will only

touch the ground at the shoulder and heel, and the highest point will be at the waist. The camber guarantees that the pressure is distributed along the entire length of the ski when you stand on it. It varies considerably from one ski to another and affects the flexibility. The other factor which determines a ski's flexibility, however, is its thickness. The maximum thickness is at the waist, directly under the skier's foot, and it becomes progressively thinner towards each end by a very carefully calculated amount. Nearly all skis have a shallow "running groove" which runs along the base of the ski to help it run straight – although skis for jumping may have up to five, and skis for freestyle ballet (which need to turn easily) may not have one at all.

Ski terminology

The diagrams below illustrate the features which, although varying from one design to another, are common to all skis. The ski is divided into five sections: the shovel, forebody, waist, afterbody and tail. The top diagram shows the thickest point of the ski and its camber. The lower diagrams show the top and bottom surfaces.

Cross section through ski showing running groove and edges

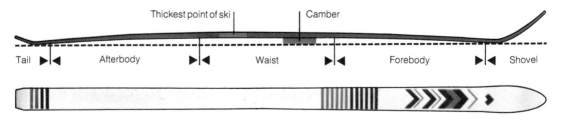

Thickest point of ski | Camber

Tail ▶◀   Afterbody   ▶◀   Waist   ▶◀   Forebody   ▶◀   Shovel

▲ Heel (second widest point)   ▲ Waist (narrowest point)   ▲ Shoulder (widest point)

Ski types

Advanced manufacturing techniques developed over the past few years have meant that skis can now be produced for specific types of skiing. Although a lot of the development has been in the area of the competition ski, skis for beginners and intermediates have also improved a great deal. There are now four main categories of ski: compact, mid-length, sport, and competition. "Compact" skis, sometimes called "shorts" because of their length, have little or no side-cut. They are comparatively wide and easy to turn at slow speeds, making them ideal beginners' skis. "Mid-length" skis are longer and narrower than compact skis, with a fairly deep side-cut, and are more suited to intermediate skiers. "Sport" and "competition" skis are used by intermediate and advanced skiers. The sport ski is a lightweight racing ski. Competition skis are longer, have varying degrees of stiffness and side-cut, and are divided into three categories: downhill, slalom and giant slalom.

Ski lengths

Skis in each of the four categories are used in different lengths. The longer the ski, the faster it will travel, and the more difficult it will be to turn. Follow the chart on p.24 to decide which ski will best suit your ability. To give you an idea of scale, a man 1.80m (5ft 10ins) tall, weighing about 75kgs (165lbs), would ski on a 170-180cm compact ski, a 185-190cm mid-length ski, a 195-205cm sport ski or a 200cm or longer competition ski – depending on his skiing ability.

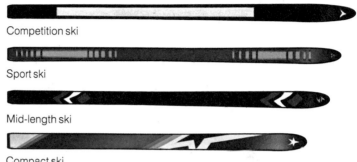

Competition ski

Sport ski

Mid-length ski

Compact ski

Ski construction

All skis have a hard plastic or "A.B.S." top surface, a polyethylene running surface, and steel "edges" which are flush to the base and slightly proud of the side-walls. The construction of the core varies and may be either foam-injected, torsion box or laminated.

Laminated ski

This type of ski has an elaborate, composite or "sandwich" construction which combines layers of a high-strength material, such as aluminium, with layers of low-strength materials. This makes a very strong but fairly heavy ski with good rigidity.

Foam-core ski

In its simplest form, this is a very cheap method of ski construction. The core material, polyurethane foam, is injected into a mold already containing the pre-assembled top and bottom layers. Some foam skis have extra reinforcement in or around the core.

Torsion box ski

This type of ski has its core material, whether laminated wood, foam or aluminium honeycomb, surrounded by a fiberglass "torsion box". This box sometimes has additional layers of metal incorporated into the fiberglass for extra strength and weight.

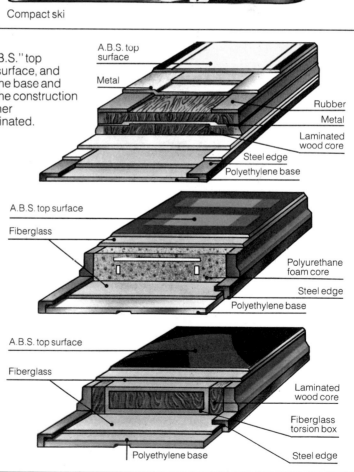

A.B.S. top surface

Metal

Rubber

Metal

Laminated wood core

Steel edge

Polyethylene base

A.B.S. top surface

Fiberglass

Polyurethane foam core

Steel edge

Polyethylene base

A.B.S. top surface

Fiberglass

Laminated wood core

Fiberglass torsion box

Polyethylene base

Steel edge

Choosing skis

Having decided that you are going to buy your own skis, it is important to go to a reputable sports shop where they will take time over your choice and will be prepared to advise you on the latest equipment. The first things to establish are the level of your skiing, what terrain and speeds you prefer, and how often you are likely to ski. In other words, establish which group of skis you are aiming at (compact, mid, sport or competition) and, within each category, what degree of flexibility or weight you are going to require.

Compact skis can be used on varying terrain but, because they are shorter and therefore easier to turn, they are used mainly by beginners and by people who ski only occasionally (although high-performance compact skis are used by some freestyle skiers). Mid-length skis are suitable for intermediate or advanced skiers who make a lot of turns or who like skiing bumpy terrain, both of which are easier on fairly short skis. The sport ski or, better still, a giant slalom competition ski is best for someone who likes to ski fast and who needs a more stable, longer ski – one that is suited for steering wide-radius turns at high speed. A good ski for fresh powder snow needs to be stiff in the center but must also have a soft, flexible forebody.

When you have chosen the skis you want, use the chart below as a guide to the correct length. Check the actual pair very carefully for any defects.

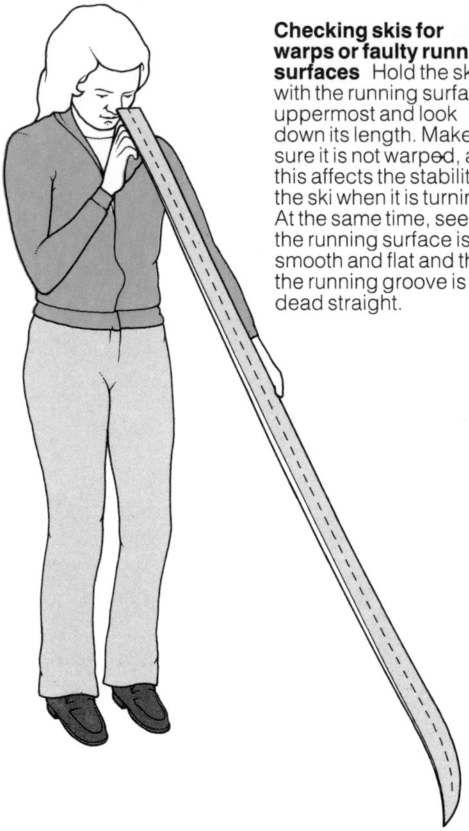

Checking skis for warps or faulty running surfaces Hold the ski with the running surface uppermost and look down its length. Make sure it is not warped, as this affects the stability of the ski when it is turning. At the same time, see that the running surface is smooth and flat and that the running groove is dead straight.

Ski length selection chart

Use the chart below as a guide to find the correct ski for your height and ability. Find your weight in the left-hand column and draw a straight line from there, through your height, to line up with a row of ski lengths. If you are a beginner, go down a row. If you are a fast, aggressive skier, go up a row as shown on the chart.

Skier's weight		Skier's height		Compact	Mid-length	Sport	Competition
kgs	(lbs)	cms	(ft/ins)	190	195	203	210
45	(99)	190	(6' 3")	190	195	203	207
50	(110)	185	(6' 1")	180	190	200	207
55	(121)	180	(5' 11")	180	185	195	203
60	(132)	175	(5' 9")				
65	(143)	170	(5' 7")	170	180	190	203
70	(154)	165	(5' 5")	170	180	180	200
75	(165)	160	(5' 3")	160	175	180	195
80	(176)	155	(5' 1")				
85	(187)	150	(4' 11")	160	170	175	190
90	(198)	145	(4' 9")	160	160	175	185
95	(210)			150	160	170	180

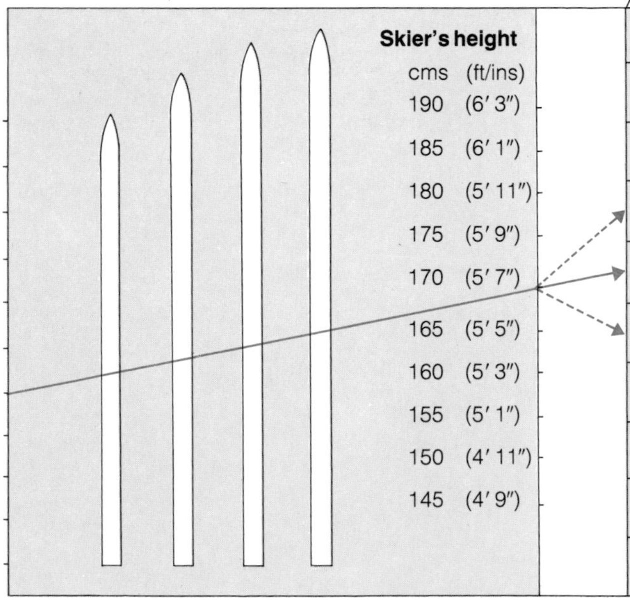

Ski length in cms

Checking that skis are pairs
Hold the skis with the running surfaces innermost, and press them together. Make sure that they are exactly the same height and width. The running surfaces must meet exactly, with no gaps in between.

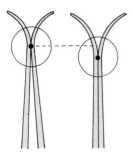

Ski contact points
When a pair of skis are held together, the running surfaces touch at the shoulder. When pressed together, the contact point should move down the ski by less than 7mm (½ inch).

Testing for flexibility
Place the tail of the ski against your foot and, holding the tip with one hand, press the center of the ski with your other hand. A good ski will spring back to shape quickly. To test the flexibility of ski shovel and forebody, move your hand further up the ski; the softer the ski, the easier it is to flex.

Caring for your skis
You will need to look after your skis carefully if you are going to get the best out of them. If you are putting them away for any length of time, spread petroleum jelly or paraffin wax on the steel edges to prevent them rusting.

New skis should be correctly prepared by a specialist before they are given to you. However, whether old or new, examine your skis carefully before using them. First, look over the running surfaces for any holes or scratches; they will need to be filled in. This can be done using a special "candle" made from a mixture of polyethylene and wax. Light the candle and drip the mixture into the hole, leave to set, then scrape the surface smooth again. Larger holes are best repaired using pure polyurethane; if in doubt about how to do this, take the skis to a good repair shop.

The next thing to check is the steel edge of the ski. On new skis, the edges are often slightly proud of the base; if so, file them flush as shown below. Edges must also be sharp, with a clean smooth surface, along the section of the ski which will be in contact with the ground, but *not* at the tip or tail where they can be dulled with a file or wire wool if necessary. You can buy special files to sharpen your edges but, again, if in doubt, take the skis to a good repair shop.

Lastly, you may want to wax your skis. This is not, as is often thought, just to make your skis faster, but also because a ski with a good running surface is much easier to turn. There are several ways of applying the wax. The most efficient is to "hot wax" the skis. In this method, the wax is dripped onto the base of the ski, ironed in, and the excess then scraped off. Other types of wax come in tubes, aerosols or blocks. These are rubbed onto the base of the ski but will need re-applying often. There are three main waxes: one for dry, cold snow; one for wet, warmer snow; and one universal wax.

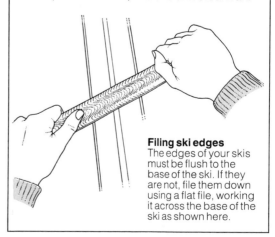

Filing ski edges
The edges of your skis must be flush to the base of the ski. If they are not, file them down using a flat file, working it across the base of the ski as shown here.

Carrying your skis

Skis and poles are awkward things to carry about. The easiest way to carry skis any distance is to balance them on your shoulder, but you must be careful, particularly when turning around, not to hit someone. Special devices are available for carrying both skis and poles together, but these are often bulky and difficult to use.

The first thing you must do before picking your skis up is to "bind" them together to prevent them sliding apart. Stand the ski tails on the ground and, with the running surfaces face to face, "lock" the ski brakes together, or wrap safety straps around them, or secure them with rubber straps as shown below. Ski poles can also be "clipped" together (see opposite) to make them easier to carry.

Carrying skis on your shoulder

Bind skis together and balance them on your shoulder, either flat or on their edges, the tips facing forwards, the tails up, and the toe-piece of the binding just behind your shoulder. Loop your arm over the front of your skis to keep them in place. Clip your poles together and use them for support as you walk.

Binding skis together

Safety straps
If you have these on your bindings, tie them around your skis to hold them firmly together.

Rubber ski straps
These inexpensive straps are wrapped around each end of a pair of skis to keep them firmly together.

"Locking" ski brakes
If your bindings have ski brakes you can "lock" them together. Stand the skis on the ground, holding one slightly higher than the other. Press them together and slide the top ski down until the brakes interlock with one another.

Carrying skis in a confined space

When there are lots of people around (in a lift line, for example), carry skis upright instead of over your shoulder. Bind them together and stand them on their tails. Loop your pole straps over ski tips if you want to use both hands to carry your skis.

Ski poles

These are the least complicated items in your ski equipment. Ski poles are used for support and to aid balance and, when you make a turn, to help you transfer your weight from one ski to the other. It is therefore important that you use poles which are exactly the right length: when you plant your pole vertically in the snow, your forearm must be parallel to the slope.

Ski poles vary slightly in quality and shape, but basically they all consist of a tapered "shaft", made of a strong, lightweight material such as aluminum,

with a steel tip, a handle or "grip" which is made of molded plastic and which should fit the contours of your hand perfectly, and a plastic or metal ring near the tip known as the "basket".

The construction of a ski pole must meet certain safety standards to minimize the risk of injury: the tip must not be a single point; the design of the grip must facilitate quick release of your hand if you fall; the diameter of the top of the grip must be larger than an eye socket; and the pole should bend, not break or splinter, if you fall on it.

Choosing the correct length of pole

If your pole is too long or too short, you will be unable to plant it properly, and this will affect your body position adversely. Methods for testing the length are shown below.

Checking length in shop Grip pole upside down, just beneath basket; forearm should be parallel to ground.

Checking length on snow Plant pole right way up in snow; forearm should be parallel with ground once again.

Carrying ski poles

All plastic baskets have at least one hole cut in them so that you can clip poles together when carrying them. The tip of one pole is simply inserted through the hole in the basket on the other pole. The grips may also clip together.

Grips

There are two different types: the traditional grip with adjustable wrist strap to prevent you losing the pole in a fall; and the "sword" grip without a strap. Try out both while wearing ski gloves.

Straight ski poles

This standard type of pole is used by virtually every skier, from beginners to experts.

Bent ski poles

Used by downhill racers, these are shaped to fit around the body to reduce wind resistance (p. 156).

Baskets

Generally made of plastic, rubber or metal, these prevent the ski pole going too far into the snow when it is planted. Variations in design are purely cosmetic.

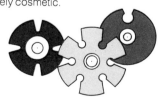

Tips

The shapes vary, but most have either four small points or a dish-shaped tip to grip the snow or ice.

Boots

The most important items of your ski equipment are your boots. They form the link between you and your skis, and bad boots will mean bad transmission of force and poor control of your movements. Your boots must fit exactly and must be as comfortable as possible. At the same time, they must be rigid enough to prevent any sideways movement of your ankle yet be soft enough to flex forwards.

Originally, ski boots were made of leather and were tied with laces, although, later, the laces were replaced by metal buckles. The leather boots got gradually higher in the search for more ankle support, but this made them much less comfortable. The problem was eventually solved with the development of plastic boots. At first the prototypes were stiff and uncomfortable. Now, nearly all ski boots are made of plastic, and consist of two parts:

the outer shell and the inner boot. The outer shell is rigid and supports the foot and ankle. It should be made of polyurethane (although cheaper boots are sometimes made of thermoplastics). The inner boot, which cushions your foot, is soft and can be made from a variety of materials.

Boots are made to suit different types of skier, and some manufacturers divide them into such categories as beginners, intermediates, sport, and high-performance or racing to correspond with the ski classifications.

Careful treatment of your boots will extend their useful life. Always store them with the buckles done up and, if for any reason they get wet, take the inner boot out and dry it separately. Do not put boots near any form of direct heat, but do not leave them outside either.

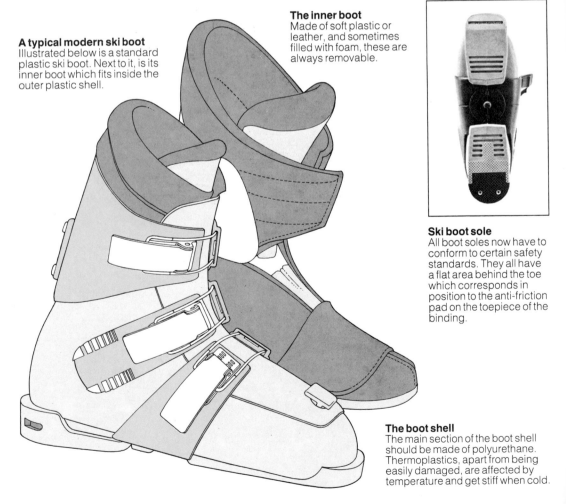

A typical modern ski boot
Illustrated below is a standard plastic ski boot. Next to it, is its inner boot which fits inside the outer plastic shell.

The inner boot
Made of soft plastic or leather, and sometimes filled with foam, these are always removable.

Ski boot sole
All boot soles now have to conform to certain safety standards. They all have a flat area behind the toe which corresponds in position to the anti-friction pad on the toepiece of the binding.

The boot shell
The main section of the boot shell should be made of polyurethane. Thermoplastics, apart from being easily damaged, are affected by temperature and get stiff when cold.

Boot types

Like skis, there are ski boots to suit every skier. However, there are two main types: rear-entry (where the buckles are at the back) and front-entry. And within each group there are "soft" and "rigid" boots. A soft boot is generally hinged at the ankle; a rigid boot is fixed in position and should therefore be raked well forwad to encourage the correct stance (p.42).

High-performance or racing boots tend to be tall and stiff, whereas a beginner's boot is lower and has a softer forward flex. There is a wide range of boots for intermediate skiers which are generally fairly high in the leg and have a varying degree of flexibility.

Simple two-buckle boot
This is a lightweight beginner's boot. It has a comfortable, fairly soft flex, and is high enough in the leg to support the ankle.

Intermediate four-buckle boot
Also flexible and with a moderate forward lean, this is a good all-purpose boot. The outer shell is made in two parts and is hinged.

Lightweight rear-entry boot
On this boot the buckles are at the back, eliminating unnatural pressure points over the top of the foot.

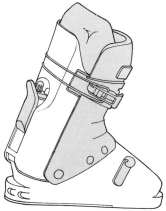

Adjustable rear-entry boot
This rear-entry boot has adjustable internal straps operated by levers to hold the foot in place.

High-performance competition boot This is a very high, stiff boot, chiefly for racers, and is adjustable in almost every direction.

Ski boot buckles

These vary a great deal and they are all adjustable to a certain extent. Most designs consist of a piece of wire which is looped around a notch on one side of the boot and a ratchet-type clip on the other side which tightens it. Many boots, however, have additional means of adjustment, either an extra notch around which the wire can be looped, or some finer method such as those shown here.

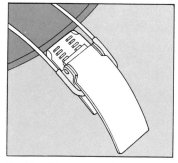

Buckle with extra ratchet
Minute adjustments can be made by moving the buckle up the ratchet.

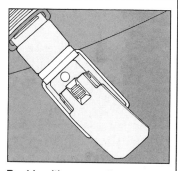

Buckle with screw adjustment
Very small changes in tension can be made by turning the screw.

Putting on your boots

The procedure for putting on boots is always the same, and you should follow the method described here. It is important that you do up the middle buckle first (or the one nearest your instep on a four-buckle boot) to make certain that your heel is pulled back into position in the boot; you can then go on to do up all the buckles to the right tension. Your foot should be held tightly, but not "cramped". Boots with fold-out tongues are easier to put on.

When you are trying on boots for the first time, do not wear very thick socks because, although the boot may fit exactly in the shop, the lining of the inner boot will "flatten" with wear.

1 Open the boot completely – both the inner boot and the outer shell – and push your foot down into it. If necessary, pull the inner boot out slightly to make this easier.

2 When your foot is right down inside the boot, tap the heel gently on the ground to push the heel of your foot firmly into position in the heel of the boot.

Choosing boots

When you buy ski boots, take plenty of time, go to a reputable shop, and get the best ones you can afford. Consider how well you ski and what terrain you like, and choose from the range of boots which will best suit your needs.

The boot you choose, whatever the type, must fit properly if you are to get an efficient transmission of force to your skis. Put the new boots on, stand up and walk around. They should feel comfortable, there should be no upward or lateral movement in the heel, and yet your toes should be able to move freely. The point at which the boot is angled or hinged must correspond exactly with the point at which your ankle bends. This is most important: the boot *must* give you the right amount of forward lean or flex. Bear in mind also that boots which can be opened are more comfortable to stand and walk about in when you are not skiing.

If you cannot find a boot that fits your foot exactly, minor adjustments (such as adding or removing foam padding) can be made to the inner boot by any good ski shop.

Points to look for when trying on boots When choosing a new pair of boots, consider each of the following parts of your foot in turn.

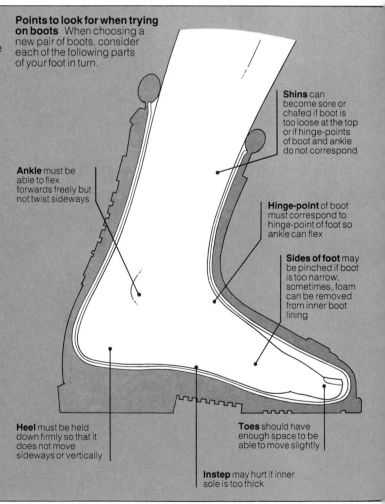

Shins can become sore or chafed if boot is too loose at the top or if hinge-points of boot and ankle do not correspond

Ankle must be able to flex forwards freely but not twist sideways

Hinge-point of boot must correspond to hinge-point of foot so ankle can flex

Sides of foot may be pinched if boot is too narrow; sometimes, foam can be removed from inner boot lining

Heel must be held down firmly so that it does not move sideways or vertically

Toes should have enough space to be able to move slightly

Instep may hurt if inner sole is too thick

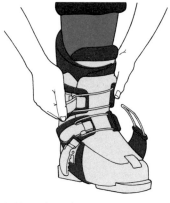

3 The first buckle to fasten is the middle one, or the one nearest your instep. When you have done this one up, bend your knees and ankles forward to drive your heel right back in the boot.

4 Next, close the top buckle as tight as is comfortable; this may mean that the middle buckle will need to be tightened again.

5 Lastly, do up the bottom buckle. The boot should now feel tight all over but should not "pinch" your foot: walk around in new boots for at least ten minutes to check that they are still comfortable.

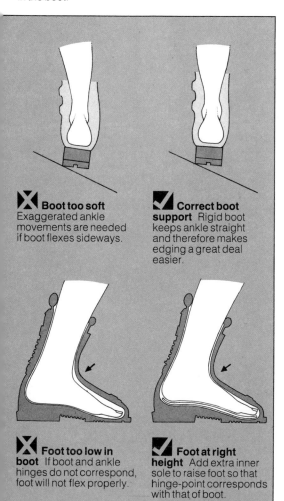

☒ Boot too soft Exaggerated ankle movements are needed if boot flexes sideways.

☑ Correct boot support Rigid boot keeps ankle straight and therefore makes edging a great deal easier.

☒ Foot too low in boot If boot and ankle hinges do not correspond, foot will not flex properly.

☑ Foot at right height Add extra inner sole to raise foot so that hinge-point corresponds with that of boot.

Wedging or canting

If you are slightly bow-legged or knock-kneed you will find that, when you stand on your skis, the running surfaces will not be flat on the snow, making movements such as edging more difficult. In general, differences in physical shape mean that men are likely to be bow-legged and women to be knock-kneed (p.261). Some boots are designed specifically for men or for women, and they sometimes have a degree of canting incorporated. If this is not enough, there are two ways of correcting the problem: one is to put so-called "cant-plates" onto the ski; the other is to make some adjustment to the boot such as fitting an "inner-sole". Some boots, however, have a screw on the side allowing you to adjust the angle.

Bow-legged skiers Men with bow-legs tend to stand on their outside edges. To get their skis flat on the snow, they need one of the systems shown below.

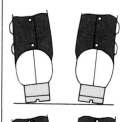

"Inner soles" Wedge-shaped inner soles inside boot help flatten skis on snow.

Ski "cant-plates" Wedge-shaped plates are placed between ski and binding.

Bindings

The device which attaches your ski to your boot is the *binding*. It is designed to hold your boot firmly in place when you ski but to release it safely and promptly should you fall over.

There are two types of ski binding: the heel-and-toe system and the plate system. The former, sometimes called a "step-in" binding, consists of two separate units: a toe-piece and a heel-piece. Plate bindings, however, consist of three units: a plate which is attached to the boot, and toe- and heel-pieces which hold the plate onto the ski.

Skiers of different weights and abilities need bindings that are designed and adjusted to release under different "stress" conditions. A lightweight beginner needs a binding that releases more easily than that of a heavy, expert skier. To conform to certain safety regulations, the German Industrial Standards Association (D.I.N.) has produced a simple "release-load" scale of 1 to 10 which indicates the weight range for which a particular binding is designed (p.34). This must now feature on every binding made in Europe. Also compulsory on every binding is the "anti-friction" pad just behind the toe-piece, which corresponds to a flat area on the sole of a ski boot. This means that the boot can still slide sideways if, for any reason, you are pulling up on your heels and therefore increasing the forward pressure on the toe-piece.

It is very important that your bindings are kept well lubricated and that they are serviced often.

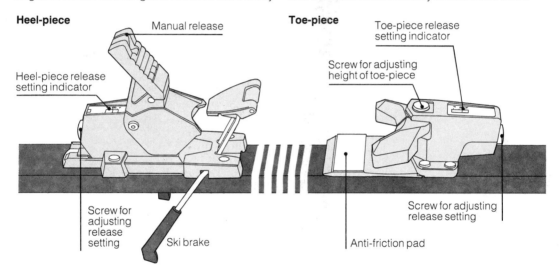

Heel-piece

Manual release

Heel-piece release setting indicator

Screw for adjusting release setting

Ski brake

Toe-piece

Toe-piece release setting indicator

Screw for adjusting height of toe-piece

Screw for adjusting release setting

Anti-friction pad

How the binding works

The ski boot is clamped into the binding by a toe-piece at the front and a heel-piece at the back. Both are adjustable.

All bindings are designed to release your boot when you fall so that your ski comes off just *before* your leg reaches the limit of its capacity to bend or twist without injury.

Most bindings release sideways at the toe and up at the heel. But, at the same time, they have a certain amount of movement or "elasticity" so that they can absorb the shocks encountered in normal skiing without releasing unnecessarily.

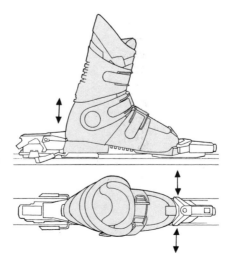

Binding "elasticity"
If a binding is to absorb bumps in uneven terrain without releasing, it must have a certain amount of "elasticity". In some cases the heel-piece can move as much as 30 mm (1¼ ins) and the toe-piece 25 mm (1 in) before releasing, yet still be able to "re-center" fast enough to cope with the next shock. A fast return-to-center speed is very important because unnecessary release at speed can be just as dangerous as no release occurring at all.

Heel-and-toe bindings

Although these bindings look similar, there are basic differences. The toe-pieces vary in that some are "single-pivot", where the pincer unit which holds the boot moves on a central screw, and others are "double-pivot", which means that two pincers work independently of each other. Heel-pieces differ in the way they fasten and unfasten, and some use the so-called "turntable" system.

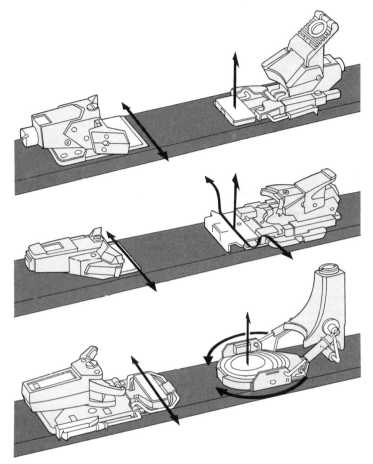

Binding with single-pivot toe-piece This binding has a standard heel release and a toe-piece that works as a single pivot. It also incorporates a special compensation system to prevent any upward pressure of the boot on the toe-piece interfering with the sideways release mechanism.

Diagonal heel release binding The heel unit of this binding releases diagonally as well as upwards. This is useful in forward twisting falls where the sideways release of the toe-piece may be prevented. The toe-piece itself operates on the double-pivot system – which means that, if necessary, each "arm" of the unit is capable of releasing independently.

Turntable binding The principle of the "turntable" system is that, in addition to the usual upward release, the whole heel unit rotates. Moreover, as well as giving additional support to the heel of the boot at the sides, the heel-piece of this type of binding pivots on a point directly beneath the pivot point of a skier's heel, thus aiding the release of the toe-piece in twisting falls.

Plate bindings

In this system, a flat rigid plate is attached to the bottom of the ski boot and the whole unit is then held onto the ski by a heel-piece and a toe-piece; the plate can be removed from the boot. It is the plate and not the boot which is in contact with the ski. This has the advantage that the condition of the boot sole, which on a conventional binding can prevent the release-mechanism from functioning, does not make any difference to the efficiency of the binding.

The main advantage of plate bindings is that they are "multi-release", often releasing sideways at both toe and heel, as well as forwards and backwards. The only inconvenience is that they are awkward to put on, particularly if you are standing on a slope after a fall.

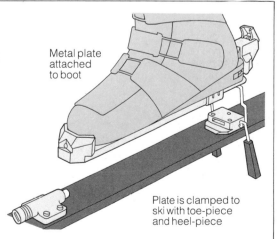

Metal plate attached to boot

Plate is clamped to ski with toe-piece and heel-piece

Choosing bindings

Selecting the right bindings depends on three factors: your weight, the strength of your leg bone, and your skiing ability. Each binding is designed to cope with a different weight range and, providing your weight is within that range, the binding will be suitable. The strength of your leg bone determines how much strain it can take before you hurt yourself. This can be ascertained by using calipers to measure the width of the top of your shin bone when your knee is bent. Then this measurement, together with your weight, will tell the ski shop what type of binding you will need. The standardization of the release-load setting by D.I.N. means that choosing bindings has become relatively simple; use the chart below as an approximate guide.

Always buy your bindings from an approved shop so that you can be sure that they will be fitted properly and adjusted to your own requirements.

Mounting bindings

Only matching pairs of binding units can be used together. It is not a good idea to try to mount bindings yourself; always take them to a shop which is authorized by the manufacturer to fit the bindings to your skis.

Bindings are fitted according to reference points marked on most skis. These are then matched to a point on the ski boot (if you do not have your own boots make sure you tell the workshop your normal boot size). The heel- and toe-pieces are then screwed onto the ski. The heel piece is usually mounted on short "runners" so that small adjustments can be made for different boot lengths. It can be loosened, slid backwards or forwards, and then tightened again.

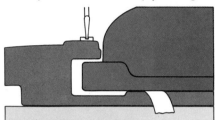

Adjusting height of toe-piece Position boot in binding with piece of paper underneath, on the anti-friction pad. Adjust height so that you can just remove the paper, leaving a very small gap between top of boot lip and binding.

The release setting

On a heel-and-toe binding, the release setting is clearly marked by a series of numbers which correspond to the D.I.N. scale range of that particular binding. Each unit is adjusted separately and the settings must be identical at front and back or the binding will not release properly.

Follow the binding setting chart (left) for the correct reading. The chart is set for intermediate skiers who ski at moderate speeds; an "aggressive" skier could probably go up the scale by 1 or 1.5 points, but a beginner should reduce the setting by the same amount. Before you make any adjustments yourself, test the release mechanisms as described opposite.

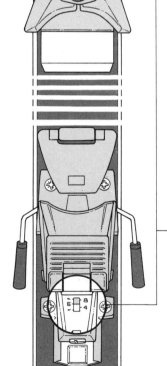

Adjusting the release settings These diagrams illustrate typical positions of the release-load indicators. There is normally a change of color or an arrow on the dial to indicate the actual setting. Make any adjustments by turning the screw on the front of the toe-piece or the back of the heel-piece.

Binding setting chart

Skier's weight		D.I.N. setting
Men	**Women**	
kgs (lbs)	kgs (lbs)	
10 (22)	10 (22)	1
15 (33)	15 (33)	1
20 (44)	20 (44)	1.5
25 (55)	25 (55)	2
30 (66)	30 (66)	2.5
35 (77)	35 (77)	2.5
40 (88)	40 (88)	3
45 (99)	45 (99)	3.5
50 (110)	50 (110)	4
55 (121)	60 (132)	4.5
60 (132)	70 (154)	4.5
65 (143)	80 (176)	5
70 (154)	90 (198)	5.5
75 (165)		6
80 (176)		6.5
85 (187)		6.5
90 (198)		7
95 (209)		7.5
100 (220)		8

Testing the release settings

The release load should have been set for you when the bindings were fitted. Before you ski, however, you must make certain that it is correct.

First check the sideways release of the toe-piece. This can be done by "kicking" or "twisting" your boot out of the binding. The "kick" test should only release the boot after a hard kick; the "twist" test should release the boot without hurting your leg.

To test the heel release, put on both skis and lean forward; your boots should come out one at a time fairly easily.

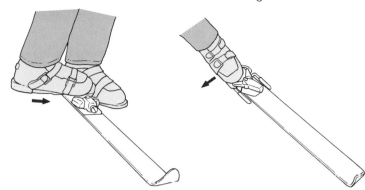

The "kick" test
With one ski flat on ground, make certain you can kick boot out of toe-piece with your other foot.

The "twist" test
Stand on one leg, lift other foot, edge ski tip in snow, make certain the boot releases as you twist foot.

The "fall forwards" test
Support yourself on ski poles, lean forwards over ski tips to make certain that both heel-pieces release upwards properly.

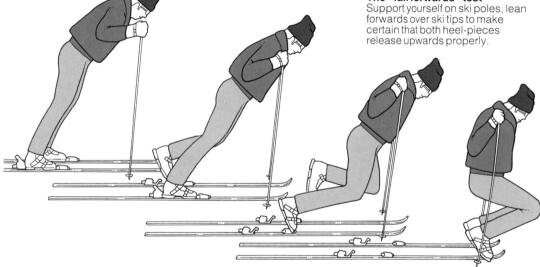

Ski brakes and safety straps

When you fall and come out of your bindings, "ski brakes" or "safety straps" stop your skis from hurtling downhill. Most modern bindings now have integrated ski brakes. These consist of two "prongs" which are lifted clear of the snow when you are wearing your skis, but which dig into it when your bindings release. Safety straps tie your skis to your legs. Their disadvantage is that they allow your skis to flail around when your bindings release.

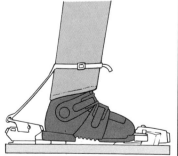

Ski brakes
These spring down and dig into snow to stop ski sliding when boot comes out of binding.

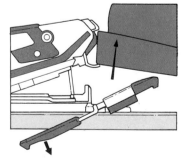

Safety straps
Their advantage is that you are less likely to lose skis if they come off in deep snow.

Ski techniques

The aim of this chapter is to help you master the basic skills of skiing. It covers the whole range of Alpine skiing techniques – from a beginner's first steps on a pair of skis to the advanced turns which have been adapted from modern ski racing for use on and off the specially prepared trails. It will also explain techniques that enable advanced skiers to ski safety in any situation.

The importance of good ski technique cannot be over-emphasized. It is vital right from the start in teaching beginners balance and control, natural body positions, simple movements, and the principle of independent leg action.

However, ski technique is not an end in itself. It is the means to an end. Its object should be the development of a natural, effective and safe skiing style. This is something that we explain in more detail in the chapter called "Functional skiing" (p.210). The techniques advocated in this book are all functional rather than "ideal". This means that we are concerned with showing skiers the best way to deal with multiple skiing situations rather than with the idea of stylistic perfection. And this is why we concentrate throughout this chapter, not only on how the basic movements are performed, but also on how they can be adapted and applied to different skiing situations and to varying terrain and snow conditions.

Watch how good skiers ski. Their movements are never unnecessarily exaggerated, flamboyant or risky. They are relaxed, controlled and efficient. Good skiers ski functionally and naturally. If you master the basic skills set out in the following pages and assemble them into an extensive "repertoire" of ski techniques, you will instinctively choose the right line down a slope and the right movement for every situation.

This chapter is based on the teaching methods used by the Swiss Ski School – which have themselves evolved from years of practical experience by its thousands of ski instructors – and it is organized in the form of a natural learning progression. As you develop and as your skiing improves, you will find that one movement leads directly to the next. Thus, snowplow turning evolves naturally into stem turning, which then leads to open-stance parallel turning and so to the more refined closed-stance parallel turning. From there, the advanced techniques are simply different ways of *initiating* parallel turns. They differ because they are functionally suited to specific snow, terrain and weather conditions or to the requirements of speed. Our teaching method is based on the belief that, from stem turning, or even from snowplow turning onwards, turns are all basically similar. The outside ski is always the steering ski, even in the advanced stepping techniques, and the turns are always steered in the same way. The difference lies in the initiation, in the way you *begin* to turn.

The concept of natural skiing is central to our method. By this we mean skiing that is effective and versatile and which is based on movements that are as simple and natural as possible, not skiing that strives to conform to strict teaching doctrines. Our ski technique is formed to a large extent by the world's top ski racers. For them, the *effectiveness* of their technique is always more important than the perfection or beauty of their style. As we show on p. 264, we can learn a lot by watching how children ski and by comparing their technique to that of ski racers. We have found that the movements which racers strive to perfect through intensive training and practice are performed instinctively by children. Simplicity, then, is one of the keys to the secret of good skiing. Throughout this chapter, we have tried to emphasize that, if you trust to your instinct, you will *feel* when you are doing something right and when you are doing it wrong. Experience has shown that this is more important than trying to enforce such ski-teaching clichés as "knees and skis together!" in situations where these movements are unnecessary.

Throughout this chapter, you will come across words which may not be familiar to you. Some of these (for example, "fall line", "schuss", "snowplow", "side-slip", "traverse", etc.) have been in use in ski terminology for many years. Their meanings are now almost universally accepted and they are explained clearly in the following pages. However, some words are entirely new (for example, "up-extension", "down-flexion", "banking", "stepping against or onto", etc.). They represent an attempt to use a terminology which is clearer and more precise in those areas of ski technique where terminology in the past has been vague and confusing. They are the result of the Swiss Ski School working closely with "Ski Interterm", an international body set up to discuss and establish an international terminology for ski technique. You will find these terms explained where they occur in the text and, in more detail if necessary, in the chapter on "Ski Mechanics" (p. 178).

Finally, the aim of all the words, diagrams, drawings and photographs in this chapter is to help you understand what it is you should be doing – and together they form as accurate a verbal and visual representation of skiing movements as possible. However, it should be emphasized that they are useful primarily as *aids* to understanding, and that they should be used in conjunction with proper ski school instruction. There is no substitute for personal experience if you want to learn to ski well.

The methodology of ski techniques

The way in which ski techniques are classified and the way in which they are taught varies from country to country throughout the world. However, with the increasing popularity of skiing as a recreational sport, attempts have been made to establish a more unified, international ski technique. National differences still exist, but the Interski Congresses, held every four years, and the work of Ski Interterm have helped to bridge the gaps. Of course, the continual changes and improvements in the design of boots, bindings and skis, as well as the observation and analysis of racing techniques and their adaptation to recreational skiing, means that the methodology is constantly being revised.

The chart below sets out a division of ski techniques into four categories – the basics, basic turning, parallel turning and stepping techniques. This reflects the methodology used by the Swiss Ski School, and it is the one followed in this book.

The basics

Standing, walking and turning around on skis

Falling and getting up

Walking uphill

Skiing down the fall line

Snowplowing

The turning snowplow

Traversing

Side-slipping and uphill turning

Skating and step turning

▼

Basic turning

Snowplow turning

Stem turning

Elementary open-stance parallel turning

▼

Parallel turning

Parallel uphill turning (open and closed stance)

Parallel downhill turning (open and closed stance)
    with an "up" initiation
    with a "down" initiation
    with a turning push-off from both legs
    in "short swinging" forms
    with an "absorption extension" initiation
    with a "jet" initiation
    with a "jump turning" initiation

▼

Stepping techniques

Stepping onto the uphill ski

Stepping against the uphill ski

Competition forms of stepping

The fall line

The term "fall line" is used almost constantly throughout this book and in any discussion of ski technique. Put simply, the fall line is the steepest, shortest and fastest line down a slope. Of course, it is rarely a straight line, because slopes are not regular; they undulate and change direction, and there are, in fact, as many fall lines as there are points on the slope. Although the fall line is an invisible, imaginary line, you will be able to *feel* it as soon as you stand on a slope. Unless you "edge" your skis at right angles to the fall line (p.44-5), they will slide downhill towards it.

All skiing movements are described in relation to the fall line. When *schussing* you ski straight down or close to the fall line. In a *traverse* you ski across the slope at an angle to the fall line. An *uphill turn* is a turn into the slope away from the fall line, and a *downhill turn* is one in which you ski in a continuous swing from a traverse, into the fall line and then away from it again into a new traverse in the other direction.

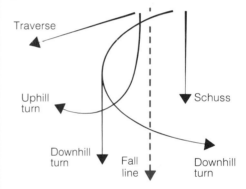

Fall line is always indicated by blue dotted line.

The terminology

There are two areas of ski terminology which need explanation right from the outset. They are used throughout this book and in ski schools all over the world. The first concerns the words "uphill", "downhill", "outside" and "inside" when used to describe which ski or which leg is which; and the second concerns the way in which any turn can be divided into four phases – the "preparation", "initiation", "steering" and "end" phase. Both are illustrated and explained below.

Uphill, downhill, outside and inside These terms are used when describing almost all ski techniques. They are less confusing than referring to, say, a skier's "right" ski or "left" leg and shoulder. When you are standing across a slope, traversing or side-slipping, your "uphill" side is the one nearest the top of the mountain, and your "downhill" side is the one nearest the valley. As you begin a turn and steer into the fall line, your "outside" is the side furthest from the center of the turn, and your "inside" is the side nearest the center of the turn. In other words, your uphill ski becomes your outside ski, and your downhill ski becomes your inside ski. As you steer out of the fall line into a new traverse, your outside ski becomes your downhill ski, and your inside ski becomes your uphill ski.

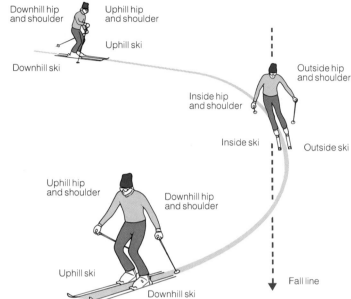

Downhill hip and shoulder
Uphill hip and shoulder
Uphill ski
Downhill ski
Outside hip and shoulder
Inside hip and shoulder
Inside ski
Outside ski
Uphill hip and shoulder
Downhill hip and shoulder
Uphill ski
Downhill ski
Fall line

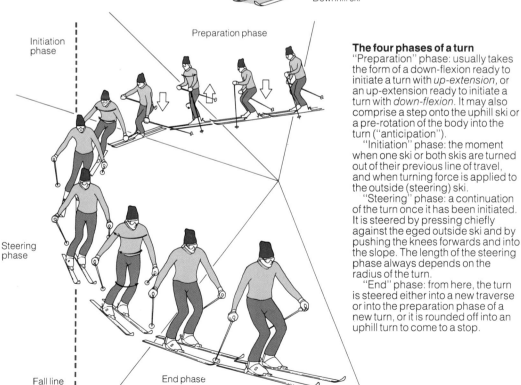

Initiation phase
Preparation phase
Steering phase
Fall line
End phase

The four phases of a turn

"Preparation" phase: usually takes the form of a down-flexion ready to initiate a turn with *up-extension,* or an up-extension ready to initiate a turn with *down-flexion.* It may also comprise a step onto the uphill ski or a pre-rotation of the body into the turn ("anticipation").

"Initiation" phase: the moment when one ski or both skis are turned out of their previous line of travel, and when turning force is applied to the outside (steering) ski.

"Steering" phase: a continuation of the turn once it has been initiated. It is steered by pressing chiefly against the eged outside ski and by pushing the knees forwards and into the slope. The length of the steering phase always depends on the radius of the turn.

"End" phase: from here, the turn is steered either into a new traverse or into the preparation phase of a new turn, or it is rounded off into an uphill turn to come to a stop.

The symbols and graphics

Where possible, every ski technique has been illustrated with both drawings and photographs. The photographs show the movement in its real context – on the trail, in deep snow, or on slopes of varying gradients. But the drawings are used to explain specific technical details, such as the rotary motion or counter-rotation of the body, the up-extension or down-flexion of the legs, and the weighting of the skis. For this reason, the following symbols have been employed.

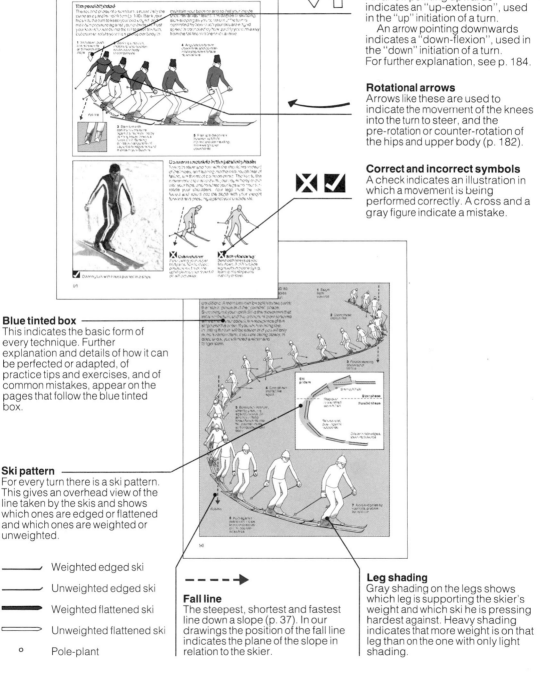

Unweighting arrows

An arrow pointing upwards indicates an "up-extension", used in the "up" initiation of a turn.

An arrow pointing downwards indicates a "down-flexion", used in the "down" initiation of a turn. For further explanation, see p. 184.

Rotational arrows

Arrows like these are used to indicate the movement of the knees into the turn to steer, and the pre-rotation or counter-rotation of the hips and upper body (p. 182).

Correct and incorrect symbols

A check indicates an illustration in which a movement is being performed correctly. A cross and a gray figure indicate a mistake.

Blue tinted box

This indicates the basic form of every technique. Further explanation and details of how it can be perfected or adapted, of practice tips and exercises, and of common mistakes, appear on the pages that follow the blue tinted box.

Ski pattern

For every turn there is a ski pattern. This gives an overhead view of the line taken by the skis and shows which ones are edged or flattened and which ones are weighted or unweighted.

——————⌐ Weighted edged ski

——————⌐ Unweighted edged ski

━━━━━▶ Weighted flattened ski

═════▷ Unweighted flattened ski

° Pole-plant

Fall line

The steepest, shortest and fastest line down a slope (p. 37). In our drawings the position of the fall line indicates the plane of the slope in relation to the skier.

Leg shading

Gray shading on the legs shows which leg is supporting the skier's weight and which ski he is pressing hardest against. Heavy shading indicates that more weight is on that leg than on the one with only light shading.

Putting on skis

Putting on skis is a simple routine. It is easier on flat terrain than on a slope, since you will find that your skis stay still instead of sliding away from under you. It is also easier with "ski brakes" (which most modern skis now have), since these dig into the snow and stop your skis from slipping until you step your boot into the binding. However, many skiers still use "safety straps" –

and these must be tied around the ankles when the skis are put on. With modern bindings, there is usually no difference between the left and the right ski, but check that yours are not an exception. You must also always check before you set off that your bindings are adjusted correctly so that they will release quickly and safely if you fall.

Putting on skis on the flat

Knocking snow from boot Apply short, sharp taps with the shaft of your pole to remove any snow – otherwise your boot will not fit into the binding.

1 Place both skis flat on snow, lean on poles for support, and rub one boot against the edge of ski or scrape it with ski pole to remove any snow.

2 Step into binding, toe first, and center boot over ski. Press down hard on heel until binding clicks into position and boot is securely fastened.

Treading down ski brakes When you are not wearing your skis, the ski brakes stop them running downhill. When you put your boot into the binding, they swing up and let your ski slide freely.

Scraping snow from boot Use the edge of the binding you are standing in for scraping snow off bottom of second boot. Lean on ski poles for support.

3 Place your other ski flat on snow parallel with the first. Scrape snow off your other boot along the edge of binding or ski you are standing on.

4 Step other foot into binding, toe first, center boot, and step hard onto the heel until you hear it click firmly and securely into place.

Tying safety straps Check that both boots are correctly in position. Then bend down and do up safety straps around your ankles.

Putting on skis on a slope

You will find that your skis tend to slide away from you when you try to put them on when standing on a slope. To prevent this from happening always place your skis across the hill, at right angles to the fall line, try to stamp out a flat platform in the snow for them, and put on the downhill ski first – then the uphill ski can rest against it without sliding away. A loose ski, without ski brakes, shooting down the trail is a great hazard to other skiers and may get lost or damaged if it goes off the trail.

1 Stamp out a ledge or platform in the snow at right angles to fall line, so that ski will lie flat and not slide away when you put it on. This is easier in soft snow than on a hard-packed or icy trail.

2 Clean snow off boot and put on downhill ski first. Ski brakes prevent ski from sliding as you click binding into place. Use poles for support.

3 Place uphill ski against downhill ski. Stand across the slope with weight on downhill ski.

4 Check to see that boot is free of snow and put on second ski. If you have safety straps, bend down and do them up. Ski brakes will automatically lift as you press down heel piece.

Taking off skis

Binding-release mechanisms vary: some are pulled upwards to disengage, but most are pushed down – either with your pole or your foot. If you are on a slope, always take off your uphill ski first. If you are wearing safety straps, do not undo them until you have released your boots from their bindings.

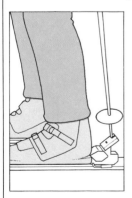

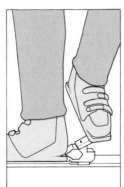

1 Use your pole to press down on the heel piece of the binding and lift up your foot. Step out of the binding heel first.

2 Press down on other heel piece with free foot to release binding. Bend down to undo safety straps if you are using them.

Tips for putting on skis

● Put on your skis out of the way of other skiers or you may cause an accident. If you are on a trail, go to the edge

● Before putting on your skis, clean off any snow stuck to the soles of your boots so that the binding will function properly

● Always check before you ski that your boots are properly centered in your bindings – otherwise the release mechanism will not function properly

● If possible, use ski brakes rather than safety straps. Ski brakes grip into the snow and make putting on skis easier, whereas straps allow the ski to slide freely as you put your toe into the binding. If you do not have ski brakes, stick your skis tails-downwards into the snow so that they cannot slide away downhill

● Stick your poles into the snow leaning uphill – so that, if they fall, they will fall into the slope, not downhill

● In powder snow, clear a ledge in the snow with your foot so that the skis can lie flat

● On icy surfaces, lay your skis on their edges while you get ready to put them on

Standing on skis

How to stand correctly when wearing skis is the first thing to learn in skiing technique. When you put on a pair of ski boots for the first time, you will realize that they force you to adapt your normal stance. The upper boot is built so that it forces your ankles and knees to flex, and the heel is deliberately high, so that you are pitched forwards slightly onto the balls of your feet (women who are used to wearing high-heeled shoes will find this more natural at first). In other words, the boots themselves make it easier to stand correctly. Relax your shoulders and back, keep your head up and your arms loosely in front of you. Keep your skis parallel, but slightly apart – the most comfortable and natural position is at about hip-width – and adopt a relaxed, balanced stance which will allow you to look ahead and react quickly. If you get the basic stance correct from the start, you will find that you will be able to ski more comfortably, efficiently and safely.

The pole grip
If your ski pole has a strap on the handle, loop it over your wrist; it will stop your pole from disappearing downhill if you fall and let go of it.

1 Slip hand through pole strap, palm facing downwards.

2 Grip handle firmly, over top of strap.

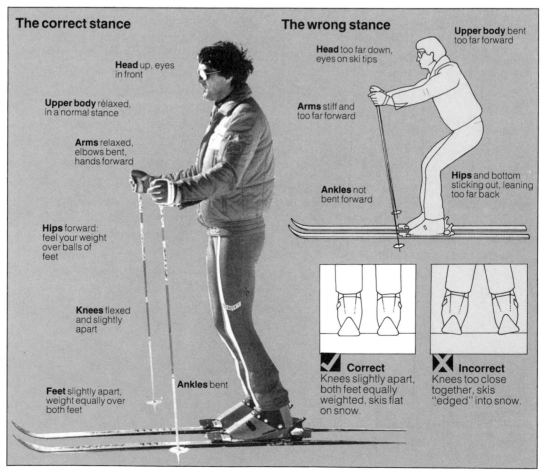

The correct stance

Head up, eyes in front

Upper body relaxed, in a normal stance

Arms relaxed, elbows bent, hands forward

Hips forward: feel your weight over balls of feet

Knees flexed and slightly apart

Ankles bent

Feet slightly apart, weight equally over both feet

The wrong stance

Upper body bent too far forward

Head too far down, eyes on ski tips

Arms stiff and too far forward

Ankles not bent forward

Hips and bottom sticking out, leaning too far back

✓ **Correct**
Knees slightly apart, both feet equally weighted, skis flat on snow.

✗ **Incorrect**
Knees too close together, skis "edged" into snow.

Getting used to your boots

Ski boots always feel heavy, stiff and hard to move about in at first. However, you will soon find that their rigidity makes it easier to transfer force from your foot through your skis to the snow. In fact, very precise control is possible. The exercise shown here will help you feel how your boots function. Stand still, on a flat surface, with your skis in a comfortable parallel stance. Rock backwards and forwards in your boots so that you feel how they support you and how the pressure from your feet is exerted onto the front, the back or the whole of your skis.

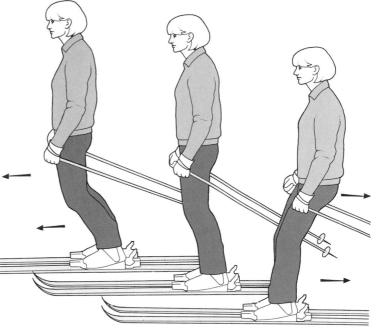

Leaning forward
When you lean forward, your weight will be on the balls of your feet. Your boots will support you and you will be exerting pressure on the fronts of your skis.

Standing upright
When standing upright, your weight will be evenly distributed on the bottom of both feet; you will be exerting pressure on the whole length of your skis.

Leaning back
When you lean back, your weight will be on your heels and you will feel your toes pressing up against the top of your boot; you will be exerting pressure on the back of your skis.

Getting used to your skis

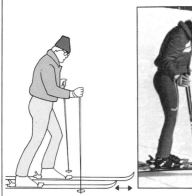

Sliding on skis
While standing on the spot, slide your skis backwards and forwards.

Jumping on skis
Either hop from one ski to the other or jump both skis off the snow.

Edging your skis
Roll your knees from side to side and feel how your skis tilt onto their edges.

Lifting one ski
To improve balance, stand on one ski, lift the other off the snow and swivel it.

Standing on a slope

The basic stance for standing on a slope is one of the foundations of all skiing technique. In order to stand on a slope without falling or slipping downhill, you must develop correct body angulation and correct edge control, keeping your skis perpendicular to the fall line. Body angulation is purely a question of balance: at first it will feel unnatural to lean away from the hill with your upper body, but it is necessary if you are to roll your hips into the slope and set your skis on their edges. The edges act as your brakes. Unless your skis are edged you will slide sideways downhill. You must always stand at right angles to the slope: if your skis are not perpendicular to the fall line, they will tend to slip backwards or forwards down the hill. This is something that you will develop with time.

At first, you will probably need to look down at your skis when setting them across the fall line; later, you should be able to *feel* the correct position instinctively. This means that, as your skiing improves, you will be able to keep your head up and look ahead. You can then concentrate on watching out for any obstacles or terrain hazards that lie ahead of you.

The correct stance for standing on a slope.

Correct body angulation

Keep your skis perpendicular to the fall line and parallel, at about hip-width for stability. Push your hips into the slope to edge your skis, then feel how twisting your uphill hip forward is more comfortable. This naturally pushes your uphill ski and uphill shoulder forward so that more weight is on your downhill ski and your upper body is relaxed, leaning out from the hill, and facing down the fall line. You will also feel how the amount of body angulation you need varies with the steepness of the slope. Do not stand knock-kneed, nor with your upper body bent forward: you are in no danger of falling as long as your skis are edged.

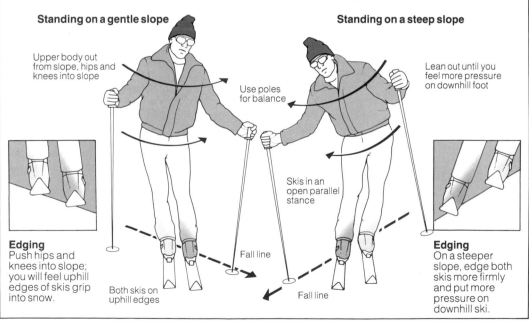

Standing on a gentle slope

Upper body out from slope, hips and knees into slope

Use poles for balance

Edging
Push hips and knees into slope; you will feel uphill edges of skis grip into snow.

Both skis on uphill edges

Fall line

Skis in an open parallel stance

Fall line

Standing on a steep slope

Lean out until you feel more pressure on downhill foot

Edging
On a steeper slope, edge both skis more firmly and put more pressure on downhill ski.

Edge control on a slope

Edging means tilting your skis onto their edges so that they bite into the snow. Edging gives you a platform to stand on and is the stance from which you initiate any movement on a slope. To set your edges, bend your ankles and push your hips and knees sideways into the slope. To maintain balance, lean out from the slope with your upper body until you feel that your edges are giving you enough grip. If you lean into the hill, your edges will not grip, your skis will slide away as they flatten on the snow, and you may fall. Edging requires precise control, but it is a vital skill that must be learned. Practice on the flat by rolling your knees from side to side to tilt your skis onto their edges.

Correct edging
Stand on your uphill edges, hips rolled into the slope, with most weight on your downhill foot.

Incorrect edging
If your hips are not pushed into the slope, your skis will flatten, lose their grip and slide downhill.

Keeping skis perpendicular to fall line

When your skis are exactly perpendicular to the fall line, you can stand motionless on a slope, without sliding backwards or forwards. Set your skis onto their uphill edges to hold your position, and push your hips into the slope, with your upper body balanced well forward over your skis and leaning away from the hill slightly for the correct amount of angulation.

Skis slide forwards downhill

Incorrect
If your ski tips are pointing down, not at right angles across the fall line, the pull of gravity will make you slide forwards.

Fall line

Skis slide backwards downhill

Correct ski position
Feel your weight on the balls of your feet: this shifts your body weight well forward over your feet. Flex your ankles and press your knees and hips into the slope to set your skis on their uphill edges in order to hold your stance.

Incorrect
If your tails are tilting back, your skis will not be perpendicular to the fall line, and you will slide backwards.

45

Turning around on the flat

On flat ground, turning around is easy. You simply use the technique known as the "star turn" and step your skis around one by one in the form of a circle – either radiating from the tips of your skis or from the tails, whichever you prefer. Turning around on a slope is more difficult, because you must prevent yourself from sliding downhill as you turn; this is dealt with on p. 57 under the heading of "herringbone turning" and on p. 58 in the form of "kick turning". If you are a beginner, star turning is usually taught first as an exercise for getting used to skis and second as a technique for turning.

The star turn

In star turning, your skis move around on the snow like the hands of a clock. It is a simple step-by-step movement. Start with your skis parallel and your poles planted on either side of your body. Lift the tip of one ski, swing it sideways, and set it down again about 30cm (1ft) away, pivoting it around the tail. Transfer your weight onto it, then lift the tip of your other ski and swing that around parallel to the first. Take small steps and continue round in the same way.

There is also a star turn variation in which you pivot around the tips of your skis instead of around your tails (see opposite).

Ski pattern

Basic technique for star turn around tails

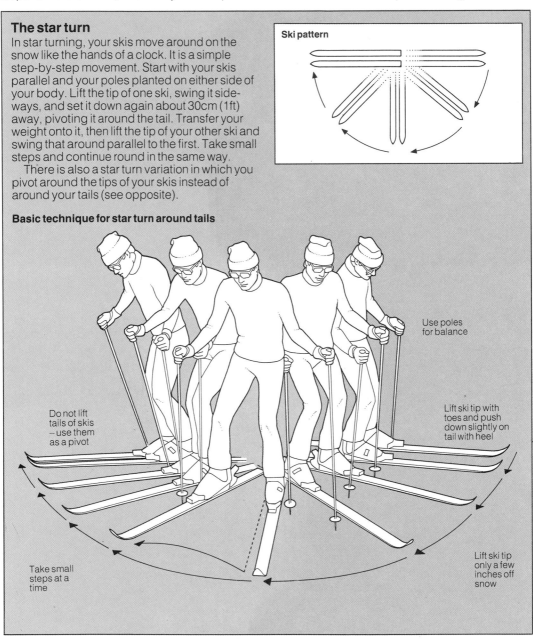

Do not lift tails of skis – use them as a pivot

Take small steps at a time

Use poles for balance

Lift ski tip with toes and push down slightly on tail with heel

Lift ski tip only a few inches off snow

A star turn in deep snow
The pattern left in the snow by the skis shows clearly how the "star turn" gets its name.

When to use the star turn

- As the simplest and easiest way of turning around on the spot when on flat terrain

- As an exercise for beginners to get used to the feel of their skis

Star turn variation

If you find it easier and more natural, do a star turn around the tips, rather than the tails, of your skis. The technique is the same; the choice is merely a question of personal preference. In this case, lift only the tails of your skis. Keep the tips firmly in the snow to act as a pivot point for your skis. This way, you will turn around in a circle instead of simply moving sideways.

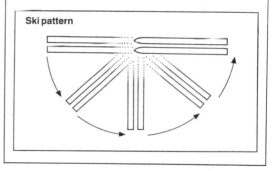

Ski pattern

Common mistakes when star turning

Treading on your own skis and getting tangled with your poles are the most common problems. These are usually caused by trying to rush the movement and by not being used to the feel of your skis and boots. Practice by lifting and swivelling one ski at a time. Then make your turn slowly, coordinate your skis and poles, take small steps, and concentrate on pivoting around either the tips or tails of your skis.

Stepping ski off snow Do not lift your ski completely off the ground. You will lose your pivot point and simply take a step sideways.

Stepping too far If you try to take too large a step in one go, you may overbalance as you try to bring your other ski parallel.

Crossed skis If pivoting around your tails, keep them firmly on the snow, otherwise you may set one ski down on top of the other one.

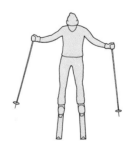

Over-reaching with poles Do not plant your poles too far away from you, otherwise you will not be able to use them to support yourself.

Walking on skis

Your first attempts to walk on skis will probably feel awkward and clumsy. You will find that your skis restrict your leg movements and your boots hold your feet rigid. Unlike normal shoes, the soles of ski boots do not flex: you cannot bend your foot and push off from your toes as usual. Although you can move your legs backwards and forwards, your ankles and feet are held firmly. Moreover, you have very little grip: the skis slide freely backwards and forwards. Walking on skis therefore requires more effort than ordinary walking. Point your skis in the direction you want to go and keep them parallel, about hip-width apart so that you feel comfortably balanced. Take short strides, and slide your skis forward across the snow. Do not try to "step" them: keep them on the snow. Lean forward and feel how this naturally forces a forward movement. Look ahead, not down at your feet. Use your poles to help you balance and to give yourself support at each step. Swing them forwards, in time with your opposite leg – left ski and right pole together, right ski and left pole together – and plant them level with your leading foot, next to your ski. Aim at coordinating your leg and arm movements so that you move fluidly and easily, without straining. Above all, do not try to rush: you will only tire yourself out. The way to travel faster is to lean forward, push off harder with your poles and *slide* forward over the snow on your skis, not try to take longer steps.

A relaxed, easy movement is best for walking on skis.

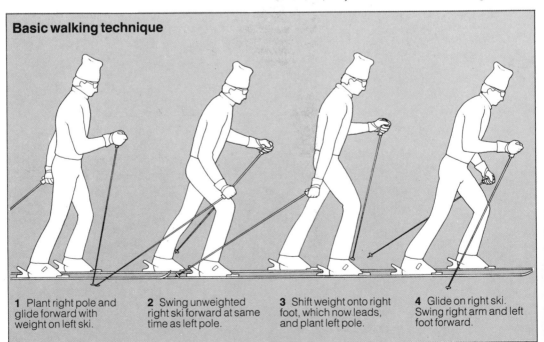

Basic walking technique

1 Plant right pole and glide forward with weight on left ski.

2 Swing unweighted right ski forward at same time as left pole.

3 Shift weight onto right foot, which now leads, and plant left pole.

4 Glide on right ski. Swing right arm and left foot forward.

Common mistakes when walking

You must bend your legs when walking on skis. If your legs are stiff, walking will feel difficult and tiring, and you will make poor progress. The unusual sensation of gliding and the fear of falling over tends to make beginners tense up their muscles. You must relax, lean forward, and flex your legs. First of all, loosen your boots slightly so that you feel more comfortable and so that you can flex your ankles freely. Try doing some exercises to get used to the feel of your skis on the snow (p. 43): slide your skis backwards and forwards, lift them up alternately, and feel how your weight is on one foot then the other, then hop on the spot. Cross-country walking is the best way to practice (p. 194).

✓ Correct walking movement Coordinate leg and arm movements in a natural rhythm, keep weight forward and slide skis across snow.

☒ Lifting skis If you lean back too far, you will lift your ski off the snow. Bend ankles and knees, lean forward and slide skis on snow.

☒ Incorrect coordination If you bring forward the same arm and leg with each step, you are doing what is called "mule walking"

☒ Stiff legs If you do not flex legs, body weight will be too far back and progress will be slow and tiring. Bend from ankles, not hips.

The double-pole push

On slightly sloping terrain, you will experience your first sensation of gliding on both skis. To travel faster and to conserve your energy, use a "double-pole push" rather than walking steps. Reach out with your arms and swing both poles forwards. Plant them in the snow just ahead of your feet, close to your skis. Then bend forward and down, and pull your body up to your poles. Follow the movement through, stay in a low crouch, and lean into the glide. When your poles are level with your hips, push hard, thrust yourself forward and rise up again. Take care not to plant your poles too far ahead or you will overstretch and not be able to pull yourself forward.

1 Rise up, swing forward and plant poles just in front of feet.

2 Sink down and pull forward on poles.

3 Push off, follow through and sink into low crouch.

4 Glide forwards and rise up ready for next pole plant.

Falling

Every skier falls—usually accidentally, but sometimes deliberately. It is an inevitable part of skiing, and there is nothing shameful about it. When you are learning to ski, you must know how to stop before you set off, and one of the most effective ways to stop in an emergency is to fall over deliberately. Knowing that you can stop when you want to by falling safely will greatly increase your confidence. Falling does not normally hurt, because snow is soft and will cushion you, but there is a safe way to control a fall, and it will help you avoid unnecessary bruises and strains if you know how to fall safely.

The safe way to fall from a traverse
In this sequence, the skier is travelling in a gentle traverse. He controls his fall by sitting down into the slope and ends up with his skis across the fall line.

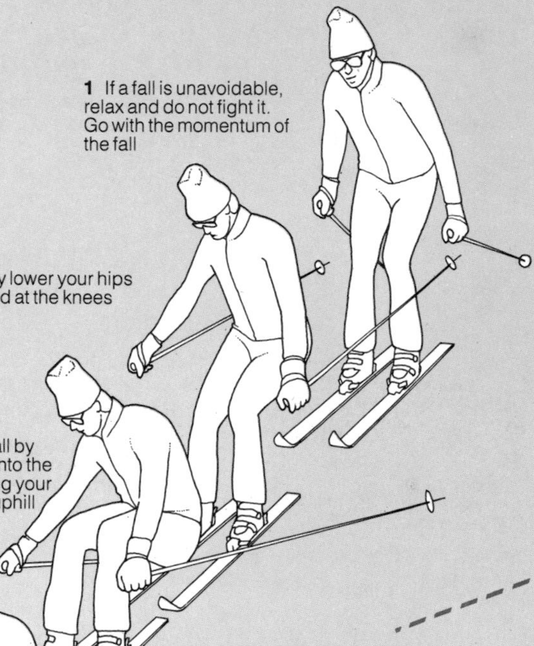

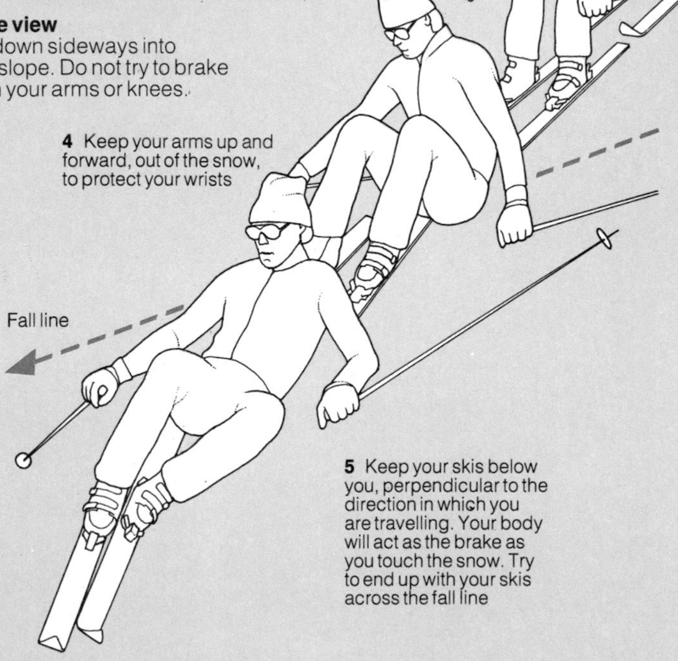

1 If a fall is unavoidable, relax and do not fight it. Go with the momentum of the fall

2 Slowly lower your hips and bend at the knees

3 Begin to fall by sitting back into the slope, twisting your hips to your uphill side

Side view
Sit down sideways into the slope. Do not try to brake with your arms or knees.

4 Keep your arms up and forward, out of the snow, to protect your wrists

Fall line

The safe way to fall from a schuss If you are skiing down the fall line, sit down sideways, to one side of your skis. Try to swing your skis around below you at right angles to the fall line.

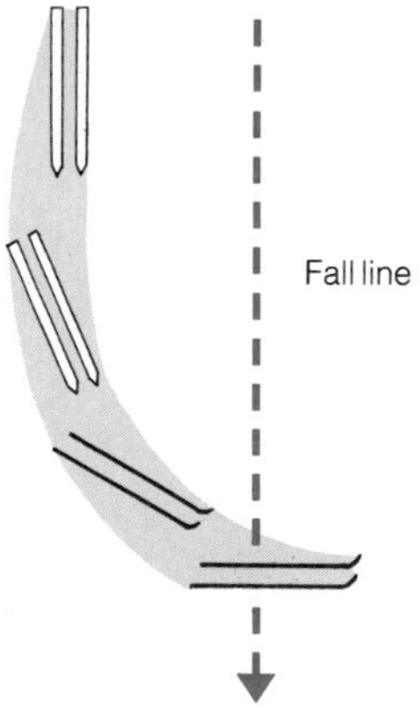

Fall line

5 Keep your skis below you, perpendicular to the direction in which you are travelling. Your body will act as the brake as you touch the snow. Try to end up with your skis across the fall line

✔ An example of a controlled, safe fall with skis perpendicular to fall line

Common mistakes when falling

It is a fact that many of the worst falls are caused by trying to stop yourself from falling. Sprained legs and arms often happen this way. Once you have gone past the point of no return and a fall is inevitable, give in to it, do not fight it. If you do fall forwards, try to roll over on your back so that your skis are below you, down the slope. If you have a bad fall, which you really cannot control, your bindings should release and your skis should come off. For this to happen, your bindings must be regularly checked and properly adjusted (p. 34) to suit your weight and skiing ability.

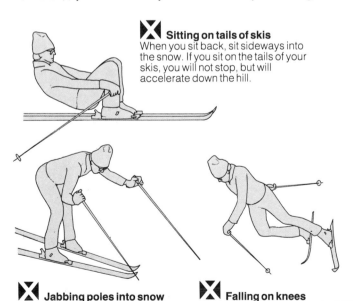

✘ **Sitting on tails of skis**
When you sit back, sit sideways into the snow. If you sit on the tails of your skis, you will not stop, but will accelerate down the hill.

✘ **Jabbing poles into snow**
If you try to prevent yourself from falling by planting your poles in front of you, you may sprain your wrists and jolt your body.

✘ **Falling on knees**
Trying to stop in a traverse by falling sideways and digging your uphill knee into the snow is always painful and is a common cause of injury.

Tips on falling

● Remember that the safest way of falling is simply to sit sideways into the slope

● Do not be afraid of falling. To gain confidence, practice by standing on soft snow and letting yourself fall sideways

● Do not stick your poles out in front of you

● Do not land on your knees or your hands

● Try to avoid falling forwards and rolling over

● Do not get into the habit of falling every time you have to attempt something difficult; always *try* to stay on your feet. But, if you are really out of control, do not fight the fall

Getting up from a fall

If you fall over, you should get up fairly promptly. Not only will you get cold lying in the snow, but you may be in the way of other skiers. However, do not rush unnecessarily; many falls are the result of fatigue, so relax for a moment and catch your breath. If you have taken a bad tumble, look around for your poles, hat and goggles. If you are lying head-first down the slope, roll onto your back and swing your legs up and over so that your skis are below you and so that you are sitting above them. Getting up is not difficult, but you must take the time to get into the right position before you start.

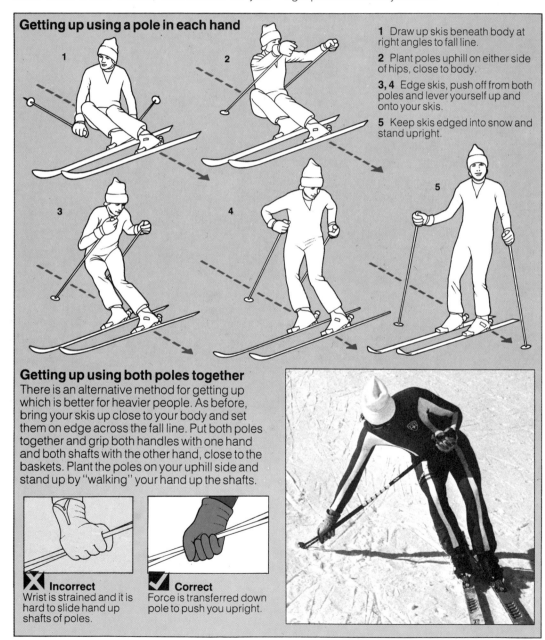

Getting up using a pole in each hand

1 Draw up skis beneath body at right angles to fall line.

2 Plant poles uphill on either side of hips, close to body.

3, 4 Edge skis, push off from both poles and lever yourself up and onto your skis.

5 Keep skis edged into snow and stand upright.

Getting up using both poles together

There is an alternative method for getting up which is better for heavier people. As before, bring your skis up close to your body and set them on edge across the fall line. Put both poles together and grip both handles with one hand and both shafts with the other hand, close to the baskets. Plant the poles on your uphill side and stand up by "walking" your hand up the shafts.

Incorrect
Wrist is strained and it is hard to slide hand up shafts of poles.

Correct
Force is transferred down pole to push you upright.

Being helped up

It is much easier to get up on a slope than on the flat, as the incline tilts you up naturally. On the flat, it is less tiring if someone pulls you up by one arm as you push off with your other hand.

What to do if your ski comes off

If one of your bindings releases, the ski brake or safety strap should stop your ski from sliding downhill. But always secure a loose ski by stamping out a ledge and edging it across the fall line.

1 Retrieve your ski and swivel yourself around so that the boot which has come out of its binding is on your uphill side.

2 Get up, stand on your downhill ski, lay the other ski above it so that it will not slip away, and step into your binding.

Common mistakes when getting up

Getting back on your feet again after a fall does not require any special strength or agility. Almost all the difficulties that beginners encounter are the result of not getting into the right position before trying to stand up. You must remember to bring your skis up close to your body, edge them across the slope and plant your poles close behind you.

Poles too far away
Keep your poles close to your body, just behind your hips. If you plant them too far apart and too far up the slope, you will not be able to put your full weight on them and you will not get enough leverage.

Skis not parallel
If you do not draw your skis up to your body, edge them and keep them parallel, your legs will be stretched out straight, and you will not be able to tip yourself over onto your skis.

Skis not across slope
If your skis are not at right angles to the fall line, they will simply slide away from under you as soon as you put your weight onto them and you will career off downhill out of control.

Walking uphill on skis

There are many occasions when you will have to walk uphill on your skis. As a beginner, you will probably not use the lifts in your first few days of ski school; instead, you will have to walk up the nursery slopes wearing your skis. So the technique has to be mastered before you begin skiing downhill. Walking uphill on skis takes a lot of effort, and knowing the correct method enables you to do it with maximum efficiency and minimum exhaustion. Apart from this, it is a good warming-up exercise: it will strengthen your leg muscles, it requires you to use the edges on your skis to create a platform for yourself on the slope, it encourages the use of the correct pole grip, and, above all, it helps you to get used to the feel of your skis.

There are two methods of walking uphill: the "side-step" and the "herringbone". Side-stepping can be used for climbing straight up the fall line or diagonally, as in a traverse. The choice of technique varies with the steepness of the slope, but it is also a matter of personal preference. Use the method which feels easiest and least tiring. The crucial thing to remember about all the techniques for climbing is that your skis will naturally gravitate towards the fall line and, unless you always support yourself – either with your poles or by edging your skis into the snow – you will slip downhill.

When to use the herringbone

● This technique is somewhat acrobatic and can be tiring: use it on gentle slopes, for short ascents, and while waiting for lifts

When to use the side-step

● On a steep slope, the least tiring method of getting uphill is the side-step. It is also the best technique for climbing in deep snow or on a slippery, icy surface. In some situations, it may be used for stepping downhill

When to use the diagonal side-step

● This is the fastest and most often-used technique. Use it for making long ascents, zig-zagging your way uphill by linking traverses with herringbone turns

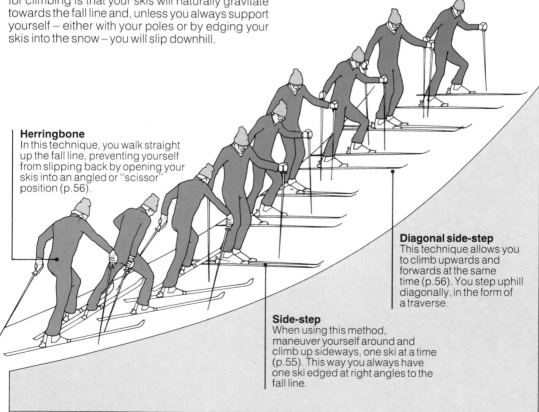

Herringbone
In this technique, you walk straight up the fall line, preventing yourself from slipping back by opening your skis into an angled or "scissor" position (p.56).

Diagonal side-step
This technique allows you to climb upwards and forwards at the same time (p.56). You step uphill diagonally, in the form of a traverse.

Side-step
When using this method, maneuver yourself around and climb up sideways, one ski at a time (p.55). This way you always have one ski edged at right angles to the fall line.

Side-stepping

On steep slopes, the most efficient climbing method is to step your skis sideways uphill; the technique is like walking upstairs sideways. You put your weight on your downhill ski and step up your uphill ski. Then transfer your weight to your uphill ski and bring your downhill ski up alongside. Do not try to go too fast, take small steps, and push your hips into the slope so that your upper body is leaning out and facing downhill – this will automatically edge your skis. Always keep your skis at right angles to the fall line, otherwise you will feel yourself slipping either backwards or forwards; and always keep your weighted ski edged into the snow.

Step 1/front view

Step 2/front view

Side-stepping in deep snow
This shot, taken from above the skier and looking down the slope, shows the clear ski print left in soft snow by side-stepping uphill.

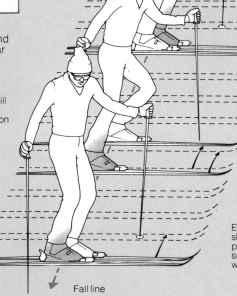

4 Repeat steps 1 to 3 and continue climbing, maintain body angulation throughout to give better edge control

3 Step up downhill ski alongside and bring up both poles

2 With all your weight on downhill ski, lift uphill ski and step it further up slope, setting it down on its edge. Now transfer weight to uphill ski

1 Stand across slope in comfortable parallel stance. Twist uphill hip forward, push it into slope to edge skis, and face down fall line

Either step up both skis and then both poles or lift poles separately, in time with each step

Fall line

Diagonal side-stepping

This is the most-often-used climbing step, since it is the quickest and least tiring technique. It is an adaptation of the side-step and is used to climb in a traverse, rather than straight up the fall line: you step upwards and forwards in one movement. There are two variations: beginners will feel more comfortable if their uphill ski always stays ahead, but better skiers may step their skis in front of each other as they would do when walking.

Ski tracks left by diagonal side-stepping in deep snow

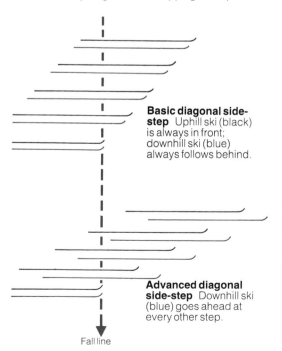

Basic diagonal side-step Uphill ski (black) is always in front; downhill ski (blue) always follows behind.

Advanced diagonal side-step Downhill ski (blue) goes ahead at every other step.

Fall line

The herringbone

This method of walking uphill on your skis is slower and more energetic than other climbing techniques. It can be very tiring, so it is best used for short ascents on gentle slopes. To stop yourself from slipping backwards, you open the tips of your skis into a wide "V" (the steeper the slope, the wider the angle of the "V") and push your knees into the slope to set your skis on their inside edges. This gives you a platform from which to push off as you take each step. Keep your poles behind your skis all the time so that you can support yourself on them. Take small steps, raise one ski at a time, and step it upwards – always keeping your weight on the ski which is edged into the slope. Move your left ski and right pole together, and your right ski and left pole together. Long skis may overlap each other, so beware of treading on the tails of your own skis.

✔ **Correct pole grip** In order to push off when poles are behind you, close palm over top of handle, thumb and fingers downwards.

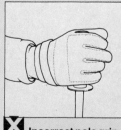

✘ **Incorrect pole grip** If you hold your poles normally, you will find it awkward to plant them behind you and you may sprain your wrists.

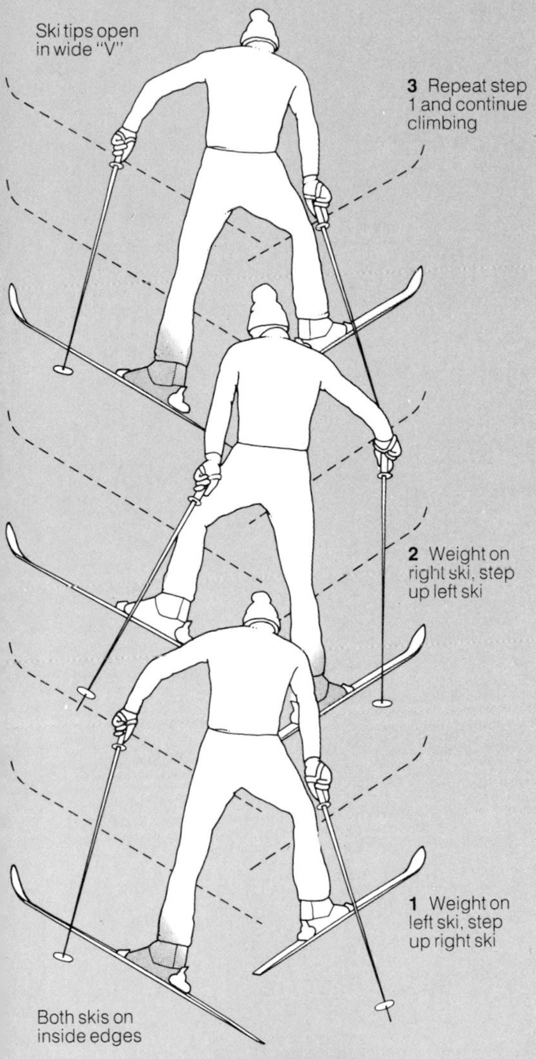

Ski tips open
in wide "V"

3 Repeat step
1 and continue
climbing

2 Weight on
right ski, step
up left ski

1 Weight on
left ski, step
up right ski

Both skis on
inside edges

Keeping your skis edged
At each step, flex your knee, push it into
the slope and set your ski firmly into the
snow on its inside edge. This will give
you a good grip and will stop you
from sliding back downhill.

Herringbone turning

If you are climbing uphill using the herringbone
technique and you want to change to side-
stepping, you must turn around so that you are
standing across the slope instead of facing up the
fall line. The "herringbone turn" allows you to do this
without slipping downhill. You step your skis
around one by one, as in a star turn, but support
yourself on your poles. The technique can also be
used for a full 180° turn on a slope.

1 Herringbone position,
poles in snow behind and
below. Put weight onto
left ski and lift right ski.

2 Pivot right ski on tail,
step it around slightly and
set it down. Lift right pole.

3 Plant right pole further
down slope, transfer
weight to right ski. Lean
into slope to edge skis.

4 Step left ski around,
use poles to stop yourself
sliding backwards.

5 Weight on left ski, step
right ski perpendicular to
fall line.

6 Step left ski parallel, so
both are at right angles to
fall line. Bring left pole
around.

Kick turning

The best technique for turning around on a slope is the "kick turn". It may feel awkward at first, as it requires mobility and a good sense of balance. Take care always to have three points of support – both poles and one leg – and do the movement fairly quickly to avoid getting stuck in an awkward position. The kick technique varies slightly according to the length of your skis: kick turning with long or normal skis is shown in this sequence; with compact skis, the movement is much easier (see far right).

1 Always do a kick turn with your back to the mountain. Start from a relaxed stance, skis parallel across the fall line and edged into the snow, your poles on either side of you.

2 Put your weight on your uphill leg and then kick your downhill ski tip up into the air in front of you. Use your poles for balance and support.

4 Immediately, lift your downhill pole out of the snow, swing it back and plant it behind you, above your uphill ski.

5 Lean back with your weight on your poles and let your vertical ski pivot around its tail. As it swings around, swivel your hips.

6 Let your raised ski pivot through 180° until it is parallel with the other one but facing in the opposite direction.

8 Twist your hips around and flex your knees comfortably so that you can lift your uphill ski, swing it around and bring it parallel.

9 Follow through with your body and your outside pole as you twist your leg around – but take care that your pole follows after your ski.

10 Set down your ski and edge it securely across the fall line. You are now facing in the opposite direction.

3 Stretch out your leg to bring your ski vertical and let the tail rest in the snow briefly – but not for too long or you will lose the momentum of the movement.

7 Now set your reversed ski into the snow on its uphill edge at right angles to the fall line and transfer your weight onto it.

When to use the kick turn

● As the quickest way of turning around while you are stationary

● For turning around while standing on a slope

● As a way of turning on a slope without losing height

● To get out of a tricky situation – such as a restricted space with no room to ski a turn

Kick turning with short skis

It is much easier to kick turn with short or "compact" skis. The technique is the same, but you do not need to rest the ski tail on the snow as you do when wearing long skis. With short skis, you can swivel your downhill ski around its tail in one movement.

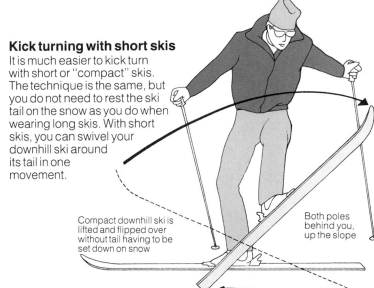

Compact downhill ski is lifted and flipped over without tail having to be set down on snow

Both poles behind you, up the slope

Common mistakes when kick turning

Although this movement does not feel as uncomfortable as it looks, it is still fairly acrobatic – requiring you to twist your body right around while standing on one leg. The important factor is to stand with your skis parallel and edged at right angles to the fall line, otherwise they will slide away as you try to turn. Always turn your downhill ski first, with your back to the hill.

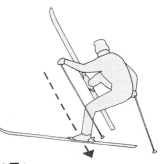

Facing uphill instead of downhill If you are on a slope, do a kick turn with your back to the mountain. This way, if you fall, you will fall into the slope, not backwards down the hill.

Poles too close to body Plant your poles far enough behind you to allow you to bring your second ski around without it hitting your poles.

Bringing pole around too early As you swing your second ski around, follow it with your pole. If you swing the pole around first, it will be in the way of your ski.

Skiing down the fall line

"Schussing" or "straight running" is the term given to straight skiing downhill. With your skis parallel, flat on the snow and equally weighted, you simply ski straight down the fall line, without turning or braking. Relax your upper body, let your shoulders hang loosely, flex your legs and lean forwards slightly. If you feel pressure over the whole sole of your foot, you will be in the correct position. Your skis should be in an open parallel stance – far enough apart to feel comfortable and natural.

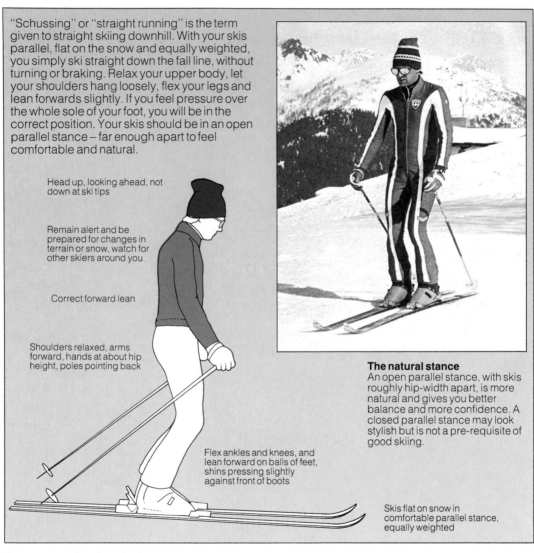

Head up, looking ahead, not down at ski tips

Remain alert and be prepared for changes in terrain or snow, watch for other skiers around you

Correct forward lean

Shoulders relaxed, arms forward, hands at about hip height, poles pointing back

Flex ankles and knees, and lean forward on balls of feet, shins pressing slightly against front of boots

The natural stance
An open parallel stance, with skis roughly hip-width apart, is more natural and gives you better balance and more confidence. A closed parallel stance may look stylish but is not a pre-requisite of good skiing.

Skis flat on snow in comfortable parallel stance, equally weighted

Common mistakes in the schussing stance

Most faults are the result of panic: fear of the fall line and fear of your own speed. If you feel you are going too fast, either try to go into a snowplow (p. 66) or sit down deliberately (p. 50). Do *not* tense up your body. Tenseness is always a sign of fear. You must relax, flex your arms and lean forward, not back, so that you can control your skis.

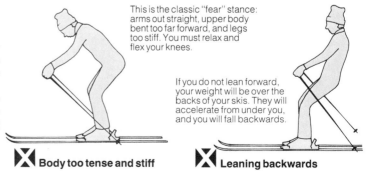

This is the classic "fear" stance: arms out straight, upper body bent too far forward, and legs too stiff. You must relax and flex your knees.

If you do not lean forward, your weight will be over the backs of your skis. They will accelerate from under you, and you will fall backwards.

Body too tense and stiff

Leaning backwards

60

Turning into the fall line

If you are standing across the slope, you must turn your skis into the fall line before beginning your schuss. For beginners, the only way to do this without sliding out of control is to plant your poles down the slope, lean on them and gradually shuffle your skis around until they are pointing downhill.

1 Stand across slope, weight on downhill ski. Plant downhill pole down slope, step uphill ski around slightly.

2 Plant other pole down slope, lean on both poles. Step downhill ski around, keeping both skis "wedged".

3 Take small steps and swivel skis around, one at a time. Lean onto poles to prevent yourself from sliding downhill.

4 When both skis are pointing down fall line, between poles, begin schussing, bringing skis parallel.

Adapting your schuss to your speed

A relaxed, upright stance is the most comfortable way to schuss at low speeds. But, as the gradient steepens, lean further forward so that your body is always more-or-less perpendicular to the slope. Flexing your legs in preparation enables you to react more quickly when you need to. The exaggerated tuck or "egg" position cuts down your wind resistance and helps you to accelerate.

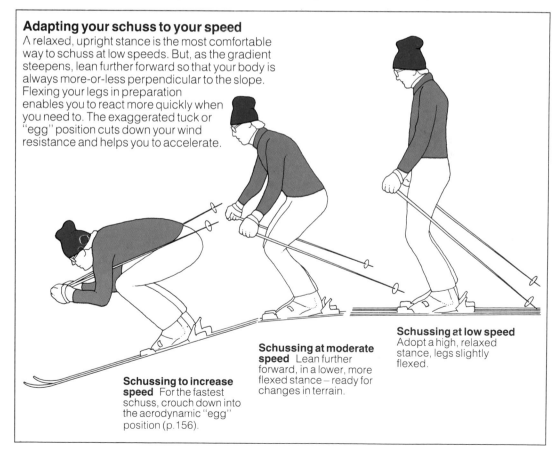

Schussing to increase speed For the fastest schuss, crouch down into the aerodynamic "egg" position (p.156).

Schussing at moderate speed Lean further forward, in a lower, more flexed stance – ready for changes in terrain.

Schussing at low speed Adopt a high, relaxed stance, legs slightly flexed.

Schussing over bumps and dips

No trail is absolutely smooth: it always comprises some gentle undulations and may contain abrupt changes of gradient or "moguls" (p. 230). These bumps and dips can easily throw you off balance unless you adapt your basic schuss position to absorb the jolts and sudden variations in speed. The secret of the technique is to "coil" your legs and body so that they act like the suspension of a car. Your head and shoulders remain steady, while your legs "soak up" the shock. At first, you must learn to do this "actively" – by deliberately flexing and extending your legs and by pushing down on your skis to keep them on the snow. Later, you will be able to

Flex on bumps
Bend forward and flex
your knees on the bump,
keep skis in touch
with snow

Schussing from a gentle to a steep slope

Slopes with variable pitches require a special technique to adjust to the changes in steepness and to absorb them smoothly. If you ski fast from a gentle slope to a steep one, you may find that you take off – because your body inertia will keep you going in the same line of trajectory, regardless of the change in slope. Then, when you land on the steeper slope, your skis will suddenly accelerate faster than your body and you will feel yourself being pitched backwards. To avoid this, flex your legs, crouch down, and push downwards and forwards over the front of your skis as you hit the lip of the slope edge. This way, you can force your skis to stay on the snow and your body will be well forward in preparation.

The same technique is used when skiing from deep snow onto a smooth trail, as your skis will accelerate on the harder surface.

✅ **Correct**
Lean forward to counteract inertia and acceleration of skis, and to stay in contact with snow.

❎ **Incorrect**
If you do not flex, you will take off. If you do not lean forward, you will be pitched back as your skis suddenly accelerate.

do it "passively" – by relaxing your body and allowing your legs to flex and extend naturally.

Approach a bump in the normal schuss position but, as you come up to the top, flex your knees and bend your legs. At the same time, lean forward for better balance and to avoid being thrown backwards. Aim to keep your skis on the snow all the time and to "swallow" the bump by letting your legs, not your upper body, absorb the shock. As you ski off the top of the bump down into the dip, stretch your legs and straighten your body so that you are fully extended as you reach its lowest point. Remember: flex on the bump, extend in the dip.

Extend in dips
Straighten up and extend your legs in the dip, upper body as relaxed as possible

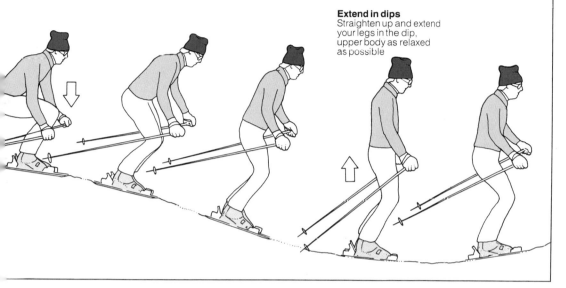

Schussing from a steep slope to flat ground

On any slope which suddenly changes from steep to gentle, you will feel yourself abruptly thrown forwards. What happens is that your skis are pushed up with a jolt as they hit the flatter slope, but your body continues travelling forward in the same line. This phenomenon is a great hazard in downhill racing and, at very high speeds, the "compression" as it is known can make a racer feel that he is being pushed forward onto his face. The answer, once again, is to be prepared for the slope edge and to be ready to absorb the shock. Just before you hit the flatter slope, lean back slightly and extend your legs. Then let yourself flex down into a crouch as you absorb the downward and forward push of your momentum.

Use the same technique to counteract the deceleration of your skis when skiing from a smooth trail into deep snow.

Correct
Stand up and lean back slightly, then let your legs flex and bend body forward to absorb jolt.

Incorrect
Skis suddenly brake as tips are forced up and you are thrown forwards by your own inertia.

Snowplowing

The snowplow, sometimes called the "wedge", can be used for stopping, braking, gliding and, in the form of the "turning snowplow", for changing direction. It is the basic technique for controlling speed in the early stages of learning to ski. However, because it is the only way to slow down without changing direction, it is also relied upon by expert skiers in bad weather or in situations where there is not enough room to brake by making a turn – for example, on narrow woodland trails. The key to the snowplow stance is the V-shape formed by the skis – tips together and tails apart. It relies upon the use of edge control and the principle of exerting pressure against the skis so that a braking force is generated by the friction between the snow and the skis. It is most successfully performed in a relaxed, natural stance in which you flex your ankles and knees. In the following pages we show how to use the snowplow to stop (p. 66), to glide at a controlled speed (p. 67) and to turn (p. 68).

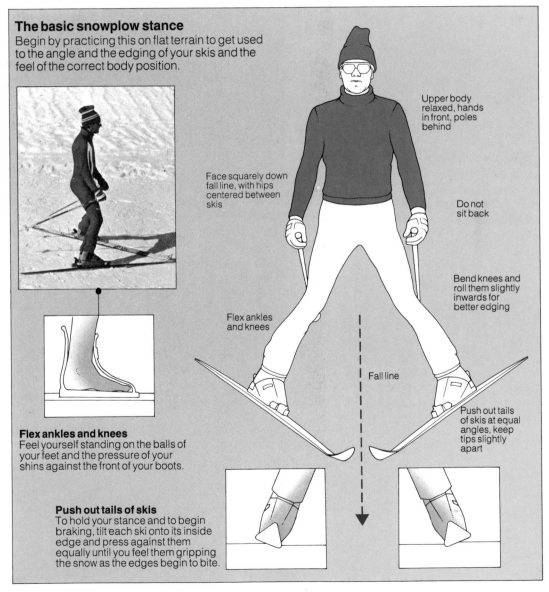

The basic snowplow stance
Begin by practicing this on flat terrain to get used to the angle and the edging of your skis and the feel of the correct body position.

Upper body relaxed, hands in front, poles behind

Face squarely down fall line, with hips centered between skis

Do not sit back

Bend knees and roll them slightly inwards for better edging

Flex ankles and knees

Fall line

Push out tails of skis at equal angles, keep tips slightly apart

Flex ankles and knees
Feel yourself standing on the balls of your feet and the pressure of your shins against the front of your boots.

Push out tails of skis
To hold your stance and to begin braking, tilt each ski onto its inside edge and press against them equally until you feel them gripping the snow as the edges begin to bite.

Developing a natural snowplow stance

The three skiers shown here are all performing the same movement, a braking snowplow – yet they appear slightly different. Children do the snowplow instinctively and look very relaxed in the stance. This child's skis are equally angled in a very wide wedge to control her speed, her arms are relaxed at either side of her body, and she looks comfortable. Children usually look more natural on skis as they are more flexible. Men and women, however, due to the physical shape of their bodies, appear slightly different in the stance. Women may have a tendency to stand in a knock-kneed position, and men may tend towards a bow-legged stance. For this reason, some women find the snowplow stance more natural: they find it easier to push out their feet and roll their knees inwards. Men who have bow-legs, on the other hand, may find a very wide wedge position uncomfortable and may have to compensate for making a narrower wedge by increasing the edging of their skis and by using more leg pressure. Your own snowplow stance should feel natural and comfortable: you will be able to feel the braking action it causes, and this will tell you how far to open your skis and how much pressure to exert on them. Do not worry if your ski tips are not level or if the angle of your skis varies from time to time. Maintaining control of your speed over changing terrain and snow conditions is more important than a "perfect" style.

The braking snowplow

This is the simplest technique for slowing down or stopping without changing direction. You will feel that, as soon as you go into the basic snowplow stance, your speed will decrease. The braking action is caused by the pressure exerted on your edged skis creating friction against the snow. The amount of braking force you need will depend on the speed at which you are travelling, how quickly you want to stop, the steepness of the slope, and the snow conditions. To brake, open out the tails of your skis into a wide wedge, flex your ankles and knees, and roll them inwards to tilt your skis onto their inside edges. Use your body weight and push out against your edged skis with your feet until you feel yourself coming to a stop. The angle of your skis and the degree of edging determine how much pressure you will need to exert. Keep your arms loosely in front of you and do not tense up. A rounded back helps you to relax your shoulders and upper body. If you have trouble with the snowplow or find it difficult to stop, read the section on how to correct mistakes; p. 71.

When to use the braking snowplow

● As the simplest and easiest method of braking

● As an emergency stop in a difficult situation or to stop without changing direction in confined spaces such as forest tracks

Sink down and press equally against both skis so that you feel yourself braking

Keep upper body relaxed and shoulders loose, arms in front at about hip-height

Open ski tails into as wide a "V-shape" as necessary, keeping ski tips slightly apart

Push knees forwards and inwards to tilt skis into snow on their inside edges

Snowplowing to a stop

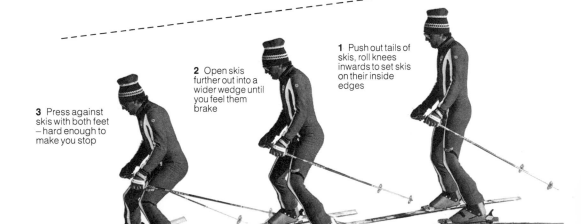

3 Press against skis with both feet – hard enough to make you stop

2 Open skis further out into a wider wedge until you feel them brake

1 Push out tails of skis, roll knees inwards to set skis on their inside edges

It is important not to tense up your body: flex your knees and let your legs do the work

Snowplowing to control speed

By alternately opening and closing your skis, and going in and out of the braking snowplow position, you can effectively control the speed of your descent in the fall line. In fact, this represents one of the best ways of learning to snowplow. You should keep practicing until you feel completely confident and until you can slow down or stop exactly when and where you want to.

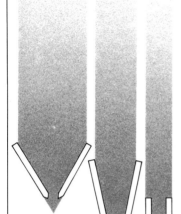

The angle of the plow

The drawing above graphically illustrates how the angle of your skis determines the amount of braking force. The wider the plow (and the harder you push against your edged skis), the more friction there is against the snow and the quicker you stop.

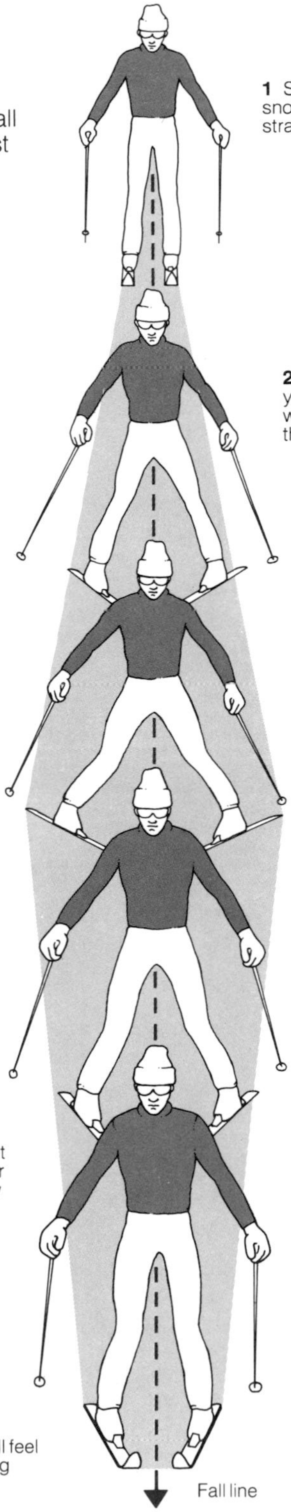

1 Skis parallel, flat on snow, high stance, skiing straight down the fall line

2 Sink down and push your skis out into a slight wedge, tilting them onto their inside edges

3 Widen the angle of your skis as far as necessary, and push against them until you feel them brake

4 Rise up again and let your skis glide together and flatten on the snow

5 As your skis come parallel again, you will feel your speed increasing

Fall line

Ski pattern

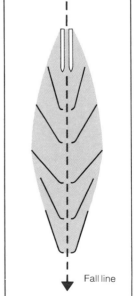

Fall line

The turning snowplow

This is the simplest turning maneuver and the first technique in which individual leg pressure is used to change direction. It also introduces the idea of turning across the fall line as a way of braking and controlling speed. In the gliding snowplow both skis are weighted equally; in the turning snowplow you alternate from one leg to the other. Press harder against your left ski to turn to your right, and against your right ski to turn to your left – first as a "stem" (or "half plow") exercise and then as a series of linked turns.

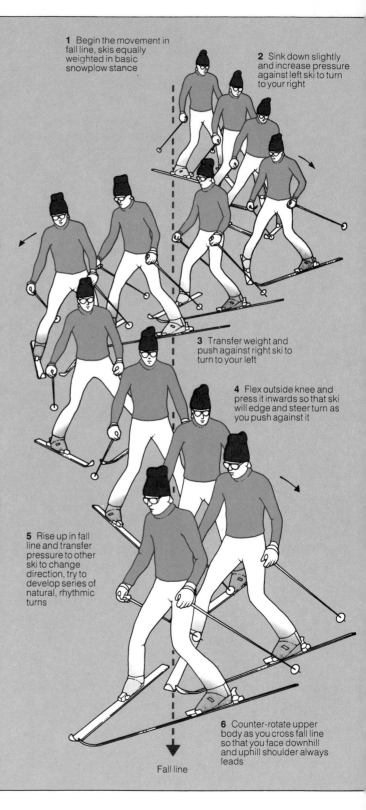

1 Begin the movement in fall line, skis equally weighted in basic snowplow stance

2 Sink down slightly and increase pressure against left ski to turn to your right

3 Transfer weight and push against right ski to turn to your left

4 Flex outside knee and press it inwards so that ski will edge and steer turn as you push against it

5 Rise up in fall line and transfer pressure to other ski to change direction, try to develop series of natural, rhythmic turns

6 Counter-rotate upper body as you cross fall line so that you face downhill and uphill shoulder always leads

Fall line

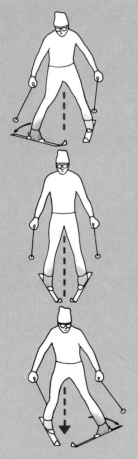

Practicing with a "stem"

Begin from a gentle schuss. Open out one ski into a narrow "stem", press against it, and feel how this steers you to one side.

Ski pattern

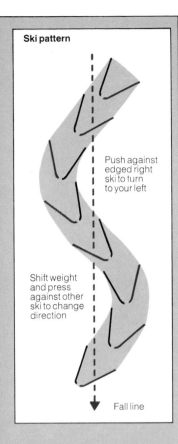

Push against edged right ski to turn to your left

Shift weight and press against other ski to change direction

Fall line

When to use the turning snowplow

- As a beginner's tool for changing direction

- As the starting point for learning more advanced turning techniques

- For controlling speed through narrow passages or on difficult terrain

- Also used by expert skiers in awkward situations, such as bad snow or poor visibility

1

2

1 The skier pushes against his right ski and steers to his left. His body is comfortably relaxed, poles held loosely at either side, knees and ankles well flexed.

2 He relaxes the pressure against his right ski and rises up slightly. As soon as he does this, it causes his skis to swing towards the fall line.

3 The skier is now facing squarely down the fall line, skis apart in the basic snowplow position, with equal pressure against each.

4 To turn out of the fall line, he flexes his left knee, rolls it inwards, and pushes down hard against his edged left ski.

5 This steers him to his right. He rotates his left knee in the direction of the turn, but counter-rotates his upper body so that his uphill shoulder leads.

3

5

4

How the turning snowplow works

The turning snowplow is based on the following principle: if you press harder against one of your skis than the other, it will turn. When you want to turn to your left you push against your right ski; to turn to your right you push against your left ski. This may seem confusing at first, especially when you are told to "counter-rotate" your shoulders and twist them in the opposite direction, but it will feel natural as soon as you start to practice.

The technicalities of how the turn works are explained fully in the chapter on "Ski Mechanics" (p.

178), but the series of illustrations below show in a simple form how it operates. In the basic gliding or braking snowplow (center drawing), both skis are equally weighted. As a result, you travel in a straight line. But, if you press harder against one edged and angled ski than against the other, it will exert a stronger force on the snow – and you will begin to turn towards the direction in which it is pointing. In other words, you always steer the turn with your *outside* ski: your right ski to turn to your left, and your left ski to turn to your right.

Counter-rotate shoulders and hips so that left (uphill) shoulder leads and comes out of turn first

Keep body centered between skis

Steer with knees and feet, not shoulders

Counter-rotate shoulders and hips so that right (uphill) shoulder leads and comes out of turn first

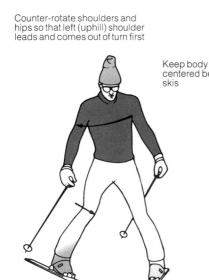
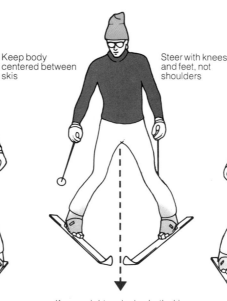

Flex right knee and push against right ski to turn to your left

If you weight and edge both skis equally, you will snowplow straight down the fall line

Flex left knee and push against left ski to turn to your right

Turning to your left

Skiing straight downhill

Turning to your right

Common mistakes when snowplowing

A naturally flexible and relaxed stance is the key to a good snowplow technique. If you find it difficult to stop or turn when you want to, the most likely cause is that you are tensing up your body. You must relax and flex your ankles and knees. If you find your ski tips crossing or if you keep doing the splits, concentrate on rolling your knees inwards and pushing against your edged skis to maintain your plow. If you keep "over-turning", the exercises below will help you to counter-rotate your upper body properly.

⊠ Ski tips crossing
Keep tips of skis slightly apart and center body between skis. If one leg is too stiff, you will lean to the side over your outside ski. As a result, it will flatten, it will not edge, and your skis will tend to cross over. Use your knees and feet to control your skis and the angle of your plow.

⊠ Leaning backwards
If you sit back, your skis will slide from under you and you will accelerate, not brake.

⊠ Tenseness
Bend at the ankles and knees, not stiffly from the waist. Stiff legs give no braking control.

⊠ Doing the splits
Roll knees inwards to edge skis and keep tips together; otherwise skis will slide apart.

"Over-turning" and how to cure it

Trying to steer the turn with your whole body, instead of just knees and feet, is very common. Prevent it by counter-rotating your shoulders so you always face down the fall line.

⊠ Over-turning
If you swing your hips and shoulders around with your skis, your inside ski may lift and you will lose control.

Touching opposite knee As you turn, touch your steering knee with your opposite hand so that your uphill shoulder always leads.

Using your poles
Hold poles horizontally and keep them facing down the fall line as you turn: you will then counter-rotate naturally.

Traversing

Skiing across the slope rather than straight downhill is called "traversing". It is one of the most fundamental of all skiing techniques. Because the quickest way down any slope is the fall line, traversing at an angle across the hill can be used to check your speed. Many descents are in fact made by "zig-zagging" down the slope in a series of diagonal traverses back and forth across the fall line. Turns are used to link one traverse with the next. The angle of your traverse will control your speed and direction of travel. If your line of traverse is perpendicular to the fall line, you will hardly move at all. But the steeper the traverse (the closer it is to the fall line) the faster you will go. In the traverse position the skis are parallel and "edged" into the snow (p. 44). This helps them grip and prevents you from sliding sideways down the slope.

A relaxed, natural stance is vital for a good traversing technique.

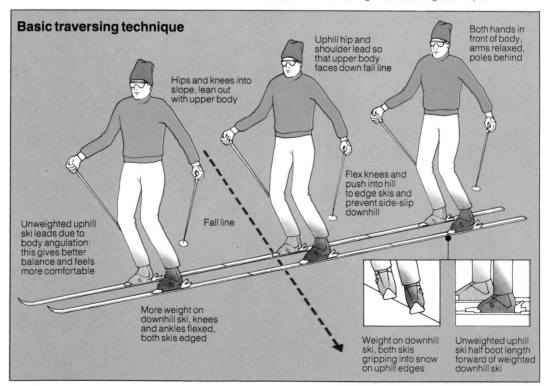

Basic traversing technique

Uphill hip and shoulder lead so that upper body faces down fall line

Both hands in front of body, arms relaxed, poles behind

Hips and knees into slope, lean out with upper body

Flex knees and push into hill to edge skis and prevent side-slip downhill

Unweighted uphill ski leads due to body angulation: this gives better balance and feels more comfortable

Fall line

More weight on downhill ski, knees and ankles flexed, both skis edged

Weight on downhill ski, both skis gripping into snow on uphill edges

Unweighted uphill ski half boot length forward of weighted downhill ski

Correct traversing stance

The skis are edged by pushing the hips and knees into the slope. To maintain balance, angulate your upper body and lean out over your downhill ski. Because of its characteristic shape, the traverse stance is known as the "comma" or "banana" position.

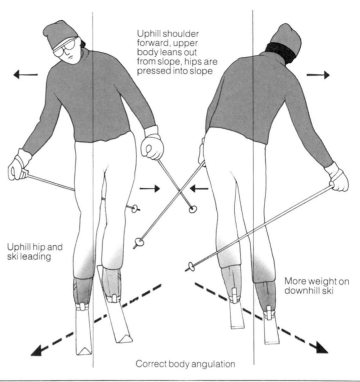

Uphill shoulder forward, upper body leans out from slope, hips are pressed into slope

Uphill hip and ski leading

More weight on downhill ski

Correct body angulation

Improving traverse technique

The exercises shown below are simple practice tips that will help you develop a natural, confident traversing style. They are each specially designed to encourage correct hip angulation, weighting of the downhill ski, and upper body position.

Body angulation
In a gentle traverse, lean out and touch your downhill ankle. This will improve your body angulation and edging by pushing your knees forward and into the slope.

Facing down the fall line
Hold your poles horizontally and point them down the fall line. This will guarantee that your upper body faces downhill and your uphill ski will be leading.

Weighting the downhill ski
While traversing, repeatedly lift your uphill ski off the snow. This concentrates your weight on the downhill ski and encourages leaning away from the hill.

Common mistakes in the traverse

Most of the problems that beginners experience stem from incorrect body angulation. You must push your hips and knees in, and your head and shoulders out from the slope, or you will not feel your skis edging properly: they will either slide sideways downhill or you will fall into the slope as they slip away from under you. You will find the correct stance easier if you twist your body slightly so that your uphill hip leads.

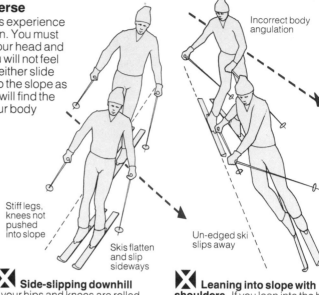

Incorrect body angulation

Stiff legs, knees not pushed into slope

Skis flatten and slip sideways

Un-edged ski slips away

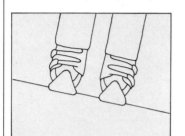

☒ Incorrect edging
This shows what happens if you do not roll your hips and knees into the slope: your skis will flatten on the snow and your edges will not grip. You will be inadvertently "side-slipping", a technique described on p. 76.

☒ Side-slipping downhill
If your hips and knees are rolled away from the slope, instead of into the hill, the edges of your skis will not grip the snow and you will begin to slide sideways downhill.

☒ Leaning into slope with shoulders
If you lean into the hill with your upper body and twist your downhill shoulder forward, your skis will have no pressure on them and they will slip away from under you.

Adapting your traverse to the terrain

When traversing, the distribution of weight, degree of body angulation and edging vary according to the type of snow and the steepness of the slope. On a steep slope or on hard snow, you will need more edging to prevent your skis from slipping and more extreme body angulation. A gentle slope or deep snow requires less edging – and therefore less angulation.

When to use the traverse

● As a universal technique for skiing across, rather than straight down, a slope

● As a means of descent: traverse across the slope, turn, traverse back, turn, etc. (many turns are initiated from and finish in a traverse)

● As a means of controlling speed: the steeper the line of traverse, the faster you go

Traversing in deep snow
Less edging and less body angulation, weight more evenly distributed over both skis as you do not need so much grip with your edges in soft snow.

Traversing on a steep slope
Increase body angulation, push hips and knees further into slope, lean out more with upper body to maintain balance, put more pressure on downhill ski.

Stepping uphill in the traverse

Lifting your skis one at a time and stepping them uphill while traversing is a useful technique for slight changes of direction or for gaining height in the traverse. Slalom racers use this step-up in between turns to get a better line through the gates (p. 136). It is also a good exercise for developing your sense of balance, angulation and mobility. If you alter the line of your traverse and turn your skis away from the fall line as you step them uphill, this technique allows you to slow down and even come to a stop. The movement is very similar to that of "step turning", described in more detail on p. 94-5.

1 Normal traverse stance, skis parallel and edged into snow, weight chiefly on downhill ski.

2 Put all weight onto downhill ski, lift unweighted uphill ski off snow and step it upwards.

3 Set down uphill ski higher up slope, edge it firmly into snow and transfer weight onto it.

4 Immediately lift up unweighted downhill ski and bring it parallel, transfer weight back to downhill ski.

Braking in the traverse

Slowing down in the traverse is usually done by slipping the skis around so that they are perpendicular to the fall line (see right and p. 79). However, if you are traversing along a narrow track or a woodland trail, or if your downhill ski is stuck in a frozen rut, this may not be possible. In such situations, brake by stemming out your uphill ski into a "half plow" position. You will feel your stemmed ski slowing you down.

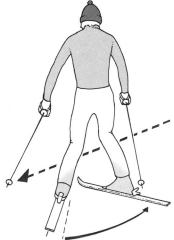

Using a half plow to brake
Weight on downhill ski, stem out uphill ski into half plow and push against it. Friction between stemmed ski and snow will slow you down.

Stopping in the traverse

The most effective way of coming to a relaxed stop in a traverse is to stem out your downhill ski into a half plow position and point the ski tip slightly uphill. Press against it and you will feel yourself swinging around in a rounded side-slip. Your un-edged uphill ski will follow until you stop with both skis parallel across the fall line. This is sometimes called a "half plow uphill".

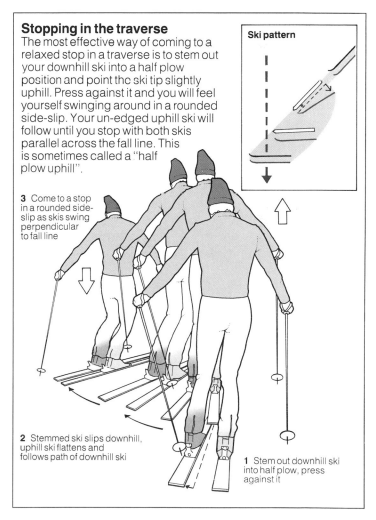

Ski pattern

3 Come to a stop in a rounded side-slip as skis swing perpendicular to fall line

2 Stemmed ski slips downhill, uphill ski flattens and follows path of downhill ski

1 Stem out downhill ski into half plow, press against it

Side-slipping

Side-slipping is a technique which allows you to skid sideways down the slope. It is a safe means of descent relied upon by all skiers on all types of terrain – especially in difficult situations where continuous turning is not possible. It also forms a vital part of turning itself, since the parallel steering phase of many turns normally includes side-slipping your skis around in a skidded arc. In skiing technique, traversing, side-slipping and uphill turning are always connected, and many movements use a combination of all three forms.

The basic technique for side-slipping in the fall line is shown opposite. It is initiated from a standing start and is used for skidding vertically, straight downhill. However, many beginners find side-slipping easier to learn if it is initiated while on the move by stemming out the downhill ski. On p. 78-9 we explain how this method is used to make a forward side-slip out of a traverse and how it can be developed into a simple uphill turn. The more advanced "diagonal" side-slipping is on p. 80.

> ### When to use side-slipping
>
> ● As a means of speed control on steep slopes or on narrow runs
>
> ● For slowing down or stopping in a traverse
>
> ● As an introduction to basic parallel turning skills – side-slipping on the move leads into parallel uphill turning (p. 100)

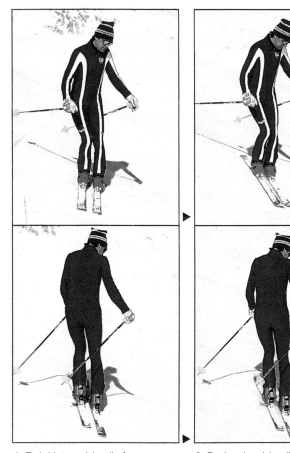

1 To initiate a side-slip from a traverse, move your knees away from the slope. This releases the edge-grip of your skis and they begin to slip downhill.

2 During the side-slip, maintain the basic traverse stance, keep your skis parallel and your upper body angled to face in the direction you are going.

3 To come to a stop, push your knees sideways into the slope so that your edges bite into the snow and stop you slipping.

Basic side-slipping technique

Side-slipping relies on edge control. An edged ski will grip, and a flattened ski will slip. You control the edging of your skis by moving your knees sideways: into the hill to edge, and away from the hill to side-slip. You may find a slight down-flexion helps you to intitiate the side-slip, but maintain your body angulation. Your uphill hip, shoulder and ski should be advanced so that you face downhill, and you should put more pressure on your downhill ski.

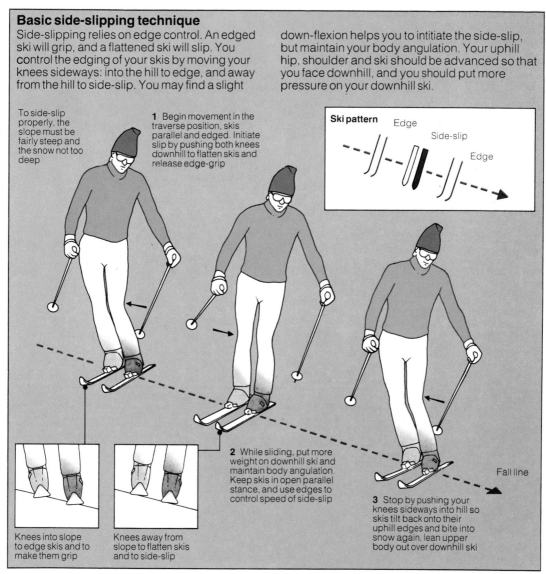

To side-slip properly, the slope must be fairly steep and the snow not too deep

1 Begin movement in the traverse position, skis parallel and edged. Initiate slip by pushing both knees downhill to flatten skis and release edge-grip

Ski pattern Edge
Side-slip
Edge

Knees into slope to edge skis and to make them grip

Knees away from slope to flatten skis and to side-slip

2 While sliding, put more weight on downhill ski and maintain body angulation. Keep skis in open parallel stance, and use edges to control speed of side-slip

Fall line

3 Stop by pushing your knees sideways into hill so skis tilt back onto their uphill edges and bite into snow again, lean upper body out over downhill ski

Learning edge control

Side-slipping looks deceptively easy at first, but in fact it requires very precise edge control. You must learn to feel with your feet and get used to the sensation of slipping. You control your movement by knee, ankle and foot action. Feel how moving your knees away from the slope releases your edges and how pushing your knees into the slope resets them so that they grip. You may find that flexing down slightly helps to release your edges when you are traversing. In the side-slip, your ski tips and tails must slide equally, so you will have to make continual adjustments by alternately weighting the tips or the tails more strongly. Eventually, you will develop a natural feel for this and will easily be able to keep your skis horizontal.

Skis edged into snow

Skis side-slipping

Learning to side-slip

As a beginner, you may find the sideways knee action required to initiate a side-slip from a standing start quite difficult. "Fear of the fall line" (that is, a fear of letting yourself go on a fairly steep slope by releasing your edges) is a common difficulty. If this is the case, you can try side-slipping from a moving traverse – by pushing out your downhill ski to initiate the skidding movement.

The technique is as follows: you begin by skiing across the slope in a gentle traverse, with most of your weight on your downhill ski and your body angulated so that your uphill shoulder, hip and ski are slightly ahead. You then push out your downhill ski and lean your body out over it so that it begins to side-slip. Your uphill ski will flatten on the snow, it will slide down alongside, and you will go into a forward side-slip. Like many skiing movements, this is easier to initiate on gently rounded terrain and on fairly hard snow. You may also find that it helps if you make a distinct push-off from your uphill to your downhill ski in order to get both skis side-slipping easily. While you are skidding, keep more of your weight on your downhill ski and try to keep your skis slipping equally, at the same speed.

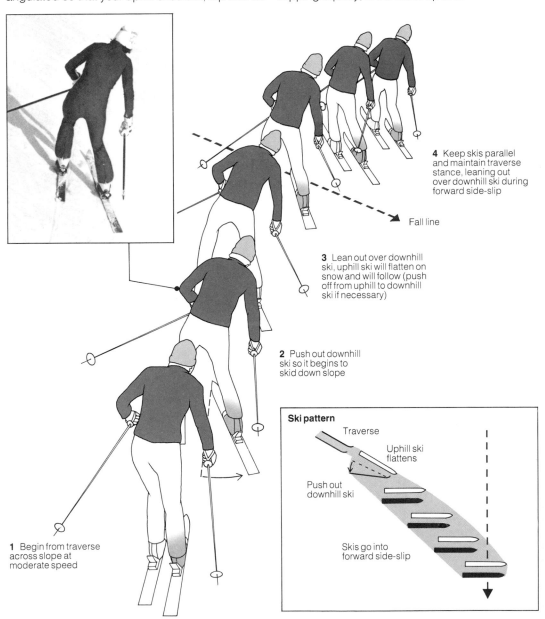

4 Keep skis parallel and maintain traverse stance, leaning out over downhill ski during forward side-slip

Fall line

3 Lean out over downhill ski, uphill ski will flatten on snow and will follow (push off from uphill to downhill ski if necessary)

2 Push out downhill ski so it begins to skid down slope

Ski pattern

Traverse

Uphill ski flattens

Push out downhill ski

Skis go into forward side-slip

1 Begin from traverse across slope at moderate speed

Learning to turn uphill

Once you have mastered the method of initiating a side-slip described on the opposite page, you can take the technique a stage further and develop it into an uphill turn. This simply means rounding off the side-slip and steering your skis uphill. It is a common method of braking or coming to a stop in a traverse (p. 75), and also forms an introduction to "parallel uphill turning" (p. 100).

The movement is initiated in exactly the same way. You push out your downhill ski and lean out over it in order to go into the side-slip. Then you push your knees forwards and into the slope and increase the pressure against your downhill ski so that your skis turn uphill. The drawing below illustrates the movement *after* the side-slip has been initiated; the photographs, the whole sequence.

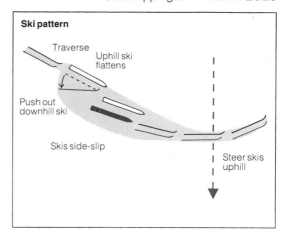

Ski pattern

Traverse
Uphill ski flattens
Push out downhill ski
Skis side-slip
Steer skis uphill

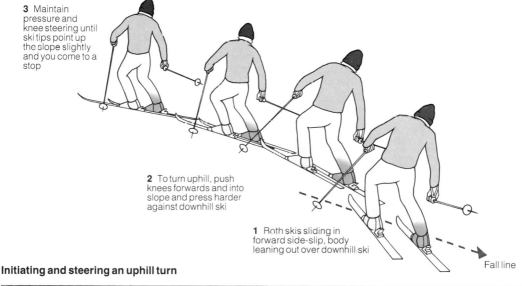

3 Maintain pressure and knee steering until ski tips point up the slope slightly and you come to a stop

2 To turn uphill, push knees forwards and into slope and press harder against downhill ski

1 Both skis sliding in forward side-slip, body leaning out over downhill ski

Fall line

Initiating and steering an uphill turn

1 Begin from traverse across slope at moderate speed and initiate side-slip as shown left.

2 Push out downhill ski and lean out over it so that both skis begin to skid forwards down slope.

3 Maintain your body angulation and keep skis parallel during side-slip.

4 Push knees forwards and into slope and press against downhill ski to turn uphill.

Side-slipping forwards and backwards

It is possible to control the direction in which you side-slip simply by leaning your body either forwards or backwards. If you lean forwards, you will feel more pressure on the balls of your feet. This exerts a rotary effect on your skis: the weighted ski tips tilt downhill and you will slide forwards down the slope in a kind of skidded traverse. Similarly, if you lean back and put more weight on your ski tails, you will side-slip backwards. Like all side-slipping, the movement is easier if initiated on rounded terrain.

1 To side-slip forwards: move knees away from slope to release edges, lean forward so that weight is chiefly on front of skis, keep knees flexed and maintain basic traverse stance

2 To initiate change of direction: straighten up and weight ski tips and ski tails equally so that skis swing perpendicular to fall line

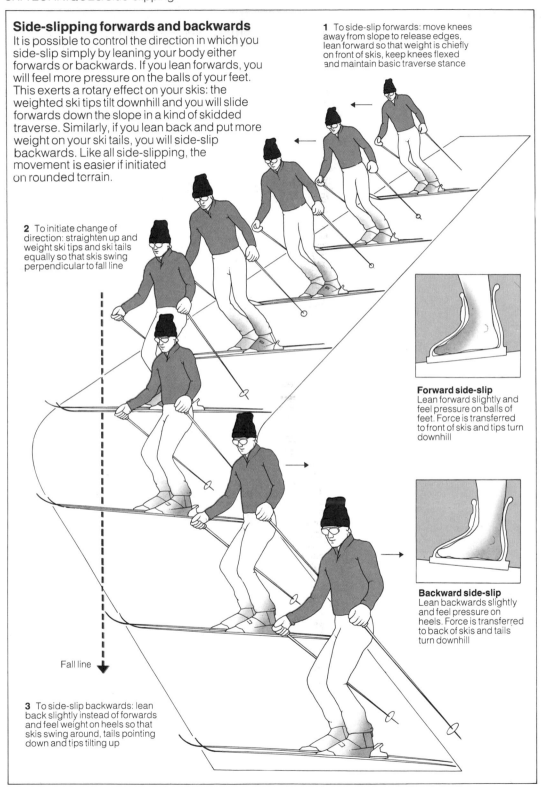

Forward side-slip
Lean forward slightly and feel pressure on balls of feet. Force is transferred to front of skis and tips turn downhill

Backward side-slip
Lean backwards slightly and feel pressure on heels. Force is transferred to back of skis and tails turn downhill

Fall line

3 To side-slip backwards: lean back slightly instead of forwards and feel weight on heels so that skis swing around, tails pointing down and tips tilting up

Common mistakes when side-slipping

Most problems with side-slipping are caused by fear of letting yourself go on a steep slope and by difficulty in getting used to the unusual sensation of skidding sideways. Practice is the only solution, since it is only with practice that you will develop an instinctive feel for edge control. You will soon find that you gain confidence, that you can keep your skis parallel and travelling at the same speed, and that you know exactly how much edge-grip and edge-release you need. Remember not to move your arms or upper body too much. Maintain a relaxed, comfortable traversing stance (see right).

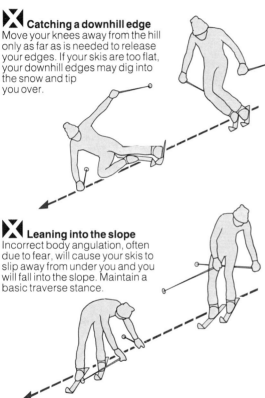

Catching a downhill edge
Move your knees away from the hill only as far as is needed to release your edges. If your skis are too flat, your downhill edges may dig into the snow and tip you over.

Leaning into the slope
Incorrect body angulation, often due to fear, will cause your skis to slip away from under you and you will fall into the slope. Maintain a basic traverse stance.

Correct side-slipping stance
The correct body angulation is the same as for traversing: hands forward, poles behind, weight mostly over downhill ski, body twisted slightly so that you face down the slope.

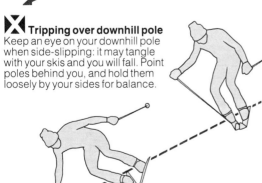

Tripping over downhill pole
Keep an eye on your downhill pole when side-slipping: it may tangle with your skis and you will fall. Point poles behind you, and hold them loosely by your sides for balance.

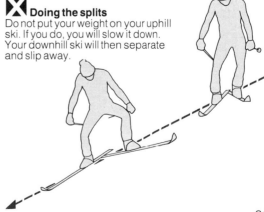

Doing the splits
Do not put your weight on your uphill ski. If you do, you will slow it down. Your downhill ski will then separate and slip away.

Snowplow turning

Snowplow turning is a very useful and highly practical slow turning maneuver. It is the simplest form of swinging in a linked sequence of turns down a slope. Often referred to as the "basic swing", it enables you to turn safely at speed. It also forms a natural progression towards more advanced turning, introducing beginners to the principles of weight-transfer and pole-planting.

Under the general heading of "snowplow turning" three categories can be distinguished: an elementary, an intermediate and an advanced form of what is essentially the same turn. The division is somewhat arbitrary since all three run into one another. But it is useful, because it helps to describe how beginners learn the technique and it explains how it can be improved with practice.

There are three phases to a basic snowplow turn: traverse, snowplow, and side-slip or uphill turn. All of these techniques have been described in the preceding pages. Snowplow turning differs from the turning snowplow (p. 68) in that it is initiated from and ends in a parallel ski stance. In other words, your descent takes the form of a zig-zag – traverse, turn, traverse, turn, etc. – and your skis do not stay in the plow position all the time. You begin from a gentle traverse, with your skis in an open parallel stance. You then push your skis out into a snowplow or "wedge" and by pressing harder against your outside ski you turn into the fall line. You complete your weight-transfer against your outside ski and bring your skis parallel to steer out of the fall line into a new traverse (as in the simple uphill turn explained on p. 79).

In the first, elementary form of the turn, you will probably travel slowly and turn around in a broad arc, maintaining a wide wedge position and finishing with a short side-slip into your next parallel traverse. As you learn to ski faster, you will not need to hold your plow for so long. You will be able to transfer your weight against your outside ski earlier, and control your side-slipping more effectively. You will also begin to use your pole. Planting your inside pole helps you to transfer your weight from one ski to the other and also encourages you to develop a sense of rhythm to your turns. This is the intermediate form of snowplow turning. The advanced form is quicker still: the wedge is shorter and narrower, the weight-transfer and pole-plant are made earlier, and the turn is finished, not so much as a side-slip, but more as a form of parallel uphill turn (p. 100). In both the intermediate and the advanced forms of the turn, you will find that an "up-extension" facilitates the weight-transfer and a "down-flexion" aids your knee-steering in the parallel phase. This movement will become very important later.

The initiation for all three forms of the turn is always the same – a turning snowplow. What differs is the point at which you make your weight-transfer and how soon you can bring your skis together to finish your turn in a parallel ski stance.

When to use snowplow turning

- As a safe, controlled turn that you can use on most gradients

- As a reliable turn often used by experts in difficult conditions

- As the first technique which allows you to link a sequence of traverses and to turn across the fall line in one fluid, continuous movement

- As a slow turn, but a less tiring technique than the turning snowplow (p. 68)

- As the traditional intermediate teaching step in the progression from the turning snowplow to stem and parallel turning

- As the way of introducing weight-transfer and pole-planting into turning

The pole-plant phase of a snowplow turn.

Elementary snowplow turning
As in the turning snowplow, open skis into a wide "V" and turn across the fall line. Transfer your weight and lean over your outside ski slightly so that all your pressure is against it. Bring your inside ski parallel when it is more-or-less unweighted and side-slip into a new traverse.

Intermediate snowplow turning
When you are facing down the fall line, plant your inside pole and, with an up-extension, transfer your weight against your outside ski. Bring your inside ski parallel and make a rounded side-slip into your next traverse.

Advanced snowplow turning
Ski faster and initiate the turn in the same way, but make a narrower and briefer plow. Plant your inside pole slightly earlier and transfer your weight sooner to make a tighter uphill turn. Use an up-extension of your legs for a more precise and faster weight-transfer.

Elementary snowplow turning

In its easiest and most basic form, snowplow turning evolves directly from the turning snowplow (p. 68). It is the simplest way of swinging across the fall line in a combined movement, and can be used to ski a sequence of linked turns to descend gentle slopes. From an open parallel traverse, the turn is initiated by pushing out both skis into a wedge. As you turn your body and press against your outside ski, you steer into the fall line. By gradually increasing this pressure, you will turn out of the fall line ready to transfer your weight completely to your outside ski and bring your skis parallel again to complete the turn in a side-slip (p. 79).

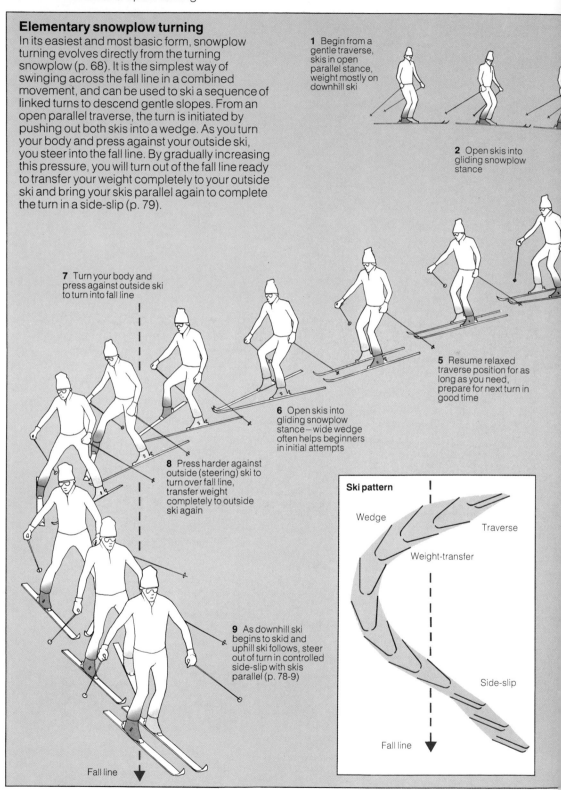

1 Begin from a gentle traverse, skis in open parallel stance, weight mostly on downhill ski

2 Open skis into gliding snowplow stance

7 Turn your body and press against outside ski to turn into fall line

5 Resume relaxed traverse position for as long as you need, prepare for next turn in good time

6 Open skis into gliding snowplow stance – wide wedge often helps beginners in initial attempts

8 Press harder against outside (steering) ski to turn over fall line, transfer weight completely to outside ski again

9 As downhill ski begins to skid and uphill ski follows, steer out of turn in controlled side-slip with skis parallel (p. 78-9)

Ski pattern

Wedge

Traverse

Weight-transfer

Side-slip

Fall line

Fall line

3 Turn your body and press against outside ski to turn into fall line

4 Press harder against outside (steering) ski to turn over fall line, transfer weight completely to outside ski by leaning out over it, downhill ski will begin to side-slip and uphill ski will follow

Comparing the other two forms of the turn

Both the intermediate and the more advanced forms of snowplow turning are shown below. Compare them with the elementary form shown on the left and you will notice how the pole-plant is introduced, how the wedge becomes narrower and briefer, how the skis are brought parallel and how the skidded side-slip develops into an uphill turn.

The intermediate form
Pole-plant is introduced as you swing out of the fall line to help you transfer your weight earlier. Wedge is still wide, but speed is a little faster.

The advanced form
With higher speed, wedge is narrower still, inside pole is planted earlier and, using up-extension, skis are brought parallel in fall line. Parallel phase is steered by pushing knees forwards and into the slope.

Intermediate snowplow turning

The most obvious thing that distinguishes this from the simple form of snowplow turning is the introduction of the pole-plant. This is the next step you must learn. You will soon feel that planting your inside pole helps you to transfer your weight more decisively against your outside (steering) ski.

Otherwise, this turn differs only in that you ski a little faster (which will make your turns easier to initiate) and you hold the snowplow stance for a shorter time. After transferring your weight, you will be able to lift your unweighted inside ski into a parallel track sooner, and you will come out of the turn in a curving forward side-slip, using your knees to steer by flexing them and pushing them well forwards and into the slope.

As your confidence and speed increase, you will find that you can make the weight-transfer against your outside ski more quickly and more precisely if you stretch your legs and extend upwards. Similarly, the initiation of the parallel phase at the end of the turn can be made more effectively by flexing your legs and sinking down slightly. Knee steering is very important in this phase of the turn, and flexing down will help you to push your knees forwards and into the hill so that you can control the direction and speed of your side-slipping.

3 Upper body relaxed, glide in snowplow stance into fall line, keep hips centered between skis

4 Begin pressing harder against outside ski to turn over fall line

1 Start from an open parallel stance in a gentle traverse, body comfortably angulated so that you have more pressure on your downhill ski

2 Open skis into wedge, keep knees well flexed

5 Plant inside pole vertically and extend upwards to transfer weight completely against your outside ski

7 Push knees forwards and, with skis in open parallel stance, try to make a controlled, rounded side-slip

6 Flex down and keep pressing against outside ski while bringing unweighted inside ski parallel

Fall line

Ski pattern

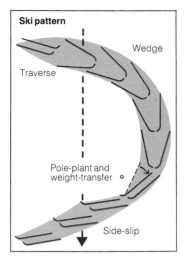

Traverse

Wedge

Pole-plant and
weight-transfer

Side-slip

Turning snowplow phase

Parallel side-slipping phase

How and when to plant your pole

Planting your inside pole enables you to transfer your weight quickly from your inside ski to your outside ski. It helps you balance and gives some support to your up-extension. Hold your pole loosely, bring it forward in good time and plant it vertically just ahead of you. Do not overstretch and do not lean on the pole or you will not be able to make the weight-transfer and you will lose control of the turn.

1

1

2

2

3

3

Intermediate pole-planting
Plant your pole after you have gone into a turning snowplow over the fall line. Then extend your inside leg, transfer your weight against your outside ski, and bring your inside ski parallel.

Advanced pole-planting
The purpose and the technique of the pole-plant are the same. It is the timing that differs: you plant your pole, make your weight-transfer and bring your skis parallel much earlier.

Advanced snowplow turning

This form of the turn, which will later lead into stem turning (p. 96), is made at a higher speed. It is initiated in the same way as the turns on the preceding pages – by opening your skis into a snowplow stance. But the wedge need not be as wide, the pole-plant is made earlier, and you transfer weight against your outside ski sooner. You should aim to bring your skis parallel while in the fall line or before and steer into your next traverse with an uphill turn (p. 79). As you improve, you will be able to maintain control at higher speeds, your turns will become tighter, and you will begin to get the feel for controlled steering instead of side-slipping in the parallel end phase of the turn.

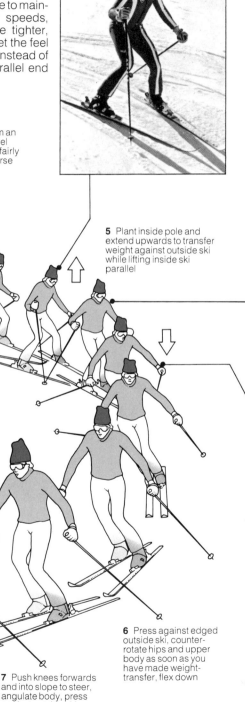

2 Initiate turn by opening skis into a wedge.

1 Start from an open parallel stance in a fairly steep traverse

5 Plant inside pole and extend upwards to transfer weight against outside ski while lifting inside ski parallel

3 Plant inside pole and extend upwards to transfer weight against outside ski while lifting inside ski parallel

4 Steer into new traverse, then initiate next turn by opening skis into wedge again

8 Try to turn around ski tips, with less skidding or side-slipping, steer into new traverse with uphill ski and shoulder leading

6 Press against edged outside ski, counter-rotate hips and upper body as soon as you have made weight-transfer, flex down

7 Push knees forwards and into slope to steer, angulate body, press against outside ski

Fall line

88

Ski pattern

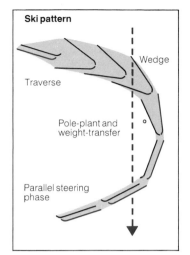

Wedge

Traverse

Pole-plant and weight-transfer

Parallel steering phase

Common mistakes when snowplow turning

Most of the problems that are encountered in snowplow turning arise from a lack of coordination and a poor sense of timing. You must develop a feeling for the right moment at which to plant your inside pole and transfer your weight against your outside ski. Use an active up-extension for the weight-transfer, then flex down as your skis come parallel and counter-rotate your upper body so that you face downhill all the time. Do not try to steer by rotating your hips and shoulders into the turn. Control your side-slipping with the usual knee pressure forwards and into the hill.

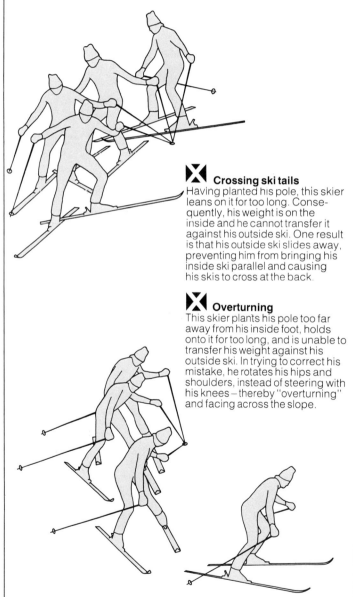

✕ Crossing ski tails

Having planted his pole, this skier leans on it for too long. Consequently, his weight is on the inside and he cannot transfer it against his outside ski. One result is that his outside ski slides away, preventing him from bringing his inside ski parallel and causing his skis to cross at the back.

✕ Overturning

This skier plants his pole too far away from his inside foot, holds onto it for too long, and is unable to transfer his weight against his outside ski. In trying to correct his mistake, he rotates his hips and shoulders, instead of steering with his knees – thereby "overturning" and facing across the slope.

Skating

Skating is an acceleration technique – used purely for increasing your speed on level ground or when skiing down a slight slope. It is sometimes used by slalom racers. Skating steps are so-called because they correspond to the technique of an ice-skater. Compare the movements of someone skating on skis with those of a speed-skater and you will see that they are the same: they both push off from one foot and then glide forwards on the other, at the same time throwing their opposite arm and shoulder forwards in the direction of the glide. Skating requires good balance and good coordination, and it teaches you to use your legs independently – skiing first on one and then on the other. It is a good all-round exercise and it forms a basis for more advanced stepping techniques.

The basic skating technique is shown here. On p. 92 we show how to learn to skate, and on p. 93 how to develop it into a powerful and effective technique for accelerating.

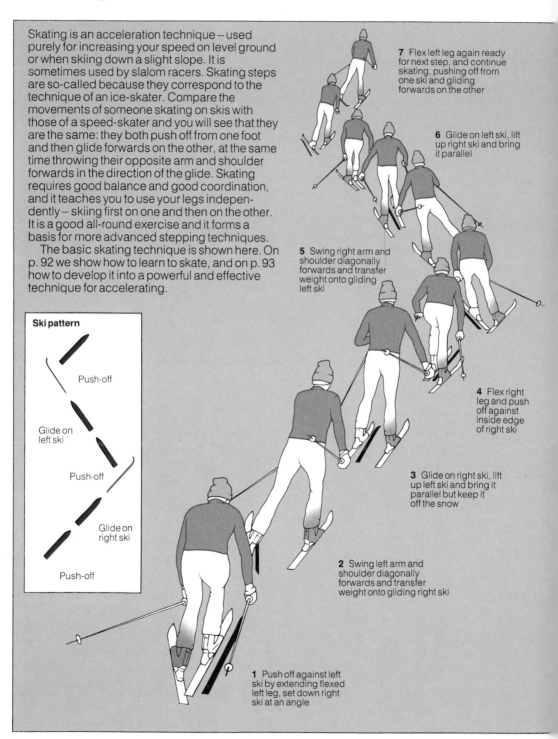

Ski pattern

Push-off

Glide on left ski

Push-off

Glide on right ski

Push-off

7 Flex left leg again ready for next step, and continue skating, pushing off from one ski and gliding forwards on the other

6 Glide on left ski, lift up right ski and bring it parallel

5 Swing right arm and shoulder diagonally forwards and transfer weight onto gliding left ski

4 Flex right leg and push off against inside edge of right ski

3 Glide on right ski, lift up left ski and bring it parallel but keep it off the snow

2 Swing left arm and shoulder diagonally forwards and transfer weight onto gliding right ski

1 Push off against left ski by extending flexed left leg, set down right ski at an angle

When to use skating

● As a way of accelerating either on the flat or down the fall line on a gentle slope

● As a way of developing balance, coordination, edge control and independent leg action

● As an introduction to weight-transfer and stepping techniques (p. 136)

5 Angle out right ski, flex left leg again and push off against left ski. The ski tracks left in deep snow show clearly the diagonal "zig-zag" pattern of the alternate forwards and outwards movement characteristic of skating.

4 Push off, swing right arm and shoulder diagonally forwards, transfer weight and glide on left ski.

3 Sink down into low crouch ready to push off strongly from flexed right leg, angle out left ski and lean body into direction of next glide.

2 Propel yourself diagonally forwards on gliding right ski, lift left ski and bring it forward so that it is parallel to right ski but off snow.

1 Flex left leg, push off against left ski, open tip of right ski at an angle ready to set it down.

Learning to skate – elementary form

When skating for the first time, you may find it difficult to achieve a fast, efficient technique immediately. The best way to learn is to choose a gentle slope and ski down, stepping from one ski to the other. This will enable you to get used to the weight-transfer and it will develop your sense of balance and coordination. Lift your left ski and angle it outwards slightly. Push off from your flexed right leg in the direction of your left ski. Set down your left ski and glide forwards on it while

bringing up your right ski. Flex your left leg, angle out your right ski while it is still in the air and prepare for your next skating step with another push-off. At this stage, the movement should be relaxed, and you will probably not glide very far or very fast. For the moment, concentrate on balance and coordination rather than speed. The sequences on the right and at the bottom of the page illustrate the technique in its advanced form with accelerating push-off.

1 Flex left leg, lift right ski and angle it out diagonally.

2 Push off from left ski, step onto right ski and glide forwards on it.

3 Lift left ski, bring it forwards and angle it out in new direction.

4 Push off from right ski, step onto left ski and glide forwards on it.

Skating with accelerating push-off/side view

1 Push off against right ski by extending right leg, swing right arm and shoulder forward and step onto angled left ski.

2 Glide forwards with weight on left ski, bring right ski up alongside, keeping it off snow.

3 Flex left leg ready for next push-off, open tip of right ski ready to set it down at an angle.

Skating with accelerating push-off – advanced form

Correct coordination of your movements, good balance and a strong push-off are vital for effective acceleration. If you lift your left ski and push off diagonally from your flexed right leg, you will feel that your body tilts in the same direction and brings your right ski onto its inside edge. This will give you a firm platform to push against. If your ski is not edged, it will simply slip sideways or backwards.

You will also feel that you can only accelerate if your push-off is directed diagonally forwards and your leading left ski is set down at an angle to your right ski. This accounts for the zig-zag track which characterizes skating. Concentrate on swinging your body forward into a long glide. Later, plant both poles to give yourself an extra push-off as you extend your gliding leg.

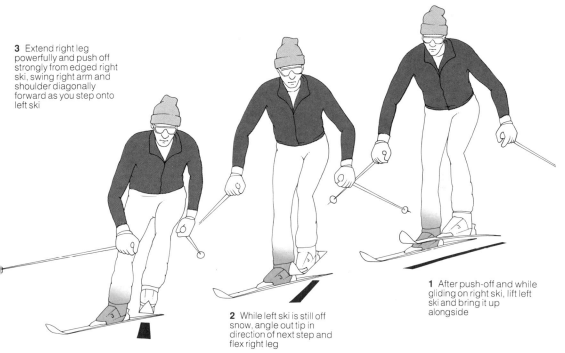

3 Extend right leg powerfully and push off strongly from edged right ski, swing right arm and shoulder diagonally forward as you step onto left ski

2 While left ski is still off snow, angle out tip in direction of next step and flex right leg

1 After push-off and while gliding on right ski, lift left ski and bring it up alongside

4 Push off against left ski by extending left leg, swing left arm and shoulder forward and step onto angled right ski.

5 Glide forwards with weight on right ski, bring left ski up alongside, keeping it off snow.

6 Flex right leg ready for next push-off, open tip of left ski ready to set it down at an angle.

Step turning

Step turning is a means of changing direction while travelling by stepping from one ski to the other. It forms a good exercise and an introduction to more advanced stepping techniques (p. 136), as well as being a useful method for turning in difficult snow conditions. Step turning is best learned in this order: first, to left and right on flat ground; secondly, uphill from a traverse; thirdly, uphill from the fall line; then as a complete downhill turn; and, finally, as a series of linked "S" turns.

When to use step turning

● For changing direction on gentle slopes

● For stopping by turning uphill

● For turning in difficult snow conditions

● As an exercise for improving your balance, mobility and weight-transfer

Basic technique for step turning

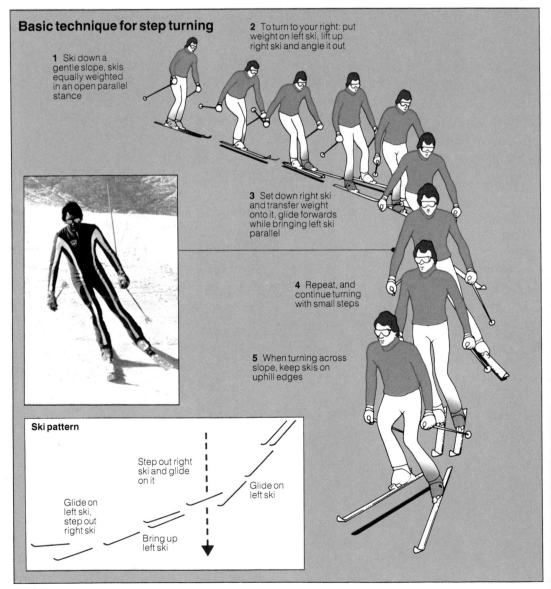

1 Ski down a gentle slope, skis equally weighted in an open parallel stance

2 To turn to your right: put weight on left ski, lift up right ski and angle it out

3 Set down right ski and transfer weight onto it, glide forwards while bringing left ski parallel

4 Repeat, and continue turning with small steps

5 When turning across slope, keep skis on uphill edges

Ski pattern

Step out right ski and glide on it

Glide on left ski

Glide on left ski, step out right ski

Bring up left ski

Step turning with acceleration

Like skating (p. 90), step turning can be used for accelerating. The technique is very similar: you increase your speed by giving yourself a firm push-off at each step. This is done by flexing down in preparation and then springing diagonally forwards, pushing off forcefully from your outside ski onto your angled inside ski.

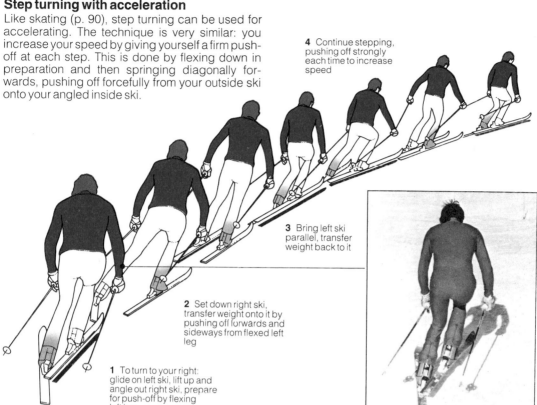

4 Continue stepping, pushing off strongly each time to increase speed

3 Bring left ski parallel, transfer weight back to it

2 Set down right ski, transfer weight onto it by pushing off forwards and sideways from flexed left leg

1 To turn to your right: glide on left ski, lift up and angle out right ski, prepare for push-off by flexing left leg

Step turning using a double-pole push

To increase your speed still further, you can use your poles. A double-pole push at each step will aid your push-off and give you even more acceleration. Propel yourself into your next step by coordinating your pole-plant with the forwards-sideways movement of your body: push off from your poles at the same moment as you push off onto your inside ski.

1 Weight on outside (gliding) ski, swing poles forward and plant them level with feet.

2 Push off from flexed leg and from both poles ready to step onto angled inside ski.

3 After the step, lift up and angle out inside ski again. Flex outside leg and plant both poles.

4 Extend outside leg and push off forwards and sideways in the direction of next step.

95

Stem turning

This is a safe, reliable technique which enables intermediate skiers to turn on moderate slopes and which is often used by experts in difficult conditions. A stem turn can be split into two parts: the "stem" phase and the "parallel" phase. Stemming out your uphill ski is the movement that initiates the turn. The amount of stem required will vary with your speed, the steepness of the slope and the snow. If you are travelling fast, initiating the turn will be easier and you will only need a narrow stem; if you are skiing slowly, in deep snow, you will need a wider and longer stem.

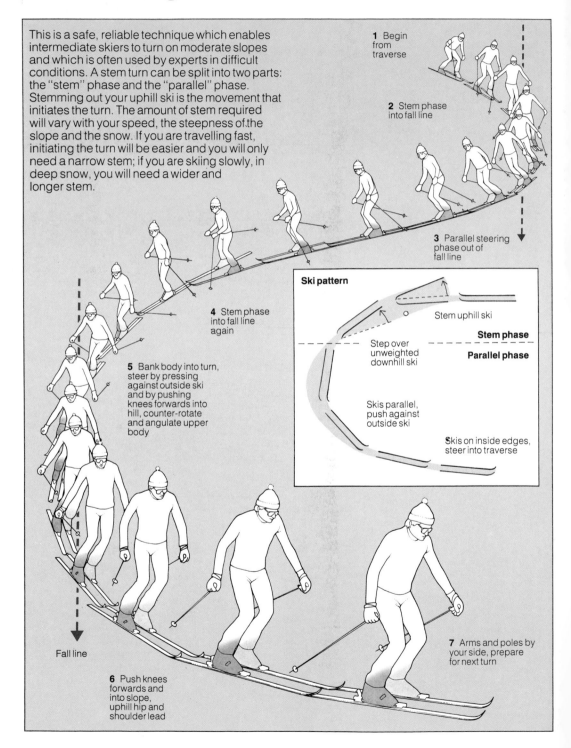

1 Begin from traverse

2 Stem phase into fall line

3 Parallel steering phase out of fall line

4 Stem phase into fall line again

5 Bank body into turn, steer by pressing against outside ski and by pushing knees forwards into hill, counter-rotate and angulate upper body

Ski pattern

Stem uphill ski

Stem phase

Parallel phase

Step over unweighted downhill ski

Skis parallel, push against outside ski

Skis on inside edges, steer into traverse

Fall line

6 Push knees forwards and into slope, uphill hip and shoulder lead

7 Arms and poles by your side, prepare for next turn

The stem phase and weight-transfer

Initiate the turn by stemming out your uphill ski (half plow). This tilts your uphill ski onto its opposite edge and helps you turn towards the fall line. Follow with your pole-plant, an up-extension and a weight-transfer against your outside ski.

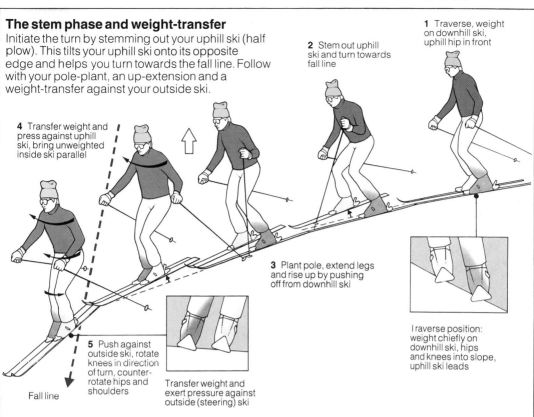

1 Traverse, weight on downhill ski, uphill hip in front

2 Stem out uphill ski and turn towards fall line

4 Transfer weight and press against uphill ski, bring unweighted inside ski parallel

3 Plant pole, extend legs and rise up by pushing off from downhill ski

Traverse position: weight chiefly on downhill ski, hips and knees into slope, uphill ski leads

5 Push against outside ski, rotate knees in direction of turn, counter-rotate hips and shoulders

Fall line

Transfer weight and exert pressure against outside (steering) ski

1 Stemming out your uphill ski "pre-turns" it and helps you to initiate the change of direction into the fall line. Flexing down acts as a preparation for the up-extension with which you transfer your weight to your stemmed ski.

2 Planting your inside pole at the right moment will help you make a decisive weight-transfer. The skier is shown here beginning to extend upwards by stretching both legs and by pushing off strongly from his downhill ski.

3 Here, the up-extension has been completed. The skier has transferred his weight completely against his uphill ski. He steps his unweighted downhill ski over ready to go into the parallel phase of the turn (see over).

The parallel phase

The second phase of a stem turn is essentially the same as a parallel uphill turn (p. 100). Bank your hips into the turn to keep your skis edged, and maintain pressure against your outside ski. Push your knees forwards into the hill to steer the turn, but counter-rotate your hips and upper body to maintain your balance and so that your inside shoulder always leads. The degree of skidding or side-slipping as you come out of the turn is controlled by how much your skis are edged. Your speed is controlled by how quickly you turn away from the fall line into the next traverse.

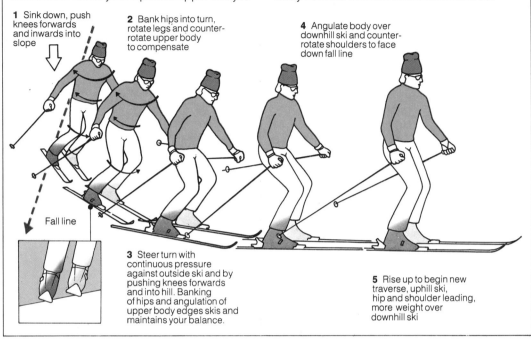

1 Sink down, push knees forwards and inwards into slope

2 Bank hips into turn, rotate legs and counter-rotate upper body to compensate

4 Angulate body over downhill ski and counter-rotate shoulders to face down fall line

Fall line

3 Steer turn with continuous pressure against outside ski and by pushing knees forwards and into hill. Banking of hips and angulation of upper body edges skis and maintains your balance.

5 Rise up to begin new traverse, uphill ski, hip and shoulder leading, more weight over downhill ski

✓ Steering turn with knees pushed into slope.

Common mistakes in the parallel phase

Trying to steer and turn with the shoulders instead of the knees, and leaning into the hill through fear of falling, are the most common errors. The key to the movement is to lean *out* with your upper body and *in* with your hips, and to rotate your legs and counter-rotate your shoulders. Your legs must be well flexed and rolled into the slope with your weight forward and pressing against your outside ski.

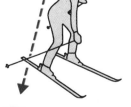

☒ Over-rotation
If you swing your upper body around into slope, pressure will be on the uphill ski and your downhill ski will slip away.

☒ Stiff outside leg
Bend both knees as you flex down. A stiff outside leg results in poor edging, leaning into slope and inability to steer.

Stem turning in deep snow

In deep or heavy snow, stem turning requires more speed and effort. To initiate the turn, make a wider stem and hold it for longer than on a smooth trail.

Then use a stronger up-extension and more rotary motion, and exaggerate your banking and counter-rotation to exert more pressure against the snow.

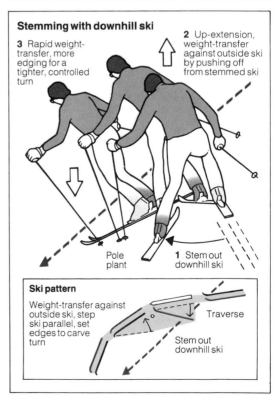

Stem turning on steep slopes

On steep slopes it is more difficult to stem out the uphill ski and transfer your weight uphill. It is therefore more comfortable and will slow you down more effectively if you initiate the turn by stemming out your downhill ski (see right). This will flatten your uphill ski on the snow so that it will change edges and you will feel that it makes turning easier. After stemming your downhill ski, rise up with a rapid up-extension of your body and push off from your stemmed downhill ski to transfer your weight against your uphill ski. To check your speed and increase your control in the fall line, flex down immediately, and make a tight turn.

When to use stem turning

● As an all-purpose means of changing direction for skiers of all levels of ability

● For situations in which you want to ski safely and in complete control

● For controlling speed in difficult skiing conditions, such as on steep terrain or when visibility is poor

● For deep snow – in an adapted form

● As an intermediate teaching step between snowplow turning and parallel turning

Stemming with downhill ski

3 Rapid weight-transfer, more edging for a tighter, controlled turn

2 Up-extension, weight-transfer against outside ski by pushing off from stemmed ski

Pole plant

1 Stem out downhill ski

Ski pattern

Weight-transfer against outside ski, step ski parallel, set edges to carve turn

Traverse

Stem out downhill ski

Parallel uphill turning

Parallel uphill turning is a technique for swinging *across* the slope away from the fall line. It is used for braking, for stopping and as a learning step towards parallel turning. It is the first technique you will learn which allows you to change direction with your skis parallel all the time.

It is possible to initiate an uphill turn by stemming out your downhill ski and going into a curving forward side-slip (a technique covered on p. 79). *Parallel* uphill turning is a more refined method: it is initiated from a parallel stance, and your skis remain parallel throughout the movement. You will

start by making the turn out of a traverse. This is shown below. Later, you will be able to turn out of progressively steeper traverses until, finally, you will master the "stop swing" out of the fall line (p. 103). This gradual learning process is known as the "fan method" (p. 102).

Parallel uphill turning is executed by flexing down, counter-rotating your hips and banking them into the center of the turn. The turn is steered by pushing your knees forwards and into the slope. This will slow you down or bring you to a stop. The movement is easier to perform on rounded terrain.

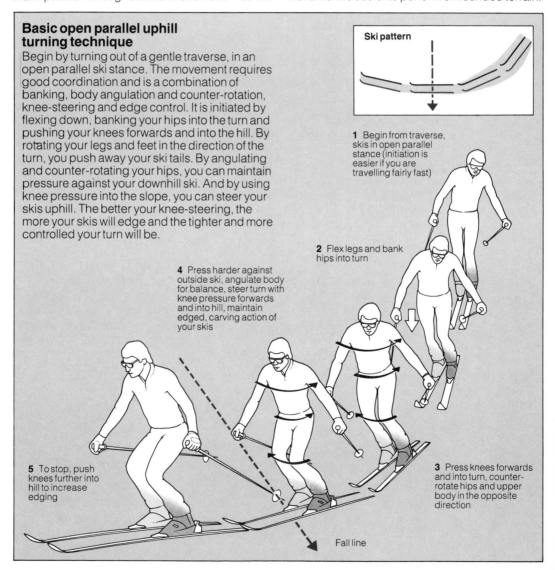

Basic open parallel uphill turning technique

Begin by turning out of a gentle traverse, in an open parallel ski stance. The movement requires good coordination and is a combination of banking, body angulation and counter-rotation, knee-steering and edge control. It is initiated by flexing down, banking your hips into the turn and pushing your knees forwards and into the hill. By rotating your legs and feet in the direction of the turn, you push away your ski tails. By angulating and counter-rotating your hips, you can maintain pressure against your downhill ski. And by using knee pressure into the slope, you can steer your skis uphill. The better your knee-steering, the more your skis will edge and the tighter and more controlled your turn will be.

Ski pattern

1 Begin from traverse, skis in open parallel stance (initiation is easier if you are travelling fairly fast)

2 Flex legs and bank hips into turn

4 Press harder against outside ski, angulate body for balance, steer turn with knee pressure forwards and into hill, maintain edged, carving action of your skis

5 To stop, push knees further into hill to increase edging

3 Press knees forwards and into turn, counter-rotate hips and upper body in the opposite direction

Fall line

Parallel uphill turning out of the fall line

Making a parallel uphill turn from a straight schuss down the fall line is more difficult than making one from a traverse. The reason is simply that you have to turn your skis further before they swing uphill. If you are schussing you will probably be travelling faster, and you will find that a higher speed makes the initiation of the turn easier. By following the "fan method" of learning outlined on p.102, you will progress naturally, through increasingly steeper traverses, towards being able to turn directly out of the fall line.

The technique for a turn from a schuss is shown here. It is essentially the same as for a parallel uphill turn from a traverse, except that it may require a more exaggerated flexion and a stronger leg rotation to swing your skis round.

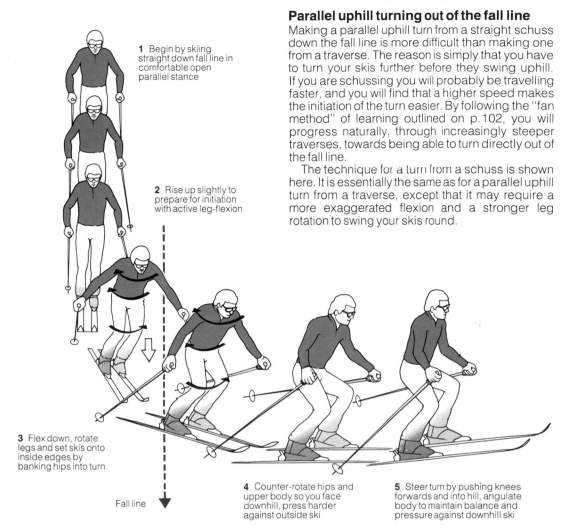

1 Begin by skiing straight down fall line in comfortable open parallel stance

2 Rise up slightly to prepare for initiation with active leg-flexion

3 Flex down, rotate legs and set skis onto inside edges by banking hips into turn

Fall line

4 Counter-rotate hips and upper body so you face downhill, press harder against outside ski

5 Steer turn by pushing knees forwards and into hill, angulate body to maintain balance and pressure against downhill ski

Closed parallel uphill turning

Learning this turn is easier in an open parallel ski stance, because this gives you better stability, but as you improve, you will be able to bring your skis closer together, as shown below.

The fan method

You should begin by turning into the hill from a gentle traverse. When you have mastered this, progress to a steeper and steeper approach until you can make a parallel uphill turn from a schuss straight down the fall line.

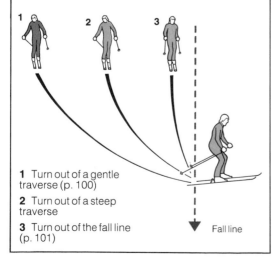

1 Turn out of a gentle traverse (p. 100)

2 Turn out of a steep traverse

3 Turn out of the fall line (p. 101)

Fall line

Common mistakes when parallel uphill turning

Most problems with the uphill turn are caused by one or more of the following: insufficient pressure against the downhill ski, not pushing the knees forwards and sideways into the slope, inadequate hip angulation (resulting in poor edge control), and incorrect counter-rotation. The last is probably the most common. You must rotate your legs into the turn and counter-rotate your hips and upper body out of the turn. Holding your poles horizontally and keeping them parallel to your skis during the turn (p. 73) will help you develop a feel for this.

When to use parallel uphill turning

- As a way of stopping

- As a way of slowing down or changing direction while traversing

- As an introduction to parallel downhill turning

- As the steering phase of turns that you already know and ones you will learn in future

- As the preparatory phase for making a "parallel turn with edge-set" (p. 111)

The stop swing

This movement is an adaptation of a parallel uphill turn out of the fall line. It is purely a stopping technique – for braking quickly and sharply – and it is done by turning your skis around at right angles to the fall line and edging them strongly. It is initiated with a rapid down-flexion and rotation of the legs, while the upper body remains facing down the fall line. You may find it helps you to keep your balance if you plant your downhill pole the moment you stop.

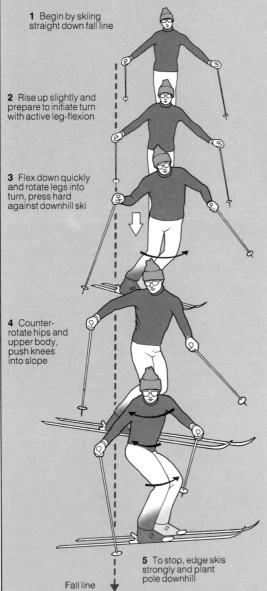

1 Begin by skiing straight down fall line

2 Rise up slightly and prepare to initiate turn with active leg-flexion

3 Flex down quickly and rotate legs into turn, press hard against downhill ski

4 Counter-rotate hips and upper body, push knees into slope

5 To stop, edge skis strongly and plant pole downhill

Fall line

Coming to a stop
Counter-rotation is vital in stop swinging. The more abruptly you stop, the harder you must press against your downhill ski and the more you must counter-rotate.

Stop swinging with "pre-rotation"

For a quicker, more dynamic stop, you can use body *rotation* as a kind of "anticipation" before initiating the turn with *counter-rotation*. Rotation into the turn, which pre-tenses the muscles of your body in the same way as winding up a spring, helps you make a more powerful and more effective counter-rotation.

1 Anticipate by rotating body in direction of swing

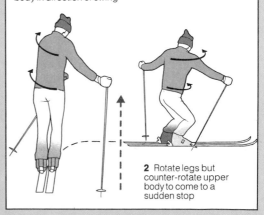

2 Rotate legs but counter-rotate upper body to come to a sudden stop

Parallel turning

One of the goals of most skiers is parallel turning. It is an economical technique which has many different forms and which can be adapted to almost all snow and terrain conditions. The essence of parallel turning is that the skis remain parallel all the time – with no angling or stemming. This is in contrast to stem turning (p. 96), where the initiation is made as a two-phase movement. This means that you first change edges on your uphill ski by stemming it out, and then change edges on your downhill ski by stepping it over. In a stem turn, the stemming itself also helps the initiation since it "pre-turns" the uphill ski. In parallel turning, the initiation is a one-phase movement in which both skis change edges together. This means that you must ski faster, bank your body into the turn and exert more turning force on your skis. At first, you will find parallel turning easier if you maintain an open stance to give you more stability. Later, as your skill and confidence increase, you can gradually close up your skis. But bear in mind that the difference is purely one of style, and that closed parallel turning is suited more to ideal conditions.

Parallel turning encompasses a wide variety of initiations, and these are set out in the next few pages. In each case, it is only the initiation that differs: the steering phase is always the same technique as for parallel uphill turning (p. 100). All parallel turn initiations are aided by either an up-extension or a down-flexion. The one you use can vary with the speed at which you ski, the tightness of your turns, and the snow and terrain conditions. The chart below sets out the different types of initiation and the situations for which they are best suited.

Parallel turns: how they differ and when to use them

Open parallel turning 	With an "up" initiation (i.e. up-extension, banking and rotary motion), p. 105-7	• The learning stage • When skiing slowly • In difficult snow conditions • For tight turns
	With a "down" initiation (i.e. banking, down-flexion and counter-rotation), p. 108	• When skiing fast • In good snow conditions • For wide turns
Closed parallel turning 	With an "up" initiation (i.e. up-extension, banking and rotary motion), p.109	• The advanced learning stage • When skiing faster • For tight turns • In deep snow
	With a "down" initiation (i.e. banking, down-flexion and counter-rotation)	• When skiing fast • In good snow conditions • For wide turns
	Initiated with turning push-off from both legs (p. 110, 111)	• In extremely difficult conditions, e.g. steep terrain, hard snow, resistant (wet) snow • When skiing too slowly

Open parallel turning with an "up" initiation

This form of parallel turn, the first you will learn, is initiated with a combination of up-extension, banking and rotary motion. It is prepared by flexing down and planting your inside pole. It is then initiated by extending both legs and banking your body into the turn. You begin by pushing off with both legs so that your downhill ski lifts off the snow slightly and your weight is transferred to your uphill ski. You then continue to extend your uphill leg and bank your body into the turn to flatten your skis on the snow. As soon as they are flat, you can begin to turn them by rotating your legs and body. The rest of the turn is then steered in exactly the same way as it is in stem turning.

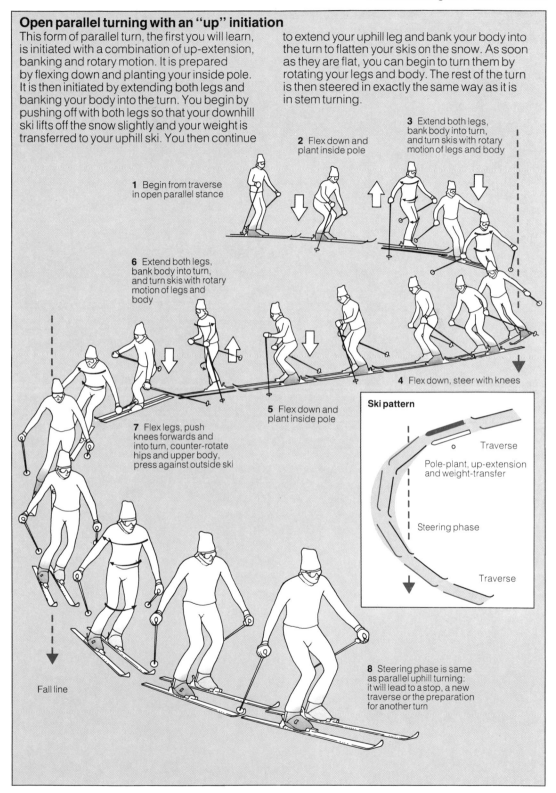

1 Begin from traverse in open parallel stance

2 Flex down and plant inside pole

3 Extend both legs, bank body into turn, and turn skis with rotary motion of legs and body

4 Flex down, steer with knees

5 Flex down and plant inside pole

6 Extend both legs, bank body into turn, and turn skis with rotary motion of legs and body

7 Flex legs, push knees forwards and into turn, counter-rotate hips and upper body, press against outside ski

8 Steering phase is same as parallel uphill turning: it will lead to a stop, a new traverse or the preparation for another turn

Fall line

Ski pattern

Traverse

Pole-plant, up-extension and weight-transfer

Steering phase

Traverse

The "up" initiation phase

Of the three elements involved in the initiation of this turn – up-extension, banking and rotary motion – it is the up-extension which momentarily *unweights* the skis, thereby releasing the pressure on them and making them easier to turn (p.184). The movement is performed with a "down-up-down" motion. You first flex down and plant your inside pole, then push off with both legs, extend upwards and bank your body into the turn. This flattens your skis on the snow and allows you to rotate them into the fall line. You then flex down again to steer. You will find that the amount of up-extension you need to initiate the turn effectively varies with the situation, your speed and the type of snow.

1 Begin from traverse, in a relaxed high stance.

2 Flex down to plant pole and prepare for up-extension.

3 Push off with both legs, extend up, bank body and turn skis.

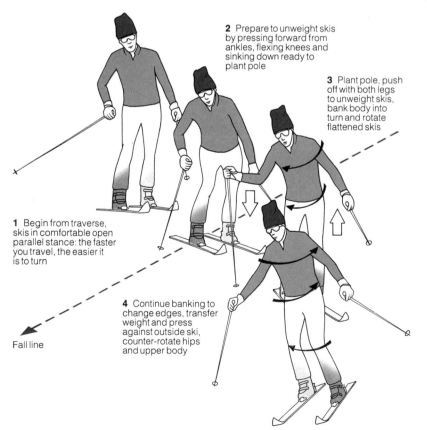

2 Prepare to unweight skis by pressing forward from ankles, flexing knees and sinking down ready to plant pole

3 Plant pole, push off with both legs to unweight skis, bank body into turn and rotate flattened skis

1 Begin from traverse, skis in comfortable open parallel stance: the faster you travel, the easier it is to turn

4 Continue banking to change edges, transfer weight and press against outside ski, counter-rotate hips and upper body

Fall line

In traverse, skis on uphill edges

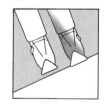

Skis flatten as you bank body

Edge-change and weight-transfer completed

Common mistakes when parallel turning

In the initiation phase of the turn, the most common problems are caused by insufficient flexion and extension, not banking far enough into the turn, and incorrect pole-planting. The inside pole-plant is very important in parallel turning. It helps relax your upper body, it acts as a pivot for your initiation, it supports the up-extension and banking of your body, and it also gives a sense of rhythm to your turning. Many skiers attempting parallel turns for the first time cannot drop the habit of stemming their uphill ski. This is incorrect since it is a two-phase, not a one-phase, initiation. The cure is to transfer your weight to your uphill ski earlier by extending high. *Then* flex down and bank into the turn. All parallel turns are easier on rounded terrain, but you will also find that to initiate them you must ski fairly fast. This is because the faster you ski the more kinetic energy you have and the less muscle strength you have to use (p.182). If you ski fast enough, you can turn largely by banking and counter-rotation.

In the steering phase of the turn, any mistakes are likely to be the same as those in turns you already know: leaning into the slope instead of out over your downhill ski, "over-turning" due to not counter-rotating your hips and upper body, and incorrect edge control, which results in poor steering.

The fan method

Begin by revising your parallel uphill turns out of the fall line (p.101). Then start from an opposite traverse, progressing from a steep to a shallow angle, and make complete downhill turns, into and out of the fall line.

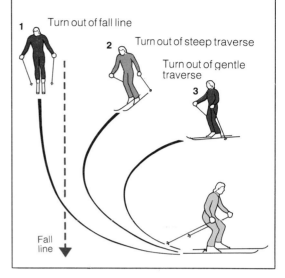

1 Turn out of fall line

2 Turn out of steep traverse

Turn out of gentle traverse

3

Fall line

A refined form of "up" initiation

As you become more experienced, you will find that your up-extension can be refined. Because you start from a traverse, your downhill ski is lower than your uphill ski. This means that, when you extend your legs, your downhill ski will lift off the snow and your weight will transfer to your uphill ski. If you then continue to extend your uphill leg and stretch not only upwards but also into the turn, then the up-extension becomes the *banking* necessary to change edges. This movement later leads to the technique of "stepping onto the uphill ski" (p.137).

1 From traverse, flex down in preparation, plant inside pole vertically in same way as for ordinary turn initiation.

2 Extend uphill leg. Downhill ski will lift off snow, all of your weight will be on uphill ski and you will find that banking into the center of the turn will be much easier.

3 Turn uphill ski into fall line with rotary motion of body, flex down and counter-rotate hips and upper body, steer turn in normal way.

Open parallel turning with a "down" initiation

This is an alternative method of initiating a parallel turn, and it is the one most often used by good skiers. Frequently taught to children, it is simpler than the "up-extension" form (p. 105) and is used for making wide turns at higher speeds in ideal conditions. From a traverse, you prepare to turn by extending up. As soon as your weight is on your uphill ski, you bank your body into the turn to change edges, bring your inside ski forward, flex down and counter-rotate your hips and upper body. The turn is then steered in the normal way.

In this case, the inside pole-plant does not act as a pivot; it can be used simply for rhythm and balance. You will find that this turn is easier to initiate on rounded terrain or on slope edges. As you prepare for your turn in the traverse, you should also find that lifting up your downhill ski slightly helps you bank into the turn – since it will no longer be supporting your weight. This early weight-transfer will lead later to the advanced technique of "stepping onto the uphill ski" (p. 136), often used by racers.

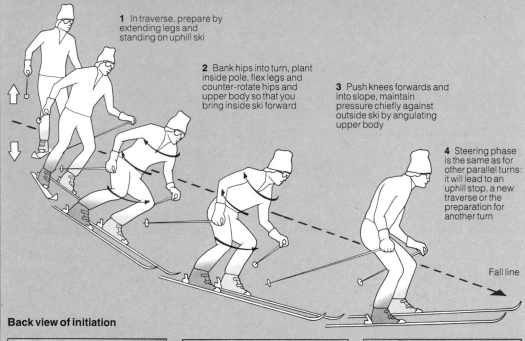

1 In traverse, prepare by extending legs and standing on uphill ski

2 Bank hips into turn, plant inside pole, flex legs and counter-rotate hips and upper body so that you bring inside ski forward

3 Push knees forwards and into slope, maintain pressure chiefly against outside ski by angulating upper body

4 Steering phase is the same as for other parallel turns: it will lead to an uphill stop, a new traverse or the preparation for another turn

Fall line

Back view of initiation

1 Prepare by extending up and transferring weight to uphill ski.

2 Flex legs quickly, bank body into turn and counter-rotate.

3 Steer turn by pushing knees forwards and into hill.

Progressing from open to closed parallel turning

Learning to make parallel turns is easier in an open stance, and all beginners start this way. At first, you will have better balance, and feel more stable, by keeping your skis about hip-width apart. Later, you will find that you can begin to close up your skis. Closed parallel turning is simply more stylish – and there is no real technical need for it other than enjoyment. But it does mean that you will have to adapt your technique slightly. The closer your stance the more difficult it is to roll your uphill ski over onto its opposite edge before turning. Consequently, *banking* becomes much more important. As you extend upwards, you must bank your body further into the turn to change edges. With practice, you will find that your up-extension becomes smoother and less exaggerated: as you might have already discovered, you may need to stretch only your uphill leg when initiating the turn (p. 107).

Parallel turning on steep slopes

One way of improving and varying your skiing is to attempt challenging terrain. Steep slopes test your nerve and your ability to control your turns. The key to turning on the steep is to keep the radius of your turns short – in other words, to get round quickly. You must also be able to use your edges effectively to check your speed – either by carving a tight turn from one traverse to the next or by preparing for each turn with a sharp "edge-set" (p. 111).

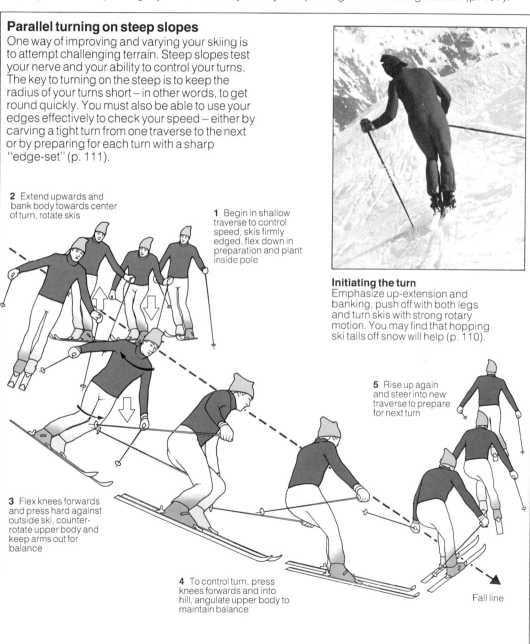

2 Extend upwards and bank body towards center of turn, rotate skis

1 Begin in shallow traverse to control speed, skis firmly edged, flex down in preparation and plant inside pole

Initiating the turn
Emphasize up-extension and banking, push off with both legs and turn skis with strong rotary motion. You may find that hopping ski tails off snow will help (p. 110).

5 Rise up again and steer into new traverse to prepare for next turn

3 Flex knees forwards and press hard against outside ski, counter-rotate upper body and keep arms out for balance

4 To control turn, press knees forwards and into hill, angulate upper body to maintain balance

Fall line

Parallel turning in light powder snow

When travelling fast enough, banking and down-flexion, together with counter-rotation, is the best initiation for parallel turning in a few inches of new snow on a firm base. This "down" technique is described on p. 108 and illustrated here. However, less experienced skiers will find that the "up" initiation (p. 105) is easier at first. In deep snow, you should ski quite fast, staying close to the fall line and linking your turns to keep going. Extend up high and bank your body well over into the turn to exert more turning force on your skis and to counteract the snow resistance. Except in much deeper snow, no further technique adaptation is necessary.

Parallel turning with "tail-hopping"

"Tail-hopping" is an extreme form of initiating parallel turns. It is used for turning in difficult conditions (such as heavy or wet snow), when you are not travelling very fast, and on steep slopes when you need to get round rapidly. After flexing down in preparation, the turns are initiated by pushing off strongly with both legs so that you hop both ski tails off the snow and unweight your skis. Together with a certain amount of banking, this allows you to pivot your skis around their tips underneath your body. You then flex down, counter-rotate and steer the turns as usual.

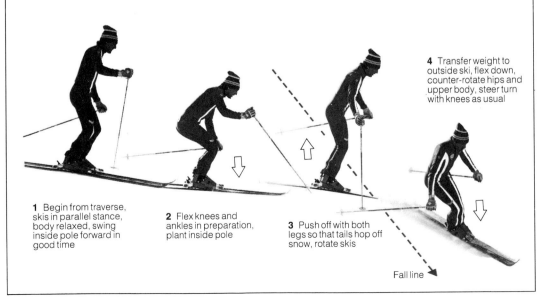

4 Transfer weight to outside ski, flex down, counter-rotate hips and upper body, steer turn with knees as usual

1 Begin from traverse, skis in parallel stance, body relaxed, swing inside pole forward in good time

2 Flex knees and ankles in preparation, plant inside pole

3 Push off with both legs so that tails hop off snow, rotate skis

Fall line

Parallel turning with "edge-set"

On undulating slopes you can use the rounded bumps to help you initiate your turns, but on very hard snow and on steep slopes where the terrain does not provide you with any natural turning aids, you should use an "edge-set" to help you brake and push off into the following turn. This forceful, exaggerated preparation is similar to making a short uphill swing (p. 100) before going into the turn. It is made with a pronounced down-flexion and pre-rotation of the body into the turn, together with a firm, sudden edge-set. This acts as a platform from which you can rebound upwards and forwards, with a strong turning push-off from both legs, to make your weight-transfer and turn your skis.

1 Parallel turning with "edge-set" can be made either from traverse or from end of previous turn

2 Flex knees and push them forwards and into slope to go into parallel uphill turn: the tighter this turn, the more effective your rebound from edge-set

3 Flex down, roll knees and hips into slope and push hard against downhill ski to increase edge pressure

The "edge-set"
At end of previous turn press hard chiefly against downhill ski and push knees and hips into slope to set edges sharply. Then push off with both legs simultaneously to initiate the next turn.

4 Plant pole, rebound upwards with strong turning push-off from both legs

6 Counter-rotate upper body and angulate out over downhill ski, steer by pushing knees forwards and into hill, rise up to resume new traverse stance or to prepare for another turn

5 Transfer weight against outside ski, bank hips into turn, steer skis with rotary leg movement

Fall line ▼

111

Short swinging

The natural progression from linked parallel turning is short swinging. Short swings are rhythmical, short-radius parallel turns in a continuous sequence, and they form an effective, stylish and enjoyable technique. Each turn has a short or "tightened" steering phase and leads directly into the next swing. Rhythm and co-ordination are the vital factors. Short swinging requires good control, since you ski close to the fall line, but speed can be determined by the diagonal placing of the skis and by the edge-setting which ends one turn and acts as a turning push-off for your up-extension into the next. As you proceed, you will feel how the amount of edge-set you need depends on the steepness of the slope and the condition of the snow. Over the next few pages, three forms of short swinging are outlined: the basic short-radius turn for use on moderate slopes; the form with pronounced "edge-set" for more braking control on steep slopes; and the fluid, relaxed "wedel" form.

When to use short swinging

- As a refined form of tight, rhythmic parallel turning, suitable for many situations

- For controlling speed on steep or moderate slopes by repeated, alternate edge-sets

- For pure enjoyment on gentle slopes in good snow

- For controlled skiing in difficult, narrow passages or anywhere where there is restricted space for turning

- For deep or powder snow

- In an adapted form, as a technique for use in special slalom racing

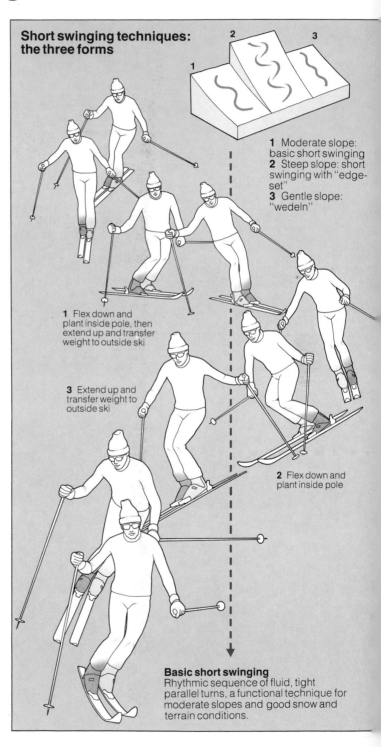

Short swinging techniques: the three forms

1 Moderate slope: basic short swinging
2 Steep slope: short swinging with "edge-set"
3 Gentle slope: "wedeln"

1 Flex down and plant inside pole, then extend up and transfer weight to outside ski

3 Extend up and transfer weight to outside ski

2 Flex down and plant inside pole

Basic short swinging
Rhythmic sequence of fluid, tight parallel turns, a functional technique for moderate slopes and good snow and terrain conditions.

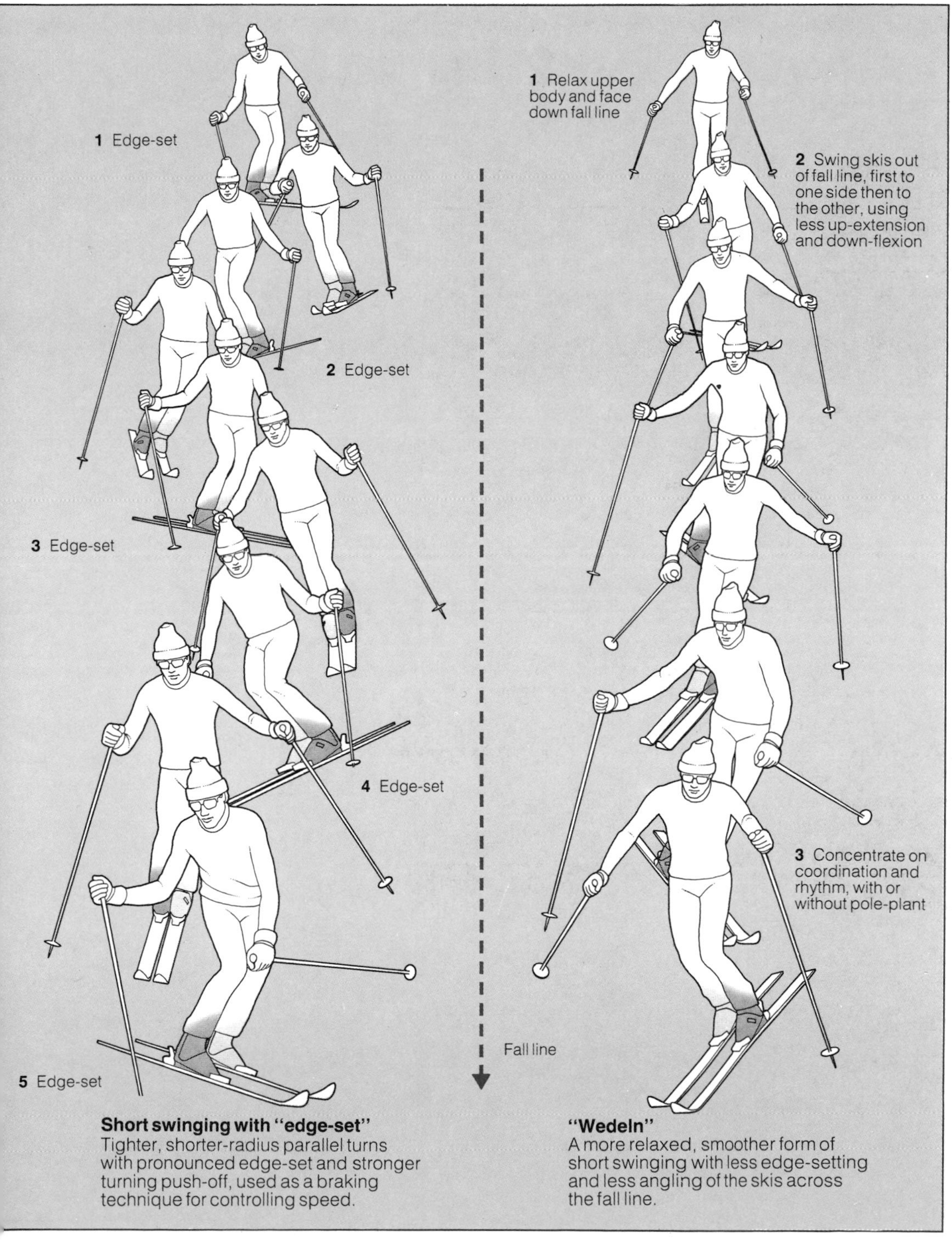

1 Edge-set

2 Edge-set

3 Edge-set

4 Edge-set

5 Edge-set

1 Relax upper body and face down fall line

2 Swing skis out of fall line, first to one side then to the other, using less up-extension and down-flexion

3 Concentrate on coordination and rhythm, with or without pole-plant

Fall line

Short swinging with "edge-set"

Tighter, shorter-radius parallel turns with pronounced edge-set and stronger turning push-off, used as a braking technique for controlling speed.

"Wedeln"

A more relaxed, smoother form of short swinging with less edge-setting and less angling of the skis across the fall line.

Basic short swinging

Short swinging is a direct progression from linked parallel turning. You simply increase the frequency and the tightness of your turns, and stay closer to the fall line. The turns flow smoothly into one another, and the end of one swing forms the preparation for the next – so a good sense of rhythm is crucial. A short swing is initiated in the same way as a parallel turn with "up" (p.105), except that the counter-rotation of your body at the end of one turn prepares you immediately for the next, and you use a stronger up-extension with both legs in order to push off and initiate the turn.

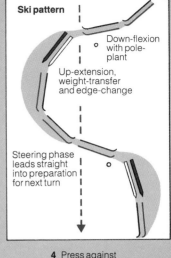

Ski pattern

Down-flexion with pole-plant

Up-extension, weight-transfer and edge-change

Steering phase leads straight into preparation for next turn

1 Skis in fairly closed parallel stance as you steer out of previous swing

3 Extend outside leg and unweight inside ski, bank hips into turn, rotate flattened outside ski and inside ski will follow

4 Press against outside ski to steer, counter-rotate, flex down again, set edges and plant pole to initiate next turn

2 Plant pole, flex down and push knees into slope so that edges grip, upper body faces down fall line

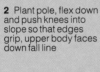

1 Bank hips into turn and press against outside ski to steer. Prepare for next turn.

2 Plant pole for pivot, and set edges to provide platform for up-extension to initiate turn.

3 Extend upwards and forwards to change edges and transfer weight to outside ski.

4 Keep upper body facing down fall line. Steer each turn with outside ski pressure.

Basic short swinging is used for relaxed, fluid turning on moderate-to-steep slopes in good snow

5 Extend outside leg and unweight inside ski, bank hips into turn, rotate flattened outside ski and inside ski will follow

Fall line

5 Aim for a smooth, controlled run, flexing and extending your legs in a natural rhythm.

Learning short swinging

Good coordination is the key to short swinging. If you find it difficult to progress from parallel turning, it may be that a poor sense of rhythm, bad timing of your pole-plant, and insufficient down-flexion and up-extension are contributing to your difficulties. The exercises below illustrate a gradual method which will enable you either to learn or to improve your short swinging technique. They will help you to coordinate your inside pole-

plant with the extension of your legs which initiates each turn. They will also encourage you to keep your body and your arms relaxed and to develop a smooth, linked motion in between turns.

If you still find short swinging difficult, try "tail-hopping" (p.110) to initiate each turn. But bear in mind that you must master basic short swinging on easy terrain before attempting steep slopes or deep snow.

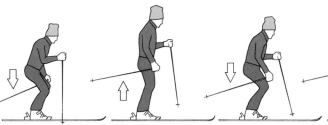

1 Pole-planting and flexion-extension

Ski slowly down the fall line on a gentle slope with your skis parallel. Flex down and plant one pole, then extend upwards. Swing your opposite pole

forwards and flex down again as you plant it, ready to extend up again. This exercise coordinates the planting of your pole with your leg movements.

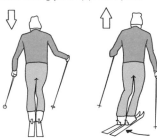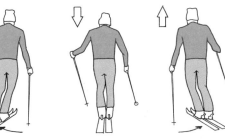

2 Turning skis out of the fall line

Repeat as above, but this time, after flexing down, extend your outside leg and unweight your inside ski. Bank your hips inwards and turn your flattened

outside ski. You should find that your unweighted inside ski will follow naturally, and that both skis will turn out of the fall line slightly.

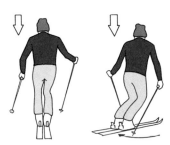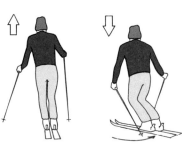

3 Turning skis across the fall line

As before, flex down and plant your inside pole, but this time turn your skis more strongly as you extend your outside leg. Then press harder against

your outside ski, counter-rotate your hips and upper body, flex down and set your skis on their uphill edges almost at right angles to the fall line.

115

Short swinging with "edge-set"

This technique allows you to turn on steep terrain and on hard snow while still controlling your speed. It is a more exaggerated and more "aggressive" form of the basic short swing, with your skis set at more of an angle across the fall line, with a sharper edge-set to slow you down, and with a stronger up-extension to rebound into the next turn. The more you want to brake, the more you angle and edge your downhill ski. As with the basic technique, you turn across the fall line as quickly as possible, keeping your turns tight and linking them together in a rhythmical sequence. In other words, on the steep, your turning radius decreases and your turning frequency increases. A closed ski stance allows more refined movements.

Short swinging with edge-set is used for safe, controlled skiing on steep and on hard slopes

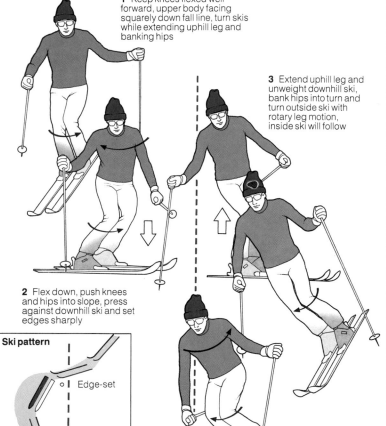

1 Keep knees flexed well forward, upper body facing squarely down fall line, turn skis while extending uphill leg and banking hips

3 Extend uphill leg and unweight downhill ski, bank hips into turn and turn outside ski with rotary leg motion, inside ski will follow

2 Flex down, push knees and hips into slope, press against downhill ski and set edges sharply

Ski pattern

Edge-set

Edge-set

4 Face downhill with upper body, flex legs and plant inside pole ready for another edge-set and for up-extension into next turn

Fall line

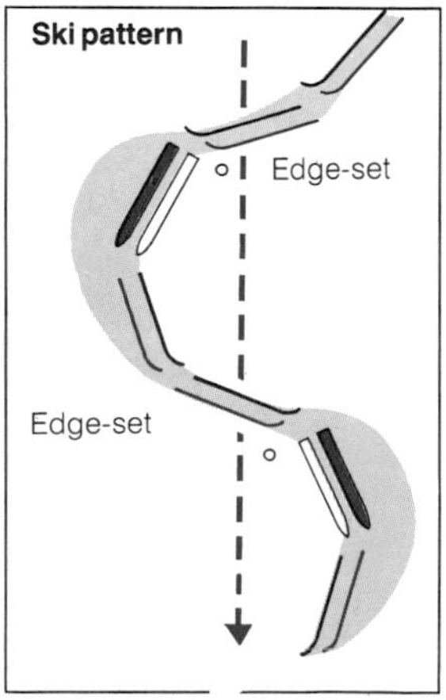

"Wedeln"

This refined form of short swinging is both enjoyable and impressive. It can be used for your own amusement and perhaps to show off a little on gentle slopes and in easy snow conditions where you might otherwise ski straight down the fall line. Basically, *wedeln* is very relaxed short swinging: the turns are smooth and flowing, and you ski quite fast, making very tight swings and using much less edging. The German word, *wedeln*, means "to wag", and you, in fact, maintain rhythm simply by swinging your ski tails out of the fall line from side to side, keeping your ski tips and upper body facing straight downhill. The regular rhythm of your turns will dictate your pole-plants and will give you the necessary balance and coordination.

Wedeln is used purely for enjoyment on gentle-to-moderate slopes when the snow conditions are good

1 Plant pole, extend outside leg to transfer weight and change edges

2 Go straight into next turn and keep skis slightly flatter on snow, set edges gently at each down-flexion – just enough to control speed where necessary

3 Upper body remains relaxed and facing down fall line, all movement comes from legs and hips: keep skis fairly close together

4 Concentrate on the two vital factors: rhythm and coordination

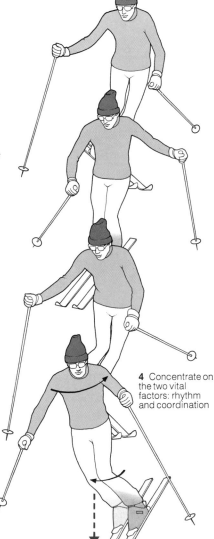

Fall line

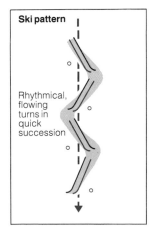

Ski pattern

Rhythmical, flowing turns in quick succession

Short swinging in powder snow

The easiest technique for skiing fresh, deep snow as well as light powder is short swinging. The fluid, short-radius turns enable you to stay close to the fall line and therefore maintain speed, and the regular rhythm of your flexion and extension makes it easier to initiate each turn. You will find that in deep snow you have to ski much more by "feel", since your skis will sink under the surface. You should exaggerate your flexion-extension move-ments (because the soft snow is more resistant to turning) and you should bank your body further into the turns. You will get used to the sensation of your skis "floating" through the snow. Keep your weight slightly further back so that your ski tips ride up under the snow. Mastering deep snow skiing will allow you to venture off the trails and give you much more freedom, variety and challenge – but always beware of possible avalanche danger.

Short swinging off-trail ▶
Two members of the Swiss Ski School demonstration team descend a powder slope in a series of fluid, linked turns – using the basic form of short swinging (p.114). For more details on adapting your technique to skiing deep or powder snow, see p.224.

◀ Fresh powder skiing
Short swinging in powder snow is functional as well as exhilarating – as these "helicopter" skiers (a ski instructor and his pupil) illustrate, high in the Alps above Zermatt, Switzerland. There are few things more satisfying than admiring the perfect tracks you have left behind in virgin snow.

Absorption-extension techniques

In order to be a good all-round skier, you should learn to initiate parallel turns and short swings with the aid of pronounced down-flexion, instead of just up-extension. This initiation is known as "absorption-extension" – although you may also find it called "bending" turning, "compression" turning, *avalement* (from the French word meaning "to swallow") or "OK technique" (from the German words, *Oberschenkel,* meaning "thigh" and *Knie* meaning "knee"). Absorption-extension techniques are ideally suited to turning on moguls or slope edges – because the skis stay in contact with the ground – and in difficult or deep snow.

In its basic form, this movement is prepared by actively flexing your legs. It is initiated by relaxing your leg muscles to momentarily unweight your skis, and by banking your thighs and knees into the turn so that you can change edges and rotate your legs to pivot your skis into the turn. The technique requires some strength, especially in the leg muscles, and you will find it easier on moguls, where the bumps will flex your legs automatically.

The pole-plant is very important in absorption-extension turning. When planted sideways, it creates a certain amount of "torque" by twisting you into the direction of the turn and helping you pivot your skis as you turn.

Basic absorption-extension turning forms the basis for two alternative forms of initiation, each adapted to different snow and terrain conditions. These are illustrated in the chart below. The basic form is described on p.121-2, the "jet" turn on p.124-7 and the "kangaroo" turn on p.128-9.

The absorption-extension initiation
This extreme stance, with the legs bent right up beneath the body and the characteristic sideways pole-plant, illustrates the initiation of the turn on top of a mogul at high speed.

Absorption-extension turns: how they differ and when to use them

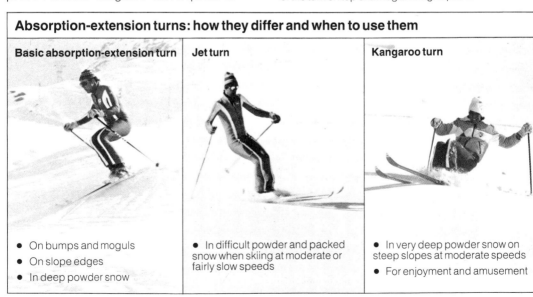

Basic absorption-extension turn
- On bumps and moguls
- On slope edges
- In deep powder snow

Jet turn
- In difficult powder and packed snow when skiing at moderate or fairly slow speeds

Kangaroo turn
- In very deep powder snow on steep slopes at moderate speeds
- For enjoyment and amusement

Basic absorption-extension turning technique

For demonstration purposes, the technique is shown below on a smooth trail – as the initiation is more exaggerated when you cannot use a bump to help you turn. The turn is prepared at the end of the previous one by gradually flexing your legs, pre-rotating your hips and upper body ("anticipation") and planting your inside pole sideways. As you ski past your pole, you initiate the turn by spontaneously relaxing your leg muscles, banking your knees downhill to change edges and rotating both skis together. Transfer your weight, rise up, counter-rotate and continue to steer the turn in the normal way.

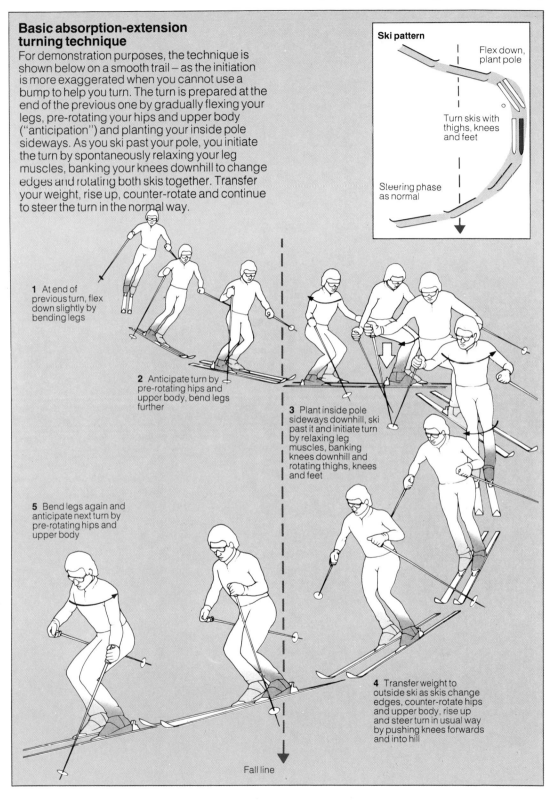

Ski pattern

Flex down, plant pole

Turn skis with thighs, knees and feet

Steering phase as normal

1 At end of previous turn, flex down slightly by bending legs

2 Anticipate turn by pre-rotating hips and upper body, bend legs further

3 Plant inside pole sideways downhill, ski past it and initiate turn by relaxing leg muscles, banking knees downhill and rotating thighs, knees and feet

5 Bend legs again and anticipate next turn by pre-rotating hips and upper body

4 Transfer weight to outside ski as skis change edges, counter-rotate hips and upper body, rise up and steer turn in usual way by pushing knees forwards and into hill

Fall line

Absorption-extension turning on moguls

When skiing moguls, bending turning is the ideal technique because it allows you to *use* the terrain to help you initiate each turn. If you turn on moguls by using an "up" initiation, you will tend to be thrown up in the air. Absorption-extension turning allows you to "suck-up" the bumps, keep your skis in contact with the snow and turn them beneath your feet. As you ski up to the top of a mogul, you will feel your knees being pushed up towards your chest: this automatically forms the down-flexion with which you initiate your turns.

Moguls take many shapes and sizes (p.230), so you must look ahead to choose your line through the bumps and dips and be prepared to react quickly. You should aim to ski against the mogul, turn on the top when your legs are fully flexed, and then extend your legs sideways to maintain snow contact as you ski down the other side.

1 Ski against mogul, pre-rotate hips and upper body in direction of new turn, absorb bump by letting legs bend as you come up to top

2 Plant inside pole sideways on top of mogul, let skis run past it underneath your body, relax leg muscles, bank knees into turn, and turn both skis together by rotating thighs, knees and feet

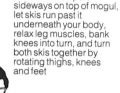

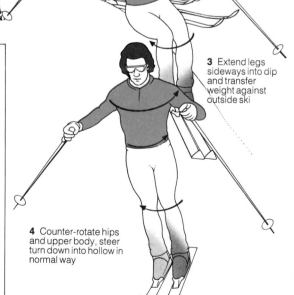

3 Extend legs sideways into dip and transfer weight against outside ski

4 Counter-rotate hips and upper body, steer turn down into hollow in normal way

How your skis pivot

Turning your skis on a bump is easier than on a smooth trail. This is because at the top of the mogul, only a small area of your skis is in contact with the snow which cuts down resistance to turning. You pivot your skis around your feet, rather than around your ski tips as you do in parallel turning or short swinging with up-extension when your skis are in contact with the snow over their whole length.

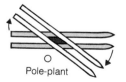

Pole-plant

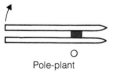

Pole-plant

Absorption-extension turning At the top of bump, skis pivot beneath your feet to make a fast, tight-radius turn.

Parallel turning On a smooth trail, turning axis is in front of feet, and turn therefore has a wider radius.

Absorption-extension turning on slope edges

Abrupt transitions in the slope gradient – from gentle to steep – can be used to aid the initiation of bending turns in just the same way as moguls. We have already shown on p.62 how to ski a slope that suddenly drops from gentle to steep. You must flex your legs and crouch forwards over the front of your skis as you hit the lip of the slope. This enables you to absorb the sudden change in gradient and to keep your skis in contact with the snow.

The sequence below shows how to use the flexing of your legs to initiate an absorption-extension turn. Anticipate the turn by pre-rotating your body, then plant your inside pole. Ski past it and bend your legs quickly, bank your knees and rotate your skis as you reach the lip of the slope. Extend your legs sideways to maintain snow contact and keep your weight well forward over your skis. Continue to steer the turn in the normal way.

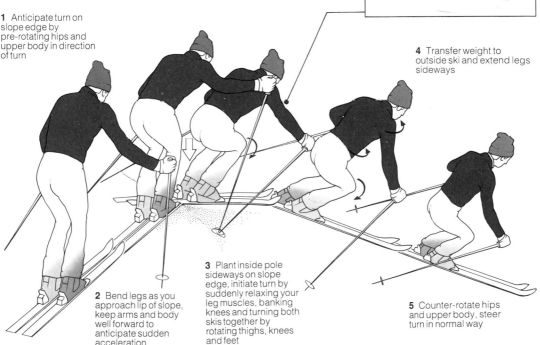

1 Anticipate turn on slope edge by pre-rotating hips and upper body in direction of turn

4 Transfer weight to outside ski and extend legs sideways

2 Bend legs as you approach lip of slope, keep arms and body well forward to anticipate sudden acceleration

3 Plant inside pole sideways on slope edge, initiate turn by suddenly relaxing your leg muscles, banking knees and turning both skis together by rotating thighs, knees and feet

5 Counter-rotate hips and upper body, steer turn in normal way

Common mistakes when using absorption-extension techniques

The great temptation in this sort of turning is to sit back over the tails of your skis instead of bending your legs and pushing your knees forwards. The extreme crouched position is used *only* for the preparation and initiation. The rest of the turn is skied in a normal stance. Your legs should be relaxed, not stiff, and, although the proper movement *is* one of lowering your seat, it is done by flexing your ankles against the front of your boots, not by sitting down or leaning against their high backs.

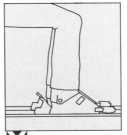

✗ Incorrect
Do not sit down. Keep weight forward by flexing ankles and knees.

✓ Correct
Down-flexion by flexing leg joints and pushing knees forwards.

"Jet" turning

This technique is an adapted form of absorption-extension turning. You will find that it helps you to initiate parallel turns in difficult conditions such as deep, heavy or windblown snow. It is known as "jet" turning because the initiation is aided by propelling or "jetting" your skis forwards beneath your body. In deep snow, this action unweights chiefly the front of your skis so that you can keep your ski tips up and turn your skis by rotating your feet. The jet movement will also act as an acceleration. For this reason, it is a good way of initiating a turn when you are skiing quite slowly. Indeed, racers often use an adapted form of the jet technique to connect two turns or to accelerate by jetting their skis as quickly as possible out of the end of a turn straight into the initiation of the following one.

This is how the jet turn works. You prepare for the turn by pre-rotating your body and by bending your legs, bringing your hips and knees as far forward as possible to build up a reserve of force – rather like coiling up a spring. You then plant your inside pole out to the side to give you support, "jet" your feet forwards to unweight your ski tips more than your tails, and rotate your feet and skis into the turn. This leads to a brief "leaning back" position – that is, a momentary weight-transfer onto the backs of your skis while you jet them forwards. However, this is only for the initiation: if you lean on your inside pole as you ski past it, you will find that your upper body banks into the turn naturally. In other words, leaning backwards is transformed into leaning inwards. You should aim to keep your upper body still and relaxed while jetting your skis forwards – the movement should come from the legs and should be prepared by leaning forward and flexing your ankles, knees and hips well in advance. The slower your speed, the more you need to lean on your pole to support yourself.

The "jet" movement

This movement is an *aid* to initiating parallel turns in circumstances which make turning difficult. It is purely a leg movement by which you propel your skis away from under you to unweight them and to rotate them in the direction of the turn.

How to "jet" your skis
Prepare by bending ankles, knees and hips forwards to build up a reserve of force. Propel feet quickly forwards to jet skis beneath body so that they are momentarily unweighted.

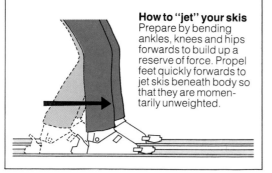

Basic jet turning technique

In the drawing on the right, the movement is demonstrated on a smooth trail so that you can see clearly how the skis are "jetted" forwards in order to initiate the turn. It is, in fact, ideally suited to deep or difficult snow where the jet movement helps overcome the snow's resistance to turning and keeps your ski tips up above the surface during the initiation phase.

To get used to the technique, practice it first on rounded terrain on a medium-to-steep trail. Begin by using a jet movement to initiate a parallel *uphill* turn from a traverse, and then from the fall line. You will start to feel how your legs must work independently of your body. Progress gradually to jet initiations of parallel *downhill* turns, first on the trail, then in light powder snow, and finally in deeper, more difficult snow.

When to use jet turning

● For initiating turns in powder, deep or packed snow where resistance to turning from the snow itself is very high

● As an aid to initiating parallel turns when skiing at slower speeds

---

Ski pattern

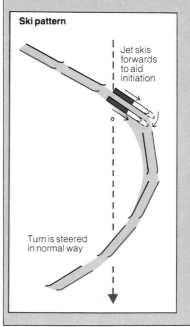

Jet skis forwards to aid initiation

Turn is steered in normal way

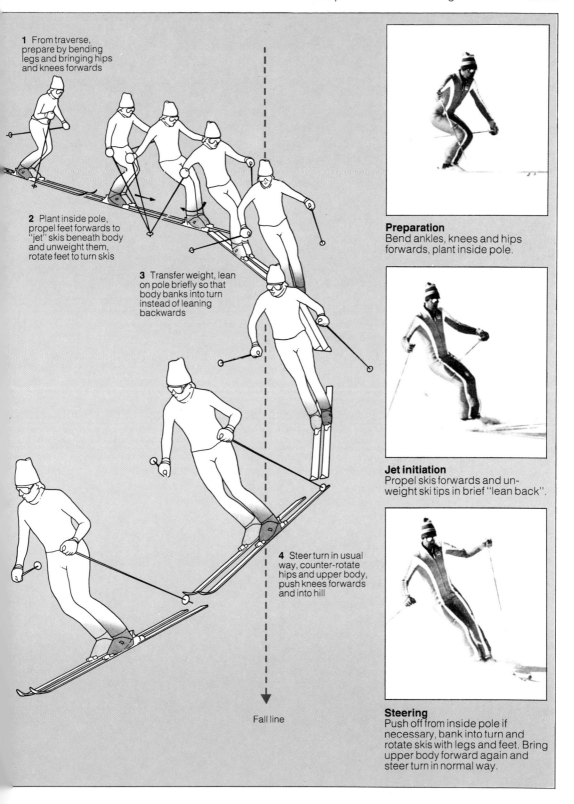

1 From traverse, prepare by bending legs and bringing hips and knees forwards

2 Plant inside pole, propel feet forwards to "jet" skis beneath body and unweight them, rotate feet to turn skis

3 Transfer weight, lean on pole briefly so that body banks into turn instead of leaning backwards

4 Steer turn in usual way, counter-rotate hips and upper body, push knees forwards and into hill

Fall line

Preparation
Bend ankles, knees and hips forwards, plant inside pole.

Jet initiation
Propel skis forwards and un-weight ski tips in brief "lean back".

Steering
Push off from inside pole if necessary, bank into turn and rotate skis with legs and feet. Bring upper body forward again and steer turn in normal way.

Jet turning in deep snow

For experienced skiers, the "jet" initiation is one of the most economical techniques for turning in deep or difficult snow conditions. Deep or packed snow exerts more lateral resistance against your skis and makes them harder to turn. The jet movement makes it easier to pivot your skis and also keeps the tips up above the surface. During the brief "sit-back" phase, you lean back over your ski tails and move the weight off your ski tips. In deep snow, too, it is more important that you *bank* into the turn as well as jetting your skis forwards; this is particularly true the faster you travel. Once you have planted your pole and jetted your feet forwards, you will have skied past it slightly and it will be planted behind you. If you then lean backwards and sideways on your pole to support yourself before coming forward again, you should be banking into the turn naturally. You will find that, if you ski fast, you will not need a lot of support from your pole, since you will be able to bank more easily; if you ski slowly, you will need more support and you will therefore lean on it with more of your weight.

Jet turning in light powder

The sequence of photographs on this page shows the jet initiation of a parallel turn in a few inches of light powder snow. Note how the skier's tips come up above the surface as he jets his skis forwards and banks into the turn, and also how he comes forward again to steer the turn in the normal way.

The "jet" stance

Many recreational skiers reach a high enough standard to ski deep snow – as this skier illustrates. His body position is characteristic of jet turning. However, the exaggerated leaning back should be only momentary. After the turn has been initiated, he will then push off from his pole, bank his body and come forward over his skis again to finish turning in a normal stance. For more details on deep snow skiing techniques, see p. 224.

Kangaroo turning

This turn gets its name from the kangaroo-like stance which the skier adopts while sitting back over his ski tails to make the initiation. Kangaroo turning is basically an extreme form of the absorption-extension and jet techniques on the previous pages, and it provides an effective and amusing way of turning. It is *possible* for good skiers to perform the movement on-trail, but its real use is as a means of initiating turns off-trail in deep powder snow and on steep slopes when travelling slowly or at only moderate speed. Indeed, as a general rule, it is only feasible in these conditions.

The characteristic "kangaroo sit-back" with which the turn is prepared and initiated transfers most of the skier's weight to the ski tails so that the tips rise up above the surface of the snow, instead of diving down beneath it. This also reduces lateral resistance to turning and makes it possible to turn the skis by pivoting them around their tails. The temporary sit-back stance is a demanding one, and requires strength in the thighs and calves. However, high-backed modern ski boots make this easier. The inside pole-plant, which is very important in kangaroo turning, provides the necessary pivot for the initiation and support for the backward and inward leaning of the body.

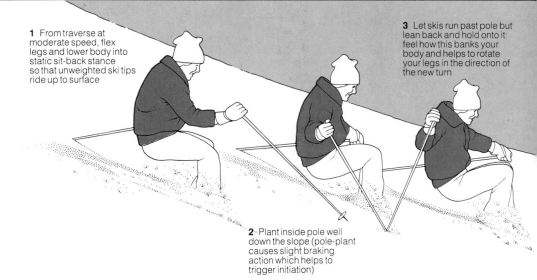

1 From traverse at moderate speed, flex legs and lower body into static sit-back stance so that unweighted ski tips ride up to surface

2 Plant inside pole well down the slope (pole-plant causes slight braking action which helps to trigger initiation)

3 Let skis run past pole but lean back and hold onto it: feel how this banks your body and helps to rotate your legs in the direction of the new turn

Basic technique for kangaroo turning

The turn is prepared by flexing the knees and ankles and adopting a static sit-back position. This unweights the ski tips so that they come up above the surface. After creating a natural pivot-point by planting and then skiing past the inside pole, the turn itself is initiated with an upwards and forwards movement together with a rotary motion of the legs. At the moment of initiation, more experienced skiers may also "jet" both feet forwards and, while still holding onto their inside pole, transform their backward leaning stance into an inward leaning one – thereby *banking* into the turn. As soon as this has happened, the turn can be steered as normal. When travelling fairly fast, the turn is easier to initiate and you may not need the pole-plant.

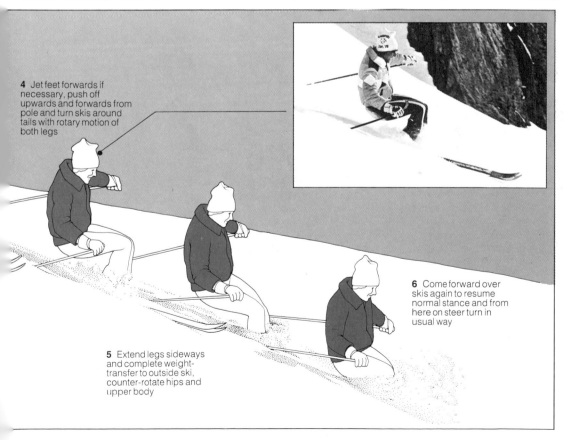

4 Jet feet forwards if necessary, push off upwards and forwards from pole and turn skis around tails with rotary motion of both legs

5 Extend legs sideways and complete weight-transfer to outside ski, counter-rotate hips and upper body

6 Come forward over skis again to resume normal stance and from here on steer turn in usual way

Jump turning

This technique can best be described as an extreme form of parallel turning with an "up" initiation (p.105). It is made by jumping both skis off the ground and turning them while they are in mid-air with a rotary motion. In other words, the turn is simply a jump straight from one traverse into another. The primary function of jump turning is to enable you to change direction in situations where almost any other kind of turn is impossible. In practice, this usually means when you are skiing slowly in deep, heavy snow on steep terrain. The pole-plant is very important in this movement, since it acts as a pivot and provides you with a necessary support while you are in the air. It can be made by planting either one or both poles on your downhill side. The most common errors when attempting a jump turn are skiing too fast and trying to rotate your skis after an insufficient push-off.

Basic jump turning technique

Prepare to turn from a slow, shallow traverse by flexing down into a low crouch, and plant your downhill pole just in front of your downhill foot. Initiate the turn by pushing off forcefully with both legs and jumping both skis up into the air. Support yourself on your pole and rotate first your whole body and then just your legs into the direction of the turn. Stretch your legs slightly and then let them flex as soon as your skis touch the snow to absorb the shock as you land in a new traverse.

When to use jump turning

- For initiating turns in difficult deep snow conditions (e.g., crust, or wet, heavy snow)

2 Push off from both legs, jump up and turn skis with rotary motion

1 Flex down and plant downhill pole

3 Extend then flex legs to absorb shock of landing in opposite traverse

Fall line

1 Flex down in traverse.

2 Jump up and turn skis.

3 Land in opposite traverse.

Jump turning in deep snow

These photographs illustrate the kind of situation in which jump turning may be useful. Although the snow is not extremely wet or heavy, the skier is approaching in a shallow traverse and, therefore, she does not have sufficient speed to initiate a normal parallel turn. She flexes down in preparation for the turn and, already, she is anticipating the initiation by pre-rotating her upper body into the new direction. By extending both legs simultaneously in a powerful push-off, she jumps up into the air. Leaning forwards and inwards slightly and using her inside pole for support, she rotates her skis in mid-air so that they land, tails first, in a new traverse. Her pole remains more-or-less vertical throughout the movement, and her pole-grip need not change. She lands with her body angulated so that more of her weight is on her downhill ski.

Terrain jumping

Jumping is enjoyable, exhilarating and impressive, as well as a useful technique which every skier should attempt to master. Being able to jump (and land) safely allows you to cope with situations such as slope edges, moguls, hidden snow fences and various other obstacles where the best way to stay in control is to make a jump. This is especially true when you are skiing fast and when you may have to react quickly and unexpectedly.

The aim of learning terrain jumping is to overcome your fear of losing contact with the ground, to build up your confidence and, perhaps, to teach yourself a little courage or daring. However, *if you lack the motivation for jumping then do not try it.* If you want to attempt it, build up your technique gradually. Begin by making short jumps (10-15 ft) from low bumps or slope edges that have a gentle landing slope and an easy run-out for you to stop. Later, lengthen your approach run, increase your speed and push off more strongly for longer jumps. Concentrate on keeping your balance in mid-air and on landing softly by using your legs as shock

absorbers. Flex down and lean your body well forward as you hit the ground so that you are not thrown backwards. You will notice that the steeper the slope the easier it is to land, and that the flatter the slope the greater the shock as you touch down.

When to use terrain jumping

- To jump from large ridges, on moguls or over bumps in the terrain

- For avoiding obstacles on- and off-trail

- As a way of coping with unexpected situations quickly and safely, especially when skiing fast

- For "pre-jumping" slope edges or bumps (a technique described on p.135)

- As a part of downhill racing technique

- For pure enjoyment

1 Flex legs and crouch forwards to prepare for take-off

2 Push off by extending legs and propel body upwards and forwards

3 Hold slight forward lean and tuck knees up to chest

Basic terrain jumping technique

As you approach the slope edge, flex your legs and crouch forwards slightly. When your ski tips reach the lip of the jump, extend your legs and body to propel yourself upwards *and* forwards with a strong push-off. At low speed, you may also boost your take-off with a double pole-push.

In mid-air, remain *relaxed,* keep your balance and lean your body forwards slightly. Do not tense up and do not lean back. Keep your skis together and in your line of travel – that is, with the tips pointing down and your skis more-or-less

parallel to the slope. While you are in mid-air, you can either pull your legs up under your body in a kind of "tuck" position then stretch them again before landing (shown here), or you can keep your legs extended all the time (as on p.134). Trick "freestyle" jumping is covered on p.174.

To land softly, let your legs flex immediately you hit the ground so that you absorb the shock, and crouch forwards over the front of your skis to avoid suddenly being thrown backwards by the force of your landing.

The "tuck" mid-air position

Although this low crouched position is somewhat acrobatic and therefore requires a fair amount of practice, it is the accepted stance for terrain jumping. As we have explained, it is not absolutely necessary for a good jump – you can also keep your legs extended while in mid-air (p.134) – but the "tuck" does serve a function. Flexing your legs and drawing your knees up to your chest after the take-off will help you keep your tails up and your tips down so that your skis are parallel to the slope. This means that you can make a smoother, less abrupt landing after extending your legs in preparation.

1 Flex legs, draw up knees beneath body and lean forward in low crouch or "tuck" position.

2 Point ski tips down. Try to keep skis together and tips level as much as possible.

3 Use arms and poles for balance if necessary, but keep body relaxed while in mid-air.

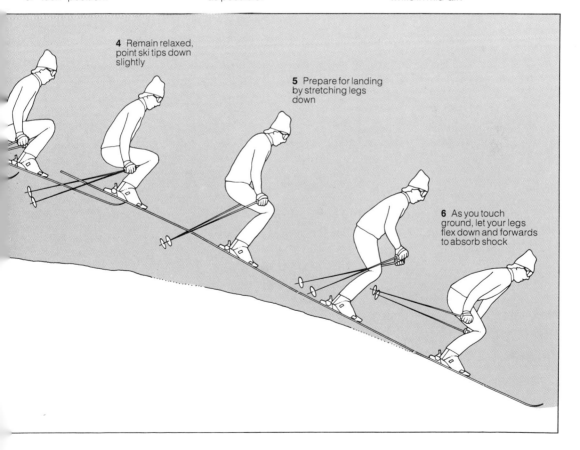

4 Remain relaxed, point ski tips down slightly

5 Prepare for landing by stretching legs down

6 As you touch ground, let your legs flex down and forwards to absorb shock

Jumping in uncertain terrain

The "extended" mid-air stance, with arms out-stretched for balance, is partly for enjoyment; it is also useful for jumping safely when you cannot see where you will land. Since your legs are extended all the time, you have no need to stretch them before landing. Even very good skiers will use this stance – as here, where the demonstrators could see the jump only from above.

1 Approach with sufficient speed to make your jump, flex knees in preparation

2 Push off by extending both legs, jump upwards and forwards

Jumping over a terrain dip

On mogul fields or undulating terrain, a jump can often be used to leap from the top of one bump right over a dip and onto the far side of the next bump. The jumping technique itself does not differ, but obviously you must be skiing fast enough to jump right over the crest of the second bump. In other words, a successful jump is mainly a question of speed. Only practice and experience will tell you whether your speed is high enough when you take off in order for you to land in the right place.

In mid-air, draw your knees up into the "tuck" position and keep your body relaxed, balanced and well forward. As you clear the second bump, straighten your legs and land softly on the other side so that your skis run downhill.

Pre-jumping

When skiing fast you will find that bumps and slope edges tend to throw you up in the air in involuntary jumps. To avoid this, you can use a "pre-jumping" technique often employed by downhill racers which cuts down your time in the air. Obviously, timing is vital: if you pre-jump at the right moment you will maintain your speed and keep your flight low and short; if you jump too soon you will land too soon — possibly before you have cleared the bump; if you jump too late you will be thrown too high in the air.

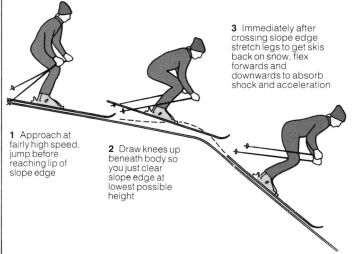

1 Approach at fairly high speed, jump before reaching lip of slope edge

2 Draw knees up beneath body so you just clear slope edge at lowest possible height

3 Immediately after crossing slope edge stretch legs to get skis back on snow, flex forwards and downwards to absorb shock and acceleration

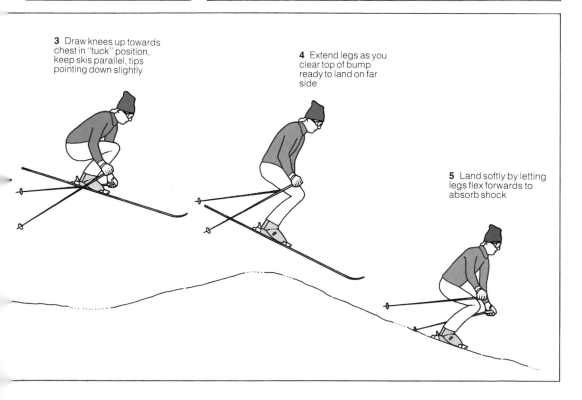

3 Draw knees up towards chest in "tuck" position, keep skis parallel, tips pointing down slightly

4 Extend legs as you clear top of bump ready to land on far side

5 Land softly by letting legs flex forwards to absorb shock

Stepping techniques

This method of preparing or initiating turns is a direct adaptation of techniques used by ski racers. The "stepping" maneuver is often used to link two turns and is a way of transferring weight to the uphill or outside ski ready to initiate and steer the second turn as soon as possible.

Two different forms of step can be distinguished: a step *onto* the uphill ski and a step *against* the uphill ski. The difference is illustrated below. Both forms can be made either with or without an accelerating push-off. All the stepping techniques discussed here can be used by racers as well as by good skiers on-trail or in snow conditions which make turning difficult.

Stepping onto the uphill ski is a method of *preparing* to turn. In a traverse, or in the end phase of the previous turn, the weight is transferred onto the uphill ski. The skier then rides on the uphill edge of his uphill ski, with his downhill ski lifted off the snow, until he wants to initiate his turn. When he does, he banks his body into the turn to change the edges of both skis in a one-phase or *direct* initiation.

Stepping against the uphill ski is a method of *initiating* a turn. In a traverse, the uphill ski is lifted off the snow, stemmed out into a "converging" position if necessary, and then set down again flat or on its downhill edge. The skier initiates the turn by increasing the pressure against his uphill ski and by banking and counter-rotating his body – this is a two-phase or *indirect* initiation.

Strictly speaking, a "step" can be made without the uphill ski being lifted off the snow. As long as there is a distinct, definite transfer of weight from the downhill to the uphill ski, this qualifies as a "step". Thus, in a manner of speaking, all the previous turns in this chapter, from the turning snowplow onwards, use a form of stepping.

When to use a step onto the uphill ski

- For making rounded, wide-radius turns
- For gaining height in a traverse

When to use a step against the uphill ski

- For making fast, short-radius turns
- For initiating turns in light powder snow
- For preparing turns in windblown or uneven snow by using your uphill ski as a "feeler" to find the best moment to initiate the turn

Stepping onto the uphill ski

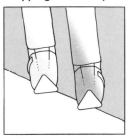 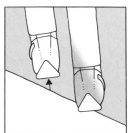 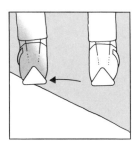 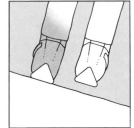

1 Traverse or end phase of previous turn, weight chiefly on downhill ski.

2 Weight completely on downhill ski, lift up unweighted uphill ski.

3 Set down uphill ski on uphill edge, transfer weight onto it.

4 Initiate turn by banking body to change both edges together.

Stepping against the uphill ski

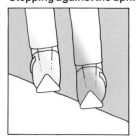 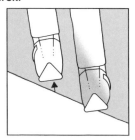 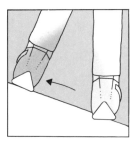 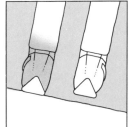

1 Traverse or end phase of previous turn, weight chiefly on downhill ski.

2 Weight completely on downhill ski, lift up unweighted uphill ski.

3 Displace uphill ski, set it down and bank body to change edge.

4 Initiate turn by then increasing pressure against uphill ski.

Basic technique for stepping onto the uphill ski

This is the basic form of the movement; its more advanced form is shown on p. 138. Here, the "step", from your downhill onto your uphill ski, forms the *preparation* phase of the turn – and its function is to transfer your weight earlier than normal to the ski which will be your outside or steering ski throughout the turn. Once the step has been made, the turn may be initiated with either an "up" or a "down" unweighting. This is how the movement is performed. It is usually started from the end phase of the previous turn

where your weight will be chiefly on your downhill ski. You then transfer progressively more and more of your weight onto your uphill ski until you are gliding on it with your downhill ski off the snow. The weight-transfer can be done with or without lifting your uphill ski off the snow. To initiate the turn, bank your body inwards so that both skis tilt onto their downhill edges, plant your inside pole for support if necessary, and pre-rotate your body in the direction of the turn. Then flex your legs and rotate them to turn your skis.

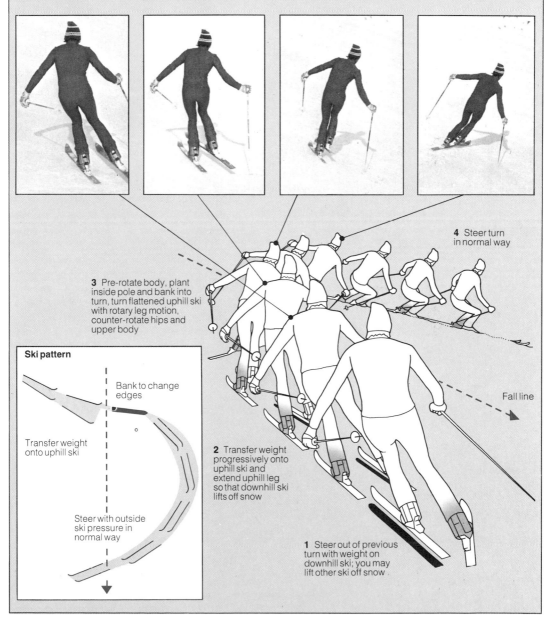

4 Steer turn in normal way

3 Pre-rotate body, plant inside pole and bank into turn, turn flattened uphill ski with rotary leg motion, counter-rotate hips and upper body

Ski pattern

Bank to change edges

Transfer weight onto uphill ski

Steer with outside ski pressure in normal way

2 Transfer weight progressively onto uphill ski and extend uphill leg so that downhill ski lifts off snow

Fall line

1 Steer out of previous turn with weight on downhill ski; you may lift other ski off snow

137

Stepping onto the uphill ski with push-off

This form is essentially the same as the basic technique described on the previous page, except that it is performed with a strong push-off from the downhill ski onto the uphill ski in order to accelerate in between turns. The movement is very like that of "skating" (p. 90) and, as in skating, the step is made *diagonally*. This means that the uphill ski is lifted off the snow and angled out slightly in the desired direction so that the push-off can be directed forwards and sideways. This is known as stepping onto the "diverging" uphill ski. Racers use it to correct their line and to gain height so that they can get up through a high gate when the layout of the course requires it.

The movement can be initiated from a traverse, but it is usually started during the end phase of a previous turn. With your weight on your downhill ski, you lift your uphill ski and push off powerfully from your flexed downhill leg. You then set down your uphill ski on its uphill edge in the desired direction and step onto it. The push-off continues upwards into an up-extension together with rotary motion

and banking. The turn initiation is therefore the same as for parallel turning with "up" (p. 105) – although racers will often refine the edge-change of their uphill ski by rotating their uphill knee inwards. The steering phase is the same as normal.

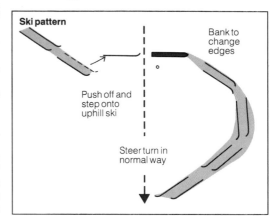

Ski pattern

Bank to change edges

Push off and step onto uphill ski

Steer turn in normal way

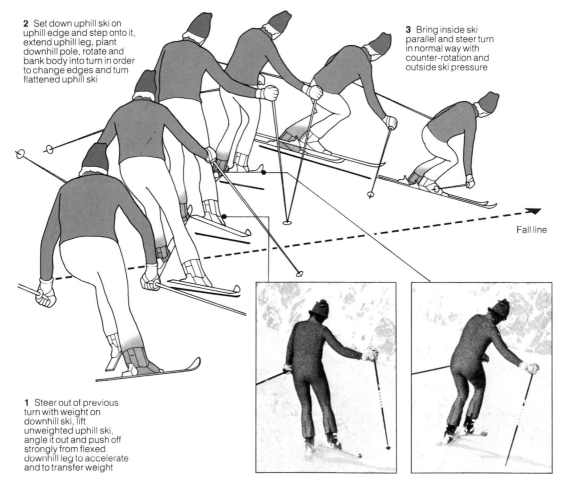

2 Set down uphill ski on uphill edge and step onto it, extend uphill leg, plant downhill pole, rotate and bank body into turn in order to change edges and turn flattened uphill ski

3 Bring inside ski parallel and steer turn in normal way with counter-rotation and outside ski pressure

Fall line

1 Steer out of previous turn with weight on downhill ski, lift unweighted uphill ski, angle it out and push off strongly from flexed downhill leg to accelerate and to transfer weight

Basic technique for stepping against the uphill ski

This turn initiation is essentially a refined form of "stem turning" (p. 96), developed by ski racers into an effective competition stepping technique. Like stepping onto the uphill ski, it can be performed either with or without a push-off to aid the turning of the uphill ski. It is shown here *without,* and it is shown *with* on p. 140. The aim of stepping against the uphill ski is to initiate turns largely by using the turning force which can be generated by your own speed or inertia (p. 182). For this reason, these turns can be initiated without a push-off when you are skiing fairly fast; when skiing slowly or when snow conditions are heavy, a strong push-off and a "converging" ski position may be needed. This is known as stepping against the converging uphill ski.

Unlike stepping onto, stepping against is normally a turning initiation, not a preparation. You begin in a traverse or at the end of the previous turn, lift your uphill ski, displace it and set it down on its opposite edge. At this point — where pressure is transferred against your

uphill ski — the "step" is made and the initiation happens. It is completed by lifting up your downhill ski, planting your downhill pole and banking into the turn.

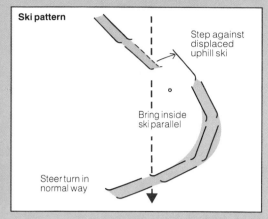

Ski pattern

Step against displaced uphill ski

Bring inside ski parallel

Steer turn in normal way

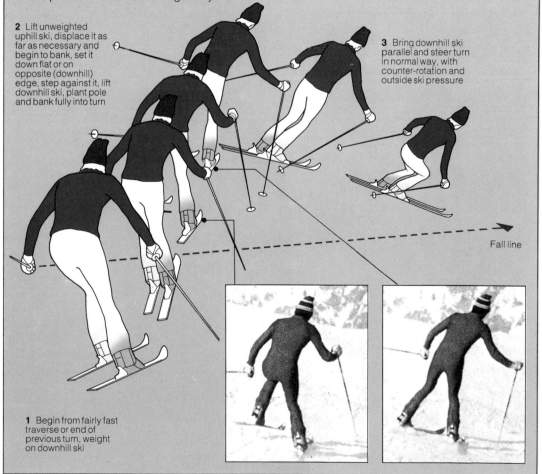

2 Lift unweighted uphill ski, displace it as far as necessary and begin to bank, set it down flat or on opposite (downhill) edge, step against it, lift downhill ski, plant pole and bank fully into turn

3 Bring downhill ski parallel and steer turn in normal way, with counter-rotation and outside ski pressure

Fall line

1 Begin from fairly fast traverse or end of previous turn, weight on downhill ski

139

Stepping against the uphill ski with push-off

This form of the technique is useful for initiating turns when your speed is slower, when the snow conditions make turning more difficult or when the slope is steeper and you therefore want to make a quicker, shorter-radius turn – in short, when your inertia alone will not supply the major part of the necessary turning force. The aim of the push-off, then, is to aid or accelerate the turning of your uphill ski and to increase the turning pressure which you apply to it. This is how the movement is performed. From a traverse, lift up your unweighted uphill ski

and displace it as far as you feel you need to – a fairly pronounced angle will make the initiation easier at low speeds. Set it down on its opposite (downhill) edge, plant your downhill pole, and push off powerfully from your flexed downhill leg. Begin to turn by transferring your weight (stepping) so that you increase pressure against your uphill ski. Bank your body into the turn, bring your unweighted downhill ski parallel and steer the turn in the normal way – pushing your knees forwards and into the hill, and counter-rotating your upper body.

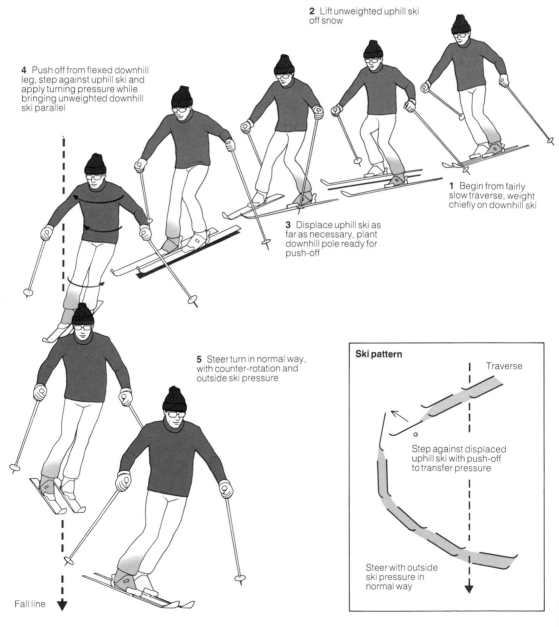

2 Lift unweighted uphill ski off snow

4 Push off from flexed downhill leg, step against uphill ski and apply turning pressure while bringing unweighted downhill ski parallel

1 Begin from fairly slow traverse, weight chiefly on downhill ski

3 Displace uphill ski as far as necessary, plant downhill pole ready for push-off

5 Steer turn in normal way, with counter-rotation and outside ski pressure

Fall line

Ski pattern

Traverse

Step against displaced uphill ski with push-off to transfer pressure

Steer with outside ski pressure in normal way

"Flying" step turning

This "flying" weight-transfer technique is a dynamic form of stepping against the uphill ski with push-off. It is used by ski racers as a form of competition stepping, and it can also help good skiers to turn over the top of moguls or to initiate turns in difficult conditions. The step against the uphill ski is made with such a powerful push-off that you jump into the air from one ski to the other and for a moment both skis are off the snow. When done in the form of short swinging, as shown here, the rhythm should be rather like a "gallop".

1 Preparation

2 "Flying step" initiation

3 Steering phase

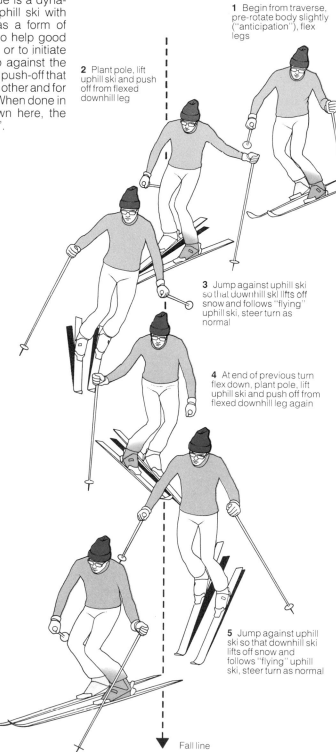

1 Begin from traverse, pre-rotate body slightly ("anticipation"), flex legs

2 Plant pole, lift uphill ski and push off from flexed downhill leg

3 Jump against uphill ski so that downhill ski lifts off snow and follows "flying" uphill ski, steer turn as normal

4 At end of previous turn flex down, plant pole, lift uphill ski and push off from flexed downhill leg again

5 Jump against uphill ski so that downhill ski lifts off snow and follows "flying" uphill ski, steer turn as normal

Fall line

Competition stepping techniques

Linking turns with a step movement is called "competition stepping". It involves steering out of the first turn into a very short traverse, and then preparing and initiating the second turn with an early step or weight-transfer to the new outside (steering) ski. It also enables the racer to ski the ideal line through the slalom gates. As we show on p.152, the ideal line is not necessarily the shortest, but the one that allows the skier to turn with minimum braking and maximum efficiency. For this reason, a slalom racer will try to make his turns as smooth and rounded as possible – from their start to their finish – and, even in special slalom where the gates are tighter and closer together, he will try to avoid sharp turns that reduce his speed.

In competition, ski racers will use both pure and combined forms of the stepping techniques described in the preceding pages – that is, both stepping onto and stepping against the uphill ski, either with or without an accelerating push-off. The choice of what movement to use depends on four things: the steepness of the slope, the snow conditions on the day of the race, how the course has been laid out, and the personal style of the racer. All racers have their own style, and a good racer varies his technique instinctively. This is a skill which can only be developed gradually through extensive training, through developing a perfect "feel" for the techniques, and through eliminating all unnecessary movements of the skis and body.

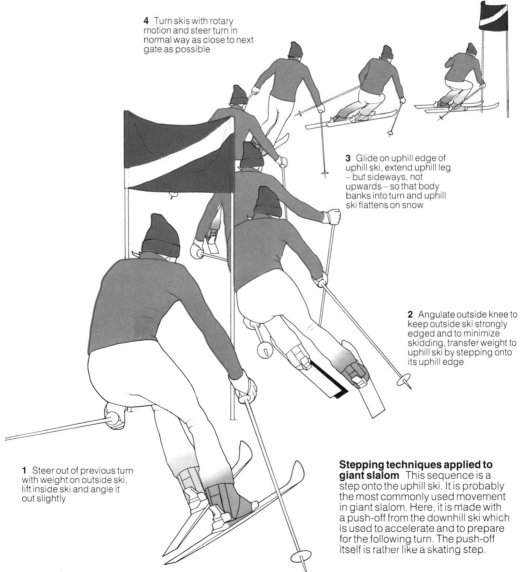

4 Turn skis with rotary motion and steer turn in normal way as close to next gate as possible

3 Glide on uphill edge of uphill ski, extend uphill leg – but sideways, not upwards – so that body banks into turn and uphill ski flattens on snow

2 Angulate outside knee to keep outside ski strongly edged and to minimize skidding, transfer weight to uphill ski by stepping onto its uphill edge

1 Steer out of previous turn with weight on outside ski, lift inside ski and angle it out slightly

Stepping techniques applied to giant slalom This sequence is a step onto the uphill ski. It is probably the most commonly used movement in giant slalom. Here, it is made with a push-off from the downhill ski which is used to accelerate and to prepare for the following turn. The push-off itself is rather like a skating step.

Various refined forms of competition stepping have been evolved to cope with specific situations. We cover these in more detail in "Slalom techniques" on p.152-7. They include: turning with minimum friction (by angulating the outside knee to try and keep the outside ski carving); cutting into the traverse on the diverging uphill ski; stepping onto/against the uphill ski in which the up-extension is made not only upwards but also sideways into the next turn; and a down-flexion with a jet movement used to accelerate out of turns.

Some of these techniques can be seen in the drawings below, where a good skier (but not a professional racer) tackles a giant slalom and a special slalom course.

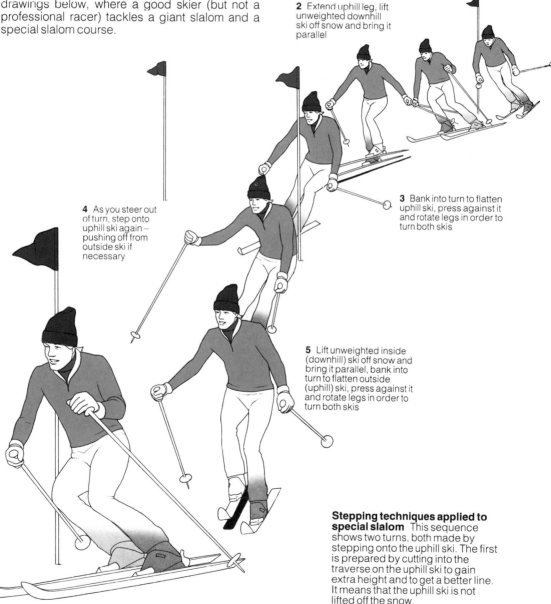

1 Steer out of previous turn, passing just inside slalom pole, push off from downhill leg and step onto uphill edge of uphill ski as it cuts into traverse

2 Extend uphill leg, lift unweighted downhill ski off snow and bring it parallel

3 Bank into turn to flatten uphill ski, press against it and rotate legs in order to turn both skis

4 As you steer out of turn, step onto uphill ski again – pushing off from outside ski if necessary

5 Lift unweighted inside (downhill) ski off snow and bring it parallel, bank into turn to flatten outside (uphill) ski, press against it and rotate legs in order to turn both skis

Stepping techniques applied to special slalom This sequence shows two turns, both made by stepping onto the uphill ski. The first is prepared by cutting into the traverse on the uphill ski to gain extra height and to get a better line. It means that the uphill ski is not lifted off the snow.

143

Competition skiing

Ski racing dates from the earliest days of skiing in Norway, and modern slalom racing is almost certainly descended from the original Nordic obstacle races. The formal composition and layout of slalom courses was not established until the 1920s when Sir Arnold Lunn drew up the first set of Alpine slalom rules. The first official race to be held under his rules was the "Arlberg–Kandahar" which took place at St Anton in 1928. In 1930 the F.I.S. *(Fédération Internationale de Ski),* the body which controls international ski racing, formally recognized Sir Arnold Lunn's rules.

Meanwhile, downhill racing, also a Nordic tradition, had caught on in the Alps and in California: a group of competitors would all set off at once from the top of a mountain and would head for a designated finish area. The first one down was the winner; otherwise, there were no rules. Giant slalom started in 1934. A downhill race on the Marmolada glacier in Italy was considered by the competitors to be too dangerous, and they asked for gates to be set on the course to control the speed.

In 1936, both slalom and downhill racing were included in the Winter Olympics for the first time; and, in 1952, giant slalom was added as well. The Winter Olympics are held every four years, as are the World Ski Championships. But they are staggered so that there is an event every two years. This means that racers can enter for both Olympic medals and F.I.S. titles. There is also an annual World Cup competition, which consists of a series of races set in Europe, America and Japan. Participation in all three disciplines – slalom, giant slalom and downhill racing – is compulsory, and the winner of the World Cup is the racer with the highest number of points awarded throughout the season. Second-strength teams race in special events, such as the European Cup, organized by the F.I.S. There is also a "lowlander" event for those whose normal residence is outside the Alps. International races are under the jurisdiction of the F.I.S., and admission to the major events is determined by an F.I.S. points system.

Competition skiing has become a highly popular spectator sport. It has also made skiing far more accessible as a recreational activity, since it promotes advances in technique and equipment, and the improvement and development of resorts.

◀ Slalom racing
This shot shows Carla Marchelli (Italy) on the slalom course at Grindelwald in 1957, competing for the Swiss Women's International title. On that occasion she came first in all three events – the downhill, giant slalom and special slalom.

Downhill racing ▶
Equipment for modern ski racing has come a long way since the 1920s. This downhill racer at the 1980 Lake Placid Olympics is using special skis and ski poles and wears a crash helmet and tight-fitting suit to cut down air resistance.
Inset Compare the lace-up leather boots, looser woollen clothing and outdated helmet worn by Christl Haas (Austria), shown here winning the women's downhill at the 1964 Innsbruck Olympics.

Special slalom racing

Slalom or special slalom courses are designed as a test of reflexes, technical versatility, agility, precision and control. Of course, speed is vital – but it rarely exceeds 25 mph. The emphasis is on turning: the flags are smaller, the gates are narrower and the turns are tighter than in giant slalom racing. The course contains between 45 and 75 gate combinations, set to produce a wide variety of different turns. Racers must complete two runs, each on a different course. Major races are timed electronically to the nearest hundredth of a second.

Training for special slalom concentrates on the most efficient way of turning and on choosing the fastest line through the gates. Although the techniques are basically the same, each racer will develop his or her own distinctive, personal style.

Body angulation ▲
As long as both feet pass through the gate, the racer is allowed to nudge or even knock over the slalom pole. Here, Paul Frommelt (Liechtenstein) cuts in as close as possible to the flag and uses extreme hip angulation to give him better edge control in his turn.

◀ The greatest slalom racer Ingemar Stenmark (Sweden) has become a legend in slalom racing. He competes in both the special slalom and the giant slalom – and wins in both, regularly. Using accelerating step turns, he combines speed with outstanding skill.

Looking ahead ▶
As Ingrid Eberle (Austria) comes out of one gate in a low, crouched stance, she is already preparing for her next turn and choosing her line through the next gate.

How slalom courses are set

Giant slalom courses

This course aims at combining turning skill with high speed, so the gates are wider apart and the distance between them (10m/32ft minimum) is greater than in a special slalom course.

Special slalom courses

The gates are fairly narrow and are set close together in different combinations to test a racer's skill and maneuverability in turns of differing radius over varying terrain.

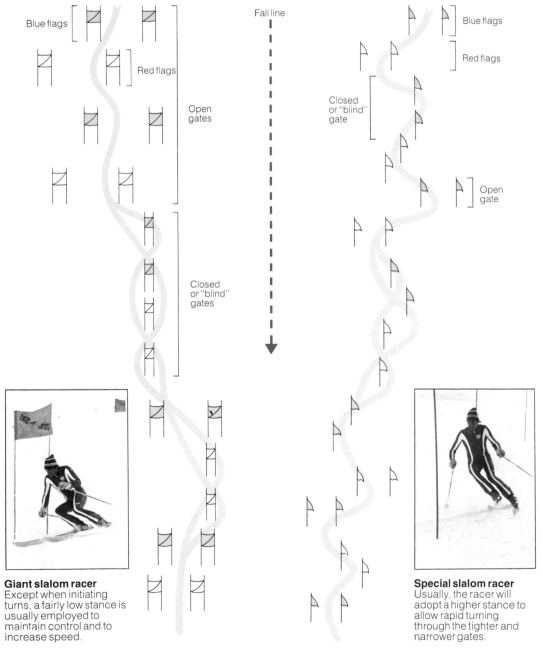

Blue flags

Red flags

Open gates

Closed or "blind" gates

Fall line

Blue flags

Red flags

Closed or "blind" gate

Open gate

Giant slalom racer
Except when initiating turns, a fairly low stance is usually employed to maintain control and to increase speed.

Special slalom racer
Usually, the racer will adopt a higher stance to allow rapid turning through the tighter and narrower gates.

Slalom variations

There are various alternative forms of slalom course, generally used for local events or for practice and training. The "single-pole" slalom makes an excellent training course as the racer has to turn around each single pole. Dual-slaloms are knock-out events in which two skiers race at once on separate courses.

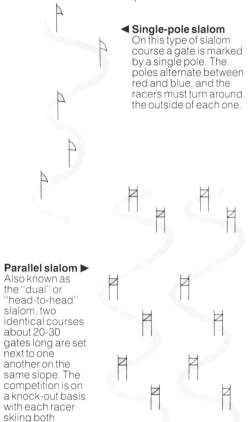

◄ Single-pole slalom
On this type of slalom course a gate is marked by a single pole. The poles alternate between red and blue, and the racers must turn around the outside of each one.

Parallel slalom ►
Also known as the "dual" or "head-to-head" slalom, two identical courses about 20-30 gates long are set next to one another on the same slope. The competition is on a knock-out basis with each racer skiing both courses.

Dual slalom
Two top Swiss racers ski against each other in a parallel slalom during training at Saas Fee.

F.I.S. slalom regulations for World Cup and Olympic championships

• Number of gates for special slalom courses: men 55 min., 75 max.; women 45 min., 60 max.
• Number of gates for giant slalom courses: 15 per cent of vertical drop, plus or minus 5 gates

• Width of special slalom gate 4-5 m. Distance between open gates 7-15 m; between closed vertical gates 0.75 m min.
• Width of giant slalom gate 4-8 m. Distance between gates 10 m min.

• Height difference for special slalom courses: men 180-220 m; women 130-180 m
• Height difference for giant slalom courses: men 300-400 m; women 300-350 m

• Gates are marked by blue and red flags on matching flexible poles; consecutive gates alternate in color. Two single poles mark a special slalom gate; two flags, each strung between a pair of poles, a giant slalom gate

• The course is set by two F.I.S. course-setters on the day of the race or the evening before and must contain open and vertical gates in varying combinations

• Special slalom courses must be set on a hard snow surface on a slope with a gradient of between 20° and 27° (33-45 per cent)

• Gatekeepers are placed alongside the course to check that each skier passes with both feet through every gate. The poles may be touched or knocked down but, if the racer misses a gate, receives assistance or does not finish on at least one ski, he is disqualified

• Three forerunners (Vorfahrer) set a track on the course before the official start

• Two separate courses are set on the same slope, and every racer skis each course once. The best aggregate time determines the winner

• The starting order is according to start number for the first run; for the second run, it is determined by the results of the first run

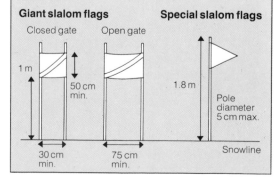

Giant slalom flags

Closed gate   Open gate

1 m
50 cm min.

30 cm min.   75 cm min.

Special slalom flags

1.8 m

Pole diameter 5 cm max.

Snowline

Giant slalom racing

In terms of ski technique, giant slalom lies in between special slalom and downhill racing — combining the speed of downhill with the turning skill of slalom. It differs from special slalom in that the gates are wider and are set further apart, the course is longer and the speed is greater. It differs from downhill in that it is more of a test of precise, controlled turning at high speed. In fact, giant slalom has evolved into a highly specialized discipline of its own. At the international level, a skier is unlikely to win in both giant slalom and downhill. Racers who excel in slalom rarely train as downhillers: the standard of competition is too high.

Ingemar Stenmark (Sweden), who has raced in the downhill only rarely, is probably the greatest slalom racer of all time. In 1979 he won seven World Cup giant slaloms and at the 1980 Olympics he took the gold medal in both giant and special slalom.

◀ **The starting gate**
Each competitor's run is timed electronically. To guarantee complete accuracy and fairness, the clock is triggered by the racer knocking aside the arm of a special "wishbone" gate at the top of the course.

Cutting a tight turn ▶
A giant slalom racer has to choose the shortest line through each gate. Maria Epple (Germany) is shown here at the 1980 Lake Placid Olympics cutting her turn as close to the gate as possible.

Accelerating out of a ▼ gate A World Cup giant slalom racer steers through the gate, banking his body into the turn. To maintain speed, he tries to let his skis run as much as possible and even in the turn he brakes only enough to keep his line.

Slalom techniques

The requirements of a giant slalom course and a special slalom course are not quite the same; in giant slalom, for example, speed is higher and the turns are further apart. However, there *is* sufficient similarity for the racers to share the same three major objectives. These are: first, skiing the ideal line through the gates; second, turning with minimum braking; and, third, accelerating between and through the gates.

Every time racers make a turn their skis exert a braking action and they slow down. They must therefore find ways of turning with as little friction as possible in order to get through all the gates as fast as they can. This involves steering with total pressure against the outside ski, with the correct amount of diagonal ski placing, and with the precise degree of edging for carved, not skidded, turns.

Acceleration can be achieved by a push-off onto the uphill ski when preparing to turn (p.138), and by a down-flexion of the body just after the initiation, followed in many cases by a forward "jet" movement of the feet towards the end of the turn.

Stepping techniques form the basis of all modern slalom racing, but racers will adapt the basic movements to the demands of each situation and to their own personal style. They will use refined forms such as completing a turn on the diverging inside ski or stepping "onto/against" the uphill ski when initiating a turn. The photo-sequences of Ingemar Stenmark and Phil Mahre on the following pages illustrate some of these techniques.

The "line"
Contrary to popular belief, the ideal line through the gates is not always the shortest. As a rule, racers aim to approach each gate from a high position and to make their turn *before* passing through it, not afterwards. Turning earlier allows them to maintain height for the next gate, and reduces the need for braking. It also means that they are able to make rounded, carved turns, which are faster than abrupt, skidded ones.

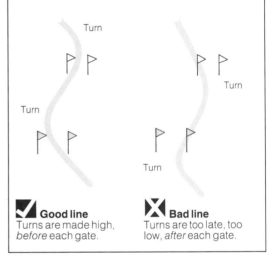

Good line
Turns are made high, *before* each gate.

Bad line
Turns are too late, too low, *after* each gate.

Slalom starts
In an event which can be lost or won by as little as a hundredth of a second, a fast, aggressive start is vital. At the top of the course, there is a "wishbone" starting gate, with a hinged arm or wand which the racers kick aside to start the electronic clock. The racer must begin from a standing start, but the aim is to come out of the gate with the maximum force and acceleration to gain speed as quickly as possible. The most common technique for doing this is shown here: a strong push-off from both legs and both poles which leads to a "catapult"-style jump and one or more skating steps.

The start technique
Plant poles downhill of "wand", flex down, spring up on ski tips, kick wand aside with one leg and push off into skating steps in direction of first gate.

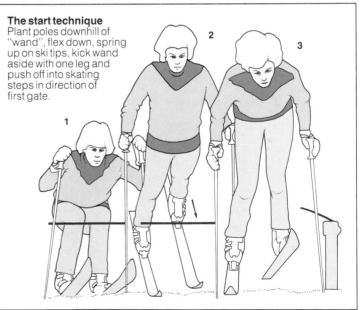

Giant slalom techniques

On a giant slalom course, the emphasis is on rounded, fluid turns. Racers will use both stepping onto and stepping against the uphill ski according to the situation. But, because speed is high, so is kinetic energy. This means that turns are easier to initiate and require less unweighting of the skis. Most racers therefore turn largely by banking and counter-rotation of the upper body, rarely needing to plant their downhill pole. They also often use a down-flexion and a jet movement as a means of accelerating while steering their turns. The down-flexion utilizes the skier's body mass for a sudden acceleration and also increases pressure against the outside ski. Jetting the feet forwards after the down-flexion causes the skis to accelerate, and the temporary back-lean can be transformed into an inward banking of the body for the next turn initiation. Our photo-sequence shows Ingemar Stenmark (Sweden) in action on the giant slalom course at Arosa in Switzerland during a World Cup race.

3 The transfer of pressure onto uphill ski has now been completed, and downhill ski is in air, totally unweighted.

4 He extends uphill leg and, while both skis are in air, turns them and banks his body.

2 Still controlling his line by outside ski steering, he begins to transfer pressure onto uphill ski ready for it to become outside steering ski for next turn.

1 Stenmark steers out of turn with extreme angulation of hips and outside knee to maintain pressure against edged outside ski.

5 Stenmark has made his turn well in advance of next gate and can now ski a good line through it. His body stance is still high as he begins the steering phase of the turn.

7 Weight is completely on outside steering ski; inside ski is off snow again. Stenmark's extreme angulation of outside knee keeps his outside ski precisely edged for maximum carving and minimum skidding in the turn.

6 He flexes down quickly in order to accelerate, and he both counter-rotates and angulates hips and upper body to maintain pressure against outside ski and to control edging.

153

Special slalom techniques

Although the gates are closer and the turns tighter and more frequent, special slalom racers have virtually the same objectives as they do in giant slalom. They aim to ski the best line through the gates and to turn with as little braking action as possible. In special slalom, there is little opportunity for the down-flexion and jet acceleration tech-niques used by giant slalom racers, so more depends on choosing and holding the best turning line. The racers must try to let their skis run as freely as possible and must use just the right degree of edging for their skis to carve, not skid. As soon as their skis begin to skid they slow down, and the racers lose height and time. This is not only be-

1 Ingemar Stenmark steers out of his previous turn, his body angulated over his edged and weighted outside ski, his inside shoulder brushing the slalom pole aside.

2 He prepares to turn again by getting ready to step onto his diverging uphill ski.

3 Extending up, he transfers pressure, plants his pole and banks into the turn.

4 Stretching his uphill leg, Stenmark has extended *into* the turn instead of merely upwards. This means that he has both transferred pressure to his uphill ski and tilted it onto its opposite edge in one movement. This is known as "stepping onto/ against the uphill ski" (p. 142).

5 Steering with carefully controlled outside ski pressure, flexing down and counter-rotating hips and upper body, Stenmark skis around the inside pole. As long as both feet pass through the gate, it does not ·matter if he knocks over the pole with his body.

cause a skidding ski creates more friction against the snow, but also because, as it skids, it swings further across the fall line and therefore becomes more difficult to turn in the opposite direction before the next gate is reached. In general, the rapid changes of direction in a special slalom course require a more pronounced unweighting of the skis and a regular pole-plant. This means that racers will use both stepping techniques and short swinging.

The photographs on these pages come from a sequence I shot at Montana in Switzerland to make a comparison between Ingemar Stenmark (Sweden) and Phil Mahre (USA) skiing the same section of the course during a World Series race.

1 Phil Mahre steers through the gate in the same way. The two racers' body positions are almost identical, and they both illustrate the same characteristic angulation of the outside knee which maintains the carving action of the outside ski and minimizes its tendency to skid.

2 Mahre seems to have overturned slightly: his skis are too square to his line of travel.

3 Recovering, his up-extension unweights his skis and for a moment both are off the snow.

4 Mahre makes the same step "onto/against" his uphill ski by directing his up-extension into the turn (banking). This early weight-transfer to what is now his new outside steering ski means he can make his turn before he reaches the next gate.

5 Crouching into a lower stance than Stenmark, but already transferring pressure to his inside ski, Mahre steers through the gate, following almost exactly the same line. He, too, counter-rotates but, unlike Stenmark, he leans out with his upper body to avoid the pole.

Downhill racing

The fastest and most challenging of the three racing disciplines is the downhill. It is basically a speed contest in which the fastest descent determines the winner, and it demands a high level of technical skill and a great deal of strength and courage. Speeds can reach 140 kph (90 mph), and maintaining control depends on instant reactions to sudden changes in snow conditions and visibility, as well as coping with the turns, jumps and changes of gradient. Safety precautions are as stringent as possible, but the accident rate is fairly high. At one point during the winter of 1980-81, twenty per cent of the world's top downhill racers were in hospital recovering from bad falls, and a deputation led by Canada's Ken Read appealed to the F.I.S. for stricter safety controls.

Downhill racing technique concentrates on ways of increasing speed and on turning accurately and efficiently without any unnecessary braking. When schussing, two of the most important aims are to minimize wind resistance and to keep the whole ski as flat as possible on the snow – since a ski in contact with the snow can be controlled better than a ski in the air. The basis of the technique is the low, crouched stance called the "egg", aerodynamically the best position (see below). However, steering is difficult in a low tuck, and racers will therefore adopt a looser and higher crouch to allow more leg and hip movement and to give better balance and quicker reactions over rough terrain. Initiating turns is easier at high speed: the racers' higher kinetic energy supplies a lot of the turning force (p.182) and they can usually turn simply by banking to change edges and by counter-rotating. However, steering turns at high speed is more difficult: greater muscle strength is needed to counteract the centrifugal force and hold an accurate line. Over bumps, racers will often "pre-jump" (p.135).

Racing equipment and clothing

The equipment a downhill racer uses, and the clothes he or she wears, must conform to F.I.S. rulings for safety and fairness. All racers use lightweight one-piece suits designed to cut down wind resistance. Skis are long (220-230 cm) and heavy and must be carefully prepared.

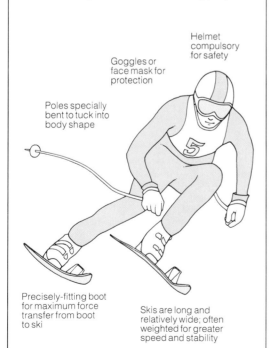

Helmet compulsory for safety

Goggles or face mask for protection

Poles specially bent to tuck into body shape

Precisely-fitting boot for maximum force transfer from boot to ski

Skis are long and relatively wide; often weighted for greater speed and stability

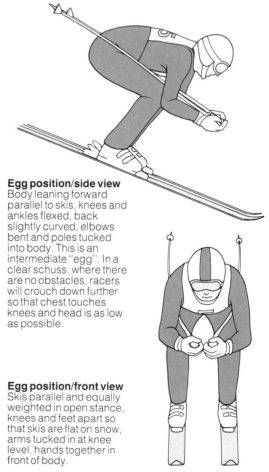

Egg position/side view
Body leaning forward parallel to skis, knees and ankles flexed, back slightly curved, elbows bent and poles tucked into body. This is an intermediate "egg". In a clear schuss, where there are no obstacles, racers will crouch down further so that chest touches knees and head is as low as possible.

Egg position/front view
Skis parallel and equally weighted in open stance, knees and feet apart so that skis are flat on snow, arms tucked in at knee level, hands together in front of body.

F.I.S. downhill racing regulations

- Different courses must be set for men and women

- Vertical drop: men 800-1,000 m; women 500-700 m

- One run per competitor (but a re-run is allowed if a racer is obstructed)

- Minimum best descent time: men 2 mins; women 1 min 40 secs

- "Direction flags" denote course boundary: red flags on left side, green flags on right side

- "Control gates" to limit average speed; minimum width 8 m; red or orange flags mark men's gates, alternating red and blue flags mark ladies'; all competitors must pass with both feet through each gate

- Course must be lined with crash areas of soft snow, straw bales or nets; woodland sections must be minimum 30 m wide

- Wearing of crash helmets is compulsory

The "Lauberhorn" downhill course Wengen, in the Jungfrau region of the Swiss Alps, is the site of the longest and one of the best-known downhill courses in the world. It is known as the "Lauberhorn". It is 4,620m (15,158ft) long and has a vertical drop of 1,028m (3,373ft); its average gradient is about 27 per cent (15°), but there are sections as steep as 90 per cent (42°). In 1980, Peter Müller (Switzerland) skied it in a time of 2 mins 31 secs. The drawing here shows how the course was laid out for the men's World Cup downhill race in January 1981

Key

Helicopter landing pad

Ski patrol

Radio

First aid post

SOS telephone

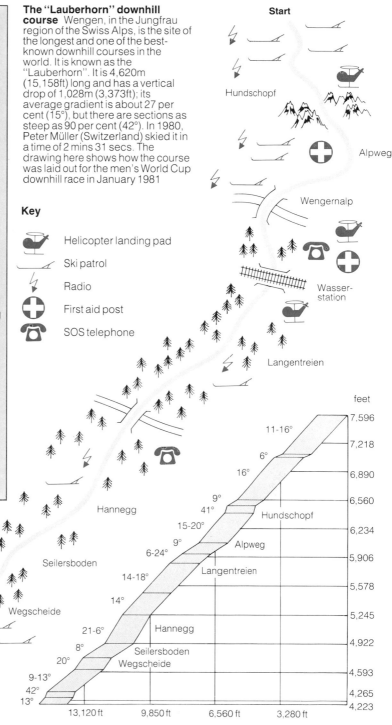

Start

Hundschopf

Alpweg

Wengernalp

Wasser-station

Langentreien

feet	
11-16°	7,596
6°	7,218
16°	6,890
9°	6,560
41°	Hundschopf
15-20°	6,234
9°	Alpweg
6-24°	5,906
14-18°	Langentreien 5,578
14°	5,245
21-6°	Hannegg 4,922
8°	Seilersboden
20°	Wegscheide 4,593
9-13°	4,265
42°	
13°	4,223

Hannegg

Seilersboden

Wegscheide

13,120 ft 9,850 ft 6,560 ft 3,280 ft

Finish

Homologation

Every downhill course must have an official F.I.S. "homologation", a graph indicating the gradient of each section (see p.222 for how this is calculated). It is used as a means of classifying and grading the run. The one shown here is of the Lauberhorn downhill course.

COMPETITION SKIING/Downhill racing

◀ Being airborne
Franz Klammer (Austria),
one of the greatest
downhill champions, flies
into the air as he skis over
a bump. Seconds can be
lost while airborne
because the line of travel
is longer, so the racer
must "pre-jump" to try to
keep his skis in contact
with the snow.

The fastest man on ▶
skis In 1978 an
American, Steve
McKinney, became the
first man to ski at over 200
kph (124 mph). He holds the
world speed record for
the "flying kilometer".
Inset Pietro Albertelli in the
egg position, skiing the
flying kilometer course on
the Plateau Rosa, Zermatt,
Switzerland.

Steering out of a turn ▼
Evi Mittermaier (West
Germany) has risen up
slightly from the low,
crouched egg position to
set her skis on edge and
to steer her turn with her
outside leg.

The flying kilometer

On the Plateau Rosa glacier, which stretches between Cervinia in Italy and Zermatt in Switzerland, a special speed trial takes place. It is called the "flying kilometer" or "K.L." *(Kilometro Lanciato)*. The course on which it is held is 2 km (1.2 miles) long and 8 m (26 ft) wide. It begins as a gentle slope, then accelerates to a 45° gradient where the competitors' speeds are recorded over a 100 m (328 ft) "time-trap". At the end of the course, the slope flattens to form a run-out. This is known as the "compression stage" and is perhaps the most dangerous: the change of gradient and direction contracts the skier's muscles and drives his body forwards and downwards. Bad falls here are common, and the skier must maintain his crouched egg position. Equipment is highly specialized – long skis, tight-fitting boots, figure-hugging suits and aerodynamically designed crash helmets – and has to conform to F.I.S. requirements. On the Plateau Rosa, it is easy to reach 160 kph (100 mph), but every kph after that is harder. The record now stands at 200.22 kph (124.4 mph).

Ski jumping

Competitive ski jumping is very highly specialized, and for most skiers it is solely a spectator sport – and undoubtedly one of the most dramatic. It originated in Norway about a hundred years ago and is a Nordic discipline. Ski jumping competitions are held not only as events in their own right but also as part of the "Nordic Combined" (p.206), where entrants must compete in cross-country racing as well. The jumps are made from specially constructed jumping hills which vary in height according to the length of the jumps: 70m ("normal"), 85 to 90m ("large"), and over 90m (a separate discipline known as "ski flying"). This means that a jump from a normal hill, for example, will be expected to measure about 70m (230ft). Jumps from ski flying towers, however, can exceed 120m (394ft): the official world record stands at 180m (591ft), although in 1977 Bogdan Norcic (Yugoslavia) made an unofficial jump of 181m (594ft).

Ski jumping requires great skill as well as courage. Every effort is made by F.I.S., the governing body, to make it as safe as possible, and all competitors must undergo intensive, lengthy and specialized training. In competition, each jump is marked by five qualified judges. and scores are given for a combination of two things: the length of the jump and the competitor's style.

The in-run
Relaxed "egg" position, skis parallel in hip-width track, upper body rests on thighs, hands back touching sides of body. Ski poles may not be used to increase speed.

The take-off
Jump is made by quick stretching of legs and push-off with feet to propel body upwards and forwards over ski tips.

The "ideal" jump

When it comes to scoring, style is as important as the length of the jump. The F.I.S. has laid down guidelines for its judges: "the ideal jump shall be executed with power, boldness and precision. It shall at the same time give an impression of calmness, steadiness and control." Each jump is divided into five phases: the *in-run*, where the skier gathers speed and adopts a crouched, aero-dynamic position; the *take-off*, which largely determines the length of the jump; the *flight*, during which the skier tries to "ride the air" with his body well forward over his skis (the Nordic cable bindings allow this); the *landing*, which must be soft and steady in the "telemark" position; and the *out-run*, where the skier must straighten up and come to a stop safely and without losing balance.

Ski jump construction

All ski jumping towers are specially built and must be approved by the F.I.S. to make jumping as safe as possible. The landing slope must be clearly marked with a blue line for the "norm point" (70m/230ft from the take-off on a normal hill, 85 to 90m/280 to 295ft on a large hill, and over 90m/280ft on a ski flying tower) and a red line for the "critical point" which marks the beginning of the transition curve or out-run. Midway between these is the "table point" (green line). The length of the in-run is varied according to the snow conditions and wind speed so that the jumpers land on or around the table point.

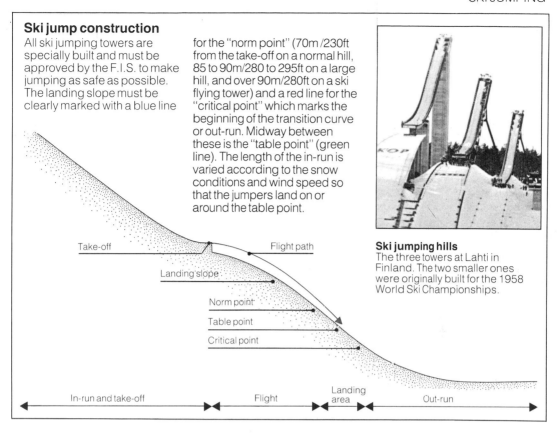

Ski jumping hills
The three towers at Lahti in Finland. The two smaller ones were originally built for the 1958 World Ski Championships.

Take-off

Flight path

Landing slope

Norm point

Table point

Critical point

In-run and take-off   Flight   Landing area   Out-run

The flight
Skier should be calm, steady and in complete control. Skis parallel and fairly close together, body leant forward over skis. Arms by sides, ski tips up slightly in first phase of jump for aerodynamic "lift".

The landing and out-run
Shock of landing must be absorbed softly and steadily, with skis together. To prepare for landing, legs are extended and arms outstretched. On landing, one ski is brought in front of the other ("telemark" position) and knees flexed to absorb impact. Hands are not allowed to touch snow. After landing, the skier should finish straight and come to a stop in a safe, steady position, skis together, without losing balance or falling.

◀ The in-run
The ski jumper emerges from a starting hatch at the top of the hill and crouches down into the "egg" position on the steep in-run, reaching speeds of up to 65 mph (105 kph) at the take-off. In this shot, he is seen from the top of the jumping tower as he skis away from the camera and down towards the lip of the jump.

The take-off ▶
The skier should aim to push off with a powerful extension of his legs and body just as he hits the lip of the jump. He must spring straight out over his skis and at the same time lift his ski tips slightly so that he can "ride" the air currents to get maximum height and distance. Here, the jumper has been photographed from the top of the tower a split-second after his take-off. In front of him can be seen the landing slope and the out-run.

The flight ▼
This lean-forward stance is not only necessary to score well on style points. It also enables the jumper to ride the air aerodynamically rather like an "airfoil". The position should be held until just before landing and the angle of the skis should be matched as closely as possible to the angle of the landing slope.

Freestyle skiing

The branch of skiing known as "freestyle" started in America in the late sixties and early seventies. It was largely an attempt to get away from such strictly stylized forms of skiing as "perfect" closed parallel turning or short swinging and to introduce more freedom, more fun and more of a challenge into skiing. Freestyle skiing is free-form, and offers a means of unrestricted self-expression. It has borrowed many of its movements from figure-skating, ballet and gymnastics, but, technically, almost anything is allowed, and new techniques are being invented by skiers all the time.

In its early days, freestyle was known as "Hot Dog Skiing". There are two explanations of this. One says that it came from surfing, where the term is used to describe surfers who pick the biggest waves and take the most chances when riding them. The other says it was coined by a skier who, eating a hot dog at the top of a mogul slope, dropped the "Dog" out of his bun and watched it hurtle downhill, picking a perfect line through the bumps and dips.

There is some controversy over who can really be said to have invented freestyle skiing. Its growth and popularity owe much to the two Americans, Doug Pfeiffer and Tom Corcoran, who organized the first freestyle competition at Waterville Valley, Vermont, in 1971, but the history of "trick" or "stunt" skiing goes a lot further back. It can be traced back to 1929, when Dr Fritz Reuel wrote a book called *New Possibilities in Skiing*. This book applied the principles of figure-skating to skiing and contained photographs of its author performing some of his new techniques – including the Reuel turn which later came to be called the "Royal christie". He was followed by other key figures: Stein Erikson, who regularly demonstrated front and back somersaults during the 1950s; Hermann Goeliner, with his "moebius flip" (a somersault with full twist) in the 1960s; Art Furrer, inventor of many of the basic ballet movements; Wayne Wong, perpetrator of the "Wongbanger"; and Heinz "Fuzzy" Garhammer. In 1973, after two very bad accidents, I.F.S.A. (International Freestyle Skiers Association) was formed in order to establish competition rules and more effective safety controls.

Today, freestyle skiing is divided into three disciplines: *ballet, mogul skiing* (or "bump" skiing) and *aerials*. All three are illustrated here and they are covered individually on the following pages.

Freestyle mogul skiing
Also called "bump skiing", this event takes place on a steep, heavily mogulled slope. Competitors aim to ski down at the fastest speed while displaying the greatest amount of skill – jumping and turning as quickly and as often as possible (p. 170-3).

◀ Aerials

Mid-air acrobatics, performed from specially constructed jumps, are the most spectacular and most daring aspect of freestyle (p. 174-7). This skier is in the middle of a "front tuck somersault".

Ballet ▼

This freestyle discipline is basically figure-skating on skis (p. 166-9). It is performed on a smooth, gentle slope and, like mogul skiing, is usually done to music. The skier here is pirouetting on one ski tip.

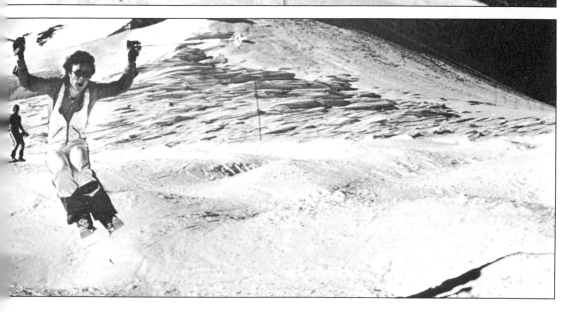

Ballet

Freestyle ballet skiing falls midway between figure-skating on ice and gymnastics; its movements owe a great deal to both. Its aim is to develop a series of skiing tricks and stunts into a graceful, choreographed routine which is then performed to music from a loudspeaker system set up on the snow. Freestyle ballet events are held on smooth, gentle slopes where the snow is fairly dry, well packed and easy to ski. Speed is not high, but the level of technical versatility is. Competitors are awarded marks by the judges on the basis of skill, originality and a flawless, perfectly controlled routine.

It is the freedom of ballet which appeals to most skiers. It offers the chance of trying something new, it is fun, and anyone can attempt it – although being a competent skier with a good sense of balance will certainly help. there are no limits – beyond those of your own imagination and physical fitness – to what can be done; and new tricks are being invented all the time.

The origin of ballet skiing can be traced back to Dr Fritz Reuel's book *New Possibilities in Skiing* (1929). He was probably the first man to see the possibilities of figure-skating and gymnastics on skis, and his influence survives today in the corruption of his name from "Reuel" to "Royal christie". But it was not until the 1960s, when Doug Pfeiffer set up his "School of Exotic Skiing" in America that ballet

techniques really became popular. As we have explained, most ballet is a question of individual ingenuity, and there are no strict technical guide-lines, but most of the movements can be classified into the following basic types: crossovers and kick turns; spins and waltzes; pirouettes and jump turns; turns made on one ski; and rolls and somersaults. All of these have an infinite number of variations, and their names are as flamboyant as the movements themselves. The most common are illustrated on p. 168-9.

If you want to try ballet skiing, begin with the simpler techniques – such as crossovers or snow-plowing backwards or kick turning while on the move. Practice these thoroughly before attempting the complex maneuvers, and bear in mind that ballet skill relies a great deal on balance, on being able to ski on one leg, and on being in good physical shape.

Ballet skiing is usually done on short, light skis – about chin-high is a good guide – which will turn easily and will spin while flat on the snow. Some ski manufacturers make special ballet skis which are shorter and stronger than normal, with only a slight "camber", which turn up slightly at the tails and which do not have a running groove on the base. Bindings are best mounted in the middle of the skis. Boots must be both light and flexible.

A ballet sequence
This freestyle skier illustrates a sequence made up of a "reverse 360° crossover", with a "tip drag" at the beginning and an "inside ski turn" at the end. He comes out of his previous stunt on his right ski with his left ski tip dragging in the snow (1). He then spins round on his right ski and brings his left ski down behind him so that he is skiing backwards with his legs crossed (2 and 3). He transfers his weight to his left ski and continues to spin around while uncrossing his right ski (4). He jumps onto his right (inside) ski (5) and then steers round on it while bringing his other ski parallel (6, 7 and 8). The photograph on the opposite page shows the final phase – turning out of the reverse crossover on the inside ski.

Kick turns, crossovers and waltzing

In ballet, "kick turns" are often made while moving – rather than while standing on the spot (the technique described on p. 58). They are used for changing direction around 180° and for linking other turning and stepping maneuvers. The illustration below shows a reverse kick turn, initiated while skiing backwards. "Crossovers" or "stepovers" have many variations:

they can be done forwards or backwards or while spinning around 360°. The drawing shows a simple forward crossover. The skier lifts his left ski, crosses it over in front of his right ski and sets it down. Transferring his weight to it and planting his poles for balance, he then uncrosses his right ski behind him ready to bring it around and parallel again. "Waltz" movements

are used for spinning around on the snow in a full circle. The first half of the spin is made by rotating around the ski tips, and the second half of the spin by leaning back slightly and rotating around the tails. Waltzing is easiest while skiing on both legs, but it can be performed while on one leg and also while dragging one ski tip in the snow (a "tip drag") to form a natural pivot-point.

Reverse kick turn

1 2 3 4 5 6 7

Forward crossover

1 2 3 4 5 6

Waltzing

1 2 3 4 5 6 7 8

Tip roll

1 2 3

Pirouettes

Although ballet skiing is not always done with ski poles, they are necessary for "pirouettes". A pirouette is performed by planting both poles, jumping up in the air and pivoting through 180° or 360° around either the ski tips or ski tails. The "tip roll", which is probably the simplest pirouette and which is shown here, is made around the ski

tips with both skis parallel. There are numerous variations: pirouettes with skis crossed, 540° tip rolls, and tip rolls that lead into crossovers, waltzes, spins and jumps. In all pirouettes, the standard pole grip is modified so that the palm is over the top of the handle and the fingers and thumb point down the shaft.

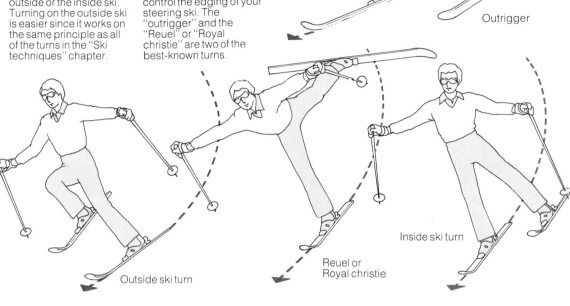

Turning on one ski
This is one of the basic freestyle maneuvers. It requires a high level of turning skill, a great deal of strength and a good sense of balance. One-ski turns can be made either on the outside or the inside ski. Turning on the outside ski is easier since it works on the same principle as all of the turns in the "Ski techniques" chapter.

Turning on the inside ski is more difficult: it relies heavily on exactly the right amount of banking into the turn, on the rotary motion exerted by your inside leg, and on the knee pressure which will control the edging of your steering ski. The "outrigger" and the "Reuel" or "Royal christie" are two of the best-known turns.

Outrigger

Inside ski turn

Reuel or Royal christie

Outside ski turn

Rolls and somersaults
These are the stunts which owe most to gymnastics. Often called "snow contact" stunts, most of them are performed by rolling over in the snow and by doing headstands, handstands or forward and backward somersaults. They should all be practiced first on grass or on a soft tumbling mat before being attempted on the snow with skis and ski poles. Our drawing shows one of the most difficult freestyle ballet tricks: a front pole-flip, sometimes called the "Wongbanger" after its inventor, Wayne Wong. The photograph illustrates a handstand on the snow with the skis in the "daffy" position.

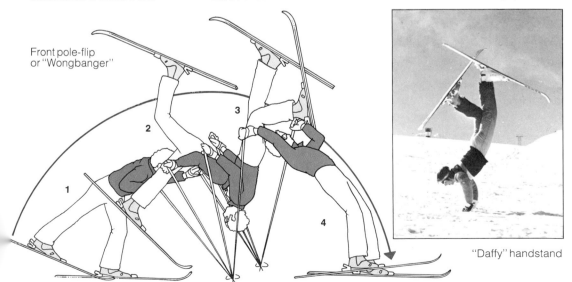

Front pole-flip or "Wongbanger"

"Daffy" handstand

Freestyle mogul skiing

In freestyle, mogul skiing is known as "skiing the bumps". As we show on p. 230, mogul slopes are steep slopes covered with bumps, dips, ridges and ruts. They are formed by the continual turning of skiers "carving" out the snow on slopes too steep to be beaten down by the trail machines. Bump skiing – fast, skillful mogul skiing where the aim is to turn and jump as often as possible while still maintaining control at high speed – tests a skier's technique to the limit. It demands great technical skill, physical strength and fitness, and lightning-fast reactions. But in mogul skiing there has always been a strong element of showmanship as well. Mogul skiers encourage each other to "go for it", to develop their own personal style and to attempt the most spectacular acrobatics.

In the early days, bump skiing had no set rules, and the competitors would be cheered not only for successful stunts but also for spectacular falls and recoveries. Now the sport is more organized and the emphasis has changed. Events are held on a specially selected course. It is about 1,000 ft long and between 100 and 150 ft wide, with a smooth, clear finishing area at the bottom where competitors must make a controlled stop. The course is fenced off to keep the spectators at a safe distance, and the judges stand at the bottom where they have a clear view of the whole slope. Scores are awarded on the following criteria: speed, the number and type of turns, jumps (two of which are compulsory), overall control, and the "continuity" of the whole run. Competitors are penalized for falls or for loss of control, and they are disqualified if they lose a ski or fail to get to the bottom of the course. All this is done to fast, loud music – usually chosen by the freestyle mogul skier himself.

The technical basis of all mogul skiing, whether freestyle or not, is "absorption-extension" (p. 120). It is the most efficient way of turning quickly and smoothly through a mogul field – although, as we show on p. 172-3, the basic technique has been transformed into the exaggerated "jet" and "shield wiper" turns and has been adapted to include spectacular jumps and ballet stunts.

No special equipment is needed for mogul skiing. The best guideline is simply to use the skis and boots that you feel you ski best with. Some freestylers advocate short skis (about 170 cm) because they are easier to turn quickly, but others seem quite happy with longer (210 cm) skis. Probably, the average is somewhere around 190 cm. A few ski manufacturers make special bump skis which are softer and more flexible than normal and which have a deeper side-cut in the middle. Whatever skis you choose, keeping them in good condition is probably the most important factor.

A mogul course ▲
Spectators line the special course
for this bump skiing contest in the
French Alps. Competitors, who ski
down one at a time, are
electronically timed and are judged
according to both speed and
technical ability.

◀ **Turning off the top of a mogul**
Most bump skiers aim to ski against
the moguls and turn on top of them.
The extreme form of "jet" turning
shown here, in which the ski tips
come right up in the air, is a special
mogul technique and has many
variations.

"Going for it" ▶
At the original bump skiing contests
in the late sixties and early
seventies, falls and recoveries were
part of almost every freestyler's run:
the more spectacular, the better.
Nowadays, falls and any loss of
control count against the
competitors.

"Jet" turning

The standard technique for "jet" initiations is shown on p. 124. Here it is adapted to bump skiing and used for turning on large moguls at high speed. The skier plants both poles as he comes up to the top of the bump (4), then bends both knees and jets his feet forwards so that his ski tips rise high up in the air (5). Leaning right back on his poles, he banks into the turn, pivots on his ski tails (6) and swings his skis around as he extends his legs into the dip on the far side of the mogul (7, 8 and 9).

Jumping from mogul to mogul

Most bump skiing involves terrain jumping (see p. 132 for the basic technique) but, as with jet turning, the technique has been developed into an advanced, highly acrobatic form. The skier in this sequence is making a series of fast jumps from the top of one mogul to the top of the next, while turning in mid-air. He skis at high speed up to the top of the first mogul (1), plants his pole and twists his uphill shoulder downhill (2), and then lets the mogul throw him up in the air (3). In mid-flight he stretches his legs, banks his body and turns his skis into the new direction (4 and 5). As he lands on the next mogul (6), he pushes off with his legs and makes another jump over the next dip (7 and 8). The technique requires great strength in the legs to absorb the shock from the repeated landings, as well as a perfect sense of timing.

Aerial acrobatics

Acrobatic jumps score highly in mogul skiing – as long as they do not break the continuity and the rhythm of a competitor's run. But they are very difficult to perform well: although it is easy to take off from the top of a bump (2), it is not easy to maintain control when landing on a steep mogul slope (6 and 7). Split-second timing and faultless judgment of speed are called for The skier is shown here doing a "mule kick" in mid-flight. Other forms are shown on p. 174-7.

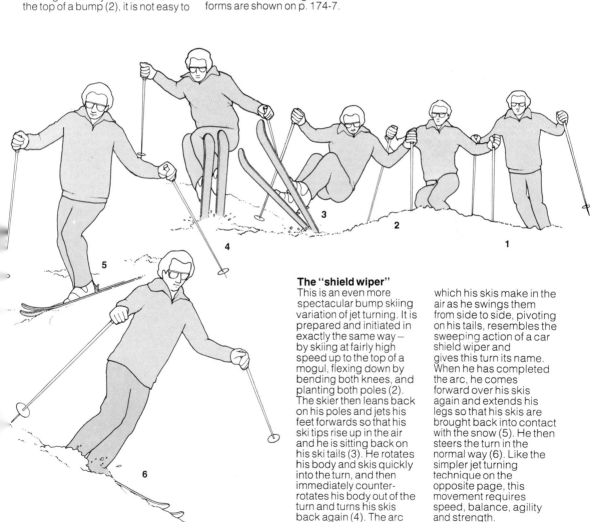

The "shield wiper"

This is an even more spectacular bump skiing variation of jet turning. It is prepared and initiated in exactly the same way – by skiing at fairly high speed up to the top of a mogul, flexing down by bending both knees, and planting both poles (2). The skier then leans back on his poles and jets his feet forwards so that his ski tips rise up in the air and he is sitting back on his ski tails (3). He rotates his body and skis quickly into the turn, and then immediately counter-rotates his body out of the turn and turns his skis back again (4). The arc which his skis make in the air as he swings them from side to side, pivoting on his tails, resembles the sweeping action of a car shield wiper and gives this turn its name. When he has completed the arc, he comes forward over his skis again and extends his legs so that his skis are brought back into contact with the snow (5). He then steers the turn in the normal way (6). Like the simpler jet turning technique on the opposite page, this movement requires speed, balance, agility and strength.

173

Aerials

Freestyle jumping is the most exciting and, potentially, the most dangerous of the three disciplines. In its early days, the crowd's cries of "Go for it!" and "More air!" spurred on the jumpers to an increasingly wilder and more reckless combination of acrobatics, gymnastics and ski jumping. But bad falls were common, and in 1973 two Americans were paralyzed after attempts at double back somersaults. In 1974 strict rules were introduced:

the construction of the special jumps is now rigorously controlled; each jumper who wishes to attempt a somersault in competition has to have a certificate from a qualified judge or an experienced jumper; and the emphasis of the judging has changed from the "daring" of the jumpers to the "perfection" (and, therefore, safety) of the jump. Nowadays, freestyle jumpers train on trampolines and into swimming pools before jumping on snow.

Back layout somersault ▲
Freestyle jumps can be classified into three types: uprights, twists and somersaults or "flips" (p.176-7). Somersaults like this one require a highly developed "air sense".

◄ Pair-jumping
Jumping with a partner demands perfect timing and coordination – as shown by these two skiers performing a joint front layout somersault.

Spread eagle ▶
In competition, freestyle jumpers are judged according to the difficulty of the maneuver and the height and length of the jump. The "spread eagle" (p. 176) is one of the easier upright jumps.

Spread eagle

This is an "upright" jump. It is one of the easiest aerial maneuvers and probably the one to learn first. As soon as the skier takes off, he spreads his arms out wide above his head and stretches his legs out to either side as far as possible. He brings his legs back together just before landing.

Daffy

Another popular but slightly more difficult upright jump is the "daffy". It is made by taking a "walking step" in mid-air. Right after take-off, the skier stretches his left leg forwards and his right leg backwards so that one ski tip points up and the other points down. To maintain balance, he stretches his right arm forwards and his left arm backwards. This is the classic "daffy" position; when several daffys or steps are done in a row, the stunt is most often called a "space walk".

Backscratcher

Because of the more extreme body position, this is one of the more difficult upright jumps. The skier begins with a strong push-off (or "pop") from the lip of the jump, then tucks his legs up behind him and throws his arms up and backwards. This leaves his ski tips pointing vertically down and his ski tails up behind his shoulders. Stretching his arms and shoulders back stops him from falling forwards and helps him maintain balance in mid-air. The landing is made in the normal way, with the skis flat on the snow and the legs absorbing the shock. This jump should be practiced first on a trampoline or into water until you are sure you can bring your tips up before landing every time.

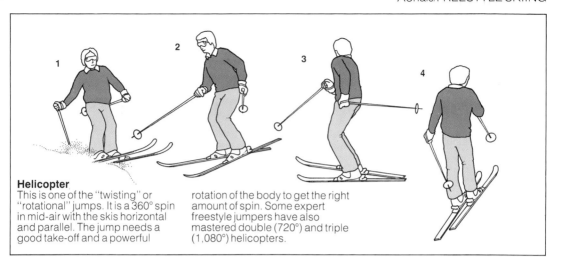

Helicopter
This is one of the "twisting" or "rotational" jumps. It is a 360° spin in mid-air with the skis horizontal and parallel. The jump needs a good take-off and a powerful rotation of the body to get the right amount of spin. Some expert freestyle jumpers have also mastered double (720°) and triple (1,080°) helicopters.

Back somersault
Somersaults, or "inverted" aerials, are the most difficult stunts. They *must* be practiced on a trampoline or into water before being attempted on a ski jump, and they *must* be learnt from a professional, qualified instructor. Somersaults can be done forwards or backwards, and with or without a twist. They can also be done in the crouched "tuck" position or in the slower, outstretched "layout" position. A back tuck somersault is shown here; layout somersaults are pictured on p. 174. Both types are difficult and not for the inexperienced.

How freestyle jumps are constructed

All jumps for aerial freestyle must be specially built to conform to safety regulations. They vary slightly according to the skill of the jumpers who will use them and the type of jumps being attempted. The differences lie in the design of the ramp or "kicker" and in the gradient of the landing slope. A kicker for "upright" jumps will be fairly straight and almost horizontal; a "somersault" kicker will be curved and somewhat steeper in order to throw the skier higher into the air. The gradient of the landing slope should correspond closely to the flight path of the jumper to reduce the shock of landing: too steep and the skier will fall from too high; too flat and he will land with a sharp, dangerous jolt.

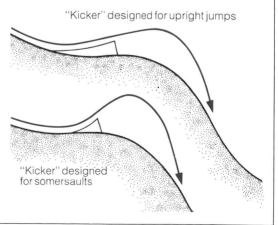

"Kicker" designed for upright jumps

"Kicker" designed for somersaults

Ski mechanics

The mechanics of skiing is all about "forces" - how they operate, how they are applied and what their effects are. Knowing something about mechanics will help you to ski better: you will understand how your skis accelerate, brake and turn, what you must do to make them grip or skid, why unweighting will help you to initiate turns and why banking and angulation will help you to steer them. All in all, an understanding of ski mechanics will enable you to make your movements precise and effective.

Forces

The study of mechanical forces is highly complex, but for the purposes of this chapter it can be greatly simplified. Forces are "pushes" or "pulls", and they alter the state of any body to which they are applied. For example, they can change its shape, they can affect its speed, they can start it moving if it is stationary or they can bring it to a stop if it is in motion, they can change its direction of travel, and they can make it turn or rotate.

A force is conventionally shown by a "force arrow". This indicates at what point it is being applied and in which direction. The length of the arrow also represents the strength of the force.

Gravity

The mechanical force on which all Alpine or down-hill skiing relies is *gravity*. It is the force of gravity which pulls you down the slope. Gravity is based on the attraction of masses – which, in practice, means that everything is attracted towards the center of the earth. The earth's pull acts on every particle of a body, but, in fact, all these separate, parallel forces can be represented by a single, net force formed by the combination of all the smaller ones. This net force is said to operate from the "center of gravity" of the body.

Gravity is related to the *mass* of a body; it is also the force by which we determine its weight. A stronger force of gravity is exerted on a dense object, such as a piece of lead, than on one that is not so dense, such as a bag of feathers. This is why a piece of lead feels heavier than a bag of feathers.

Gravity also depends on the distance to the center of the earth. This is because the attraction or pull of gravity which the earth exerts decreases as you move further away from it. All things being equal, gravity would pull you down vertically towards the center of the earth – and. if you were free-falling, you would accelerate as you went. Of course, in practice, when you ski down a mountain, gravity is modified or controlled by the gradient of the slope, by the friction between your skis and the snow, by air resistance, and by the forces you, yourself, exert to turn or to brake.

The laws governing forces

Newton's third law of motion states that for every force there is an equal force in the opposite direction. This principle is known as *force and opposing force* or *action and reaction*; if you exert a force against something, it will exert an opposing force back.

Two parallel forces acting on different parts of the same body and in opposite directions will produce a rotary motion, as shown below. Known as a "couple", this principle is very important in the turning of skis.

Parallel turning forces
Force a operates on front of ski and force b operates in opposite direction on back of ski. The result is that ski pivots or turns.

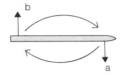

Two forces acting on a body at the same point but in different directions will combine to produce a single, resultant force. This principle is known as the *resolution of forces*, and the strength and direction of the resultant force can be found with a "forces parallelogram".

Forces parallelogram
The resultant force r from two forces a and b is the diagonal of the parallelogram formed by force arrows (a + b = r). Conversely, an individual force may be broken down in two component forces (r = a + b or a = r − b).

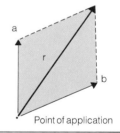

Point of application

Inertia

Newton's first law of motion defines *inertia*: "if a body is at rest it will remain at rest, or if it is moving in a straight line at constant speed it will continue to do so, unless a force acts on it." So, inertia is a force which tends to keep an object doing whatever it is already doing: it will stay stationary until something sets it moving; and, if it is in motion, inertia will tend to keep it going.

When you are skiing, you will feel inertia most often as a force of *resistance* to the change that you are trying to make - in either your speed or your direction of travel. For this reason, inertia is described as a *force*. When you want to slow down or stop, you will feel it trying to keep you travelling, and, when you want to turn, you will feel it trying to keep you moving in a straight line.

Ski position and edging

Every movement you make when skiing is transmitted to the snow through your skis. The way in which it is transmitted, the effect it has, and the amount of friction it creates between your skis and the snow depend on two things: your skis' *position* in relation to one another, and whether they are flat on the snow or *edged*. Edged skis create more snow resistance and, therefore, more braking or turning force than skis which are flat on the snow. Various ski positions, together with their names, are shown below. The snowplow and stem are also known as "converging" ski positions, and the scissor or herringbone as a "diverging" ski position.

Open parallel stance

Closed parallel stance

Snowplow or angled position

Stem or half-plow position

Herringbone or scissor position

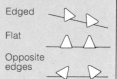
Edged

Flat

Opposite edges

The mechanics of skiing in the fall line

If you stand on a slope, facing down the fall line with your skis parallel, you will slide downhill. This much is obvious. But we can understand more about how it happens if we look at the mechanical forces involved. The force which produces the movement is gravity. It acts from the skier's center of gravity, vertically downwards towards the center of the earth. However, in reality, it resolves into two component forces (according to the principle of the forces parallelogram, opposite). One force operates through the skier's feet onto the snow at right angles to the slope, whatever the gradient. It is the result of *pressure* from the skier's body weight and it is called the "normal force". The second force operates downhill and acts parallel to the slope. It can be called "forward momentum". Working against these are two forces of resistance – from the air and from the snow. Provided that the force of forward momentum is greater than the combined forces of resistance from the snow and the air, the skier will slide downhill.

It follows that, if the skier wants to slow down or stop, he must act against his own inertia by increasing the resistance to his travel. Snowplowing achieves this. By opening the skis into a snowplow position and by tilting them onto their inside edges, more friction is created between the skis and the snow. In soft snow on a gentle slope, with the skis in a narrow angle, the skier's own weight or "normal force" may create sufficient resistance to slow him down; on hard snow on a steeper slope, he may have to push his skis out into a wider angle.

Schussing
Gravity, the combined weight of skier plus equipment, operates vertically downwards. It resolves into two component forces, normal force and forward momentum, which, when schussing, are greater than the forces of snow and air resistance.

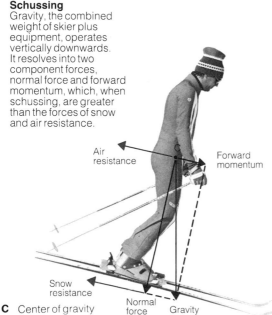

Air resistance

Forward momentum

Snow resistance

Normal force

Gravity

C Center of gravity

Snowplowing
Normal force (pressure of skier's weight) and forward momentum created by gravity still apply, but snow resistance is increased by opening skis into snowplow and edging them to generate stronger opposing force.

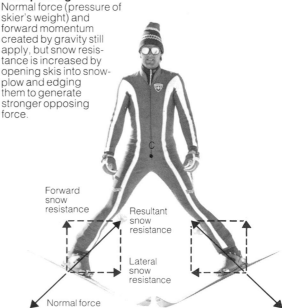

Forward snow resistance

Resultant snow resistance

Lateral snow resistance

Normal force

The mechanics of traversing and side-slipping

When seen from the side, the mechanics of traversing are similar to the mechanics of schussing (p.179). Gravity resolves into "normal force" (acting through the skier's feet as pressure on the snow) and "forward momentum". If the angle of the traverse is steep enough for the skier's forward momentum to overcome snow (and air) resistance, he will ski downhill, across the slope. However, because the body must be angulated to maintain balance while edging the skis, "normal force" resolves into two sub-component forces: a pressure force acting *into* the slope, and a force of momentum acting *down* the fall line. The second force is cancelled out by snow resistance as long as the skis are firmly edged. As soon as the edge-grip is released, the skier begins to side-slip.

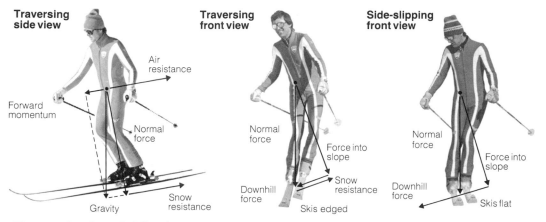

Traversing side view

Air resistance

Forward momentum

Normal force

Gravity

Snow resistance

Traversing front view

Normal force

Force into slope

Downhill force

Snow resistance

Skis edged

Side-slipping front view

Normal force

Force into slope

Downhill force

Skis flat

The mechanics of skiing bumps and dips

Skiing down the fall line over bumps and dips involves the same basic mechanical forces as schussing – but with the difference that "inertia" comes into play. Whenever a skier goes over a bump or down into a dip, he is forced to make a vertical change of direction. However, as we have seen on p.178, inertia is a force which tries to keep him going in the same direction – that is, in a straight line. Therefore, in the dip, he will feel inertia as a downward push which he must counteract by extending his legs and exerting a muscular force against the "centripetal force" acting up towards him from the slope. On the bump, he will feel inertia as the upward lift of "centrifugal force". This time he must counteract it by flexing his legs and letting his body fall to avoid being thrown into the air.

How to ski bumps and dips with minimum effort In the first drawing, skier maintains same stance throughout. The curve through which his center of gravity travels has a short radius: inertia is felt as strong force and skier must exert correspondingly powerful force to counteract it. In the second drawing, he extends legs in dip and flexes them on bump. The curve therefore has longer radius (i.e., more like a straight line): inertia is not as strong and skier has to use less muscular force.

G Gravity
N Normal force
F Forward momentum
T Track followed by center of gravity

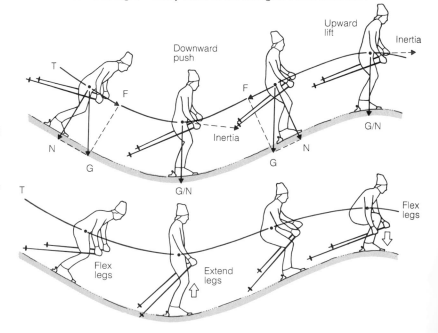

Upward lift

Inertia

Downward push

F

F

Inertia

T

N

G

G/N

G/N

T

Flex legs

Extend legs

Flex legs

The mechanics of turning

This is a highly complex subject. Although the basic principle, which we explain below, is fairly simple, the mechanics of how turns are initiated and steered, how unweighting works, and why the shape of the ski is important, are very technical. These topics are covered on the following pages.

To understand the forces involved in turning, we must look again at Newton's definition of inertia: "... if a body is moving in a straight line at a constant speed it will continue to do so, unless a force acts on it." Therefore, to make any change of direction, a skier must exert a *turning force* – one which counteracts his own inertia – or he will continue to travel in a straight line. In turning, the force which he exerts is called *centripetal force*. He must exert it sideways, into the center of the turn, and he must continue to exert it, in the right amount, throughout the turn. As soon as centripetal force is removed, inertia takes over again and the skier will ski straight, off at a tangent to the turning arc. In the mechanics of turning, inertia is usually described as *centrifugal force*. Centripetal force is the turning force applied *towards* the center of the turn; centrifugal force is the force of inertia action *away from* the center of the turn.

How does the skier create a centripetal turning force? In fact, he does it by pressing against his edged skis in order to exert a force against the snow. The snow resists and generates an equal "opposing" force which acts sideways, at right angles to the direction of travel. This is centripetal force and it is what keeps the skis turning in an arc.

The forces involved in turning

The turning force which counteracts the skier's inertia is centripetal force. It is produced by pressure chiefly against the edged outside ski. The resulting increased snow resistance which this causes creates an opposing force directed sideways into the center of the turn.

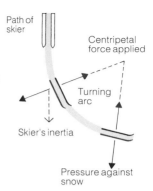

Path of skier

Centripetal force applied

Turning arc

Skier's inertia

Pressure against snow

The phases of a turn

A turn is made up of four phases: preparation (a), initiation (b), steering phase (c) and end phase (d). Centripetal force operates as soon as the turn has been initiated and continues acting throughout the steering phase. It is removed in the end phase where the skis resume a straight line once more.

Traverse

Centripetal force from snow resistance

Skier's inertia

a

b

c

d

Centripetal force removed

Traverse

Fall line

A demonstration of "parallel turning forces"

These photographs illustrate two turns based on the principle of "parallel turning forces" or "couples" (p.178), whereby two parallel forces operating in opposite directions on different parts of a body will make it rotate. In the first example, the skier lifts the tail of his right ski and lets the tip drag in the snow. This creates a force of resistance from the snow acting in the opposite direction to his forward momentum. As a result, his left ski pivots beneath his left foot, and he turns to his right. The second example, called "scissoring", works in the same way.

1 Lift right ski, press tip into snow to create force of resistance.

2 Forward momentum on left ski plus friction on right initiates turn.

1 Angle out right ski to create friction between tip and snow.

2 Forward momentum on left ski plus friction on right initiates turn.

How turns are initiated

This is one of the most complex and also one of the most controversial areas of ski technique. The study of turn initiations is concerned with the problem of how skis can be turned out of their initial position and into a new direction. The methods by which this can be done vary according to the situation and the snow conditions, the speed at which the skier is travelling, and the type of turn being made. We have made a broad distinction here between six different possibilities.

1 By lifting or "jumping" skis off snow

The simplest way to change direction is to lift your skis off the snow, either one at a time or both together (in a jump), swivel them around and then set them down again in a new direction. You supply the force required simply by employing the muscle strength in your own legs, and the movement can be made either while standing still (as in a star turn, p.46) or when moving (as in step turning, p.94, 203). Parallel turns with "up", as well as jump turning (p. 130) – where the skis are rotated while unweighted or while in mid-air – might also be said to come into this category.

2 By displacing body weight forwards or backwards in a traverse

When you are in a traverse – again, either stationary or moving – you can turn your skis by releasing your edge-grip to flatten them on the snow and then shifting your body weight forwards or backwards. Leaning forwards moves your center of gravity nearer your ski tips, puts more weight on the front of your skis, and turns them into the fall line. Leaning backwards shifts your center of gravity back, your tails slip down, and your skis swing uphill. This form of turn initiation, which works on the principle of "parallel turning forces" (p.178), forms the basis of forward and backward side-slipping (p.80).

3 By displacing one ski

In the early stages of learning to ski, most turns on the move are made by displacing or "pre-turning" one ski and then pressing against it to make it turn. The ski which is displaced into the angled or "converging" position becomes the outside, steering ski. As we show below, the displaced ski is turned by exerting pressure against it to create a centripetal force; and this pressure is produced by a combination of body weight and muscle strength. The amount of pressure can be increased by a push-off from one ski to the other, i.e., from the inside to the outside ski.

In certain situations, however, *kinetic energy* may work together with or replace muscle strength as the turning force exerted against the displaced outside ski. The faster a skier is travelling, the greater his kinetic energy. The formula for kinetic energy is $\frac{1}{2}mv^2$ (where m=mass and v=velocity). Therefore, a skier weighing, say, 175lbs and travelling at a speed of 20mph has a kinetic energy of 4,000 joules; but a racer of the same weight skiing at 60mph has a kinetic energy of over 30,000 joules. By displacing one ski (stepping against the uphill ski, p.139) and banking, this kinetic energy can be exerted against the ski to make it turn. Moreover, at very high speeds, the displacing may not even be necessary; both skis can be banked and turned together while parallel – although, in this case, some leg rotation and body counter-rotation is also required.

The mechanics of the turning snowplow
Both skis are displaced to initiate turn. Centripetal steering force is created by pressing against outside steering ski.

Center of gravity moves over outside ski as skier bends outside knee and leans out

Greater pressure against outside ski creates more snow resistance: this provides centripetal turning force

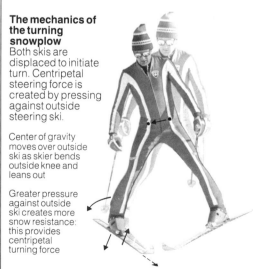

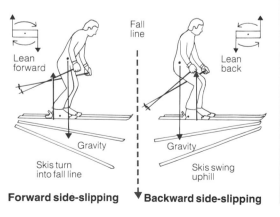

Fall line

Lean forward

Lean back

Gravity

Gravity

Skis turn into fall line

Skis swing uphill

Forward side-slipping   **Backward side-slipping**

4 By rotary motion of body

Parallel turns are made without displacing or pre-turning either ski. In the initiation, two things must therefore happen: the skis must be tilted onto their inside edges, and they must be rotated into the turn. In this category, which includes most forms of parallel turning with "up" (p.105), the edge-change is normally made by banking during an "up-extension unweighting" (p.184), and the skis are turned with a *rotary motion* of the body. As soon as the skis have begun to turn, the body stops rotating and begins to counter-rotate. The term "rotary motion" (which most Americans call "turning motion" and the French call *projection circulaire*) was mis-used in the past and consequently went out of fashion. However, in our Swiss instruction method, we continue to use it, making clear what we mean by it: a rotation of the whole body into the direction of the turn in order to transfer a turning force to the skis.

5 By counter-rotation of body

This category also employs the skier's own muscle strength as the force which initiates the turning of the skis. However, in this case, it is only the legs which rotate in the direction of the turn. The hips and upper body go the opposite way – that is to say, they *counter-rotate*. Parallel turning with "down" (p.108) and stepping onto the uphill ski (p.137) are the significant turns in this category. The edge-change is normally made by banking during a "down-flexion unweighting" (p.185) – although, when speed is high enough, banking alone may suffice. The turning of the skis is then initiated by rotating just the legs *against* the mass of the rest of the body. Counter-rotation is based on the principle of force and opposing force (action and reaction): if the lower body twists in one direction (into the turn), the upper body will remain static or twist the other way (out of the turn).

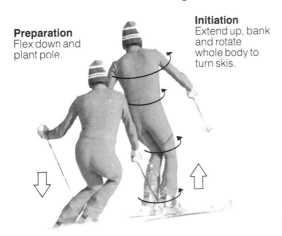

Preparation
Flex down and plant pole.

Initiation
Extend up, bank and rotate whole body to turn skis.

Preparation
Extend up and plant pole; some pre-rotation ("anticipation") may be used.

Initiation
Flex down, bank, rotate legs, counter-rotate hips and upper body.

6 When short swinging

High-frequency short swings, such as *wedeln* (p.117), are a special case. What happens is that the upper body remains more-or-less static, facing downhill all the time. Both un-weighted skis are then turned beneath the body and are dis-placed almost directly from one edge-set into the next. The skis may be unweighted with either an up-extension or a down-flexion, and mixed forms are possible. The legs *rotate* to turn the skis and the upper body does not move – except to make the regular inside pole-plant.

Legs and feet rotate unweighted skis beneath body.

Upper body faces downhill (passive counter-rotation).

Unweighting

All parallel turns rely on "unweighting" as an aid to their initiation. Unweighting works on the principle that skis with your full weight on them are hard to turn, because you are pressing them down onto the snow, whereas skis without your full weight on them are easier to turn.

We can distinguish between two types of ski unweighting: "active" and "passive". In active unweighting, you make a sudden body movement which momentarily takes your weight off your skis, allowing you to turn them. The movement may be either a quick "up-extension" or a "down-flexion" (see below).

In passive unweighting, terrain forms such as bumps or slope edges will unweight your skis, since, when your ski tips and tails are not in contact with the snow, resistance to turning is decreased (p.122-3).

The chart on the right shows how the forms of unweighting vary and how they depend on the way each turn is initiated.

		Preparation	
Snowplow turning		Snowplow ski position	
Stem turning		Stemmed ski position	
Uphill turning		Downhill stem or parallel ski position	
Parallel turning	With "up"	Parallel ski position, legs flexed	
	With "down"	Parallel ski position, high stance	
Short swinging		Parallel ski position, legs flexed	
Absorption-extension turning		Parallel ski position, legs begin to flex	
Jet turning		Parallel ski position, knees and hips pushed forwards	
Kangaroo turning		Parallel ski position, static sit-back stance	
Stepping techniques	"Onto" the uphill ski	Parallel or diverging ski position, transfer of pressure onto uphill ski	
	"Against" the uphill ski	Converging or parallel ski position	

Up-extension unweighting
In this form of unweighting, you spring upwards to momentarily take the pressure off your skis. Unweighting of this kind always has two phases: the preparation and the initiation. In the preparation, you sink down; in the initiation, you quickly extend your legs and body so that for a split-second there is hardly any weight on your skis. At this moment – while you are fully extended and before you flex down again – you change edges and rotate your skis into the turn.

Up-extension unweighting is the form used to initiate parallel turns with "up" (p.105) and short swinging. Refined forms also exist in which the extension is made chiefly with the uphill leg (p.107) and in which it is made sideways as well as upwards, to bank into the turn (p.142).

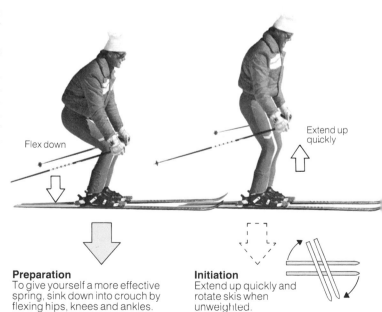

Flex down

Extend up quickly

Preparation
To give yourself a more effective spring, sink down into crouch by flexing hips, knees and ankles.

Initiation
Extend up quickly and rotate skis when unweighted.

Initiation	Unweighting	Pole-plant	Ski pivot
Outside ski pressure	None	Yes (if possible)	At front
Outside ski pressure	None	Yes	At front
Turning pressure or leg rotation	Down-flexion	No (although downhill pole-plant for stop swinging if necessary)	At front
Rotary motion and banking	Up-extension	Yes	At front
Banking and counter-rotation	Down-flexion	If necessary	At front
Rotary motion and banking, or turning push-off with leg rotation	Up-extension	Yes	At front
Pivot on pole, banking of knees and rotation of lower legs	Down-flexion	Yes	Beneath feet
Jet movement, leg rotation and banking	Down unweighting	Yes	At back
Extension up and forwards, leg rotation, banking, jet movement if necessary	Sit-back to unweight ski tips	Yes	At back
Rotary motion and banking	Up-extension	Yes	At front
Banking and counter-rotation	Down-flexion	If necessary	At front
Transfer of pressure against uphill ski, together with counter-rotation	Usually none, but various forms are possible	Yes (usually)	At front

Down-flexion unweighting

Sudden down-flexion creates the same effect as sudden up-extension: it takes the pressure off your skis. This works because, when you rapidly contract or fold up your body, your head and trunk drop but your feet rise up, thereby unweighting your skis. This movement must be made even more quickly than the upward spring of "up-extension" and its unweighting effect lasts for an even shorter time, only while your body is falling. So choosing the moment to rotate your unweighted skis is crucial.

Down-flexion unweighting is the technique for parallel turning with "down" (p.108) and it forms the basis for all the absorption-extension initiations (p.120-27). It is often used together with the "passive" unweighting supplied by bumps and slope edges.

Extend up

Flex down quickly

Preparation
Get ready to flex down forcefully by adopting relaxed, high stance, with legs extended.

Initiation
Bend knees, flex down rapidly, rotate skis when unweighted.

How turns are steered

As we have seen on p.181, *centripetal force* is required to make skis turn. It is generated by exerting pressure against the skis to create a force of resistance from the snow which is directed towards the center of the turning arc. Centripetal force must be maintained throughout the turn. As soon as it ceases to act, the skis stop turning.

The study of how turns are steered concerns the way in which a skier generates and controls centripetal force during the steering phase of a turn.

If we compare a simple, basic turn such as the turning snowplow (p.68) with a more advanced one such as parallel turning (p.104), we can see that there are certain differences. In the turning snowplow, the whole turn is made with the skis in a converging wedge position. The centripetal turn-ing force is produced by pressing *wholly* against the outside ski, and the turn is steered by pushing only *one* knee – the outside knee – forwards and into the turn. In a parallel turn, however, the skis stay parallel all the time: centripetal force is generated this time by pressing *chiefly* against the outside ski (some pressure acts on the inside ski as well), and the turn is steered by pushing *both* knees forwards and into the slope.

Snowplow turning (p.82), stem turning (p.96), and some stepping techniques (p.136) are different again and so fall in between the two categories. They have what might be called two initiations: first, an initiation to make the initial change of direction, and, second, an initiation of the parallel steering phase once the skis are already turning.

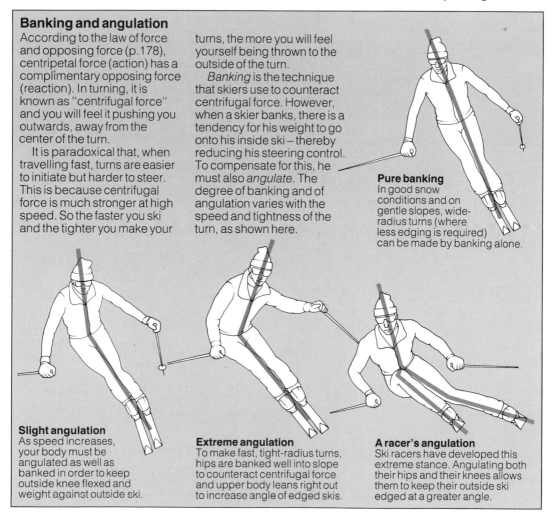

Banking and angulation

According to the law of force and opposing force (p.178), centripetal force (action) has a complimentary opposing force (reaction). In turning, it is known as "centrifugal force" and you will feel it pushing you outwards, away from the center of the turn.

It is paradoxical that, when travelling fast, turns are easier to initiate but harder to steer. This is because centrifugal force is much stronger at high speed. So the faster you ski and the tighter you make your turns, the more you will feel yourself being thrown to the outside of the turn.

Banking is the technique that skiers use to counteract centrifugal force. However, when a skier banks, there is a tendency for his weight to go onto his inside ski – thereby reducing his steering control. To compensate for this, he must also *angulate*. The degree of banking and of angulation varies with the speed and tightness of the turn, as shown here.

Pure banking
In good snow conditions and on gentle slopes, wide-radius turns (where less edging is required) can be made by banking alone.

Slight angulation
As speed increases, your body must be angulated as well as banked in order to keep outside knee flexed and weight against outside ski.

Extreme angulation
To make fast, tight-radius turns, hips are banked well into slope to counteract centrifugal force and upper body leans right out to increase angle of edged skis.

A racer's angulation
Ski racers have developed this extreme stance. Angulating both their hips and their knees allows them to keep their outside ski edged at a greater angle.

How the shape of the ski helps you turn

Skis are designed to make the initiating and steering of turns easier. They are not simply flat, narrow boards. As we show below, they have a "side-cut" which means that they are narrower in the middle than they are at the front or back, and a "camber" which means that, when there is no weight on them, they bow up in the middle. Both these properties help to control the way a ski makes skidded turns at low speed and the way it tends to make carved turns at high speed. But other factors are important too: its length, weight and thickness, its degree and distribution of flexibility, and its torsional stiffness (resistance to twisting). All these things vary from one ski to another, and they all affect the way it behaves – that is, how fast it is, how easy or difficult it is to turn, how well it steers when edged, and how forgiving or demanding it is on the skier.

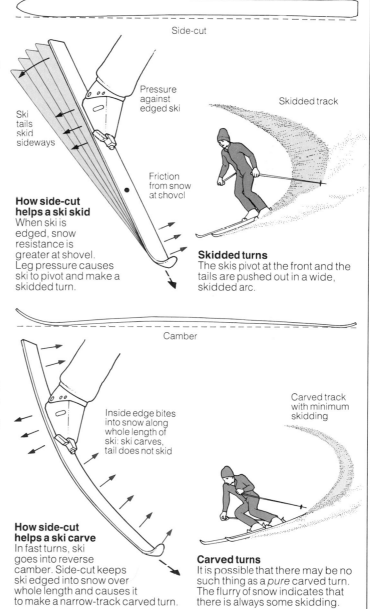

Side-cut

All skis are widest at the front (or "shovel") and tapered (or "waisted") in the middle. This feature is called the *side-cut* of the ski. It means that, when you set a ski on edge in order to turn, the shovel digs deeper into the snow than any other part of the ski. This in turn means that, when you press against the edged ski, more snow resistance is generated at the shovel. Your leg pressure acting in one direction, together with the snow resistance acting in the opposite direction, creates a "couple" or two "parallel turning forces" (p.178). This causes the ski to turn around the shovel. Your leg pressure pushes or "skids" the tail sideways and the ski pivots.

Camber

All skis are cambered. The purpose of the camber is to distribute your weight over the whole length of your skis when you stand on them. However, it is an added feature of skis that, when turning at high speed, the pressure you exert on them makes them go into what is called *reverse camber*. Here, the side-cut comes into play once again. It guarantees that, if an edged ski goes into reverse camber, the entire length of its inside edge stays in contact with the snow. As a result, the ski tends to make a carved rather than a skidded turn – it cuts a groove through the snow and it travels in a smooth, carved arc.

Side-cut

Ski tails skid sideways

Pressure against edged ski

Friction from snow at shovel

Skidded track

How side-cut helps a ski skid
When ski is edged, snow resistance is greater at shovel. Leg pressure causes ski to pivot and make a skidded turn.

Skidded turns
The skis pivot at the front and the tails are pushed out in a wide, skidded arc.

Camber

Inside edge bites into snow along whole length of ski: ski carves, tail does not skid

Carved track with minimum skidding

How side-cut helps a ski carve
In fast turns, ski goes into reverse camber. Side-cut keeps ski edged into snow over whole length and causes it to make a narrow-track carved turn.

Carved turns
It is possible that there may be no such thing as a *pure* carved turn. The flurry of snow indicates that there is always some skidding.

Cross-country skiing

Cross-country or "Nordic" skiing pre-dates Alpine skiing by centuries. In contrast, Alpine skiing is still in its infancy. Cross-country skiing grew out of simple necessity: it is claimed to have originated over four thousand years ago in Scandinavia and Russia as a means of travel and communication during the long, snowbound northern winters. It was – and in some places still is – a way of life rather than a sport. References exist in the Norse sagas to the use of skis by the Vikings, and in the Norwegian Civil War the king's army scouts were all equipped with skis for reconnaissance. In the mid-nineteenth century, Norwegian immigrants heading for the mining towns in the mountains of the West brought skiing to the United States and to Australia. It was early races there – and back in Scandinavia – which led to the development of modern cross-country skiing competitions.

Cross-country or "XC" skiing differs from Alpine skiing in the following ways. Alpine skiing is all downhill; cross-country is on the flat, uphill *and* downhill. You propel yourself forwards under your own steam over any kind of terrain, you are not restricted to areas served by ski lifts and you can ski almost anywhere you like. Alpine skiing equipment is fairly sophisticated, heavy and expensive; cross-country equipment is simpler, lighter and cheaper, and it differs in design (p. 190-3). The longer, thinner skis are attached to your feet by bindings which are hinged at the toe to allow your heel to lift up off the ski. This is because cross-country ski techniques, although very similar, are not the same as Alpine techniques. The basic cross-country step is fundamentally a form of walking, or rather gliding, on skis. Later, it can be developed into a more athletic form called *langlauf,* meaning "running on skis". These and other techniques for accelerating, braking and stopping, climbing uphill and turning are covered on p. 194-203.

Today, recreational cross-country skiing has become enormously popular throughout the world and is said to be one of the fastest-growing sports. It can take three forms: "ski touring" on specially prepared trails; skiing off-trail; and competition racing on tracks (called *loipes).* These three disciplines are illustrated here and explained later in the chapter. In its basic form, cross-country skiing is not strenuous and it is not difficult to learn. This is its greatest appeal. You can pick it up in a few days, you can choose your own routes and set your own pace, and there is very little risk of injury. It is an ideal family sport and one that is suited to all ages. There are fewer crowds, no ski lifts and no long lines of people. On top of all this, it is a fine way of enjoying the winter landscape while taking beneficial, healthy, all-round exercise.

Skiing on marked trails ▲
Official "ski touring" trails and cross-country tracks are specially prepared circuits, formed by a machine which lays down parallel tramlines or tracks for your skis to run in (p. 204). These are where most beginners learn, they are more-or-less flat, and almost all Alpine ski resorts now provide at least one. Alternatively, they may be longer trails, over more varied and undulating terrain, still well planned out and signposted but perhaps without the prepared ski tracks. These are much more common in Scandinavia where, as shown above, the whole family may go for a day's skiing together.

◀ Cross-country ski touring
This sport, more common in Scandinavia, is similar to hiking or backpacking on skis and is often done in a group. Short tours can be made over marked trails, but longer ones – possibly lasting several days – will probably be off-trail (p. 204) and may include snow camping. Long-distance touring requires detailed planning and accurate navigation. These skiers, in characteristic single file, are touring in Kilpisjärvi, Finland.

Cross-country racing ▶
The top cross-country racers or *langläufers* are highly specialized athletes. Competitive events take various forms (p.206-9), but they all demand perfect technique, strength, fitness and endurance. This picture was taken during the men's 50km race at the 1978 World Championships in Lahti, Finland.

Equipment

The most obvious difference between cross-country equipment and that used for Alpine skiing (p. 16) is that it is much lighter. It is also simpler and, therefore, less expensive. Cross-country equipment falls into three broad categories: recreational skiing, off-trail touring, and racing. In general, touring equipment is heavier and fairly rugged; racing equipment is light and fast; and the equipment used by ordinary recreational skiers lies somewhere in between. It is possible to rent most of the equipment, but, because the correct fit of the boots is so important, and unless you are trying out cross-country skiing for the first time, it is advisable, at least, to buy your own boots. In recent years, technical innovations have changed the look of

cross-country equipment. This is especially true of the skis, which now tend to be made of fiberglass rather than wood. It is also true of boots, which are now lighter, warmer and better waterproofed, and of bindings, which are now standardized.

Clothing must be light and warm. It should also be fairly loose-fitting (so as not to restrict your movements), wind- and waterproof, and should allow your body to breathe if you get hot. Traditionally, skiers wear knee-breeches and long woollen socks (with perhaps a thinner pair of socks underneath), a warm sweater, a jacket, a hat and gloves. However, you may wear a tracksuit, ski pants, or whatever you like: technique is more important than clothing.

Bindings

Cross-country bindings all work on the same principle: the boots are attached to the ski with a hinged toe-piece that holds the foot firmly in place but which allows the heel to lift up off the ski. However, designs differ. The oldest form, the cable binding, has a metal cable running around the heel. The most common design is the 3-pin binding, in which metal pins protruding from the binding slot into holes in a lip on the front of the boot. A metal clip then clamps down over the toe. This type is also available in a 2-pin and 4-pin variety but, unfortunately, in different widths as well. Until recently, this has meant that boots and bindings were not all interchangeable. Attempts to standardize the systems have now resulted in a 75mm wide "Nordic norm" (with 71mm and 79mm variations) for general skiing, and a 50mm wide "racing norm" which is lighter and narrower. However, there are still anomalies: the 38mm Adidas system and the "push-button" system shown opposite.

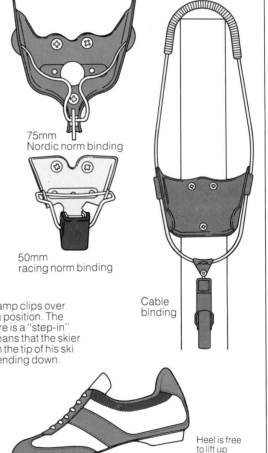

75mm
Nordic norm binding

50mm
racing norm binding

Cable
binding

How the binding works

In cross-country skiing, the heel must be free to rise up off the ski. For this reason, there is no heel binding and the boots are secured only by a hinged toe-piece. Metal pins center the boot in place and a spring-loaded clamp clips over the toe to hold it in position. The design shown here is a "step-in" binding which means that the skier can release it with the tip of his ski pole instead of bending down.

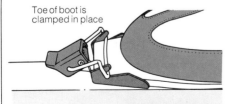

Toe of boot is
clamped in place

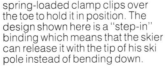

Heel is free
to lift up

Boots

Modern cross-country boots resemble running shoes – except that they have a protruding lip on the toe which fits into the binding. Your choice of boot depends on two things: the type of binding you have and the sort of skiing you intend to do. For ordinary recreational skiing, you will need a boot that is warm, waterproof and cut at or just above the ankle. You should probably go for the standard 75mm Nordic norm. For off-trail touring, you will need a boot that is slightly stronger and one that comes higher above your ankle to give you more protection against snow. For the more athletic *lang-lauf* skiing or for racing, where speed is more important than warmth, you will need a very light, low-cut boot. All boots should fit exactly and should be perfectly comfortable. The soles, usually made of nylon or polyurethane, should be flexible vertically (so that you can bend your foot) but rigid horizontally (so that your foot does not twist sideways.

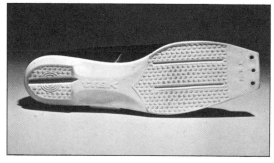

How the sole "grips"

Many of the newer boots now have holes or grooves (above) in the sole which fit over conical "studs" (right) or "ridges" on the ski. They prevent your heel from slipping sideways off the ski when turning.

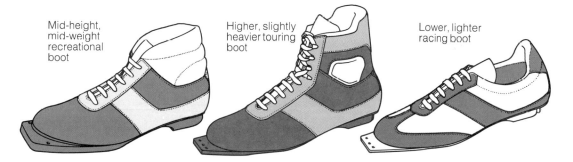

Mid-height, mid-weight recreational boot

Higher, slightly heavier touring boot

Lower, lighter racing boot

"Push-button" boots and bindings

Simpler and more effective cross-country bindings are introduced from time to time. The one shown here is manufactured by Dynafit and is called the "LIN system". It works on a push-button principle. The boot has a narrow, extended toe-piece with a flexible hook on the end. The toe-piece simply snaps into an opening in the binding and the hook springs up to catch at the top as you step down on the ski. To step out of the binding, you press down the flexible hook.

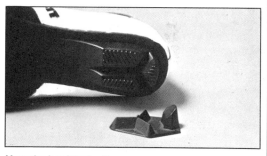

How the heel "grips"

A star-shaped wedge mounted on the ski fits into a star-shaped cavity in the heel of the boot to stop it slipping sideways.

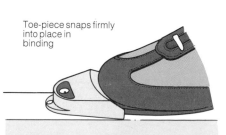

Toe-piece snaps firmly into place in binding

The advantage of this system is that toe is hinged further forward so foot will lift higher off ski and skier can take longer steps

Skis

Cross-country skis are narrower and lighter than Alpine skis. They also have more of a curve at the tip – which is important when lifting the tail of the ski off the snow while gliding. Until a few years ago, all cross-country skis were made of wood. Wooden skis are still widely used, but synthetic skis have become increasingly popular. Usually made of fiberglass, and with some form of plastic base, they are easier to use and stronger than wooden skis. Moreover, the new fiberglass skis are also available in a "non-wax" form.

The point about cross-country skis is that they should slide forward when you are gliding or skiing downhill, but that they should *not* slip backwards when you push off against them or when you are climbing uphill. In other words, they should both grip and glide. Wooden skis and standard fiberglass skis must be treated with special wax to give them this property; non-wax skis have special surfaces on their base to make waxing unnecessary.

All cross-country skis have a pronounced "camber" (p. 187), which means that they curve upwards in the middle, beneath your foot. This is so that the "kicker" or center section of the ski rises off the snow slightly when you are gliding. Go for a ski with a soft camber for recreational and off-trail skiing, and for one with a harder camber (or a "double camber") for racing. Some cross-country skis have a "side-cut" (p.187), which makes them easier for turning, but skis with parallel sides are better if you ski mainly in prepared tracks.

"Non-wax" skis

Skis that do not need waxing are a relatively new innovation. They are all made of fiberglass and they all have a special base, beneath the center of the ski, which allows them to slide forwards easily, but stops them from sliding backwards. The bases vary but include mohair strips (fine hairs facing backwards which lie flat when gliding but grip the snow when pushing off), fishscales and step patterns, and tiny mica chips (embedded in the base of the ski and slanting backwards).

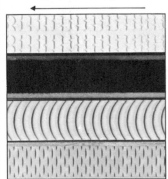

Step plus fish-scale patterns

Mohair strips

Curved step pattern

Cambered step pattern

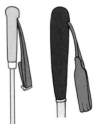

Choosing skis

The most important things to consider are length and width, and whether you want waxable or non-wax skis. Non-wax skis are better if you do not ski regularly and do not need high performance. To test for length, stand with one arm raised up above your head: your skis should reach to about your wrist. You can also take these figures as a rough guide. For recreational skiers: men 200-210cm, women 190-205cm. For *langlauf* or racing: men 210-215cm, women 200-210cm. As for width, use 50-55mm skis for recreational skiing; wider 55-60mm skis for off-trail touring; and narrow 44-50mm skis for racing.

Ski poles

These must be light and strong. For this reason, they are usually made of fiberglass or aluminum – although the cheaper ones may be bamboo. They are longer than Alpine ski poles – the top of the handle should reach up to your armpit when the pole is in the snow – and the tips are angled forwards slightly so that the poles are easier to pull out from behind. Basket designs vary, but they are usually asymmetric because you need support only at the back. A larger basket is better for deep, untracked snow when off-trail touring. Handles are leather or plastic with a longer wrist strap than Alpine ski poles.

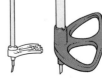

How to choose and apply ski waxes

Put simply, waxing improves the performance of the cross-country ski. Some waxes help it to grip and some waxes help it to glide. In reality, the study of waxing is highly complicated and can be very confusing. If you use a non-wax ski, you may decide to ignore waxes altogether. But if you have a waxable wooden or fiberglass ski, waxing is unavoidable; and if you are a racer, the correct choice of wax can be crucial.

Broadly speaking, there are two categories of wax: base waxes and running waxes. *Base waxes* are used to prepare the base of a ski so that the running waxes used later will stick to it properly. They are sometimes applied from a tin and then "ironed" on with a warm iron, or they are sprayed on from an aerosol can. A wooden ski also needs a layer of "tar", before the base wax is applied, to seal it against water.

Running waxes are the waxes that grip or glide. The "grip" waxes are the most important, and they come in two types: hard waxes and soft waxes. All grip waxes are applied only to the center of the ski (the "kicker" section) where you need the ski to grip the snow when you press down on it and push off for each gliding step. Hard waxes come in small cans and are rubbed onto the base of the ski and then smoothed out into a thin film with a piece of cork. Soft waxes (also known as "klisters") are stickier, give more grip and come in small tubes, like toothpaste. They are easier to apply when warm.

The choice of a hard or a soft grip wax depends on the condition of the snow – whether it is old or new, dry or wet – and the temperature. As a general rule, hard waxes are used when the snow is new and dry and when the temperature is low; the stickier soft waxes are used when the snow is older, when it is wet or thawing, and when the temperature is higher. Some manufacturers produce a simplified, general waxing kit containing just two waxes: a soft "plus" wax for temperatures above zero, and a hard "minus" wax for temperatures below zero (see right-hand column in chart below). Others produce a much more complicated range of specialized waxes. These are all color-coded according to snow type and temperature. For the best results, follow the manufacturers' instructions carefully, but the chart below will act as a rough guide. Take care that your skis are dry before you wax them, that you scrape off old wax before putting on a different type, and that you apply the wax evenly in a fairly thin layer.

"Glide" waxes, the other type of running wax, are used to make the ski glide more easily. For this reason, they are applied only at the tip and tail of the ski, not in the center. They are availble both as a general glide wax and as specialized, color-coded glide waxes for specific conditions.

To re-cap, a non-wax ski need not be waxed at all – although you may like to add a glide wax to the tips and tails; a waxable fiberglass ski needs a base wax and then the correct type of running wax for grip and glide; and a wooden ski needs first a tar preparation, then a base wax, and then the grip and glide waxes as appropriate.

Wax choosing chart

Snow conditions	°C	Specialized waxes			General waxes
		Glide wax	Grip wax	Glide wax	
Very wet, melting snow, slush	+1°	Red glider	Red klister	Red glider	Plus
Transitional, wet, mushy snow, large crystals or crumbling clumps of old snow	0°	Violet glider	Red wax / Violet wax / Violet klister / Silver klister / Yellow klister	Violet glider	Minus
Moderately cold dry snow, new dry flakes or hard crust of old snow	−1° to −7°	Blue glider	Blue wax / Blue klister	Blue glider	
Cold dry snow, new powdery flakes or small, fine crystals		Green glider	Green wax / Green klister	Green glider	

Basic techniques

In its simple, recreational form, cross-country skiing is known as "ski touring" or "ski rambling". It is neither difficult nor dangerous; indeed, it is a sport that virtually anyone can do.

We have divided this section into two parts. The first part, *basic techniques* (p. 194-7), covers ski touring, and includes the transition from walking to gliding, the double-pole push, and the most commonly used techniques for walking uphill. The second part, *advanced techniques* (p. 198-203), deals with the more athletic *langlauf* skiing used in racing and covers some movements which may be needed when touring off the prepared tracks.

On the whole, beginners pick up cross-country skiing very quickly – much faster than Alpine skiing. Nevertheless, it is best to learn from an instructor at a *langlauf* school. Not only will you be taught the techniques properly from the start; you will also learn on terrain that is suitable for beginners. Most schools have a special learner's loop which is flat, relatively straight and out of the way of other skiers.

As soon as you attempt your first steps on cross-country skis, you will see that it is in many ways just like walking. In fact, as a beginner, this is what you should aim for: to move across the snow in a relaxed, leisurely way just as you would when walking normally. Later, you will be able to develop this into the slightly faster technique known as the "gliding step" or "diagonal striding". A simple form of the gliding step, together with the double-pole push, are probably the only techniques you will need to go ski touring. The machine-made tracks will keep your skis parallel and stop them straying, and the trails avoid sharp changes of direction and steep ascents or descents which may require different techniques. Turning around while stationary can be performed by making a "star turn" on the spot (p. 46), either around your ski tips or around your ski tails.

If you compare the drawing below with the one on p.48, you will see that walking on cross-country skis is almost identical to walking on Alpine skis. The difference is that cross-country equipment is actually designed for walking, whereas Alpine skis, boots and bindings are not. This makes the technique much easier. Cross-country skis are lighter, the boots or shoes are flexible, not rigid, and the bindings hold your foot onto the ski only at the toe so that your heel is free to lift up as it does when you are walking. Moreover, cross-country poles are longer in order to give you more leverage, better balance, and a stronger push-off at each step.

From walking to gliding

When you begin walking, only your unweighted ski moves forward. As soon as you go a little faster, you will feel that both skis are moving at once. This is the point at which you begin to glide

and when simply walking on skis becomes the basic *gliding step*. The important points to remember are these. Keep your ski tips in contact with the snow all the time, and resist the

1 Plant left pole and transfer weight from left ski to slowly gliding right ski.

2 Glide forward on right ski and push off slightly from left pole.

3 Slide unweighted left ski forward in time with right arm.

4 Transfer weight from right ski to left ski. Plant right pole and glide on left ski.

The pole grip

The standard cross-country pole grip is the same as it is in Alpine skiing. However, as your technique develops, you will find that once you have pushed off from your pole and swung your arm backwards, you can release your grip (as shown below) until your arm comes forward.

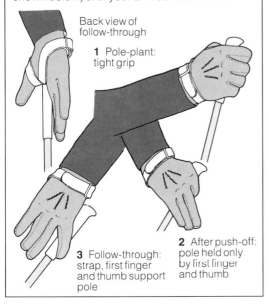

Back view of follow-through

1 Pole-plant: tight grip

3 Follow-through: strap, first finger and thumb support pole

2 After push-off: pole held only by first finger and thumb

Walking on cross-country skis
The simple "gliding step" is easily mastered, and it forms a relaxed, effortless technique in which the skis glide smoothly over the snow.

temptation to lift them at each step. Instead, push forwards so that you *glide* them over the snow. Coordinate your movements so that your right arm and left leg work together, and your left arm and right leg do the same. Keep your weight slightly forward, balanced over your gliding ski, and plant your poles close to your side. Above all, try to maintain an even, natural rhythm.

5 While gliding on left ski, start to bring right ski forward.

6 Slide unweighted right ski forward in time with left arm.

7 You have now made two complete steps and you are back at the beginning of the sequence again.

Basic gliding steps can be used on most gently undulating terrain.

Climbing techniques

As with Alpine skiing, the method you use to walk uphill should vary according to the steepness of the slope. Because cross-country skis are either specially waxed or provided with a non-slip running surface (p.192), they are much less prone to slip backwards than Alpine skis. This means that gentle slopes can be negotiated using the basic *gliding step* – adapted by taking shorter strides and by supporting yourself on your pole at each step.

As soon as the gradient increases to the point where your skis no longer grip, change to *side-stepping*, either diagonally or straight up the fall line. Alternatively, for short, steep ascents, you can use the *herringbone*: open your skis out into a wide "V" and edge them into the snow as far as you can in order to prevent them from slipping backwards downhill. As with side-stepping, the movement is performed in the same way as the corresponding Alpine technique (p.55-6).

Uphill gliding steps

Climb gentle slopes by taking slightly shorter steps with a briefer glide phase. Keep your weight forward and maintain pressure on leading ski so that "kicker" grips. Push harder on poles.

Double-pole pushing

Over flat ground or on gentle descending slopes, you can increase your speed by using the *double-pole push*. Like so many of the cross-country movements, this is the same as the Alpine technique (p.49). Instead of making a gliding step, keep both feet level, and use both your poles to propel yourself forward. At first, do not try to glide too far. Concentrate on coordinating your various movements and keeping your balance. The more dynamic *langlauf* form will come with practice (p.201).

1 Plant both poles together, just in front of your feet.

2 Press down firmly on both poles with arms flexed.

3 Follow through and push off finally as you glide forwards.

Walking straight uphill on a gentle slope.

The herringbone

On short, steep slopes, herringboning is an alternative climbing method. The diverging ski stance – tips apart and tails together – forms a "wedge" which stops you slipping backwards. Plant your poles behind you for support and push your knees into the hill to make use of the inside edges of your skis.

Side-stepping

When the slope becomes too steep for walking straight uphill, turn your skis around so that they are at right angles to the fall line and climb up sideways. Take one step at a time: first, lift your uphill ski and set it down a little higher up the slope; then bring your downhill ski up alongside. This way, one ski is always edged into the snow.

Advanced techniques

Though some of the appeal of recreational cross-country skiing lies in its unhurried, leisurely pace, it would be a mistake to suggest that this sport is *slow*. Modern cross-country racers can now ski a kilometer (0.6 mile) in around three minutes – that is, at average speeds of around 20 kph (12½ mph) – and can, moreover, maintain these speeds over very long distances.

The more athletic, more competitive branch of cross-country skiing is sometimes called *langlauf*, and the skiers who practice it are known as *langlaufers*. Obviously, it is much more demanding than recreational skiing, but it is a logical progression from the more relaxed, more leisurely style. As a general rule, the techniques are the same as those described on the previous pages – but, in *langlauf*, they are refined and perfected. A high standard of fitness and a good training program are necessary, but what is also important to the amateur *langlaufer* is a thorough mastery of the gliding step and the transition from merely walking to running on cross-country skis.

Over the following pages, we cover some of the more advanced *langlauf* techniques. These include the athletic forms of the gliding step and the double-pole push (together with their variations), how to ski bumps and dips effectively, and how to change direction on cross-country skis.

Langlauf courses are not flat like ski-touring trails; they are designed to undulate and to contain uphill and downhill sections, so that some of the time is spent either using climbing steps or "schussing" downhill. The stance for a schuss is the same as it is in Alpine skiing (p. 60) and it can be varied according to speed and terrain in the same way. On steep sections, *langlaufers* will use the "egg" position (p. 156) to increase their speed and also to rest their arms and legs briefly.

Many of the techniques in this section also apply to skiing off the machine-made trails or *tracks* – in particular, the bumps and dips technique and the various methods of turning. When touring, you may encounter all kinds of snow and terrain conditions. As well as the gliding step, the schuss and a variety of turns for different situations, you will probably also need to know how to traverse (p. 72) and how to snowplow (p. 64) to control speed. Bear in mind that all of these Alpine techniques are more difficult to perform well on the light cross-country skis with their single toe-piece bindings.

Advanced technique for gliding steps

If the simple form of the gliding step illustrated on p. 194 is like walking on skis, then the advanced form shown here is like running on skis. There is a much stronger push-off or "kick" with the thrusting leg, the pole-push is more powerful, the step is larger, and the glide is longer and faster.

Although the complete movement should be smooth and uninterrupted, two distinct phases can be distinguished: the *push-off* and the *glide*. The push-off is made by rapidly extending ("kicking") your rear leg, then giving a strong final thrust from the ball of your foot and a push with

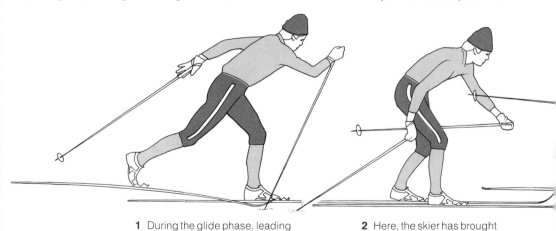

1 During the glide phase, leading knee must be bent so that weight is well forward and angle between lower leg and front of ski never exceeds ninety degrees.

2 Here, the skier has brought right ski and left pole loosely forward. He now pushes off from his right pole and flexed left leg.

The gliding stance

The forward body lean during the glide phase is very important. You must keep your leading knee flexed so that your weight is over the ball of your gliding foot and so that your push-off is directed diagonally forwards, not upwards. As you extend your rear leg, the heel will lift and the ski tail will come up, but a good forward lean will also help to keep the ski tip in contact with the snow.

✗ Weight too far back
Leading knee is stiff and foot too far forward. Therefore, rear ski comes down onto snow too soon and glide phase is shortened.

✓ Correct stance
Flexing leading knee keeps center of gravity over gliding foot: body extends diagonally forwards, balance is better, and new pole-plant can be made at correct angle, with pole slanting backwards.

✗ Body too stiff
You must bend your legs and body. If you do not, your push-off will extend upwards, not forwards, and you will not be able to accelerate in long, effective glides.

your arm from your opposite pole. This propels your body *diagonally* forwards so that you are fully stretched, with your weight well over your gliding ski. During the glide phase, you plant your pole, pull yourself forward and slide your unweighted ski in front. You flex the leg on which you are gliding and sink down slightly in preparation for the next push-off and extension. An effective gliding step technique depends largely on timing and rhythm – that is, on pushing off from leg and pole at just the right moment and on coordinating your movements precisely.

3 Next glide phase follows the push-off, body is extended and relaxed, and weight is balanced over gliding foot again.

4 The actual push-off is the only moment when skier's body is tensed. Here, he pushes off from left pole and "kicks" from ball of right foot.

5 The skier has now made two complete steps and is gliding again. He will make next step as soon as he feels acceleration beginning to slow.

Developing a racing technique

Langlauf racers train extensively to perfect their gliding steps technique. Cross-country racing is considered to be one of the most physically demanding sports, so stamina and strength are essential. As well as training on snow throughout the winter, racers may also practice on special "rollerskis" during the summer months.

Of course, style varies slightly from one racer to another, but the basic technique can also vary according to the demands of the terrain. On undulating ground, you may want to alter your rhythm and, on long, gentle slopes, you may want to miss out one or two of your pole-plants in order to give your muscles a momentary rest (these techniques are sometimes known as the "Finnish step", the "swinging step" or "triple striding").

The drawing on this page – of the gliding steps movement seen from the front and back – may help you to refine your technique and develop the right rhythm for the push and glide and for the transfer of weight from one leg to the other.

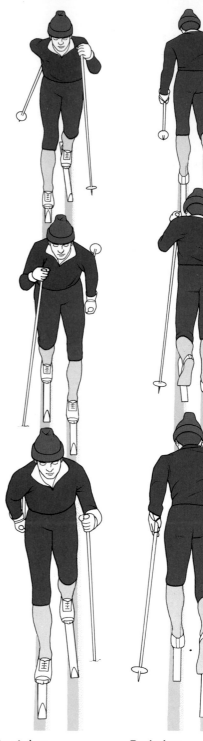

A *langlauf* racer in action
Zinaida Amosova (USSR) competing in the 10km event during the 1978 World Nordic Games, held at Lahti in Finland. Note how powerfully she pushes off from her right leg and left pole in order to glide forward on her left ski.

Front view
In the gliding step, poles are planted just in front of leading foot, close to ski track. Arms move close to upper body.

Back view
Machine-made tracks guarantee that skis are kept parallel and in an open stance – at about hip-width.

Advanced techniques for double-pole pushing

Like gliding steps, the basic double-pole push (p. 197) can also be developed into a more athletic, more effective technique. Racers frequently use double-pole pushes both to increase their speed on the flat and on descents, and to relax their muscles briefly during the glide phase: it is the second most commonly used acceleration technique in cross-country skiing.

For the double-pole push to be effective, it requires good timing, an accurate pole-plant and a lot of strength in the shoulders and arms. In our first drawing, it is begun from a fairly upright stance. Both poles are planted together just in front of the feet. The skier then presses down on them and drops his upper body forward to increase the force of the final push-off which he makes as his arms follow through. In our second drawing, the skier goes into the double-pole push from what is known as a "one-step" – that is, a single gliding step during which both poles are swung forwards.

The double-pole push in competition
Another racer in the 1978 World Nordic Games bends into a low, forward stance as he pushes off from his poles to propel himself forward.

The advanced double-pole push

1 With feet level, and in a fairly upright stance, swing arms forward and plant both poles.

2 Bend upper body forward to increase pressure on poles, then push off strongly.

3 Follow through with arms. Glide forward with knees flexed and upper body bent forwards.

4 Rise up gradually as glide phase slows down and bring arms forward ready for next pole-plant.

The double-pole push from a one-step

1 Make one gliding step as normal but bring both arms forward during the movement.

2 While gliding, plant both poles at once so that they are pointing backwards slightly.

3 As feet come level, bend upper body forward and push off as strongly as possible from both poles.

Skiing bumps and dips

On *langlauf* courses and when skiing off-trail, you will have to cope with undulating terrain. The way to do this is to combine your gliding step and double-pole push techniques, and to vary your rhythm so that you follow the rhythm of the bumps and dips. In the sequence below, the skier times his first double-pole push just *after* he has cleared the first bump, when his skis are already

2 One-step into double-pole push at bottom of dip

1 Double-pole push down into dip

Turning

Turns on cross-country skis fall into two categories: those made on more-or-less flat terrain, and those made while skiing downhill. "Step turning" is the technique used for changing direction on the flat or on very gentle slopes – and it can be performed by angling out either the ski tips or the ski tails.

All downhill turns were once made by using the "Telemark turn", in which the skier adopted a kind of kneeling position, with his outside ski leading and his inside ski trailing behind. This turn is still used in places, but it is now seen only rarely. Much more common today are the many turns used in Alpine skiing – snowplow turning, stem turning and, even, parallel turning. All of these can be performed on cross-country skis, although, because the skis are narrow and often edge-less, the boots are soft and low, and your heel is not fixed to the ski, they are much more difficult to control.

1 Open skis into wedge ("V") position

2 Plant pole and transfer weight against outside ski to turn

Snowplow turning

The technique is identical to the form used in Alpine skiing (p. 82) except that you put more weight on your heels to keep them on your skis. Open your skis into a V-shaped snowplow stance. Plant your inside pole and begin to press against your outside ski. Keep both legs flexed, but push your outside knee forwards and into the direction of the turn to steer. As you turn out of the fall line, bring your inside ski parallel to steer.

3 Bring skis parallel at end of turn

pointing downhill. This propels him forcefully down into the hollow. He brings his left leg forward and, at the bottom of the dip, he makes a one-step into a second double-pole push. This gives him added momentum, but, for the climb up the other side of the dip, he must change to single gliding steps, with quite short strides and a more exaggerated forward lean.

3 Uphill gliding steps with single pole-plants

4 Transition to normal gliding steps as terrain levels out again

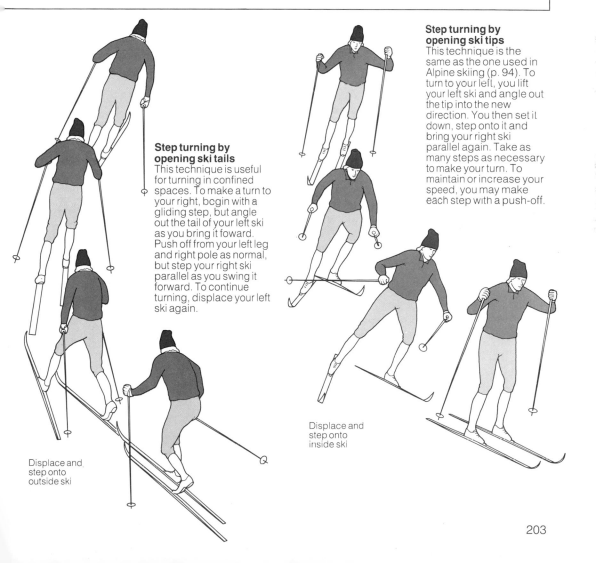

Step turning by opening ski tails
This technique is useful for turning in confined spaces. To make a turn to your right, begin with a gliding step, but angle out the tail of your left ski as you bring it foward. Push off from your left leg and right pole as normal, but step your right ski parallel as you swing it forward. To continue turning, displace your left ski again.

Step turning by opening ski tips
This technique is the same as the one used in Alpine skiing (p. 94). To turn to your left, you lift your left ski and angle out the tip into the new direction. You then set it down, step onto it and bring your right ski parallel again. Take as many steps as necessary to make your turn. To maintain or increase your speed, you may make each step with a push-off.

Displace and step onto outside ski

Displace and step onto inside ski

203

Trails and touring

In the Alps, nearly all cross-country skiing is done on prepared trails. These are called "ski touring" trails or tracks. They are made by vehicles similar to the Alpine trail machines (p.214). The difference is that as well as beating down any new snow into a firmer surface, the machines cut out parallel grooves or tracks for the skis to run in. There are usually two sets of parallel tracks: one for skiers going in one direction, another for skiers going the opposite way. Almost all ski touring trails are flat; although they may undulate slightly, there are no steep gradients and no points at which you have to use "side-stepping" or

"herringboning" (p.197). They travel in more-or-less straight lines – which removes the need for making difficult turns.

In Scandinavia, where cross-country skiing first originated, the tradition is different. Specially prepared trails do exist (especially around well-known ski resorts and on the outskirts of large towns), but cross-country skiers are much more likely to go off into the countryside and make their own tracks. In other words, off-trail touring is more common. The tours vary in length from one-day excursions to trips lasting several days, in which case the routes are planned in advance to take in overnight stops.

Skiing off-trail ▶
Cross-country skiing is the ideal
way to enjoy the remoteness and
quietness of the winter landscape –
at whatever pace you choose.

◀ The prepared tracks
Parallel hip-width tracks make the
skiing easy – as this youngster
demonstrates. Your skis do not
wander from side to side and you
concentrate only on propelling
yourself forwards.

Skiing on-trail ▼
Most Alpine ski resorts now provide
ski touring trails. They are
usually sited on the flat valley floor,
but there may be others on the
higher slopes (p.216) and some that
offer slightly more varied and
challenging terrain.

Scandinavian touring ▶
In Scandinavia, it is common to see
a group of ski tourers pulling special
sledges (called *pulki*) that carry
everything they might need for a trip
of several days. Twenty miles
(32km) in a day is quite possible on
skis. The routes may or may not be
marked, and North American
tourers often follow the course of
summer footpaths.

Alpine touring
Although it is not seen very often,
off-trail cross-country touring is
possible in the Alps. In fact, there is
a famous 100-mile (160km) tour,
called the *Grande Traversée*, over
the Jura in eastern France and
Switzerland. The skier shown here is
skiing some of the terrain used for
langlauf racing in the 1976
Olympics near Seefeld, Austria.

Racing

Racing on cross-country skis is probably as old as skiing itself and, in modern competition, it has developed into one of the toughest and most demanding sports in the world. Like Alpine competition skiing (p. 144), cross-country racing is governed by the *Fédération Internationale de Ski* (F.I.S.). It is divided into five separate disciplines: individual racing, relays, the biathlon, the Nordic Combined, and marathons (although the *Committee Internationale de Sports Militaires* also run four-man "patrol" races). F.I.S. establish the rules and also supervise the design and construction of the courses. These should be laid out over varied, fairly rugged terrain with a specified mixture of uphill, downhill and level sections in order to test the racers' technical skill, tactical ability and physical fitness. The courses should be clearly marked with boards, arrows, flags or ribbons and should have a distance marker every kilometer. They should be well prepared with, if possible, two sets of machine-made parallel tracks for the skis to run in – except around turns where racers make their own skating

Individual racing
A tense moment as the competitors close on one another near the finish of a race in the World Championships at Lahti, Finland, in 1978.

tracks. On courses of 15km, at least one refreshment station must be provided where the racers can take drinks or hot soup; on 30km courses there must be at least two, and on 50km courses at least four. The competitors themselves must follow the marked track using only their own means of propulsion. Techniques are a combination of diagonal gliding steps with single- or double-pole pushes, downhill running, step turning, uphill climbing and herringboning. If a racer finds himself being overtaken by another competitor, he must give way. During the race, both poles may be exchanged at any time, but only one ski if it is broken or damaged.

Individual cross-country races are held for both men and women. Distances vary from country to country, but the F.I.S. norms for World Championships and for the Winter Olympics are as follows: for men, 15km, 30km and 50km; for women, 5km, 10km and 20km. Competitors leave the starting line at thirty-second intervals and race against the clock. The fastest time determines the winner. Strategy is as important as technique and stamina, and the racers must pace themselves carefully.

Cross-country relays are by far the most exciting events for spectators (p. 10-11). Each team contains four members: men ski a 4 x 10km relay; and women ski a 4 x 5km relay. The race begins with a mass start, the first members of each team ski one complete lap, and then they hand over to the second members by touching them while they are both in a 30m exchange zone. The first competitor over the finishing line determines the winning team.

The biathlon event is a highly specialized combination of skiing and shooting and has its origins in the use of skis for hunting and for military purposes. The Olympic and World Championship races are held over a distance of 20km. Each competitor skis a 4km loop five times, carrying his rifle on his back in a special sling, and comes into the shooting range four times during the race, once after each lap. He takes five shots at the target each time, and his score is based on a penalty system whereby extra time is added to his time for the cross-country run. Biathlon events also take place as 30km relays and as 10km "sprint" races.

Finally, the Nordic Combined event includes both ski jumping and cross-country racing. The competition, which some people feel determines the real *meister* of Nordic skiing, is only open to men. On the first two days, entrants make three jumps from a 70m hill (p. 161), of which the best two count, and on the third day they enter a 15km cross-country race. The results are combined to find the winner.

Ski marathons

Also called "citizen racing", these long-distance mass events have become increasingly popular. They are open to anyone and they attract thousands of skiers of all abilities – a few international champions who win regularly and many recreational skiers who aim simply to complete the course. Ski marathon courses can vary in length from about 25 miles to 95 miles, and each race begins with a mass start.

The first marathon, held in 1922, was the now-traditional Swedish "Vasaloppet" race, stretching for over 53 miles between Sälen and Mora. It still attracts over ten thousand entrants every year and, to date, has been won in under five hours. Telemark, in Wisconsin, is the home of North America's most popular ski marathon, the annual 22-mile *Birkebeiner*. The picture on the right shows the start of the 47-mile "Finlandia Ski Race".

◄ Individual racing

Sweden's Sven-Åke Lundbäck in action in the 1978 World Championships in Finland. Cross-country racing is a gruelling sport and racers must be in peak physical condition. They train throughout the summer – in gymnasiums, on cross-country runs and on special "roller skis". During the race, waxing (p. 193) is vital, and all the international teams have waxing experts.

Biathlon ▶

Biathletes are judged on a combination of skiing speed and marksmanship. During each race they must come into the shooting range four times. They shoot twice lying down and twice standing up. In the 20km race, the target is a bull's-eye surrounded by two circles. Penalty time is added to the racer's skiing time according to how he shoots. In the 10km "sprint" race, the targets are glass circles. For each circle that the racer does not hit, he must ski a 150m penalty loop. The photograph on the right shows Andy Pittendrigh (Canada) in the 10km event at the 1979 World Championships.

Citizen racing ▼

Ski marathons are open to any skier who wishes to enter. This picture shows the start of the well-known "Finlandia Ski Race", held every year between Hämeenlinna and Lahti in Finland. The course is 75km long, takes on average about eight hours to ski and attracts nearly ten thousand competitors – not all of whom reach the finish.

Functional skiing

The aim of functional skiing is to ski safely, without taking unnecessary risks, without falling over and without wasting energy. It is a mix of three things: skill, adaptability and experience. Learning the basic movements of skiing is only half the battle; the other half is knowing instinctively when and where to apply them. Skiing conditions can change constantly in the course of a single run – the type of terrain, the weather and visibility, and what the snow is like. The way you ski will also depend on the altitude, the number of other skiers around you, whether you are skiing on- or off-trail, your fitness, and your mood or "motivation" on any particular day. All these things will affect your *speed;* and speed is the most important factor. In this chapter we examine all these situations and supply you with the information which, together with your own practical experience, will enable you to make the right decisions and adapt your technique to ski safely and efficiently – that is, *functionally.*

Undulating slopes ▶
On slopes like this, whether on-trail or in deep powder snow, you must constantly be aware of sudden surprises and always judge how fast to ski the bumps, dips and slope edges that you encounter.

◀ **Wooded slopes**
In Europe, where this picture was taken, the "tree line" is lower than it is in, say, the North American Rockies and, in general, the slopes are not very difficult. However, avalanches can still occur in wooded areas.

Smooth, open slopes ▼
On slopes where the gradient is fairly constant and where you can see well ahead, your only concern will be how to turn. In these conditions, short swinging may be the most effective and enjoyable method of controlling speed.

Ski trails

Every ski resort provides specially prepared ski runs: these are called "trails". They are designed to be as safe as possible and to create good but varied skiing conditions for all grades of skier. They are clearly signposted and graded according to their difficulty, they are patrolled regularly, and the trail service will send a rescue team in the event of an accident. They are also made safe from avalanches. Moreover, trails are "groomed" – which means that, except on very steep slopes, machines are used to break up ruts and bumps and pack down freshly fallen snow to produce a smooth and consistent surface for skiing.

At most resorts, there will also be a choice of off-trail "descent routes". These are really for expert skiers only. They differ from trails in that they need not be signposted, they are not patrolled, and they are not specially prepared or groomed. You ski them at your own risk, and you must make up your own mind about avalanche danger. Check the local bulletins before you start.

Mid Alpine trail ▼
Lower down the slopes become more heavily wooded – although trees are often cleared to create the trail.

High Alpine trail ▶
Here, high above the tree line, the trails are open and spacious. The snow cover will also last longer into the spring.

How trails are graded

Trails are almost always color-coded according to their degree of difficulty. The grading is based on the average difficulty of the run in "normal" conditions, so you must take account of the fact that poor weather and snow conditions can make them much trickier to ski. Despite attempts to make the color-coding system international, there are still variations from country to country.

In Europe, trails usually fall into three categories: *black* for a difficult run, *red* for an intermediate run, and *blue* for a fairly easy one. Some resorts may also indicate very easy beginners' slopes in *green*. These color-codes appear as colored disks attached to poles, and they are placed at the beginning of a run and on either side of the trail throughout its length. They often carry a trail number and a smaller "location" number (in order to locate the site of an accident when reporting it). Normally, the grading of the trails should match the colors used on the "piste map" (p. 216) available at the resort.

In the United States, the color system differs: a black diamond for a difficult run, a blue square for intermediate, and a green circle for easy.

Some resorts mark "descent routes" in yellow. The yellow may then be combined with black, red or blue to denote the degree of difficulty.

Easy trail

Intermediate trail

Difficult trail

Color-coded trail markers
Blue, easy trails are usually no steeper than 25 per cent; red, intermediate runs vary from 25 to 40 per cent (although they may include short, steeper sections); black, difficult trails are generally 40 per cent or steeper.

Trail signs

As well as the color-coded poles which tell you how a trail is graded, many resorts also use signposts which resemble the familiar international road signs and display markers (like the one below) indicating where the unpatrolled skiing areas begin.. Signs that warn of avalanche danger or state that a trail is closed should *never* be ignored.

 Danger

 Crossing

 Run narrows

Trail closed

 Sharp curve

 Ski lift crossing

Road crossing

Avalanche danger/ trail closed to skiers

Trail closed

Unpatrolled ski area beyond this sign

 SOS telephone

 First aid post

Trail changes direction

Note Closed-off areas are also indicated by fluorescent-colored flags on a cord strung between orange poles.

How trails are maintained

The trails which most skiers take for granted require a great deal of complex and expensive maintenance. The work, often carried out by the resort authorities or the ski lift companies, begins during the summer months when there is no snow at all. During this period trees are cleared to make the trail wider, rocks, boulders and tree stumps are removed, and bridges are built. During the winter, most of the work on the slopes centers on marking and signposting the trails and on making the snow surface as consistent and safe as possible. This "grooming" is done by special machines. These vehicles, with their wide caterpillar tracks and rollers, are used to beat down freshly fallen snow into a firm surface, to spread the snow evenly over bare patches, to flatten bumps and fill in dips, and, in spring, to break up dangerously icy or crusted snow. They go to work immediately after a new snowfall and at the end of each day when the lifts have closed down. There is, however, a limit to the steepness of the slopes on which the machines can operate (see "Mogul skiing", p. 230).

Trail maintenance also means preventing avalanche danger. Although most trails avoid areas which are known to be avalanche-prone, the risk can never be entirely eliminated. The responsibility for avalanche safety lies with the resort's "ski patrol" (p. 247), which must inspect the trails and the surrounding mountains constantly. They will close a run if there is any risk, and they will often trigger avalanches deliberately to make the runs safe.

"Artificial" snow

Artificial snow is *real* snow produced by a machine. It is an expensive process, and its product is like old snow, somewhat heavy and wet, but it can extend the skiing season in areas with low snowfall, and it may be used to provide good snow cover where necessary for ski racing (e.g., the Lake Placid Olympics).

There are two systems: "air/water" and "airless". The latter produces more snow and is more energy-efficient, but if the temperature rises above −4°C (26°F) compressed air systems allow more control of the water content and produce drier snow. Computers are sometimes used to monitor the air and water flow ratios.

Artificial snow-making machine

A trail-maintenance machine These vehicles, a Swiss invention made by a company called *Ratrac*, are sometimes known as "trail bashers". They run on wide caterpillar tracks to which rollers or blades can be attached, and their purpose is to "groom" the trails. This means packing down soft, new snow, breaking up hard, rutted snow, spreading out uneven snow, and levelling off bumps and dips. They are highly versatile and can negotiate slopes as steep as 60 per cent on a solid snow base. In deep, soft snow or melting slush, they are more handicapped.

Safety on the trail

The hazards of skiing cannot be eliminated solely by preparing the trails. The ski patrols can grade them and signpost them, and issue warnings when there is a danger of avalanches, but if you ignore these then you are putting yourself, and possibly other skiers, at risk. The best they can do for you then is to send out one of the rescue teams.

Follow the code of conduct outlined below and ski functionally – within the limits of your own ability. Do not ski fast unless it is safe to do so, and pay attention to what other skiers around you are doing – especially on crowded trails (see right). Take special care when snow conditions are treacherous, when visibility is poor and when skiing difficult or narrow sections of the run (see p. 235 for how to cope with situations such as these). If you are tired, stop and rest – instead of skiing on and risking a bad fall. Bear in mind that many skiing accidents occur on that "one last run of the day".

If you are skiing in a group – whether as a ski school class or with a number of friends – try to observe the following guidelines. Do not cut across the turn of the skier in front of you. If your group is coming to a halt, stop *below* the skier in front of you (i.e., on their downhill side); if you try to stop above them and you miscalculate, the chances are that your colleagues will all go down like dominoes as you slide into them. If there are two experienced skiers in the group, one should lead and the other should bring up the rear. Decide on the order in which the rest of you will ski, and then stick to it.

Crowded trails
This picture of a Japanese resort demonstrates that a large number of people on the trails is the price to be paid for the boom in popularity of skiing. Special care and attention to safety are required.

Skier's code of conduct

Good manners and a concern for other skiers on the trail is largely common sense, but to encourage safe behavior and to help prevent accidents, the following code of conduct has been formulated by the International Ski Federation. You should treat it like you would the Highway Code.

- Consideration for others: you must ski in such a way that you put no-one else on the slope at risk of danger or injury

- Control of speed and movements: you must adapt your speed and movements to your own ability and to the prevailing weather, terrain and snow conditions

- Choice of route: if you are approaching another skier from behind, you must choose your route so that you do not endanger the skier in front of you

- Overtaking: you may overtake another skier on the uphill or downhill side and from the right or from the left, but you must leave sufficient room for the other skier to maneuver. The skier in front of you always has the right of way

- Joining a trail and traversing: if you wish to enter a trail, or ski across a slope, you must check beforehand that the slope is free of skiers, both on the uphill and downhill side

- Stopping: except in an emergency, you should avoid stopping in the middle of the trail, at narrow points, or in places where you cannot be seen. If you fall, move out of the way quickly

- Climbing a slope: if you are climbing a slope, stick to the edge of the trail. You should avoid even this if visibility is bad. The same applies to skiers who descend on foot

- Trail markers: you must observe all signs, markers and instructions from the ski patrol

- Behavior in accidents: in the event of an accident, it is your duty to stop and help wherever possible – also to guarantee that the rescue service has been notified and the precise location of the accident given

- Identification: in the event of an accident, you must give your identity, whether you are a participant or a witness

Trail maps

Every ski resort publishes its own trail map. The one shown here, of Engelberg in Switzerland, is a typical example. It tells you where the slopes are in relation to the resort, how the lift system is laid out and, by employing the color-coding explained on p.213, how each of the trails is graded. Trail maps should also indicate the altitude, not only of the surrounding mountain peaks, but also of the intermediate lift stations and the resort itself. There should be a compass on the map so that you can tell which way the slopes face. If there is not, then check

with a geographical map, since this affects the snow conditions. And bear in mind that the best resorts have slopes facing both north and south.

A good map, one which includes a lot of detail, should also give you an impression of what the trails themselves are like – whether they are open or wooded, wide or enclosed by exposed rock walls, high up above the resort or lower down, nearer the valley floor. If you have a lift pass which allows you to ride all the lifts at the resort, use the map to plan out a varied day's skiing.

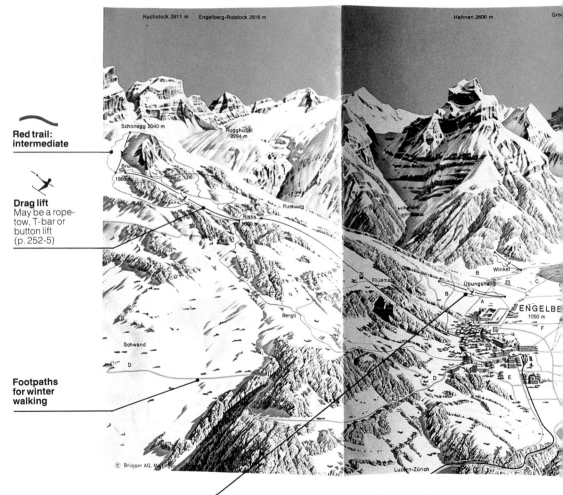

Red trail: intermediate

Drag lift
May be a rope-tow, T-bar or button lift (p. 252-5)

Footpaths for winter walking

South-facing slopes
In winter, slopes that face south or south-west receive more sun (p. 218), and, as the map shows, the tree line is higher. In December and January, they are warmer and more enjoyable to ski than north-facing slopes, but, in spring, conditions may deteriorate and the snow will not last as long into the season.

Beginner's nursery slope
These are often sited away from the main trails. They are fairly flat and fairly gentle and usually have their own simple nursery slope lifts.

The resort
Engelberg is an old established resort situated in a valley at a height of 1,050 m (3,445 ft) and surrounded on three sides by mountains. The map shows that it offers access to a variety of trails, from a cable car that starts in the center of the town and also from a funicular railway situated on the outskirts.

Cable car
Here, two cars run up to the intermediate lift station side by side. A new one has been built alongside the original one, which is now no longer in commercial use.

Black trail: difficult

Summer skiing
At this altitude (the map shows the height of the top lift station to be 3,020 m or 9,910 ft), snow will lie all year round and skiing may be possible in the summer months.

Ski touring trail
These are prepared trails for cross-country skiing (p. 204). Most Alpine resorts now provide them. They are usually on the flat valley floor, but, as here, they may also be on the higher plateaux.

Chairlift
Here, the lift brings skiers back up to the pass from the other valley (p. 256)

Blue trail: easy

Funicular railway

Toboggan run

Restaurant
All Alpine resorts have restaurants up on the mountain (often at the lift stations). This means that skiers do not have to go back down to the resort in the valley for lunch.

North-facing slopes
These slopes are more shady in winter, although they get the afternoon sun if they face more west or north-west. The lifts go up to the top station in four stages. From there, the run down to the valley is about 12 km (7½ miles), and from Trübsee can be skied by beginners on fairly easy "blue" trails.

Ski jumping hills
(see p. 161)

217

Weather and snow conditions

Skiing depends entirely on the weather – not simply because you can only ski when there is snow, but because the weather determines the condition of the snow *after* it has fallen. It therefore controls directly the kind of skiing you will get.

Mountain weather is probably the most changeable and most unpredictable of all. It can switch from one extreme to the other, with little or no warning, within half an hour or so, and it can be entirely different a few miles further down the valley or on the other side of the mountain. The study of mountain weather is the study of "microclimates" (that is, the prevailing conditions within a small, localized area). The best thing you, as a visiting skier, can do is to check the local weather bulletins, take the advice of the people who live there, and be prepared for the unexpected.

When the moisture in the air cools to below freezing point, it crystallizes and forms snow. If it is not cold enough, it will simply rain. The formation of snow is highly complex; it depends on a number of factors, including the amount of moisture or "humidity" in the air, the exact temperature at which the snow crystallizes, and then what happens to it after it has fallen. This is covered on p. 220-21.

As a skier, the things which most affect the conditions in which you ski are the time of year, the altitude of the slopes and the direction in which they face, and the presence or absence of winds.

At high altitudes, the sun is very strong indeed, and reflection from the surface of the snow will multiply the glare and the amount of ultra-violet light. Use skin protection creams, and wear goggles or sunglasses.

Skiing in fog, in a so-called "white-out", or when the light is flat and casts no shadows is difficult and potentially dangerous. Whenever visibility is bad, ski slowly and carefully.

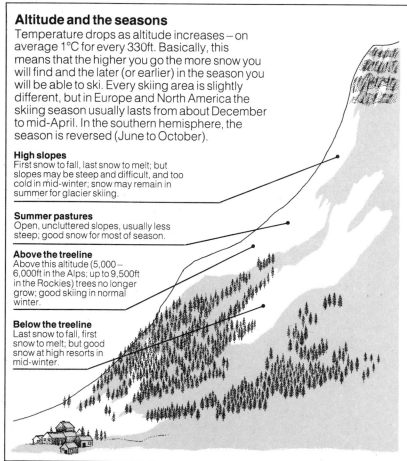

Altitude and the seasons

Temperature drops as altitude increases – on average 1°C for every 330ft. Basically, this means that the higher you go the more snow you will find and the later (or earlier) in the season you will be able to ski. Every skiing area is slightly different, but in Europe and North America the skiing season usually lasts from about December to mid-April. In the southern hemisphere, the season is reversed (June to October).

High slopes
First snow to fall, last snow to melt; but slopes may be steep and difficult, and too cold in mid-winter; snow may remain in summer for glacier skiing.

Summer pastures
Open, uncluttered slopes, usually less steep; good snow for most of season.

Above the treeline
Above this altitude (5,000 – 6,000ft in the Alps; up to 9,500ft in the Rockies) trees no longer grow; good skiing in normal winter.

Below the treeline
Last snow to fall, first snow to melt; but good snow at high resorts in mid-winter.

November
First snowfalls, but no base for skiing.

December
Heavier snowfalls, colder temperatures, snow settles; skiing may be uncertain but season begins officially.

January
Can be very cold, but conditions often very good – especially for powder snow.

February
High season for skiing; good, plentiful snow; more sun, longer days.

March
Warmer weather, spring snow conditions begin (p. 228) but south-facing slopes may be wet in afternoons.

April
Snow melting; best skiing on high-altitude north-facing slopes.

May
Season over; skiing usually only possible at high altitudes.

Note This season applies only to the northern hemisphere.

The direction of the slopes

The type of skiing and the condition of the snow on a particular slope is determined not only by its altitude but also by the way in which it faces. In the nothern hemisphere winter, the sun tracks from east to west across the southern half of the sky. This means that south-facing slopes receive more sun than north-facing slopes. In the southern hemisphere, the situation is reversed.

In mid-winter, the effect of the sun on the snow is less important. Snow conditions tend to be good everywhere, but, because the temperature is so low, the south-facing slopes, exposed to the sun, will be warmer and more pleasant to ski than the shady north-facing slopes. Later in the season, however, those slopes which get the most sunshine will be the first to deteriorate: the snow will be frozen in the morning and wet in the afternoon (p. 228).

Of course, slopes rarely face directly north or directly south. East-facing slopes get the sun in the morning and west-facing slopes in the afternoon, and in cold weather this is probably when you should ski them. Slopes that are exposed to the north-west tend to be similar to those that face north, and south-east-facing slopes have more-or-less the same characteristics as south-facing ones.

North-facing slopes
During the winter, these receive less sun and more shade. The tree line may therefore be lower. Around about Christmas, the sun may hardly reach them and they will be very cold. But they will have a longer season and better, drier snow during the spring months.

South-facing slopes
These are the slopes that receive sun throughout most of the day. In mid-winter, this makes them warmer and more popular. However, the snow does not last as long into the spring, and the constant freezing at night and melting during the day can produce icy conditions in the mornings and wet, slushy snow in the afternoons. Powder snow tends not to last.

Wind

The movement of air masses causes wind. In general, air masses move in a fairly predictable way from high pressure areas to low pressure areas, bringing warm air or cold air, fine weather or rain or snow. General trends, such as a prevailing wind from the west or from the south, can be used to forecast an overall change in the weather, but in mountain areas the situation is very complex. Differences in altitude (and, therefore, in temperature) are extreme, and air currents are forced up by the mountains or channelled in certain directions along the valleys. Conditions change rapidly and the effects of the wind can be extremely localized. This can give rise to the infamous winds known in the Alps as the *föhn* and in the Rockies as the *chinook* – very dry, warm winds which blow down from the mountains into the valleys, causing the temperature to rise and the snow to melt.

Strong winds can alter the condition of the snow – forming drifts, windslabs, cornices and, sometimes, a hard crust. They also reduce the effective temperature. This is known as the "wind-chill factor" and it means that the stronger the wind the colder you will feel at a given air temperature.

Clouds, fog and mist

Humidity is the amount of water in the air. It depends on the temperature. Clouds, fog and mist occur when the air cools and can no longer absorb moisture. To some extent, clouds can be used to forecast the weather, but in mountain areas this is difficult and unreliable. Most skiers are concerned with clouds only when they affect visibility or cause the weather to change. Low cloud or mist can suddenly blanket the slopes, turning everything white (a "white-out"), cutting visibility completely and making skiing almost impossible.

A "cloud ocean"
Also known as a *Wolkenmeer* or *Nebelmeer,* this cloud formation is the result of temperature inversion. From a high peak in brilliant sunshine, you can look down onto an ocean of clouds caused by cold air trapped in the valley.

Snow types

When a snow crystal first forms, high up in the cloud layer, it takes the basic shape of a six-pronged "star". As it falls, it grows (becoming either "feathery" or needle-like) and joins together with other crystals to form snowflakes. The size of the flakes depends on the temperature. The colder the air the smaller they are; the warmer it is the more likely the crystals are to form large flakes.

Once snow has fallen, it begins a long period of metamorphosis. To some extent it will settle under its own weight – although the colder and drier it is the less this happens (in the western Rockies where the snow falls through very cold, very dry air, it forms the classic bottomless, light "Rocky Mountain powder"). At the same time, it will melt and re-freeze in a continuous cycle according to the warmth from the sun and the changes in temperature between day and night. This breaks up the snow crystals into more rounded granules, packs them down and makes the snow cover harder and more compact. The same thing happens when the snow is blown by the wind or skied over. The friction causes a slight rise in temperature and the crystals melt. As they melt they release "latent heat", the temperature drops again, and they immediately re-freeze – leaving a harder and more compacted surface.

Most snow types can be simply classified into those that are pleasant to ski and those that are not. On-trail, the snow is specially prepared (p. 214); but before the machines have done their rounds, or when skiing off-trail, you may encounter any of the following snow types.

Powder snow is dry, new snow which has settled only slightly. When it is about 1 ft (30cm) deep and is lying on a solid base of older snow, it is enjoyable and easy to ski (p. 226); when it is between 1 ft and 3 ft (30 to 95cm) deep and there is no solid base, it is still enjoyable but more difficult and may require an adapted technique (p. 227). *Spring snow* or *corn snow* covers a variety of snow types – from some of the best to some of the worst. These conditions are described in detail on p. 228-9.

Windblown snow is snow that has been blown into "waves" by the wind. It is very uneven – sometimes packed, sometimes soft – and usually has a hardened crust on the top. It is difficult to ski, because the crust will not always support your weight. *Crust* is also formed by the sun melting the top surface of the snow which then re-freezes overnight. *Icy snow* is also formed by the rapid freezing of wet snow; it is sometimes found during off-trail touring and should be avoided if possible as it is very difficult to make your edges grip on it. *Heavy, wet snow* (also known as "porridge" or "mashed potato") is soft, sticky and unpleasant. It is basically melting snow and it is common in spring, especially on sunny south-facing slopes where the temperature is higher. It can also be caused by a fresh snowfall when the weather is warm or by rain falling on powder snow.

Light powder snow ▲
Here, a few inches of new powder snow has fallen on a firm base of older snow. This makes for ideal skiing conditions.

Melting powder snow ▶
The small lumps beside the ski tracks indicate that this powder is already changing under the influence of the sun.

Deeper powder snow ▼
Perhaps knee-deep, but still dry and light, this powder snow is enjoyable and fairly easy to ski.

Windblown snow ▶
When snow is blown into "waves" or small drifts by the wind (as shown here), it can produce highly treacherous skiing conditions. Often, a hard, icy crust forms on the top. This varies in thickness, making the surface uneven, and it may be impossible to tell in advance whether or not it will break under your weight. Windblown snow makes skiing conditions unpredictable and, hence, difficult.

◀ Very deep powder snow
Seemingly bottomless powder like this is a rare skiing experience. It can be found in the Alps but is more common in the North American Rockies, where the very cold, dry atmosphere at high altitudes encourages it to stay light and feathery, without settling. It may require a certain adaptation of technique (p. 227).

Powder snow on-trail ▼
Until the "trail bashers" beat it down to form a more compacted surface, a fresh snowfall of between 4ins and 1 ft (10 to 30cm) can lie on the trail as powder snow. Here, it has been churned up by the many skiers on the slope, but it still throws out the distinctive swirls or sprays of snow as you turn on it.

Learning to adapt your technique

As we explained at the beginning of this chapter, *functional skiing* is largely a question of adaptability. To ski both safely and efficiently, you must be able to choose the most appropriate technique for the situation. And the situation depends on the following factors. The *terrain* – are the slopes steep or gentle, open or wooded, smooth or mogulled, well-covered with snow or dotted with outcrops of rock? The *weather* – is it warm or cold, is visibility good or bad, are the shadows clear and the terrain well-defined or is the light flat and gray, making it difficult to see ahead and to pick out the contours? The *snow conditions* – is the snow hard or soft, new or old, wet or dry, even or uneven in consistency, easy to ski or difficult to turn in? You must also consider such other factors as the altitude of the slopes, the number of skiers on the runs, and whether you are skiing on or off the trail.

The chart on the opposite page sets out many of these conditions and indicates how they may affect the speed at which you ski. Speed is not only important in terms of safety. It also determines the

technique you use. This is because many turn initiations are only effective at a certain speed. The turning snowplow is basically a slow turning maneuver; parallel turning, on the other hand, can only be initiated properly when skiing fast enough. So, when conditions are poor and it is only possible to ski slowly, even the best skiers will use snowplow or stem turns. Remember that, in general, it is better to ski slowly and be over-cautious than to ski too fast and take unnecessary risks.

To some extent, the amount by which you will be able to vary your technique will depend on your level of skill. But, even as a beginner, you should be able to pick out the slopes where you can schuss quite safely, where you can make a series of linked snowplow turns, and where you may have no alternative other than to side-slip down.

Learning to analyze the terrain, to take into account the weather, and to be sensitive to changing snow conditions is something that is difficult to teach. It is a faculty that develops with experience, almost like a sixth sense.

How slope gradients are measured

The steepness of a slope affects whether it is graded as a beginner's, an intermediate or an expert trail (p.213). Its gradient should therefore give you some idea of how easy or difficult it is to ski. Consequently, it is useful to know how the gradients are calculated. There are two methods

in general use. One measures the slope in degrees; the other measures it as a percentage. The percentage system is easier to work out, but the degrees system is perhaps more immediately understandable to the skier. A simple conversion table is included below.

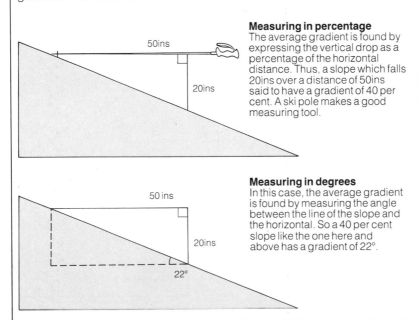

Measuring in percentage
The average gradient is found by expressing the vertical drop as a percentage of the horizontal distance. Thus, a slope which falls 20ins over a distance of 50ins said to have a gradient of 40 per cent. A ski pole makes a good measuring tool.

Measuring in degrees
In this case, the average gradient is found by measuring the angle between the line of the slope and the horizontal. So a 40 per cent slope like the one here and above has a gradient of 22°.

%	Degrees
100	45
90	42
80	39
70	35
60	31
50	27
40	22
30	17
20	11
10	6

Factors which control skiing speed	Good skiing conditions: ski fairly fast if you wish	Poor skiing conditions: ski slowly and carefully
Visibility	Clear light, good visibility	Diffuse light (no shadows)
	Bright sunshine	In shade, poor visibility
		Fog or mist
		Snowing or gale
Terrain	Open terrain where you can see well ahead	"Unknown" terrain where it is difficult to see ahead
	Slopes that are less than forty per cent steep	Slopes that are steeper than forty per cent
Snow conditions on-trail	Smooth, even surface	Uneven or rutted surface
	Medium-hard snow	Hard or icy snow
	Equal, consistent snow quality	Unequal, inconsistent snow quality
	Good snow cover, well prepared	Poor snow cover, stones, rocks or bare patches
	New snow on a solid base	New snow on an unequal, inconsistent base
Trail traffic	Fairly empty, plenty of room to turn	Crowded, restricted space
		On easy slopes where you must look out for beginners who may be learning to ski
Snow conditions off-trail	Consistent, soft snow	Inconsistent, soft snow
	Dry, soft snow	Wet, soft snow
	New snow on a solid base	Windswept snow
		Melting snow
		New snow covering rocks, bushes, trees, etc.
In spring	Good snow-crust which will carry your weight	Soft, thin snow-crust which is not strong enough to carry your weight
		Frozen, icy snow-crust
		Slush (wet, melting snow)
		New snow covering icy surface

Deep snow skiing

Deep snow comes in many forms. It can be very deep or only about ankle-height, it can be dry and light or wet and heavy, or it may be the classic waist-deep, feathery snow known as "powder" (p.220). Apart from the times when you are able to catch a fall of fresh snow on the prepared ski runs before the trail machines beat it down, all deep snow skiing is found off-trail.

There is no sense in talking about a specific deep snow technique. After conquering initial nervousness, any experienced skier with a very good technique on-trail should be able to transfer it to deep snow without too much difficulty. Maintaining speed, keeping your skis parallel and the tips up are the main points to bear in mind.

Deep snow off-trail ▼
In very deep snow, your skis will plane below the surface. You must adjust to the sensation of "floating" – like waterskiing – and learn to ski by feel, without seeing your skis.

Skiing down edge of trail ▲
You should be a proficient parallel skier before attempting deep snow. But, to get used to the feeling, practice directly after a fresh snowfall or down the trail-edge.

North American powder snow ▶
Powder conditions like these provide good skiers with the most exciting and exhilarating skiing. They are mostly found in North America and always off-trail.

Turning in new powder snow on a firm base

When the snow is light, fresh and only a few inches deep, and when it is lying on a solid base, hardly any change of technique is necessary – although the extra resistance which the snow creates may make turns a little harder to initiate. Any movement which you use on-trail can be used in these condi- tions – although the easiest and most enjoyable is parallel turning with "up" (p.105). This is shown below. Link your turns to maintain speed and, if necessary, exaggerate the unweighting motion slightly and bank your body well into the center of the turns, without too much edge pressure.

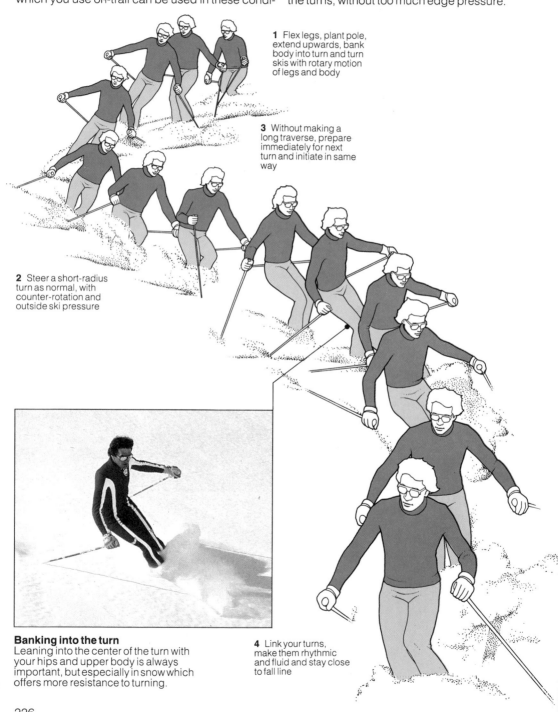

1 Flex legs, plant pole, extend upwards, bank body into turn and turn skis with rotary motion of legs and body

3 Without making a long traverse, prepare immediately for next turn and initiate in same way

2 Steer a short-radius turn as normal, with counter-rotation and outside ski pressure

4 Link your turns, make them rhythmic and fluid and stay close to fall line

Banking into the turn
Leaning into the center of the turn with your hips and upper body is always important, but especially in snow which offers more resistance to turning.

Turning in deep powder snow without a firm base

In very deep snow, turns are harder to initiate and you must prevent your ski tips from diving down beneath the surface. A certain amount of technique adaptation is therefore required. Experts will use a variety of movements according to what the situation demands but, in general, deep snow is best skied at a fairly high speed in a series of linked short-radius turns. Often, a combination of initiation elements (down-flexion, up-extension, absorption-extension and jet) will all be involved in these turns. Short swinging with an absorption-extension initiation is illustrated below.

1 Pre-rotate upper body, bend legs, plant pole and let body sink down as you feel resistance from snow: this unweights ski tips causing them to come up to the surface

2 Bank knees and body to change edges and initiate turn by rotating legs

4 Initiate turn with rotary leg movement as before, extend legs sideways to push snow away

3 Extend legs sideways to displace ski tails and steer turn. Without making a long traverse, prepare immediately for next turn

5 Steer turn and prepare immediately for next initiation

Keeping your ski tips up

In light powder, you should use the same normal stance that you use on-trail. This way, you will be more relaxed and better able to move. But, in deep snow, you must sit back to lift your ski tips up if they dive down into the snow. As the drawings below illustrate, your stance is therefore different in deep snow because your skis do not run parallel to the line of the slope.

Ankle-deep powder
Normal stance, legs flexed, weight over balls of feet, skis run parallel to slope on firm base beneath powder.

Knee-deep snow
When you sit back, your tips will rise up and your skis "plane" through snow – but this makes deep snow skiing tiring.

Spring snow skiing

At the end of the Alpine skiing season, during late March and April, or when skiing on the high glaciers in summer, snow conditions are quite different from those in mid-winter. The days are warmer and longer, and the continuous process of melting and re-freezing "ages" or "metamorphoses" the snow so that the flakes change into granules or small round particles of ice. This is known as "spring" or "corn" snow. Spring skiing on hot, sunny days can provide you with some of the best and most enjoy-able conditions you are likely to encounter, but it can also provide you with some of the worst. This is because spring snow changes from one extreme to another during the course of a day. The process can be divided into three phases: the very early morning, when the snow is still frozen and icy (sometimes called "hardpack"); the mid-morning, which gives slightly softer, excellent snow conditions as the ice begins to thaw; and the afternoon, when the snow may turn wet, heavy and slushy.

Snow conditions in the early morning

After a cold night, during which the temperature has dropped and snow which was wet and slushy the previous afternoon has been re-frozen, early morning conditions are likely to be difficult. The snow will be hard and icy, and, although it is tempting to ski fast, falls in which you skid downhill unable to stop are common. You must take special care, ski slowly and adapt your technique. As a general rule, ski in a more open stance than you might normally use. This will allow you to increase your angulation when traversing and give you better edge-grip, particularly over your downhill ski. When turning, avoid abrupt movements: strong unweighting is unnecessary since on hard snow there is very little friction and skis are easier to turn.

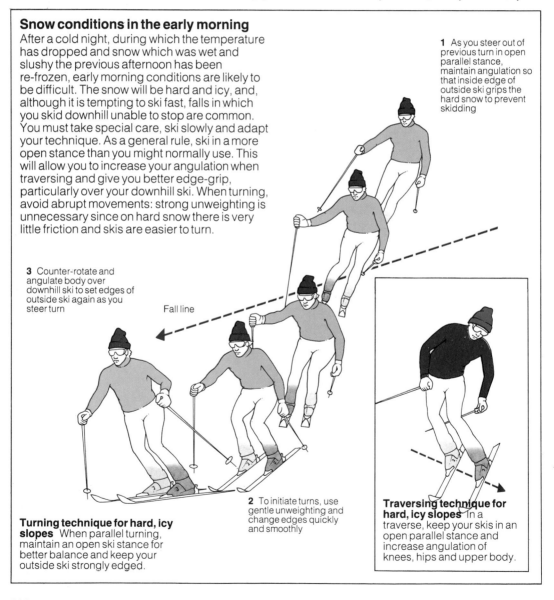

1 As you steer out of previous turn in open parallel stance, maintain angulation so that inside edge of outside ski grips the hard snow to prevent skidding

3 Counter-rotate and angulate body over downhill ski to set edges of outside ski again as you steer turn

Fall line

2 To initiate turns, use gentle unweighting and change edges quickly and smoothly

Turning technique for hard, icy slopes When parallel turning, maintain an open ski stance for better balance and keep your outside ski strongly edged.

Traversing technique for hard, icy slopes In a traverse, keep your skis in an open parallel stance and increase angulation of knees, hips and upper body.

Snow conditions later in the day

By about ten o'clock in the morning the sun will be warmer and the temperature will probably have risen enough to melt the top surface of the snow. These conditions are ideal for skiing. The slopes are no longer treacherously slippery, the snow is slightly softer but still has a good solid base, and it is fast and easy to turn on. Even the "singing" sound that the skis make is different. No other snow conditions provide such easy, enjoyable skiing.

However, conditions like these may not last long – perhaps only from ten to about twelve o'clock. If the temperature continues to rise, the snow will continue to thaw, and the "perfect" spring snow will turn rapidly into slush. This is particularly true of south-facing slopes. North-facing slopes, which are shaded from the sun, are cooler and the snow is often better. North-east or north-west-facing slopes, of course, have the advantage of good snow plus some sun in the early morning or in the late afternoon and evening.

Skiing in wet, heavy snow is difficult and can be dangerous. Bad falls, in which the skis dive below the surface and legs get twisted, are common. If you *have* to ski in these conditions, ski slowly and make stem turns (p.96).

"Ideal" spring snow skiing
The best time for skiing is in mid-morning when the sun has just begun to melt the very top surface of hard snow. The slopes then have the distinctive mirror-like sheen which these pictures illustrate, and your skis will edge well, turn easily and leave barely any tracks behind you.

Mogul skiing

The term "mogul" is thought to derive from an Alpine dialect word, *mugel*, meaning a "small hill". Moguls are simply bumps in the snow, but they vary in size and shape from small, rounded humps which are easy to ski to high, virtually sheer-sided ridges that are much more difficult. A "mogul field" is a steep slope completely covered with bumps and dips of this sort.

To a beginner, mogul slopes can be a very daunting prospect, and having to traverse or side-slip down them because you are unable to turn can be a nightmare; to an experienced skier, they can be challenging and enjoyable. Indeed, mogul skiing forms the basis of one of the three freestyle disciplines (p.170-73).

The ideal technique for skiing moguls is absorption-

extension (p.120-23). The down-flexion during which all these turns are initiated helps you absorb the bumps and keep your skis in contact with the snow. The bumps themselves also aid the initiation of each turn (see opposite). If you are skiing a mogul field for the first time, it is a good idea to try and follow a good skier and turn where and when he or she turns. This is because choosing a good line is half the secret (p.233). Do not be afraid to stop for a few moments and plan out the best way to ski down. Try to let the moguls dictate your rhythm and the flexion and extension of your legs.

The sequence below shows a skier using the absorption-extension technique at high speed. But moguls can be skied slowly just as easily if you initiate your turns on top of the bumps.

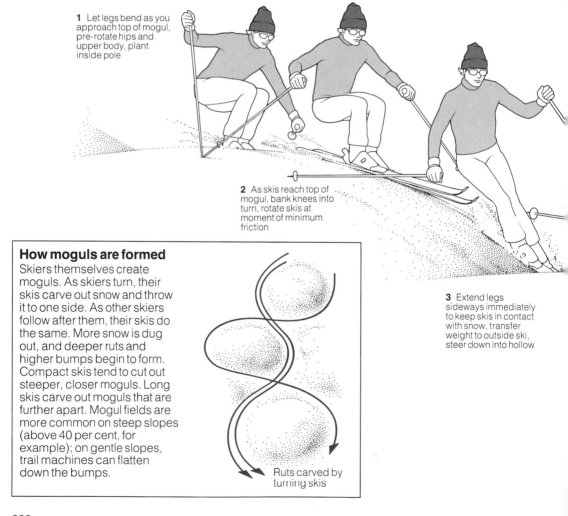

1 Let legs bend as you approach top of mogul, pre-rotate hips and upper body, plant inside pole

2 As skis reach top of mogul, bank knees into turn, rotate skis at moment of minimum friction

3 Extend legs sideways immediately to keep skis in contact with snow, transfer weight to outside ski, steer down into hollow

How moguls are formed
Skiers themselves create moguls. As skiers turn, their skis carve out snow and throw it to one side. As other skiers follow after them, their skis do the same. More snow is dug out, and deeper ruts and higher bumps begin to form. Compact skis tend to cut out steeper, closer moguls. Long skis carve out moguls that are further apart. Mogul fields are more common on steep slopes (above 40 per cent, for example); on gentle slopes, trail machines can flatten down the bumps.

Ruts carved by turning skis

Turning on top of the moguls

Bumps provide a natural pivot for absorption-extension turning. There are two reasons for this: first, because the counter-pressure as you ski up the side of a mogul flexes your legs automatically into the correct position for the turn initiation; second, because a ski on top of a mogul offers less resistance to turning than a ski that is flat on the snow.

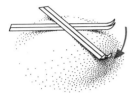

Using the bump as a pivot-point
On top of bump, only center of ski is in contact with snow. There is no resistance or friction at either front or back, and ski will pivot easily.

The turn initiation
Choosing his moment exactly, this skier initiates his turn when his skis are hardly in contact with the snow at all.

4 Let legs bend again, plant other pole, turn skis on crest of bump by banking knees and rotating feet

5 Extend legs sideways into dip, flex them as you ski up side of next mogul, keep legs working as shock absorbers to "suck up" bumps and dips while upper body remains still and relaxed

6 Plant inside pole and initiate turn on top of mogul again

Choosing a line through the moguls

The essence of mogul skiing is to make the terrain work for you, not against you. This means picking a line through the bumps and dips which allows you to link your turns and ski fluidly and rhythmically. Perhaps the classic way to ski a mogul field is to turn on top of a bump, steer down into the trough between the next moguls and then turn again after skiing up to the top of another bump. However, you may like to make quicker, shorter-radius turns, staying closer to the fall line and turning from crest to crest – that is, on the top of *each* mogul. Alternatively, you can ski the hollows between the bumps, as shown below. This is similar to skiing a rutted slalom course, and you must ski faster because there is more resistance to turning than when on the top of the bumps. You will also need good edge control to hold your line. In each case, timing is critical. You must look ahead, plan your movements, judge your speed carefully and react quickly. Mogul skiing is easier on compact skis, which are quicker to turn, than on long skis. Since mogul fields are formed mostly by compact skis, you will also find that long skis do not "fit" so well – the tips and tails tend to catch.

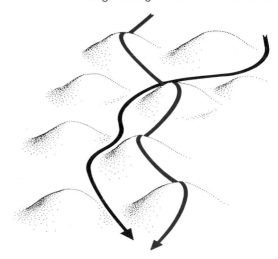

Skiing the hollows
The black line illustrates the path of a skier who stays in the dips and turns through the hollows in between the bumps.

Skiing the bumps
The blue line shows the "athletic" way of turning frequently, with more extension-flexion, on top of each mogul.

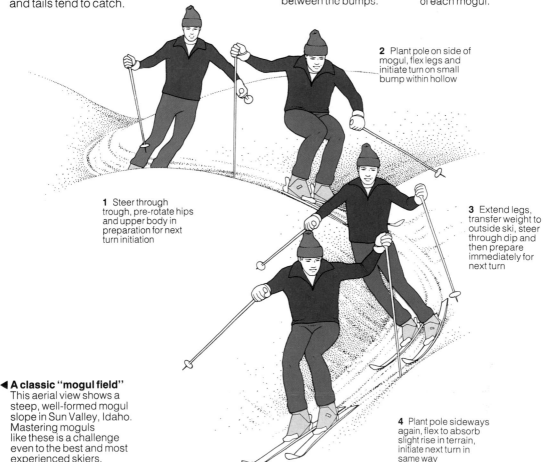

1 Steer through trough, pre-rotate hips and upper body in preparation for next turn initiation

2 Plant pole on side of mogul, flex legs and initiate turn on small bump within hollow

3 Extend legs, transfer weight to outside ski, steer through dip and then prepare immediately for next turn

4 Plant pole sideways again, flex to absorb slight rise in terrain, initiate next turn in same way

◄ A classic "mogul field"
This aerial view shows a steep, well-formed mogul slope in Sun Valley, Idaho. Mastering moguls like these is a challenge even to the best and most experienced skiers.

Skiing difficult situations on-trail

Pitting yourself against situations which demand skill and control is part of the appeal of skiing. Sometimes, you may deliberately wish to seek out challenging terrain and snow conditions – for example, moguls (p.230), deep snow (p.236) or steep slopes (as shown here). At other times, just skiing on the marked trails will present you with situations that require extra care and, perhaps, a slightly different technique. Two such situations are illustrated in the photographs on the opposite page. However, they are special examples, and it is well worth knowing in general how to cope safely with such things as a series of undulating bumps and dips or "slope edges" – points where the gradient suddenly changes from steep to flat or from flat to steep. These are covered on p.62-3.

"Gunbarrels" or "funnels" are steep-sided ravines where the trail narrows and is often hemmed in on either side by rock outcrops. If the gradient is not too steep and if the surface is fairly smooth, gunbarrels can be skied by making linked turns – zig-zagging down by turning against the walls on either side. However, if the gunbarrel is very narrow, very steep and heavily mogulled, then side-slipping down the edge, close to one wall, may be the safest technique.

Narrow woodland paths are another common hazard. They often contain dangerous, icy patches, and they may be deeply rutted; if the snow cover is not good, there is always a risk of catching a ski tip on a tree root. When the path is too narrow to use turns to control your speed, it is best to resort to snowplowing (p.64), or a "half plow" (p.75); when too steep, use side-slipping (p.76).

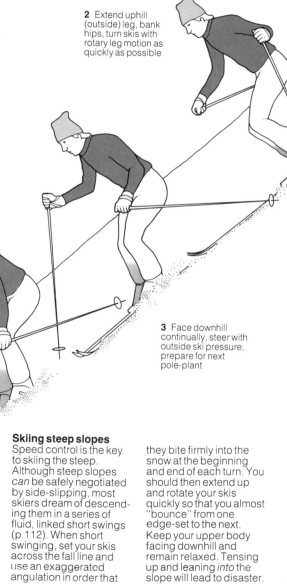

2 Extend uphill (outside) leg, bank hips, turn skis with rotary leg motion as quickly as possible

3 Face downhill continually, steer with outside ski pressure, prepare for next pole-plant

4 Flex down, push knees and hips into slope, press against downhill ski to make another strong edge-check

5 Extend uphill (outside) leg, bank hips and rotate skis again to initiate another fast, short-radius turn

Skiing steep slopes
Speed control is the key to skiing the steep. Although steep slopes *can* be safely negotiated by side-slipping, most skiers dream of descending them in a series of fluid, linked short swings (p.112). When short swinging, set your skis across the fall line and use an exaggerated angulation in order that they bite firmly into the snow at the beginning and end of each turn. You should then extend up and rotate your skis quickly so that you almost "bounce" from one edge-set to the next. Keep your upper body facing downhill and remain relaxed. Tensing up and leaning *into* the slope will lead to disaster.

◀ **A "ski road"**
Here, a kind of man-made "ledge" has been built to carry the trail across the side of the mountain. There is a fairly steep "headwall" on one side, and an equally steep, fenced-off drop on the other. In situations like this, it is dangerous to ski fast: although *you* may be able to maintain control, other skiers around you may not, and most accidents which occur in such places are caused by collisions. If you choose to descend by making linked turns, try to stay in the middle of the run. If you decide to snowplow or side-slip down, keep to one side – where the snow will probably be softer anyway.

1 Flex down, press against downhill ski and set edges to check speed, plant downhill pole

A narrow run through rock ▶ outcrops Where the trail narrows in order to wind through steep areas of exposed rock, care and control are essential. There are two reasons for this. First, the snow conditions are likely to be poor because the constant passage of skiers tends to create ruts and throws much of the snow to either side of the trail, leaving icy or bare patches in the middle. Second, these situations are inevitably "bottlenecks", with the result that large numbers of skiers, all travelling at different speeds and all of varying ability, find themselves forced into the same restricted space. If the run is very crowded, it may be best to wait at the top for it to clear slightly before skiing down. When you set off, remember that, according to the "code of conduct" (p.215), the slower skier in front of you always has the right of way. It is up to you to avoid him, not his responsibility to avoid you. On the steep, man-made section of trail in this photograph, the skiers are of all types (adults, youngsters and a very small child) and the techniques vary from snowplow turning to schussing and side-slipping.

Off-trail skiing

All off-trail skiing is potentially dangerous and must be approached with *respect*. Off-trail descent routes are *not* patrolled by the rescue teams, and the risk of avalanches always exists. You should therefore never ski off-trail alone. Travel in a group and, if you are unfamiliar with the area, get an experienced guide or a ski instructor to go with you. Check the local avalanche bulletins before departing, find out which slopes are dangerous, and avoid them. In short, *inform yourself* and follow all the safety precautions against being caught by avalanches (p. 248).

So, having emphasized the risks, what are the attractions of off-trail skiing? Ask any good skier and they will probably answer with one or all of the following: the challenge of skiing unprepared, untracked snow; the desire to get away from crowded trails and deeply rutted mogul fields; and the peace and silence of the winter atmosphere.

Off-trail skiing can take three forms: travelling up by way of the normal cable cars or lifts and then skiing down the descent routes rather than the trails; "helicopter skiing" (p. 238); and "touring", which is done under your own steam (p. 240).

Powder snow skiing ▲
Most off-trail skiing is done in deep snow – in fact, the exhilaration of skiing deep, fresh powder like this (above Verbier, Switzerland) is perhaps its greatest appeal. A good, solid technique is required and, as we show on p. 224-7, some movements are more effective and more functional than others.

◀ **Off-trail skiing below the tree line** Not all off-trail skiing is done on the open, high-altitude slopes. Off-trail descent routes often run down through woodland – where, especially in North America, some of the best powder can be found.

High-altitude touring ▶
All ski touring is off-trail. Some of the tours are well known; others are not and must be navigated by the skiers themselves. Here a ski tourer descends an off-trail slope high in the Canadian Rockies.

Helicopter skiing

"Heli-skiing", as it is also known, has opened up huge areas of otherwise inaccessible terrain. Helicopters take the place of ski lifts. They can transport skiers up to the top of a specially chosen off-trail run within a few minutes, meet them again at the bottom, after their descent, and immediately take them up again for another run. Most helicopter skiing takes place in North America, especially in the Canadian Rockies of south-eastern British Columbia where conditions are usually very good indeed. It can be found in the Alps – although not in France, where environmentalists have had it banned – but there are stringent safety regulations to minimize accident and avalanche dangers.

◄ The start of the run
Here, the helicopter hovers above the skiers as they begin their descent. All heli-skiing parties *must* be led by a highly experienced, specially trained guide.

Heli-skiers in action ▶
Because of the cost of operating the helicopters, heli-skiing is very expensive – and it is not for inexperienced skiers. However, the scenery is magnificent, the skiing exhilarating and the snow conditions often unparalleled. All the photographs here were taken in the Canadian Rockies.

The setting down ▼
The helicopter lands on a flat area at the top of the descent route to deposit the skiers and their equipment. It is fitted with special skis for landing on snow.

Alpine ski touring

Also known as "ski mountaineering", ski touring is the perfect way to explore the mountains in winter, and it is the logical progression for anyone who enjoys off-trail skiing. It is a little like cross-country skiing, except that it is high-altitude, involves steep ascents and descents, and is done on specially modified Alpine equipment.

Its chief appeal lies in the silence and the isolation of skiing away from the crowded trails, and in the fact that ski tourers are totally independent: they travel under their own power, climbing uphill as well as skiing down, and have no need of lift installations or trail machines. They carry everything they need (food, extra clothing and equipment, etc.) in backpacks. Indeed, many European ski tourers are also Alpinists during the summer months. However, ski touring is not for beginners. It requires solid skiing experience and, if there is no guide, a sound knowledge of the mountains. The routes are not marked, and navigation must be done with a map and, in bad weather, with a compass.

Circular tours that can be completed in a single day are common, but there are also various famous routes which last several days. These include the *Haute Route* (p.244-5), the *Tour Soleil* (from Andermatt to Zermatt in Switzerland), and the *Oetzal Rundtour* and *Stubai* circuit in Austria. In Europe, overnight stops can be spent in Alpine Club mountain huts, but in North America these are rare and most tourers must carry tents to camp out in.

The ascent ▶
Three skiers climb uphill in the Bernina mountain range on the Swiss-Italian border. Alpine tourers invariably climb in single file so that their skis can run in each other's tracks. The leader of the group goes first and sets the pace. On long ascents, a certain amount of strength and stamina is required – especially at heights of over 3,000m (9,843ft) where the air becomes thin.

◀ The descent
After the long climb up, either wearing his skis with skins attached to them or carrying them over his shoulder, this ski tourer skis down from one of the high peaks above Zermatt in Switzerland. Special care must be taken when skiing unpatrolled off-trail slopes. Notice must always be taken of avalanche warnings, since no skier can afford to take unnecessary risks.

Safety when ski touring

All ski tourers should travel in a group, with an experienced leader or a mountain guide who will take responsibility for safety. The equipment should be organized and the route planned well in advance. There is often a danger of avalanches when ski touring and the strictest precautions should be taken when skiing in a high-risk area (p.248). Each skier should carry a radio bleeper switched to "transmitter" and an avalanche shovel (in some countries this is in fact an official recommendation). When crossing glaciers, the group should rope themselves together in case someone falls into a snow-covered crevasse.

All ski tourers must be proficient, experienced skiers. The skiing may be difficult and conditions are not always good. The weather can change rapidly from one extreme to another, and you may come across every snow type, from deep power to hard, icy snow, in the course of a single day's skiing. Most tourers start skiing at first light and stop early in the afternoon when the snow begins to deteriorate.

Climbing technique ▲
Ascents are usually planned to avoid steep climbs and to be on as even a gradient as possible. A regular, steady climbing rhythm helps prevent exhaustion and conserve energy. Most climbs are made in the form of a zig-zag (an uphill traverse, a turn, then another traverse, etc). It is quite possible to climb 300m (1,000ft) in about an hour.

◄ The climbing step
The technique used for ascents is basically the same as the cross-country climbing step (p.196). Skins stop the skis from sliding backwards and the binding unlocks at the back to allow the heel to rise up.

Ski touring equipment

The boots and bindings used for ski touring are similar in principle to those used by all skiers earlier this century. This is because they must be adaptable for both downhill skiing and for climbing. The boots are softer than normal Alpine ones and have a ridged sole so that they grip well when walking on snow. The bindings hold the toe and heel of the boot firmly in place when skiing downhill, but can be "unlocked" at the back to allow the heel to rise when walking or climbing. Touring skis are usually shorter than average and fairly lightweight, but they must be strong as well as flexible at the front. Some have a hole in the tip so that they can be used to make an emergency sledge. Skins, made of nylon or mohair, are stuck or strapped to the bottom of the skis to make them grip when climbing. Special ski touring poles are available which are telescopically extendable and which have an adjustable strap to make climbing easier. Some may have detachable handles so they can be used as avalanche probes. Finally, the backpack. It must contain extra clothing, food, maps (and, in the case of the leader, a compass), reserve sunglasses, skin cream, first aid and repair kits, rope, a snow shovel and an avalanche bleeper.

Boots

Standard Alpine ski boots can be used for short tours, but for long treks special boots like the one shown here are essential. They are warm, waterproof and much more comfortable, and have "Vibram" profiled soles and adjustable hinges which allow them to flex backwards and forwards when walking uphill.

Mountaineering equipment

Tourers like these who tackle the high glaciers and mountain peaks should also carry ropes, ice-axes, crampons and pitons and a lightweight nylon bivouac.

"Harscheisen"

This toothed metal plate, also called a *Firn* or *Harsch* blade, fits onto the ski beneath the binding to give additional edge-grip when climbing on steep or icy slopes.

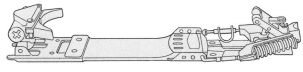

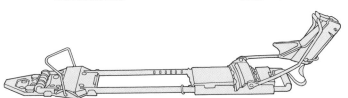

Bindings

These consist of a toe-piece and a heel-piece, either all in one or in two separate sections. There is usually a simple clip which allows the heel to lift off the ski for walking uphill but which locks it tight for downhill running. The hinge at the front should be as close as possible to the toe of the boot to make walking easier.

The "Haute Route"

One of the most famous of all the Alpine ski tours is the one known as the *Haute Route*. It is about 120km (75 miles) long, it stretches between Argentière, near Chamonix, in France and Saas Fee in Switzerland, and on the way it takes in some of the highest and most dramatic peaks in the Alps. The classic route is indicated on the map below, although it can be varied. There is some controversy over the direction in which the route should be skied but, as a rule, it is best to travel from west to east. The complete tour can be done in about a week, although if diversions are made to climb some of the high peaks, such as Monte Rosa, Pigne d'Arolla or Grand Combin, it will take a few days longer. Overnight stops are spent in French or Swiss Alpine Club huts. The ones most frequently used are also marked on the map – although there are many others dotted throughout this region.

The *Haute Route* is not signposted in any way and navigation must be done with Swiss maps (to a scale of 1:50,000) and a compass. It is essential to travel with an experienced guide. Much of the route is over glaciers and there is always danger from crevasses and avalanches. The tour is not usually attempted until May. Before that, temperatures are too cold, the weather is unreliable, the days are too short and snow conditions can be dangerous.

Apart from very steep climbs where skis must be carried, and the section between Orsières and Bourg St Pierre where it is customary to take a bus, virtually the whole journey – including ascents and descents – can be completed on skis.

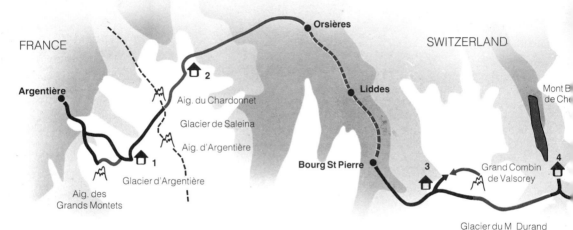

FRANCE

Argentière

2

Aig. du Chardonnet

Glacier de Saleina

Aig. d'Argentière

1

Glacier d'Argentière

Aig. des
Grands Montets

Orsières

SWITZERLAND

Liddes

Mont B
de Che

Bourg St Pierre

3

Grand Combin
de Valsorey

4

Glacier du M Durand

The climbs

On fairly gentle slopes, ascents can be made in a straight line, heading directly uphill. The skins which tourers attach to the bottom of their skis are nowadays usually made of nylon or polypropylene instead of the original seal skin and are claimed to give a good "grip" on slopes of up to 70 per cent (35°). On slopes that are steeper than this, it is more effective and less tiring to climb in a series of traverses linked by "step turning" (p.94), zig-zagging uphill.

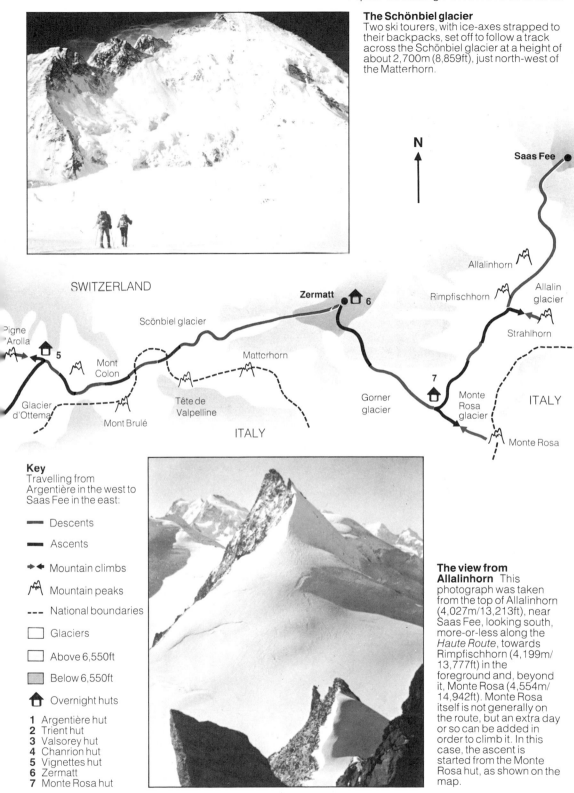

The Schönbiel glacier
Two ski tourers, with ice-axes strapped to their backpacks, set off to follow a track across the Schönbiel glacier at a height of about 2,700m (8,859ft), just north-west of the Matterhorn.

N

Saas Fee

SWITZERLAND

Allalinhorn

Zermatt 6

Scönbiel glacier

Rimpfischhorn

Allalin glacier

Pigne Arolla 5

Mont Colon

Matterhorn

Strahlhorn

7

Glacier d'Ottema

Tête de Valpelline

Gorner glacier

Monte Rosa glacier

ITALY

Mont Brulé

ITALY

Monte Rosa

Key
Travelling from Argentière in the west to Saas Fee in the east:

— Descents

— Ascents

►◄ Mountain climbs

⩕ Mountain peaks

--- National boundaries

☐ Glaciers

☐ Above 6,550ft

▨ Below 6,550ft

⌂ Overnight huts

1 Argentière hut
2 Trient hut
3 Valsorey hut
4 Chanrion hut
5 Vignettes hut
6 Zermatt
7 Monte Rosa hut

The view from Allalinhorn This photograph was taken from the top of Allalinhorn (4,027m/13,213ft), near Saas Fee, looking south, more-or-less along the *Haute Route*, towards Rimpfischhorn (4,199m/ 13,777ft) in the foreground and, beyond it, Monte Rosa (4,554m/ 14,942ft). Monte Rosa itself is not generally on the route, but an extra day or so can be added in order to climb it. In this case, the ascent is started from the Monte Rosa hut, as shown on the map.

Avalanches

Almost all fatal ski accidents are caused by avalanches. Despite the considerable scientific research that has been put into the study of avalanches, they remain largely unpredictable. And, despite the enormous amounts of money spent on making the mountains as safe as possible – by building snow fences or planting trees and regularly patrolling high-risk areas – avalanches cannot always be prevented. Every winter in the mountains, avalanches cause millions of dollars worth of damage.

Most skiers know little, if anything, about why, when and where avalanches occur. One of the most common misconceptions is that they only happen in the high mountain areas, not on the lower slopes and on the trails where everybody skis. This is untrue; avalanches can occur *anywhere* given the right conditions.

Put simply, an avalanche takes place when the forces of friction and internal cohesion no longer hold the snow in place on the slope. It fractures or crumbles and then begins to slip downhill under the influence of gravity. The process is usually sudden and normally happens without warning. Nevertheless, there are certain terrain, snow and weather conditions which, when combined, make an avalanche more likely than at other times. Briefly, these are: *the steepness and profile of the slope –* open, exposed slopes of between 30° and 45° are the most prone to avalanches, although they can also occur on gentle 15° slopes; *the composition of the snow –* "floating" layers within the snow mass are particularly unstable; *a new snowfall –* in principle, every new fall of snow increases the risk of an avalanche; *the wind –* which can cause surface sliding avalanches and which can build up dangerous drifts of snow, especially on lee slopes; *the temperature –* a sudden rise dramatically increases avalanche risk, particularly in spring.

Whatever your level of ability, it is worth bearing in mind that a large proportion of avalanches are caused by skiers themselves, and that they are usually the result of ignorance and reckless behavior. To reduce the danger to yourself and others, follow *all* the precautions outlined on p.248.

Types of avalanche

Avalanches vary according to the specific situation in which they occur, and they are notoriously difficult to classify. However, they usually follow some sort of pattern, and three broad categories can be distinguished on the basis of their shape, consistency and the manner in which they start. These are *slab* avalanches, *loose snow* avalanches and *powder snow* avalanches. Slab avalanches are perhaps the most treacherous for skiers, and they are the type that they most often trigger themselves. The track left by a simple traverse can break the surface and cause a fracture line which may send huge compacted blocks of snow, varying in width from a few yards to more than a mile, sliding downhill with tremendous force. Loose snow and powder snow avalanches are composed of snow which does not stick together in clumps.

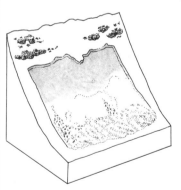

Slab avalanche
Usually marked by a jagged breakaway line, these are always caused by a "cut" made across the slope. This releases blocks of compacted, unstable snow which slide rapidly downhill.

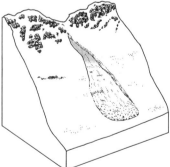

Loose snow avalanche
These may occur when the snow is either wet or dry. Usually triggered by a temperature rise and often occurring beneath rocks, they start from a single point and are of loose snow.

Powder snow avalanche
Less common, these occur when the snow is thrown into the air. The effect is more like an explosion than a conventional avalanche: the dry, cold, airborne snow can reach 320kph (120mph).

The ski patrol

It is the responsibility of the ski
patrol to make the trails safe for
skiers, to close them when there
is avalanche danger, and to put
out reports and warnings for
high-risk off-trail areas. They
often set off avalanches deliberately to avoid them starting
accidentally and unpredictably.
When necessary, the ski patrol
also acts as a rescue team. Portable radio "bleepers", worn by
skiers and transmitting to receiv-
ers carried by the ski patrol,
make the problem of locating a
buried avalanche victim much
easier, but the traditional
methods of specially trained avalanche dogs and metal sounding
rods are still widely used.

Searching for survivors ▶
A Swiss avalanche rescue team
search for buried skiers using long
metal rods to probe beneath the
surface of the avalanche.

Early morning patrol ▲
At first light, the ski patrol is out on
the mountain checking the snow
conditions for the possibility of
avalanches during the day. The
job is highly dangerous.

◀ Triggering an avalanche
In certain situations, the ski patrol
will release an avalanche on
purpose – when they know that
there are no skiers on the slopes
below. They do this by either
cutting a traverse across the slope
or by using explosives. A Swiss ski
patrol is shown here above a
typical slab avalanche, two to
three seconds after the explosion.

Avalanche precautions

When going off-trail skiing, you have a choice of where you ski. Consequently, *do not ski in areas where there is an avalanche risk*. This is the simplest and most obvious rule – but the one most frequently ignored. When ski touring, you may find you *have* to cross a dangerous or suspect area. If so, take the following precautions. Even if there appears to be no risk, take care.

● Inform yourself: check the bulletins and the ski patrol, and avoid slopes similar to those where avalanches have already occurred

● Wear a radio transmitter, switch it to "transmitter", and carry an avalanche shovel and probe

● If you do not have a transmitter, wear a 10m (33ft) avalance "trail cord": it will float to the surface of the snow if you are buried

● Never ski alone. Travel in a group if possible, but keep a slight distance from the other members

● Always have a possible escape route in mind

● Loosen your bindings, remove safety straps (if you have them), and slip hands out of pole straps

● Choose your route carefully: if you have to traverse, follow the procedure shown below, and move into the center of the slope only when safe

Traversing a potential avalanche slope

Groups should stop at a safe point on the edge of the slope. One member traverses across as high as possible, then a second member makes another traverse, 1-2m (3-6 ft) below the first. If there is no snow-slip between the two lines, the others follow. They all ski down the side of the slope so they can move away quickly should an avalanche start.

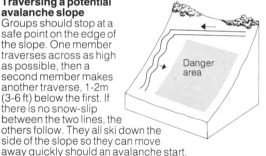

Danger area

What to do in an avalanche

The most important thing is to react quickly and calmly. First of all, try to ski away to one side out of the path of the avalanche. If you cannot, then release your bindings, let go of your poles and try to hold on to any trees or rocks so that the snow flows past. If the avalanche overtakes you, close your mouth and try to keep to the surface by making "swimming" movements. Shortly before the avalanche stops, use all your strength to stretch upwards with your arms and try to create an air cavity around your face and chest so that you can breathe. Call or shout out as soon as you can hear rescuers above you. Above all, do not struggle needlessly; reserve your strength. Remember that help will be on its way and that past experience shows that skiers *can* survive avalanches.

Avalanche rescue procedure

There is a time limit to how long a buried skier can survive beneath an avalanche. Speed and a systematic, organized procedure are therefore vital if the rescue is to be successful.

If you witness an avalanche, this is what you should do. Watch those who have been caught up in the slide. If they have been buried, use ski poles or articles of clothing to mark the exact spots where the snow overtook them and where they disappeared. Discuss where the buried skiers may be located (bearing in mind that they are most likely to be lying in the flow direction of the avalanche, below the point where they disappeared), and search the surface of the snow for any pieces of equipment, clothing or signs of an avalanche cord. If you find any, mark the point where they were discovered and begin searching the surrounding area immediately. If you find nothing, and if you have not got a radio transmitter, try listening for cries of help. Sound carries well, and, if you kneel down with your ear to the snow, you may hear something.

At this point, send for help from the rescue services. Do not hesitate; it is better to call them out even if ultimately they are not required. If possible, send two people rapidly to the nearest telephone with the following information: the precise location, the time the avalanche occurred, the number of victims, and the number of helpers already at the site.

Those left behind should begin probing beneath the surface of the avalanche. the rescue service will bring an avalanche dog and special sounding rods with them. Until they arrive, use upturned ski poles, skis or any other suitable objects. It is important that this is done systematically. Begin by probing at intervals of every 75cm (30ins), mark off the areas you have covered and then, if you have no success, go back and probe again at intervals of every 25cm (10ins).

If you discover any buried skiers, first free their head and remove any snow from their mouth, nose and throat so that they can breathe freely. Then dig them out completely, keep them warm with extra clothing, and, if you can, attend to any minor injuries. If they are conscious, move them to a safe place. However, keep an eye on them. If they show any sign of vomiting, turn them quickly onto their stomach.

If the victims are unconscious, first see whether or not they are breathing and check for a pulse-rate. If there seems to be no sign of life, clear their air passages of snow, give artificial respiration and, later, heart massage until they begin breathing again. Meanwhile, keep them as warm as possible.

First aid for skiers

The very nature of skiing means that injuries do sometimes occur, although they are much less frequent and less serious than they once were. This is largely due to the introduction of modern safety-release bindings. However, bindings only work efficiently if they are adjusted properly. In fact, nearly all serious leg injuries are caused by the skier's bindings not being correctly set.

Most accidents are the result of falls or collisions, and almost always might have been avoided by taking the few, simple precautions outlined below. The chief cause of falling amongst beginners is tenseness, itself due to fear. The only solution to this is not to attempt speeds and situations which are far above your ability. The chief cause of collisions is reckless behavior. The solution, here, is careful and considerate skiing.

It is the responsibility of the ski instructor to guarantee the safety of the class. Every instructor has a first aid certificate and should always carry a first aid kit. However, if the accident is serious, the rescue service must be called out. Rescue teams, usually made up of specially trained local skiers and mountain guides, have a remarkable reputation. Once notified, they can reach injured skiers very rapidly, and will transport them down to the valley by sled (the infamous "bloodwagon"), by snowmobile or, if necessary, by helicopter. These rescue methods are expensive and a good reason for taking out accident insurance.

Accident precautions

● Check, maintain and correctly adjust all of your equipment

● Warm up before you begin skiing (p. 278)

● Stop skiing as soon as you feel tired

● On-trail, take note of all signs and markers, and follow the "code of conduct" (p. 215)

● Off-trail, avoid areas where there is a risk of avalanches, and never ski alone

● Learn to fall safely (p. 50)

● Ski within the limits of your own ability and always adapt your speed to the situation

● In bad weather and poor visibility, ski slowly and take special care

● Choose a safe line of descent, pass any hazardous points swiftly and one skier at a time, and try to avoid skiing on hard, steep trails and in melting, heavy spring snow

Accident procedure

If you are present at the scene of an accident or if you come across an injured skier, it will help if you know in advance what to do. Begin by marking the spot and protecting the victim by crossing skis and ski poles and sticking them into the snow on the uphill side. This will give other skiers plenty of warning.

If the victim is conscious, ask him where he feels pain. Take off his skis carefully, but do not remove his boots. Let him lie in the position he feels to be most comfortable, but keep him warm (possibly using your own jacket). Send someone to inform the rescue service as quickly as possible – telling them the nature of the accident and exactly where it is according to the number on the nearest trail marker. They will arrive shortly. In the meantime, if you suspect that the victim has hurt his back or trunk, do not move him – except only slightly if it is necessary to alleviate pain. This should be done by lifting him by his clothes with as many pairs of hands as possible.

If the victim is unconscious, check that his air passages are clear and lay him gently on his side with his mouth open. Check his pulse and whether or not he is breathing. If necessary, give artificial respiration. Keep him warm and wait with him until the rescue team arrive.

If the victim is bleeding, the best thing is to raise the injured limb and apply direct pressure (by hand or with a piece of clean cloth) to try and stop the bleeding.

Hypothermia and frostbite are very unlikely in the normal course of skiing. However, in an accident, where an injured skier may be lying in the snow for some time waiting to be rescued, the risk is increased. Hypothermia, in which the body temperature drops dangerously low, can be treated by getting the victim into a warm room, by wrapping him in warm clothing, and by giving him hot drinks. If necessary, he can be kept warm on the mountain by close body contact. Frostbite or "local freezing" usually occurs in the fingers and toes or on the tip of the nose and ear lobes. The skin goes white and the parts become numb. The best treatment is to keep the patient moving and warm and get him indoors. Then immerse the frozen part in luke-warm water which you can gradually heat up to about 50°C (120°F) by adding hot water. In serious cases, get the patient to a doctor as soon as possible, and *on no account* rub the frostbitten parts with snow.

Ski lifts

Perhaps more than any other single factor, ski lifts have revolutionized skiing. Before the invention of mechanized mountain transport, the only way that skiers could get uphill in order to ski downhill was to climb – either carrying their skis or wearing them with skins strapped to the bottom to stop them sliding backwards. The climb might take several hours, leaving the skier with time for only one brief downhill run per day. The new ski lifts changed all this: as a result the number of skiers grew enormously – and with them came new developments in ski techniques, ski teaching and ski equipment.

It was the Swiss who led the way. They had already built narrow-gauge mountain railways which ran up a central toothed rail, and had overcome many of the problems involved in operating them throughout the winter. They also developed "funiculars", carriages that run on much steeper tracks but which are pulled uphill by cables.

Although the idea was not new, the Swiss were also the first to build a "cable car" for skiers at Säntis in 1935. Cable cars are large cabins, holding up to 125 people, which hang from a cable suspended between pylons. They are pulled uphill by a separate traction cable which is driven from the engine houses at the top and bottom of the mountain. Two cars travel at the same time; one goes up while the other comes down, and they pass in the middle. Cable cars have opened up new heights since they can negotiate near-vertical slopes and cross the most difficult or inaccessible terrain, and they are the most spectacular form of mountain transport.

But perhaps more important to the growth of recreational skiing was the invention of the "drag lift". The forerunner of all modern drag lifts was the simple "rope tow". Driven by a petrol engine, it consisted of a loop of rope which pulled the skiers uphill. The first successful ones appeared in 1932 in Switzerland and at Shawbridge in Canada. Then, in 1934, a Swiss engineer called Erich Konstam added T-shaped wooden bars and paved the way for the modern "T-bar" lift which pulls up two skiers at a time (or one in the American variation, the "J-bar"). And in the early 1950s, a French engineer called Pomagalski took the principle a stage further by inventing the more versatile Poma "button" lift. Other forms of drag lift have also been designed specially for nursery slopes (p.252).

T-bars and button lifts are the most common form of ski lift in Europe; but in North America and Japan they are outnumbered by the "chair lift". This was invented by an American, Jim Curran, and the first one was built in the winter of 1936-7 at Sun Valley, Idaho. Chair lifts were introduced to Europe in 1948-9. Later, they were joined by "gondolas" or "telecabines", which are rather like a series of miniature cable cars or enclosed chair lifts.

Other non-standard forms of mountain transport are snowmobiles, SnoCats and light aircraft. And, for those who can afford it, helicopters have opened up the experience of off-trail "heli-skiing".

Basically, ski lifts can be divided into two categories: those that you ride with your skis on, and those that you ride with your skis off. The second type (funiculars, cable cars and gondolas) require no special knowledge or technique, but there is a certain "knack" to riding lifts with your skis on (nursery slope, T-bars, button and chair lifts). Over the next few pages we explain what you need to know and how to use them.

Lift tickets

Ski lifts are expensive. But in most resorts there is a choice of ticket systems: a single-journey ticket; a book of tickets or a punch-card entitling you to a certain number of rides; and a "pass", season ticket or "credit card" which gives you unlimited use of any lift at the resort and which is normally worn around the neck to save you hunting through your pockets each time.

22 12 79 F ⋆ 7

Weekly lift pass

Single-journey lift tickets

Types of ski lift

At any resort, the system of ski lifts should be laid out to give easy access to a variety of trails, to avoid bottlenecks, and to give you the maximum choice of routes. You will probably find that, in order to do this, the resort has installed a series of different lifts for different purposes. Some of the types you are most likely to come across are illustrated below. At a high resort, you will probably be carried up to the top in a cable car or gondola where a choice of drag lifts and chair lifts will serve the various trails. However, at Zermatt in Switzerland, the funicular has re-appeared in a new form. An underground railway has been built inside the mountain to carry skiers from the resort in the valley up to the high skiing areas. It is fast and can carry a large number of people; it is able to run regardless of the weather; and, because it is not visible from the outside, it does not spoil the environment.

Button lift
Automatic, self-service drag lift which carries one skier at a time. Short-to-medium distances on all kinds of slopes, and capable of up to three changes of direction (p. 253).

T-bar lift
Very common, fairly comfortable form of drag lift. So-called because of its shape, it carries two skiers in tandem up a straight track over medium distances on all kinds of slopes (p. 254). It can also be ridden singly – one skier at a time.

Chair lift
Single or double chair suspended from a moving cable above ground level. For longer ascents on all types of slopes. Can be cold, but usually quite comfortable. Ridden with skis on or off (p. 256).

Gondola or telecabine
An enclosed "bubble car" form of chair lift. Can handle large volume of skiers, each car carrying between two and six people up long ascents. Skis are not worn but carried in a rack outside gondola car. Often found in France, where it originated.

Cable car
Large cabin on suspension cable high above the ground, can carry up to 125 people at a time. For fastest, longest and steepest ascents to the high skiing areas.

Funicular
Oldest form of transport. Mountain railway drawn up by cable and on central toothed rail. Usually, two tracks run side by side, and one car full of skiers is pulled up as other car goes down.

How to use nursery slope lifts

At almost all ski resorts there are gentle nursery slopes where beginners first learn to ski. These easy slopes usually have their own simple lifts. Since many of the beginners are children, the lifts are often adapted to their height and strength: they are safe, fairly slow and easy to use. Although some nursery slopes may have button lifts like the one on the opposite page, most are equipped with simple rope tows. Sometimes known as "pony lifts", these consist of a continuous wire loop which runs uphill, turns around a capstan at the top and then travels back down to the bottom again. Along the wire there are attached plastic-covered metal handles. To ride the lift, you simply grab the handle

and allow yourself to be pulled uphill on your skis as shown below. Later, as you become more confident and develop a better sense of balance, you will be able to ride the lift by holding the wire itself and placing the handle behind your seat – rather like the T-bar lift (p. 254).

In some cases, however, there are no handles on the wire. Instead, you are given your own metal handle when you buy your ticket and, to use the lift, you clip it onto the wire when you are ready and un-clip it again when you reach the top. This means you must carry the handle when skiing – which is a big disadvantage, since the handle can hurt if you fall over and land on top of it.

2 Lean back ready to absorb jolt, catch hold of handle with hand nearest to wire.

1 Get into position with skis parallel, hold poles in outside hand, look over shoulder for handle.

How the lift works
Cable is in form of continuous loop on capstan drive. Empty handles therefore travel downhill, turn around and come up behind you.

How to use the "pony lift"

Getting on and getting off are the most difficult things about this lift. You begin by getting into position beside the wire, with your skis in an open parallel stance. Hold your poles in your outside hand or tuck them under your arm. Watch behind you for the handle to come round. Grab hold of it with one hand, then the other, and absorb the jolt with your arm. Lean back slightly with your legs fairly straight as the wire pulls you up, and at the top, where the slope flattens out, get off by simply letting go of the handle.

A child being taught to use the pony lift.

How to use the button lift

The button or "Poma" lift (named after its French inventor, Pomagalski) consists of a continuously moving overhead cable from which metal poles are suspended with small disks or "soup plates" on the end of them. Each bar carries one skier at a time, and you ride it by tucking the disk between your legs and letting it drag you uphill. The button lift system is fairly common in many ski resorts, as it is efficient, easy to ride and relatively inexpensive to install. It is also more flexible than, say, the T-bar: it can negotiate changes of direction instead of having to be built in a straight line, and the number of bars on the system can be regulated – thus reducing the need for waiting in line. Sometimes the lift is operated by an attendant who will engage the bar and start it moving; sometimes it is self-service.

Getting on a button lift

If you are unsure of how to ride the lift, watch the skiers in front of you. In the case of self-service Poma lifts, move into position with your skis parallel and tails against the checkboard, and with your poles in one hand. Grab the bar with your other hand, slip it between your legs and wait until the green light comes on or the barrier lifts to tell you that the bar will start moving. Lean back slightly to absorb the jerk as you start off. Do *not* sit down on the button; stand up, lean back a little and keep your legs comfortably flexed. Keep your skis in the tracks and absorb bumps and dips by bending your legs.

1 Skis parallel in tracks, both poles in one hand.

2 Grab bar and slip button between legs.

3 As bar starts moving, lean back to absorb sudden jolt.

Getting off a button lift

Hold the bar with one hand and, as you approach the top, pull yourself forward and slip the disk out from between your legs. Do not let go until the slope flattens out, and then move out of the way as quickly as possible.

1 Ride lift with your legs slightly flexed. Hold onto bar tightly.

2 Flex knees, pull yourself forward and slip button out from between your legs.

3 At top, let go of bar gently and ski off to one side out of way of other skiers.

How to use the T-bar lift

The T-bar lift is common in Europe, but less so in America. It is a medium-range lift which may span up to a mile in length and which travels in a straight line over a specially prepared trail. The T-bar is so-called because it consists of a "T-shaped" wooden bar on the end of a spring-loaded wire. The bars are attached to a moving cable which runs up and down the slope in a continuous loop. To ride the lift, you pull the bar down, tuck it behind you and let it drag you uphill. At the top, you release the bar, and it springs back up above head-height before turning around a capstan to travel back downhill.

The T-bar is usually ridden in pairs, but it is possible to ride solo as well. If you are riding up on your own, use exactly the same technique as if you had a partner: keep your skis parallel and your knees flexed; do not put the bar between your legs as this could be dangerous if you fall. The most common reason for falling is sitting down on the bar. If you do fall, move quickly to one side, out of the path of other skiers.

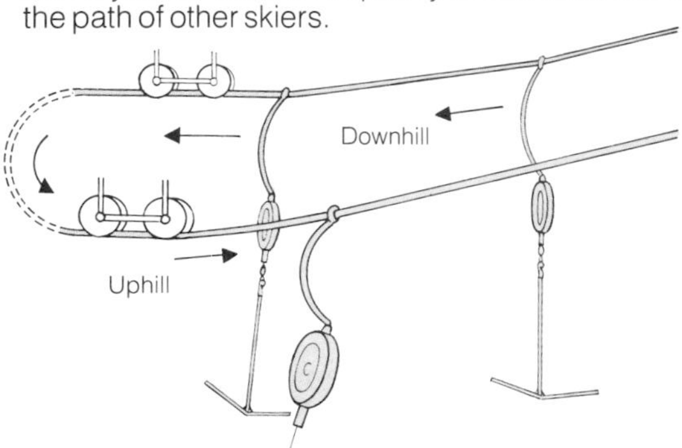

Downhill

Uphill

Attendant-operated lifts
On some lifts, there is an attendant who will pull the T-bar down and hand it to you. Move quickly into position, reach behind you, and take the bar from him.

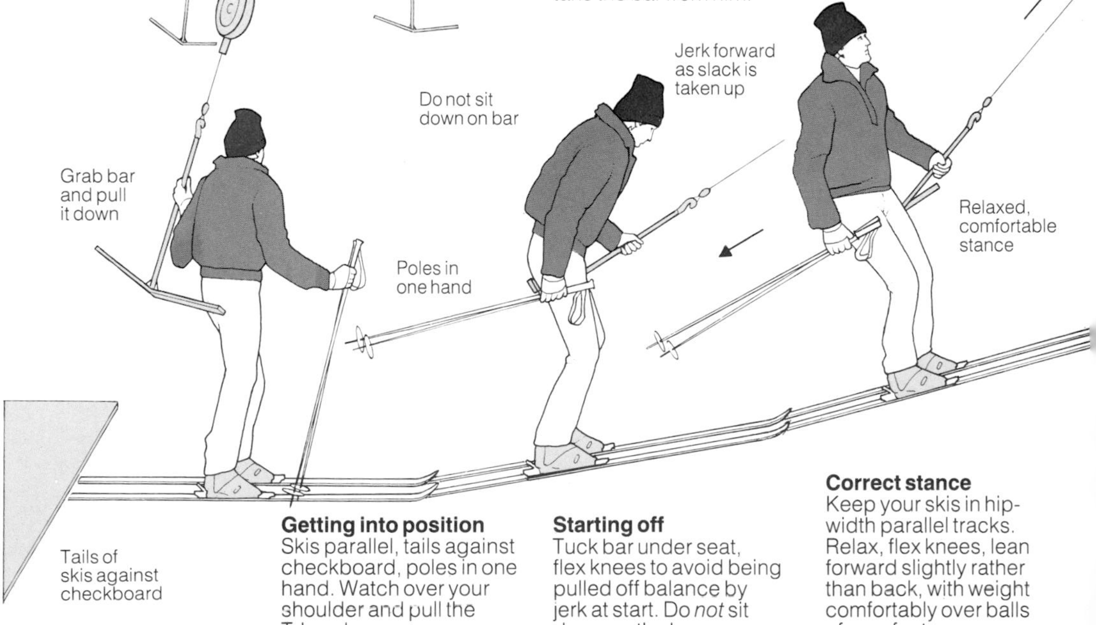

Grab bar and pull it down

Do not sit down on bar

Poles in one hand

Jerk forward as slack is taken up

Relaxed, comfortable stance

Tails of skis against checkboard

Getting into position
Skis parallel, tails against checkboard, poles in one hand. Watch over your shoulder and pull the T-bar down.

Starting off
Tuck bar under seat, flex knees to avoid being pulled off balance by jerk at start. Do *not* sit down on the bar.

Correct stance
Keep your skis in hip-width parallel tracks. Relax, flex knees, lean forward slightly rather than back, with weight comfortably over balls of your feet.

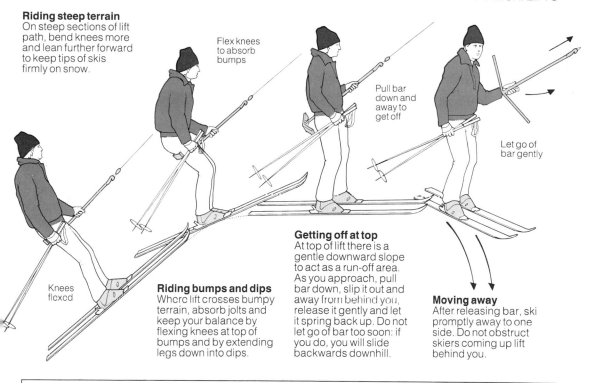

Riding steep terrain
On steep sections of lift path, bend knees more and lean further forward to keep tips of skis firmly on snow.

Flex knees to absorb bumps

Pull bar down and away to get off

Let go of bar gently

Knees flexed

Riding bumps and dips
Where lift crosses bumpy terrain, absorb jolts and keep your balance by flexing knees at top of bumps and by extending legs down into dips.

Getting off at top
At top of lift there is a gentle downward slope to act as a run-off area. As you approach, pull bar down, slip it out and away from behind you, release it gently and let it spring back up. Do not let go of bar too soon: if you do, you will slide backwards downhill.

Moving away
After releasing bar, ski promptly away to one side. Do not obstruct skiers coming up lift behind you.

Riding tandem on the T-bar
The T-bar lift is designed to carry two people at a time. It is, in fact, easier to ride if you have a partner because you will counter-balance each other. It is more comfortable if you choose a partner approximately the same height.

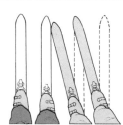

Staying in the tracks
Keep your skis parallel and stay in the tracks worn by other skiers. Lean shoulder to shoulder with your feet apart and do not let your ski tips wander over to your partner's side. If they cross, you may over-balance and fall.

Getting off when riding tandem
You should get off the lift one at a time. If you are getting off last, hold onto the bar until your partner has skied out of the way. Then move off the bar, let go of it gently and ski away.

How to use chair lifts

Originally an American invention, the chair lift was first introduced in the United States in the 1930s and in Europe in the 1940s. It consists of either a single or a double chair attached to a moving cable suspended from pylons. Chair lifts are usually fairly high off the ground. They can transport you up steeper slopes and over more rugged terrain, and they can cover great distances. They can be quite comfortable but, because the ride may take a long time and because you are exposed to the elements, you should wear plenty of warm clothing. Unlike drag lifts, chair lifts can be used for travelling downhill as well as uphill; they also run in summer when there is no snow.

Some chair lifts stop for you to get on and allow you to carry your skis in a rack on the side of the chair. But in most cases they move continuously and you must ride them with your skis on. This is more tricky. You must be in position and ready to get on the chair as it comes up behind you; and you must be ready to slide off your seat and ski out of the way when you get to the top.

Double chair lift ▼
These chairs take two skiers, although they can also be ridden singly.

Single chair lift ▶
These chairs carry one skier at a time and are ridden with your skis on.

Getting on a chair lift

If you are riding a chair lift for the first time, watch carefully what the skiers in front of you do as you move forward in the line. When your turn comes, get into position with both poles held securely in one hand. Move quickly but do not panic. Watch over your shoulder so that you are ready when the chair comes up behind you. There is often an attendant who will help you by steadying the chair as you sit down. As soon as you are on the move, keep your ski tips up to avoid them catching. Many chairs have a safety bar, although several resorts in the western United States operate ones that do not. During the ride, you should pull the safety bar down – over your head or, from the side, over your lap.

1 Move into position, side-by-side, both poles in one hand. Look over shoulder as chair approaches, reach out with your hand, and sit down as soon as edge of seat is beneath you.

2 As you move off, chair may sway slightly at first, but lower safety bar down over your head or swing it across your lap. This will stop you falling forwards out of chair. Keep your ski tips up.

Getting off a chair lift

The procedure for getting off at the top may vary slightly from lift to lift. But, unless the chair stops for you to get out, what usually happens is this: the chair reaches a special ramp, you slide yourself forwards out of the chair and stand up, and you then ski away downhill as the chair carries on uphill above your head. The important thing is to be ready well in advance. There is normally a sign on the last pylon from the top which tells you to prepare for getting off. Open the safety bar, keep your ski tips up and ease yourself forward in your seat slightly, ready to slide off and ski down the ramp – quickly, without fuss, and without getting in the way of other skiers.

1 Keep your ski tips up as you come to the top. Push yourself forwards and slide out of your seat as you reach the lip of the slope.

2 Ski down the snow-covered ramp, snowplowing if you need to control your speed. Do not stop at the bottom of the ramp: move out of the way of other skiers.

Ski instruction

Skiing is not an easy sport to do well, and in certain situations, if the skier is not properly equipped to deal with its demands, it can be dangerous. Consequently, *all skiers should take ski instruction from a qualified instructor*, whatever their level of ability. Of course, not every skier's requirements are the same, and not everyone will benefit from the same kind of teaching. But what can be said with certainty is that trying to teach yourself or trying to learn from your friends does not work and can be dangerous: your progress will be slow and you will pick up bad skiing habits which may be difficult to eradicate.

Nearly every skiing country runs its own national ski school and employs qualified ski instructors. The organization of the ski school and the way in which it teaches skiing differs from country to country. Most countries attempt to unify their methodology into a national teaching system, which is then advocated as being superior to the methods used by other rival countries. However, efforts are made by the International Ski Instructors Association (I.S.I.A.) to advance the international interpretation of ski technique. This body meets at regular congresses and holds seminars and demonstration sessions designed to promote discussion and comparison of the diverse approaches.

Most national ski schools run a local ski school at every resort. These operate by dividing their pupils into "ski classes" according to their ability (see opposite). However, the crux of the whole system is the "ski instructor. The profession of ski instructors is now much more tightly controlled than it once was. Qualified ski instructors are trained not only as skiers but also as teachers. To qualify, they must attend courses and training programs and pass a series of standard tests set by the controlling body. And, once certified, they must also keep up-to-date with new methods by attending refresher courses. In most countries, they are graded according to the level at which they are qualified to teach, they wear uniform ski suits so they are easily recognizable and badges to show that they are approved instructors. It is the ski instructors who run the ski school classes, but many can also be hired for private lessons.

Because they vary so much, the discussion of ski schools in this chapter is of necessity fairly generalized. However, throughout the rest of this book, the methodology used by the Swiss Ski School, with its emphasis on safe, functional skiing, is the one that has been followed. Its principles and its teaching progression are outlined on p.37.

Ski school classes

Ski schools normally operate six days a week; they start on Monday morning and end on Saturday. The first thing to do once you have signed up for the ski school is to select the right class. Most ski schools run six classes, and a good ski school will make it clear from the start which class covers what. Sometimes, you may be asked to demonstrate what you can do so that you can be placed in the right one. There is an international grading system, from "A" for beginners' classes to "F" for experts, but some countries may grade their classes from 6 to 1 or from 1 to 6 (see below).

Most ski classes consist of one instructor and between eight and twelve pupils, although if the resort is not busy there may be less. Except for the periods around Christmas and Easter when the ski schools are inundated with people, there certainly should not be more than fifteen skiers in a single class. Sometimes, the class will ski every morning and every afternoon. In other schools, the class may meet only in the mornings, and in the afternoons you will be left to ski on your own.

In charge of the class will be the ski instructor. To some extent, instructors will vary their methods according to the number in the class and the level of ability, but they should have some form of program for the week so that, at the end, you will have made some visible progress. Instructors are also responsible for the safety of the group, and you should find that you are not only being taught how to ski but also how to behave safely on the slopes (p.215). When introducing a new movement, the instructor will first explain it and then demonstrate it so that you understand exactly what you should be doing. You will then practice, by performing a few specially devised exercises or by following the ski instructor down the slope and imitating his or her movements. Instructors are trained to pinpoint any difficulties you may have and to show you how to correct them. They should also understand why they arise (the pupil's physical limitations, lack of confidence, mis-interpretation of the technical explanation, steepness of the slope, unsuitable snow conditions, etc.).

As we show below, the organization of ski school classes is based on a natural learning program. Although the exact order may vary, it is based on introducing new movements through a series of exercises of increasing difficulty until they can be performed satisfactorily on varied terrain and snow conditions and at different speeds and rhythms. Thus, in Class A, beginners are taught the basics of getting around on skis; in Class F, experienced skiers are taught advanced turn initiations for use on- and off-trail, competition stepping techniques and, in some cases, "trick" freestyle movements. Most ski schools operate a system of proficiency tests alongside the classes – awarding bronze, silver and gold or one-star, two-star and three-star badges or medals to those who pass.

How classes are graded

	USA Spain	Switzerland Italy Germany Gt Britain	Austria France
Beginners	A	1	6
Improved beginners	B	2	5
Intermediates	C	3	4
Improved intermediates	D	4	3
Advanced skiers	E	5	2
Experts	F	6	1

How ski school classes are organized
The charts above show how the labelling of each class differs, and what techniques are taught at each level in the Swiss Ski School system.

◄ **A children's ski class**
A group of youngsters in a ski class line up on the edge of the trail ready to watch their instructor demonstrate a movement.

The ski school learning progression

Class	Techniques covered in each class	International proficiency test
A	Walking, schussing, snowplowing, turning snowplow	Test 1 Bronze
B	Traversing, uphill turning, side-slipping, snowplow turning	
C	Stem turning, parallel uphill turning	Test 2 Silver
D	Parallel turning (open)	
E	Parallel turning (closed), short swinging (basic)	Test 3 Gold
F	Parallel turning with functional initiations (e.g., absorption-extension), stepping techniques (leading to competition skiing), deep powder skiing	

Ski school classes v. private lessons

There is a lot to be said for learning to ski in a class. Skiing with others of the same ability can be fun as well as encouraging, since, by and large, you will share the same difficulties and the same advances. This is especially true of beginners and of children.

The success of a ski class depends a lot on the instructor. Fortunately, poor instructors are rare nowadays, but some are still better than others. Good instructors will be patient and helpful, not intolerant or disinterested. They should keep the class moving as much as possible, on a variety of different runs and using various teaching methods. They should explain things clearly and demonstrate them simply, one movement at a time and at a level just a little higher than that of the pupils. They should also rotate the order in which the class skis, so that everyone has the same chance to follow behind them and imitate their movements.

However, not everything is up to the instructor. Your progress also depends on being in the right class for your ability. If you are not, you should not be afraid to change over. Being in a class whose members are all better than you can be discouraging, and you risk holding the others back. Similarly, if you are in a class where the standard is slightly too low, you may not be stretching yourself as much as you really need.

The major disadvantage of ski classes is that, however hard the instructor tries to avoid it, there will always be a certain amount of standing about, watching the others and waiting for your turn. This is particularly true when the class is large. To some extent, it can be solved by avoiding the high season, when classes are crowded, but in some cases private tuition may be the answer. Most instructors will give private lessons. You can book the amount of time you want and request a particular teacher if you have a preference – although the best instructors are often booked up well in advance. A private lesson can often help to isolate and cure a specific difficulty or a bad skiing habit. Private tuition *is* more expensive than the ski school, but you may be able to share the cost with one or two others if you are of the same standard.

How men, women and children ski

Debate rages over whether or not women ski in the same way as men and, consequently, whether or not they should be taught differently. Women are often teased about the way they look on the slopes, especially when they first learn to ski. The fact that they have a tendency to ski knock-kneed and with their bottoms sticking out is not so much due to poor technique as to their being a different physical shape. In other words, their movements and techniques are the same, but, because they are built differently, they *look* different. In general, men have a narrow pelvis and legs that tend to bow apart at the knees; women have a wider pelvis, a lower center of gravity and legs that are more knock-kneed. A man may therefore be more comfortable in a closed parallel stance, a woman more natural in an open parallel stance. Young children, as we explain in more detail on the following pages, are either unaware of, or are not interested in, style, and often ski more naturally than men or women. The photographs below, and on p.65, illustrate some of the visible differences.

Skiing in the fall line ▶
You can see clearly from these photographs how the man's bowed legs make it easier for him to keep his skis together in a closed parallel stance. The woman, with her wider hips and slightly knock-knees looks more natural in an open stance. The young five-year-old girl on the far right skis with her feet even further apart.

Traversing ▶
The woman, with a lower center of gravity than the man, angulates her upper body further out from the slope. Men, as a general rule, are able to counter-rotate their hips further and more easily than women. The child keeps her knees close together and her skis in an open stance for better balance.

Parallel turning ▶
Again, the man's skis are close together without him having to press his knees together, and the child's skis are the furthest apart. Because of her wider pelvis and different bone structure, the woman must press one knee against the other to ski in a closed stance.

◀ A ski school class
The other members watch as the first pupil sets off down the slope.

Teaching children to ski

Children learn to ski much more quickly than adults. Given as little as two weeks' ski instruction each winter, many children develop into excellent skiers by the age of about ten. They also learn by *imitation*, not by the *explanation* which adults often seem to require. Their limbs are more supple and more flexible; they have a very good sense of balance, and tend to ski much more by feel. Above all, they are primarily interested in having fun – not in developing a "perfect" technique.

All this has a direct bearing on how children should be taught. The ski school is the right place for them to begin, and many operate special children's classes in which youngsters ski with other children of about the same age and ability. Within the class, the emphasis is on *play*. Children react much better and their attention can be held for longer if skills are taught in the form of games – that is, in the way in which they naturally learn. The games may include snowplow trains, switchbacks, jumps, races, slalom runs and, perhaps, some of the basic freestyle movements.

Many ski schools try to take children straight from the turning snowplow to parallel skiing. And many youngsters, especially the more "aggressive" ones, are encouraged to learn parallel turning with a "down" initiation (p.108) – that is, with down-flexion, banking and counter-rotation. Indeed, the crucial thing in teaching children is imparting this principle of rotating the legs and counter-rotating the hips and upper body. Once they master this, all the other movements tend to follow naturally.

Buying the right equipment for children is as important as it is for adults. Skis should be about head-height and, if not, then shorter rather than longer. Some are now available with cross-country-style step patterns to stop them sliding backwards. Plastic, edge-less "play" skis are no substitute for proper skis. Safety bindings should be simple and adjustable for the child's weight; boots must flex forwards easily and must fit correctly (although they can be bought slightly larger so that they last for two seasons as long as the heel fits snugly). Small crash helmets are recommended for young children.

How children can teach adults

In recent years, a lot of careful study has been made of how children learn to ski. All children intuitively adopt a style which is natural and functional. The reason for this is almost certainly because children are more relaxed and uninhibited on skis and because they do not worry about how they look. They are pleased if their movements work and if they enjoy themselves. Adults, on the other hand, with their more intellectual approach, are continually attempting to measure their performance against some ideal of perfect technique – for example, linked parallel turning in a tightly closed parallel stance. They also tend to be more "negative", to get embarrassed about falling, and to concentrate on their mistakes instead of on what they are doing right. This often results in their tensing up, becoming self-conscious, and, ultimately, having less fun than children. Adults can therefore learn from children to forget about trying to look stylish, to relax and to trust to their own feel for what is the right movement, and to set out to enjoy themselves.

The "games theory" ▲
Many ski schools have special nursery slopes called "kindergartens" where children can get used to the snow and to their skis at their own pace. Wooden cutouts of cartoon characters, hoops, rings and switchbacks are all used to transform learning to ski into a "game".

A children's ski class ▶
Children can be taught to ski almost as soon as they have learned to walk. In many Alpine countries, skiing is now part of the school curriculum, and teachers are often trained ski instructors as well.

◀ **A "snowplow train"**
A game like this, in which the children follow the instructor down the slope in single file, makes learning enjoyable. It teaches balance, coordination and the ability to control speed with the snowplow.

The "natural" style of children and racers

Children develop their own functional style of skiing as soon as they have mastered the basic skills of getting about on skis. On the whole, they will not see the point in striving to achieve a closed parallel stance and will have little interest in attempting to do so. They ski naturally with their feet fairly wide apart, since this gives them better balance, and also in a somewhat knock-kneed position (see photographs on p.261). They tend to lean well forward, to ski quite "aggressively" and to use a lot of body movement to help them turn.

The observation and analysis of children skiing now plays almost as large a part in the formulation of ski technique and ski school teaching programs as that of the world's top ski racers. And comparisons show that *young children and racers ski in remarkably similar ways*. Effectiveness is the only criterion by which a racer judges his own technique. He is constantly looking for ways to ski faster and more accurately, and he will employ any movements or body positions that make a positive difference. The same is true of children; consequently, both they and the racers will use an open stance and transfer their weight early to their outside steering ski. This illustrates, if proof were needed, that in good skiing the closed parallel concept of ski technique should give way to independent leg movements. "Style", in the sense in which most skiers still understand it, has become increasingly unimportant.

These comparisons also point to the fact that the movements which racers strive to perfect through continuous training and practice, children will employ purely as a result of instinct. This is partly because the movements that they use are the most rational and most functional – and, therefore, the most natural – and partly because children are natural imitators and will inevitably copy the good skiers they see around them, whether on-trail or on the television. The photographs on the opposite page, which were taken on different occasions but as an almost identical slalom course, emphasize the similarity in technique and behavior between two of the top world racers, Ingemar Stenmark and Phil Mahre, and two unknown youngsters who had received no specific race training at all.

Ingemar Stenmark and ▶ a young racer Skiing a similar line on different giant slalom courses, both Stenmark (Sweden) and this unknown youngster steer out of their last turn and then make a rapid, early transfer of pressure against their uphill ski to initiate the next turn. In both cases, we can see the technique of banking the uphill knee to tilt the uphill ski onto its steering edge. Furthermore, both skiers then make their turn initiations by flexing down and rotating their legs while counter-rotating their hips and upper bodies.

Phil Mahre and a young ▶ racer Exactly the same similarity can be seen between the top racer, Phil Mahre (USA), and this untrained youngster. Both skiers initiate their turn with a transfer of pressure against their uphill ski, placed in a "converging" or "stem" position. They then bank into the turn, flex down and counter-rotate to steer. Their body positions and movements are almost identical.

◀ **Children as racers** Children who have been brought up on skis from a very early age make naturally good skiers. They may start racing at the age of five or six, and they tend to adopt instinctively the ski techniques used by top racers.

Short-ski teaching methods

These methods of ski instruction are very different from the standard teaching programs. They all share the same basic feature: beginners start off on very short skis (about 100cm) and then gradually progress onto longer ones during the next few days. Short-ski teaching was developed in the 1960s by Clif Taylor and Karl Pfeiffer in the United States, by Martin Puchtler in Germany, and by Robert Blanc and Pierre Grueneberg in France. Working independently, they evolved virtually identical methods of instruction. In America, the technique is known as *G.L.M.* (the "Graduated Length Method") or A.T.M. ("Accelerated Teaching Method"), and in Europe it is known as *Ski Evolutif* or "Mini ski". Experiments have been made with short-ski teaching throughout Europe, but it has never become part of the official program in any of the national ski schools. However, it is practiced in some of the newer French resorts, such as Les Arcs, and in parts of Germany. In America, about a third of the ski schools still use G.L.M. but, as in Europe, it is declining in popularity. The method is expensive for the ski schools, since they have to carry about two-thirds more rental skis than normal, and it is difficult to organize as people progress onto longer skis at different stages.

When short-ski teaching was first introduced, all skiers learned to ski on the same long skis used by advanced skiers. Their aim was to master the technique of skiing in a parallel stance, but, on account of the length of the skis, they had to progress towards this via learning snowplow and stem turns. Although "compacts" have largely taken the place of the long skis, this is still usually the case. With the "mini skis", however, beginners could learn to make parallel turns on their first day (a method known as "direct parallel teaching"). Its supporters claim that, for this reason, short-ski teaching is much more positive. The emphasis from the outset is on learning to ski in a parallel stance, using parallel turns to brake and to control speed.

Short skis are used because they exert less leverage on the leg. This makes them easier to turn. By increasing the length of their skis about every two days, pupils can therefore gradually get used to the sensation of moving over the snow at higher speeds and can slowly build up the power necessary to turn the longer skis. Normally, the transition from the 100cm skis, through the 135cm and 150cm skis, and onto full-length compact skis takes about a week.

Short skis for beginners ▶
Because they are so much easier to turn, sliding around on short or "mini" skis during the first few days helps to build a beginner's confidence quickly.

Skis for G.L.M. and Ski Evolutif The skis are exactly the same shape as full-length skis but are simply shorter. On the very short skis, the bindings are positioned so that the ball of your foot is exactly over the center of the ski.

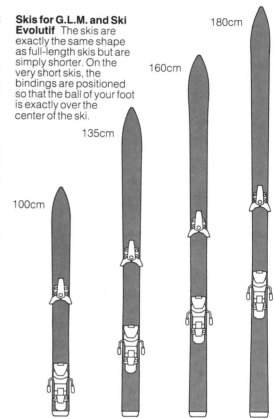

180cm

160cm

135cm

100cm

Short-ski turns

The short-ski method uses the power of the lower body to make the turns. The upper body remains more-or-less passive. There are three basic turns: the *foot* turn, *knee* turn, and *hip* or *lower-body* turn. The foot turn makes a turn about 15 degrees away from the fall line. The knee turn increases this angle to about 45 degrees. And the hip turn is used to make a wide-radius turn, up to 90 degrees away from the fall line. To make a foot turn, put your hands on your knees and "twist" your feet by jumping slightly; your knees must not move. For the knee turn, put your hands on your hips and "twist" in the same way; your hips must not move. For the hip turn, hold your arms out to the side and turn your lower body; your arms should not move.

Foot turn   Knee turn   Hip turn

The advantages and disadvantages of short-ski teaching

When short-ski teaching was first introduced, it was the only alternative to traditional instruction. The traditional method used very long skis which beginners found difficult to control. As a result, the drop-out rate was very high. The short-ski method meant that beginners could enjoy skiing with some degree of control from their first day on skis.

However, there are practical disadvantages to short-ski teaching. The ski schools find it both expensive, because of the number of skis needed, and difficult to organize.

Another major problem lies in the difference between short-ski techniques and those taught in normal ski schools. Short-ski pupils do not learn "defensive" skiing. In other words, the fact that they miss out snowplowing and stem turning is regarded as a *disadvantage*. Many skiers feel that these techniques do have a function and should be taught to beginners, since even the most expert skiers will use them when the situation demands it. Moreover, traditionalists also feel that short skis do not provide as stable a base to stand on as normal skis; this tends to result in more backward falls.

The short-ski methods are considered useful for teaching older people to ski for the first time, and also for people who have found it very difficult to learn by traditional methods. Occasionally, short skis are used to get people who have skied before but who have had a bad accident used to skiing again. In general, however, now that compact skis have become widespread, the need for very short skis has been greatly reduced.

Typical short-ski learning program

	Ski length	Program
1	100cm	*Learn:* handling equipment; stationary exercises (star turns and basic foot, knee and hip turns); climbing techniques (side-stepping and herring-boning); straight running down gentle slopes; turning out of the fall line; use of ski lift.
2	100cm or 135cm	Repeat and refine first day. *Learn:* linked turns; turning around small bumps; use of poles.
3	135cm	Repeat everything on longer skis. *Learn:* traversing; uphill turning; wide-radius turns; anticipate turning using poles.
4	135cm	Repeat and refine previous lesson. *Learn:* side-slipping; turning around larger bumps.
5	135cm or 150cm	Similar to previous day, but skiing faster on steeper slopes
6	150cm	Repeat program on longer skis.
7	160cm, compact or longer	Continue to refine techniques. Strong skiers can now try deeper snow.

Dry slope skiing

Artificial ski surfaces have made skiing possible all year round and have opened up the sport to many skiers who might not otherwise have the chance to ski on snow. Dry slopes are now common, particularly in Great Britain, France, Japan and Australia, and have been constructed not only on the sides of naturally suitable hills but also on specially built artificial mounds. Some of the urban and city-center slopes are quite short – with room for only three or four turns per run – and they are used chiefly for practice and exercise or to give beginners their first taste of skiing. But some of the larger slopes are much longer (1,300ft or more) and offer a variety of gradients and tighter changes of direction. They may be floodlit for use in the evenings and they often have mogul slopes, separate nursery areas for ski teaching and more than one lift or ski tow for taking skiers up to the top. They may also hold regular slalom races for more advanced skiers. At the larger sites, there will be a wide range of equipment for hire and regular, organized ski classes led by qualified instructors.

Artificial slope surfaces vary in design and composition, but most of them are made of some form of plastic or nylon intended to feel as much like snow as possible. One of the most successful surfaces is the "snowslope" made by a British brush-manufacturing company called Dendix. It consists of a mat made of PVC bristles or "brush strips" held together by stainless steel bands (see right), and it is claimed to reproduce the skiing characteristics of medium-packed snow. To some extent it does; but, obviously, it is not exactly the same. None of the artificial surfaces are as slippery as snow. In fact, they are slower and offer more resistance to the skis than snow does. For this reason, dry slopes are usually steeper than comparable snow slopes. Manufacturers recommend a minimum gradient of 12° (21 per cent) and a maximum gradient of 25° (47 per cent). However, the ski techniques are the same: your skis will edge, side-slip, carve or skid on an artificial surface just as they will on snow. And dry slopes can be used successfully for teaching beginners, for learning advanced turns and techniques, for race training and competitive events, for freestyle and jumping and, in the case of some specially laid-out trails, for cross-country skiing.

Outdoor dry ski slope
This artificial slope, which is at Southampton in England, is fairly typical. It is built on the side of a hill, is just under 330ft long and has its own small "rope-tow" ski lift.

What you need for dry slope skiing

Almost all dry ski slopes will rent the equipment you need – boots, skis and ski poles. For the most part these are exactly the same as for Alpine snow skiing (see p.16 for details). Renting skis in particular, is a good idea. This is because the hard plastic slope surface will tend to harm the special material on the underside of your own skis. However, if you intend to ski regularly and often on dry slopes, you will find that some manufacturers make skis designed specifically for artificial surfaces.

If you have your own boots, it is worth wearing them, because trying to rent a comfortable pair that fit as well as your own can be frustrating and time-consuming. If you do have to rent boots, look around for a good pair and remember to take along several pairs of socks of different thicknesses. Check that the bindings on the skis have been adjusted correctly and that they will release properly if you fall. the ski poles which most dry slopes rent are usually made of thicker than normal aluminum without a basket or sharp point at the bottom. If you use your own poles you may be asked to put a cork or plastic cap on the tip to avoid damaging the surface of the dry ski slope.

As for clothes, wear an old pair of pants, a long-sleeved sweater and, if necessary, an old jacket. Most importantly, take some gloves and wear them all the time. Falling over on a dry slope is harder than falling on snow and, without gloves, you may graze or cut your hands.

What to wear
If you have your own ski suit, ski pants or jacket, you can wear them for dry slope skiing, but bear in mind that they may get torn by the hard plastic surface if you fall over.

How artificial slopes are made

The earliest attempts at dry slope skiing were made on an ingenious variety of surfaces: pine needles, straw, carpets, coconut matting and plastic chips. None were satisfactory. Since then, artificial slopes have been made from plastic or nylon which feel and act much more like snow. The British and the Italians were first with a kind of carpet made from nylon bristles. Later, the nylon was replaced by PVC – to form flexible mats which look rather like upturned toothbrushes. Other cheaper, but less durable, surfaces have also been made from injection-molded plastic.

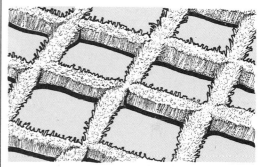

PVC brush (Dendix) is formed from bristles held together by metal bands.

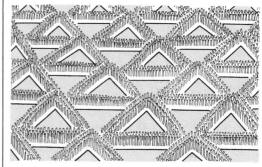

Plastic bristles (Delta), moulded into triangular shapes, is often used on short slopes.

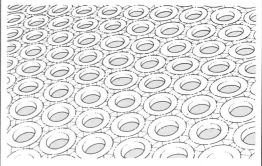

Injection-molded plastic (DriSno), an early form of slope, has not lasted as well as other surfaces.

The advantages and disadvantages of dry slope skiing

Dry slopes are probably most useful in countries like Great Britain where most skiers have to travel abroad to get good skiing. The chief *advantages* are that they are easily accessible, inexpensive and often open all year round. If you can ski already, dry slope skiing is a good way of polishing up your technique during the summer months. This is particularly important for "lowlander" racers who must keep in training for the winter. For recreational skiers, it also serves as a way of testing out new boots and of getting into shape before a winter skiing holiday – and it is almost certainly as good as doing pre-ski exercises (p. 274).

However, beginners are those who will probably get the most benefit out of dry slope skiing. Artificial slopes are ideal for learning to ski, because the slopes are slower and therefore less frightening and because the conditions are always the same. Taking a few lessons on a dry slope before going on a skiing holiday is highly advisable. It will teach you the basics (such as getting used to your skis, walking, turning around, climbing, schussing and snowplowing), give you a head start over complete beginners and, as a result, save your holiday time quite considerably.

The biggest *disadvantage* of dry slope skiing is that it is *not* the same as snow skiing. The surface is not as quick as snow and more unpleasant if you fall over, and, apart from the largest sites, the slopes are fairly short. However, if you are disappointed with dry slopes as your first experience of skiing, do not give up: try snow skiing.

Dry ski slope instruction ▶
Because the majority of people that use artificial slopes are beginners, almost all dry ski centers offer qualified ski instruction. Here, a class of youngsters are being shown how to fit and adjust their boots properly.

Chair lift ▼
Some of the larger and better dry ski slopes have chair lifts as well as drag lifts. This one is at the 400m (1,450ft) artificial slope on the out-skirts of Edinburgh in Scotland.

The layout of dry ski slopes

All artificial slopes are designed to give as good a simulation of Alpine snow skiing as possible. Their layout and construction is consequently very important. The major manufacturers of artificial surfaces offer a "consultancy" service which covers the surveying, planning and design of new sites. A good dry ski slope must not be so difficult or challenging as to deter all beginners, but on the other hand it must not be so gentle or regular as to bore experienced skiers. The best dry ski slopes therefore try to offer a variety of gradients – suitable for beginners, intermediates and advanced skiers. They will also try to incorporate undulations, sudden bumps and dips, tight changes of direction and, sometimes, specially constructed jumps for practicing freestyle "aerials" (p. 174). Some of the larger, more ambitious slopes offer a variety of routes, and some of the more attractive are built on wooded hills. Many dry ski centers have a separate nursery slope at the bottom where beginners' ski classes are held; and this may have its own simple tow lift. The main slope will probably be served by a button lift or a T-bar, but the larger sites may also have a chair lift for the longer slopes. Most dry ski centers are built fairly near large towns, have a clubhouse on the site and provide car parking space as well.

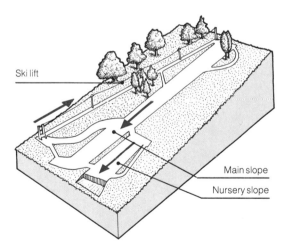

Ski lift

Main slope

Nursery slope

A typical artificial ski slope
This drawing is based on the dry ski slope at Gloucester in England. The main slope is almost 300m (1,086ft) long and has a drag lift which climbs up one side along a separate track. At the bottom there is a special nursery slope where ski classes are held and where beginners can learn the basics of skiing without getting in the way of skiers on the main slope. The nursery area has its own small lift. There is also a clubhouse at the foot of the slope where skis, boots and other equipment can be rented.

The "ski deck" machine

Attempts were first made in the 1940s to build a machine which would allow simulated skiing. The most successful model is probably the one known as the "ski deck". It is a compact, indoor slope which works on the principle of an endless moving belt. In other words, you get onto the machine and ski "on the spot" while the slope moves past beneath you – rather as if you were running down an "up" escalator.

The "ski deck" is better than most other machines because the angle and the speed of the slope can be varied. It can be used for teaching beginners (when the slope is at a low angle and the belt is travelling slowly) as well as for training more advanced skiers (when the slope is steeper and the belt is travelling faster). The surface of the belt is made of silicon-impregnated matting which allows the skis to edge and skid. The machine has fixed, spring-loaded pole holders at either side and there is an automatic stop bar which switches off the machine should the skier fall over.

Although large versions are sometimes found at ski shows, the "ski-deck" is really designed for ski teaching and ski training, and it is most commonly found in sports centers and ski shops. The machine is very useful for teaching beginners, since the instructor is right beside the pupil and can help or intervene immediately. For more experienced skiers, it is a way of practicing out of season and of getting into shape before a skiing holiday.

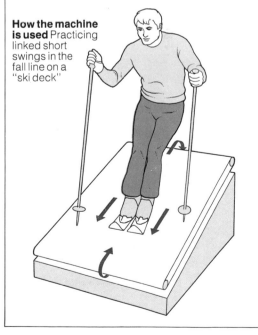

How the machine is used Practicing linked short swings in the fall line on a "ski deck"

Grass skiing

Grass skiing is exactly what it says – skiing on grass. It is supported by a small but enthusiastic minority in the United States and in Europe, but is especially popular in countries like England that do not have a regular snowfall. Grass skiing is done not only as a sport in its own right (although it has not been recognized by F.I.S.), but also as a summer alternative to snow skiing, as a way of introducing skiing to beginners, and in some cases as a form of training for ski racers. The first ever international grass ski festival was held in 1970 at Windermere in England; there is now a full calendar of competitive events every summer.

The idea of grass skiing was dreamed up by a German sewing-machine manufacturer named Kurt Kaiser, and the first prototypes were seen in the 1960s. Now several different firms produce their own designs, based on the principle of either rollers or caterpillar tracks. Grass skis can take a normal skier some time to get used to. They are much shorter than snow skis and they make you stand much higher off the ground. Standard ski boots, which simply clip into the bindings on the skis, can be used, as well as normal ski poles, although you should tape up the tips to stop them sticking into the ground. The only other essentials are an old pair of pants and jacket (because grass will stain your clothing) and some gloves to protect your hands if you fall over.

In theory, it is possible to grass ski anywhere where there is a grass-covered slope. In practice, most grass skiers belong to clubs which hold meetings at regular sites. The clubs may also run competitions, organize training and instruction classes, and rent out the equipment you will need. Uphill transport usually takes the form of a portable, motor-driven drag lift (similar to the "nursery slope" lift, p. 252) set up on the slope to take the skiers up to the top of the hill, although some permanent sites may have chair or "button" lifts. In some areas, local clubs may also organize cross-country treks.

Although the sensation of grass skiing is not really the same as snow skiing, the techniques are in many ways similar. The two major differences are these: first, it is not possible to snowplow or stem, so all turns are made with the skis more-or-less parallel; second, there is no side-slipping, because the skis are either edged or they are not, so all turns are "carved", not skidded. Good grass skiers, or racers who compete in special slalom, giant slalom or parallel slalom events, use various forms of stepping technique. In the usual instruction program, beginners go straight from basic schussing and traversing techniques to step turning as a means of swinging uphill, and then onto linked parallel turning and short swinging.

Grass skis
Modern grass skis are light, fast and very maneuverable. They are a lot shorter than snow skis: usually between 50 and 80cm – although longer skis of over 80cm have been used in special trials to reach speeds of almost 95kph (60mph). There is a binding attached to a metal plate on top of the ski, and your ski boot clips into this in the normal way. Nowadays, almost all grass skis work on the "tank-like" caterpillar-track principle (see below): a continuous belt which is always in contact with the grass runs around an endless metal track on nylon rollers. The new designs are quieter, faster and stronger than the original prototypes, and caterpillar-track skis have now largely superseded the earlier models which used a series of wide plastic wheels and were similar to large roller skates.

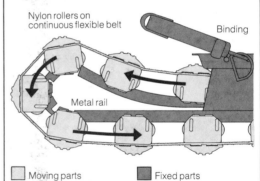

Nylon rollers on continuous flexible belt

Binding

Metal rail

☐ Moving parts   ■ Fixed parts

How grass skis work
As the ski slides over the grass, a continuous belt attached to nylon rollers runs around a fixed, endless metal "rail" or frame. Washing and oiling the mechanism is the only regular maintenance required.

Grass ski slalom racing ▶
Numerous local, national and European grass ski championships are held each year throughout the summer. Speeds can reach 50kph (30mph).

Ski fitness

Skiing is a highly demanding sport, both physically and mentally. It requires good, general physical fitness – that is, a combination of stamina, flexibility and strength. Skiing, after all, is not only downhill running; it is also falling, getting up, turning around and uphill climbing, as well as walking with all your gear on. It requires sustained effort and employs muscles which you do not normally use. This is especially true if you are a beginner and have not yet learned to control your movements naturally and easily or to ski functionally and efficiently. Beginners exert more effort and tire more easily.

Clearly, recreational skiers do not need the rigorous training that ski racers undergo. But the difference is only one of degree; the same muscles are employed. If you look, you will see that a good skier is in control of his movements all the time, whatever his speed and whatever the situation. The key to this is not just muscle strength but also alertness and agility. A good skier should be flexible and supple, since so much of good skiing relies on anticipation, on the speed of reactions and reflexes, and on a highly developed sense of co-ordination. In this way, he will be able to employ the right amount of force at the right moment.

The fitter you are, the more you will enjoy skiing. It therefore pays to get into good shape: the preparation is undoubtedly worth the time and effort. If you are *not* reasonably fit before you go skiing, you will tire easily, you will risk overstraining yourself and be more likely to fall and injure yourself, and you will probably wake up on the second morning of your vacation stiff and aching. If you *are* in good shape before you go, you will have more stamina, more flexibility and more control. The result is simple: you will ski better and you will ski more safely.

Over the next few pages, we outline a basic fitness program for the average skier. It is divided into two parts: the first comprises a series of exercises for general all-round fitness (p. 275); the second includes specific exercises designed to tone up the muscles most commonly used in skiing (p. 276-7).

If you can combine these exercises with other regular sports and activities (in particular, swimming, cycling, football, tennis, jogging, walking or mountaineering, and dry or grass skiing), then fitness should not present any real problem. Bear in mind that the best sport to prepare you for Alpine skiing is cross-country skiing – in terms of both fitness and technique.

The skier's anatomy

This drawing illustrates the parts of the body on which skiing makes the greatest demand. These are the joints and muscles which you should always aim to develop in any program of pre-ski fitness. They should be strong, to withstand the strains that skiing puts on them, and supple so that you are agile and flexible and can react quickly to changing terrain and snow conditions.

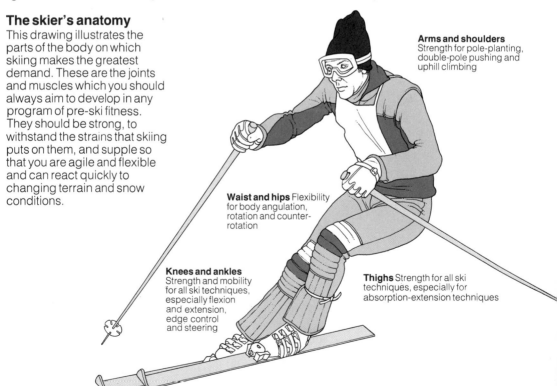

Arms and shoulders
Strength for pole-planting, double-pole pushing and uphill climbing

Waist and hips Flexibility for body angulation, rotation and counter-rotation

Knees and ankles
Strength and mobility for all ski techniques, especially flexion and extension, edge control and steering

Thighs Strength for all ski techniques, especially for absorption-extension techniques

General exercises for all-round fitness

Pre-ski exercises will help you get fit before you go on a skiing vacation. They will get your body into good shape, improve your balance and coordination, loosen up and strengthen your muscles, and increase your stamina. Provided you approach the exercises sensibly, you will not find them difficult, or painful, and you will be glad of the time you spent on them. You can, of course, make up your own individual exercise program to suit your own requirements, but bear in mind that you should be aiming at a mixture of suppleness, stamina and strength. Illustrated below are a few ideas for a well-balanced routine of general exercises designed to tone up your body. If you are not exercising all year round, begin the program about four to six weeks before going skiing and devote, say, half an hour a day to it. It is important that you do the exercises *regularly*, not in sporadic bursts, and that you begin slowly and build up gradually, without attempting to overdo it from the outset.

Leg spread

Back exercise

High kicks

Leg lifts

Toe touching

Jumping and twisting

Arm swinging

Knee bends

Special exercises for skiing

These exercises are designed to supplement those on the previous page. In most cases, they are deliberately meant to imitate common skiing movements. This is to enable you to develop those joints and muscles that have to work especially hard or which are particularly prone to stress and strain when you ski. Although playing other sports and doing a general exercise program can help to keep you fit and in good overall condition, it is worth also concentrating on the movements which are peculiar to skiing. There is probably no other sport in which so much emphasis is placed on keeping your hips, knees and ankles constantly flexed, which demands so much leg strength *and* elasticity at the same time, and which requires such good coordination of knee and ankle flexibility, leg-muscle strength and waist and hip mobility.

As with the general, all-purpose exercises, try to set yourself a program, and stick to it. Spend a few minutes on each of the exercises and do them every day. Once every week is no good whatsoever. Exercises have a beneficial effect only if they are done regularly and only if you gradually build up the time that you spend on each one. If you follow the schedule properly, you will find that your skiing will improve: you will have more stamina, you will be able to ski faster and more safely, you will fall over less often, and you will be less prone to injury.

Standing on your toes

Set a block of wood or a standard house brick on the ground. Balance on it on your toes, and alternately stretch up as high as you can and then down as low as possible, with your heels below the block. This exercise helps to develop a good sense of balance, and it stretches and strengthens your calf muscles and your ankles. It is particularly useful for the flexed-leg, forward-leaning stance of the basic schuss position (p. 60).

Schussing

Getting up

Every skier falls and it is worth practicing how to get up onto your feet again easily and efficiently (p. 52). Sit down on the floor in the corner of a room, with both legs tucked up alongside you. Push yourself upright with your legs, using your arms to support yourself against both walls. Repeat several times with your legs on either side of you. On the slopes, you will see immediately how your ski poles take the place of the walls.

Getting up from a fall

Front press-ups

All skiing techniques require the effective use of your poles – for turning, for walking on skis and for double-pole pushing (p.48) to increase speed. For this reason, you should aim to build up the strength in your arms, shoulders and upper body. The simple, familiar press-up is one of the best exercises for this – but remember to keep your back straight and your whole body rigid all the time.

Double-pole pushing

Back press-ups

Doing press-ups while lying on your back instead of on your front will also help you strengthen your arms and shoulders. Place your hands more-or-less level with your shoulders, and as you push up try to keep your legs and body as straight and rigid as you can. This exercise is particularly helpful for herring-bone climbing (p. 56), where you support yourself with your poles planted down the slope behind you.

Herringbone climbing

Rotating hips

The rotation and counter-rotation of the upper body which is a vital part of almost all turning maneuvers (p. 183) requires great mobility of the hips, waist and torso. You can develop this by standing with your hands on your hips and swinging your upper body slowly around in a wide circle, first one way and then the other. Alternatively, jump up in the air and, as you land, twist your legs in one direction and your upper body in the other.

Counter-rotation

Wall sitting

Keeping your legs flexed is an important part of all ski technique – but especially in absorption-extension (p. 120) and in its "jet" and "kangaroo" variations. These movements put a great strain on the front of the thighs. Probably the best exercise for building up strength in the leg muscles is the "wall sit". With your feet flat on the floor, sit back against a wall so that your thighs are parallel to the ground. Take it easy with this exercise: it is not as easy as it looks.

Absorption-extension

Jumping to either side

From a standing position with your feet together, jump your legs out to one side – first to your right and then to your left. Try to keep your upper body still and make your legs do the work. This will strengthen your legs and loosen up your hips and waist. It will improve your body angulation and your ability to transfer weight and edge your skis when turning. And it is a particularly good exercise for short swinging (p. 112) and slalom racing.

Slalom racing

Warming up on the slope

Before you begin skiing first thing in the morning or after lunch, or after a cold ride up on the ski lift, you should always do a few simple exercises to warm up. Although this advice is often ignored by recreational skiers, the routine is highly worthwhile. When your body is warm, not only will you ski much better, but you are less likely to fall and less likely to hurt yourself if you do. Cold muscles and stiff joints do not work efficiently: they become inflexible and lose their elasticity, and you will find that your coordination is impaired and your reaction time slowed down. As a result, you may try to ski simply by using more physical force – with the risk of tearing muscles and ligaments.

Ski racers always warm up before a run – especially in the morning when it is usually a little colder and when the body may be stiff from the day before. Simple exercises loosen up stiff joints, warm up cold muscles and get the circulation going. In other words, they get your body ready for the demands

that will be placed on it when you set off. This is especially true in the case of beginners, who may not be used to skiing, who may not have prepared themselves with a pre-ski fitness program, and who are more likely to make mistakes, fall and overstrain themselves. Warming-up exercises are also particularly helpful if you find that the unusually high altitudes make you slightly short of breath. Getting your circulation going before you begin to ski will increase your oxygen supply and make your breathing easier.

The exercises illustrated on these pages will give you a few ideas for limbering up. Of course, you can supplement them by adding exercises of your own. But the ones shown here will serve to stretch, loosen and warm up most of your joints and muscles. At the top of the trail, spend a few minutes doing these warm-up exercises, but remember that you are aiming only to limber up, not to exhaust yourself before you start.

◄ Ski class warming up
A ski instructor gives his class of youngsters some exercises designed to limber them up after a long ride up to the top of the mountain on the ski lift.

Sliding skis backwards and ▲ forwards Walk on the spot, sliding your skis over the snow beneath your body, to warm up your leg muscles and get you used to the feel of your skis.

◄ Arm and body stretching
With your skis apart in a wide parallel stance, lean over to touch your ankles with both hands, first to one side and then to the other.

Pole exercises ▲
Hold both poles together as shown. With your legs straight, bend down to touch your ankles, stretch your poles up and over your head, and twist them around to each side.

Leg stretching ▶
With your skis in a wide "herringbone" position, bend down first to one side and then to the other, trying to touch the snow with your knee. Bend just enough to stretch your leg muscles, not so far that you strain them.

Touching opposite ▲ ankles With your skis wide apart, stretch down and touch your right ankle with your left hand, then your left ankle with your right hand. Repeat until your muscles have loosened and warmed up.

Swivelling skis ▼
Stand on one leg and support yourself with your pole. Lift the other ski and swing it around behind and in front.

Rotating knees and hips ▶
With your skis parallel and using both poles for support, swivel your hips around in a wide circle, first clockwise and then counter-clockwise.

279

Ski vacations

A skiing holiday has been described as the ideal winter tonic. It combines fresh mountain air and sunshine with exercise and a totally absorbing sport. The idea of a winter vacation in the mountains is not new: it originated in Europe in the mid-nineteenth century when "lowlanders", in particular the affluent British, travelled to the mountains for the winter sunshine. At that time, they stayed in summer resorts and health spas. These were ideal because they were already well-established tourist towns and unlike the smaller mountain villages, had the necessary hotels and were accessible by road and rail in the winter.

The early winter holiday-makers took part in ice-skating, tobogganing and "curling". This laid the foundation for the idea of the "winter-sports" holiday. At first, skiing was not included; it was introduced to the Alps only gradually, towards the end of the century, and it did not become a common sight until the First World War.

In the 1920s, skiing began to take over as the most popular of all winter sports. Until that time, all skiers had had to teach themselves how to ski – perhaps with the help of the few instruction manuals that had been written and published. But, in 1920, Hannes Schneider, an Austrian, developed a method of skiing known as the Arlberg technique and established the first modern ski school in St Anton am Arlberg where he could teach his technique to groups of would-be skiers. This very important breakthrough in the development of skiing led to ski schools being started in resorts all over Europe. By the 1930s, the so-called "Golden Age of Skiing", many more resorts were developed in suitable areas to cope with the increased number of skiers. The invention and installation of ski lifts (the T-bar was first installed in Davos in 1934) made the sport more accessible and meant that skiers no longer had to climb the mountains on foot.

Traditionally, skiing holidays have been associated with the wealthy because, originally, they were the only people who had "holidays". For a long time, the tradition was perpetuated by the expense of travelling to the mountains and staying in the resort. Nowadays, with travel and holidays open to more people, specialized firms offer "package holidays" to make skiing cheaper and attract more people. Such "pre-paid" holidays include the cost of travelling to a destination and of accommodation when you get there. Many tour operators now also include the cost of the lift pass, ski instruction and equipment rental in the price of the holiday.

The ski resort

The Swiss developed the first ski resorts – places to go specifically to ski – when they winterized their summer resorts for the first skiers. Ski resorts have since grown rapidly alongside the remarkable development of the winter-sports industry. In the Alps, they can be clearly divided into three categories: first-, second- and third-generation resorts.

The "first-generation" resorts are the oldest. They include some of the most famous names – for example, St Moritz and Davos in Switzerland, Chamonix in France and Badgastein in Austria. These resorts now have some of the largest ski areas in the Alps. And, because they were developed as ski centers early this century, most of them have large old town centers with many old established hotels. They are still very popular and offer an enormous variety of leisure activities for both skiers and non-skiers – but because they are fashionable they do tend to be expensive.

As the number of skiers increased – with the introduction of the ski school, for example – more resorts were developed around small Alpine farming villages. These are the "second-generation" resorts. They had no previous tourist trade but are located in good skiing areas. The majority of European resorts fall into this category. There is normally an old village center which, depending on its age, may now be engulfed by modern buildings.

The "third-generation" resorts are purpose-built. They are complete villages which have been designed and manufactured solely for skiers in a suitable skiing area. The first purpose-built resort was built, together with access roads, in the middle of nowhere in the 1930s at Sun Valley, Idaho, in the United States. The first European purpose-built resort followed at Sestrière in Italy in 1936. But it was the French in the 1950s and 1960s who developed the idea properly. Their resorts are built either to open up previously unused mountains (e.g., Isola 2000) or to link already existing resorts.

St Moritz ▲
An old first-generation resort, it received its first winter visitors in 1865 and it remains popular.

Lech am Arlberg ▼
An early Austrian second-generation resort in the region where the first ski school was developed.

La Plagne ▶
This is typical of the modern French resorts. It is purpose-built so that everything you need is provided – but you will find that you have to sacrifice virtually all the traditional character of an old village for the modern convenience of a new one.

◀ The world's fastest growing leisure activity
Two skiers admire the spectacular view on the slopes above Verbier – one of the best organized resorts in the Alps.

Choosing a ski resort

This can be a daunting prospect, particularly if you have never skied before. Start by consulting a few holiday brochures and, if necessary, contact the government tourist offices of the countries you would like to visit. This should give you an idea of what is available. Bear in mind, however, that this is all promotional literature; contact a ski club if you want more objective information.

One of the most important factors to take into account when making your choice is your budget. Skiing is most expensive at Christmas and Easter (when the resorts are crowded), and cheapest at the beginning of December and the end of April. Basically, there are two seasons: a "low season" which runs from the beginning of January to mid-February; and a "high season" which runs from mid-February until the end of March or after Easter. In the southern hemisphere, the low season for skiing is in June and the high season is in August.

Resorts are often classified according to the size of the skiing area, the number of lifts and trails, the number of beds in the resort, and the height of the village and of the highest lift station. Tour companies sometimes "grade" resorts according to their suitability for skiers of different abilities. As a beginner you may do best if you go to the small resorts which are more likely to have suitable slopes, and avoid the large, popular ones you have heard a lot about. The latter are likely to be more expensive and have plenty of good runs for advanced skiers but only a few for beginners. The easier slopes that they do have may be at the bottom of the main runs (which means that you will constantly have fast skiers around you), and may be in shadow for much of the day.

Accommodation in each resort varies. There are three main types: hotels, chalets and apartments. The last two are sometimes self-catering or, as is popular with the package-tour operators, they are let with a cook or "chalet girl". In each case, the location is important. Ideally, your accommodation would be beside the main lift station, but, unless you are in a purpose-built resort, this is unlikely. So make certain that there is transport provided or a good local bus service, because a long walk with your skis and boots can be very tiring.

Always check that there are adequate ski school facilities and that, if you are in a foreign country, there are instructors who speak your language – your progress will be much faster if they do.

Checklist

Use this as a guide to the things you should consider when choosing a resort. Also, obtain a "trail map" of the surrounding slopes.

- Time of year
- Budget
- Country (p.282-305)
- Size of resort
- Altitude of resort, slopes, and tree line
- Lifts and trails: quantity, height, length, grading, direction (p.212)
- Accommodation
- Type of ski school
- Children: nursery slopes, kindergartens, etc.
- Extra recreational facilities

The mountain restaurant ▶
All resorts have one or more places on the mountain where you can stop for lunch without having to go down to the village.

Snow conditions at the resort

There are a number of factors which affect the sort of snow you will get, and they should all be considered when you are choosing a resort. One of the most important is the direction in which the slopes face (p.219). It is an advantage to go to a resort which has slopes facing in as many different directions as possible. In the early season, when it is very cold, south-facing slopes will allow you to ski in the sun for longer. In the late season, slopes which are north-facing will be the last to lose their snow.

The actual snowfall is unpredictable. However, there are certain snow conditions that you can expect in particular months during the season. These are discussed in greater detail in the section on "Weather and snow" (p.218-21). Basically, the season in the northern hemisphere runs from December to May. Although there is sometimes snow in November, there is generally not enough to form a good base on which to ski. The snow in December is still unreliable, but usually you should be able to ski at Christmas. In January and early February, the snow conditions are good with plenty of dry "powder snow" although it will be very cold. From the middle of February to the middle of March, the beginning of the high season, it will be warmer, with longer days and good plentiful snow. By the end of March, the conditions should still be good but you will be getting "spring snow" on the south-facing slopes and a much stronger sun. April is a good month for sunshine but you are only likely to find good snow on the north-facing slopes – and very low resorts may have no snow left at all. After May, you will have to go to very high altitudes to find any snow at all – possibly up to the glacier ski areas where you can ski all summer.

In the southern hemisphere, the skiing season runs from June to October. The seasonal snow conditions are similar, except that it is the north-facing slopes that receive the direct sun.

Altitude

The height of a resort is important for several reasons. The higher the resort, the greater the probability of finding snow early or late in the season. However, a high resort can be very cold in January and February, with more difficult slopes that are less suitable for beginners.

Altitude also has to be considered for another reason: the possibility of mild "altitude sickness". Although there is no given height above which you are likely to suffer from this, it is quite common to find slight difficulty in breathing and sleeping when you first arrive at a high resort. You may also suffer from other signs, such as headaches, nausea, dizziness or a fast pulse-rate, particularly after going up the mountain in a cable car. These often take you up over 1,000m (3,280ft) in a matter of minutes. If this is the case, be careful when you arrive at the top, and take it easy for a few minutes so that your body can adjust to the altitude before you begin skiing.

Cable cars ▲
These are used to take skiers up very steep mountain faces or over deep ravines to the high skiing areas.

Skiing at high altitude ▼
The views, looking down to the valley from the top of the mountain can be almost as exciting as the actual skiing itself.

Travel

There are several different ways of getting to a resort: by airplane (followed by a road or rail transfer from the airport to the resort); by train; by coach (this is cheaper but slower); or by car all the way. If you are organizing your own holiday, all these methods require careful planning. The main advantage of the package-holiday is that everything is organized for you. The disadvantage if you are flying is that you are normally limited to 20kgs (44lbs) of luggage, plus your ski equipment.

Travelling by car is becoming more popular, even in the case of people who live a long way from the mountains and, in particular, amongst those who are going on a self-catering holiday. The advantage is that there is no weight limit for your luggage. This means that you can carry all your equipment with you and as many provisions as you wish. You will, however, need a ski rack if you are not hiring your skis at the resort. The other advantage of going by car is that you have your own transport in the resort – although private vehicles are banned in some towns.

If you are passing through several countries, make certain, *before* you start, that you are familiar with all the different winter driving laws. In most Alpine countries, for example, it is against the law not to carry "snow chains" for the tires and driving without them in places is almost impossible. Check also that your car insurance covers the countries through which you will pass.

Insurance

It is possible to insure against almost everything that can go wrong on a skiing holiday – even bad snow – and you are well advised to take out some sort of cover. Most tour operators include an insurance policy in the price of their package-holidays, but examine the terms very carefully and make certain that they include cancellation insurance.

For a skiing holiday, the type of things you will need to insure yourself against are: medical expenses (for both short-term and possible permanent injuries); the cost of transport from an accident to the hospital (this can be very expensive – especially if a helicopter is involved); loss or damage to your ski equipment, or any other possessions; and third-party liability in the event of you injuring another skier (in a collision on the slopes, for example) and finding yourself responsible for the damages.

You can never over-insure yourself. The problem when skiing is not so much that you are *likely* to injure yourself – if you are careful you will probably not – but that, if you do have an accident, rescue and medical expenses can be very expensive.

Horse-drawn sledges ▲ At one time the only form of transport across the snow, sledges are used in some resorts to create a traditional atmosphere.

Skiing below the tree ▶ line As well as providing shelter from the wind, skiing through the trees can give you some of the best snow conditions.

Ski gazetteer

It is possible to ski anywhere where the snow lies for long enough – this need only be for a few weeks – and anywhere where the terrain is suitable for cross-country skiing or downhill skiing, or both. You can now ski at resorts or ski areas in nearly forty different countries throughout the world and, as the popularity of the sport increases, more areas are being developed to cope with the growing numbers. All that is needed to establish a ski resort are the right geographical conditions, the finances necessary to install lift systems and to maintain the slopes, and an adequate, accessible population to use the facilities.

The most recent developments have been made in the more "exotic" parts of the world: in the Near and Middle East (Iran, Turkey, Syria and the Lebanon), in northern Africa and South Africa, and in the Himalayas. In northern Africa, there are ski areas in both Morocco (near Casablanca and Marrakech) and in Algeria (between Algiers and Bouira). Skiing in Kenya is possible on Mount Kenya and Mount Kilimanjaro, although development here is severely hampered because they are so difficult to get to. In South Africa, there is a certain amount of orga-

nized skiing to be found outside Cape Town and in the centre of the country on the Lesotho border, but ski touring is more popular. There are also one or two resorts in the Himalayas, the largest of which is Gulmarg, on the Pakistan-India border between Lahore and Kashmir. Most of these ski areas, however, are fairly small, and they all share the same basic problems: first, they are not readily accessible; second, there is not a sufficiently large enough population close at hand – most of the people who use Gulmarg, for example, come all the way from Hong Kong. This means that it is difficult to raise the finances necessary for further growth.

So, apart from these "exotic" areas, the major regions of the world where you can find organized ski resorts are Europe, America, Canada, Australia, New Zealand and Japan. In this chapter we describe some of the best-known resorts in all these areas. There are maps of all the most important ski regions, and with each map is a list of the largest resorts in the region. Where possible, the height of the village and of the top lift station is given – as well as the number of lifts in the resort – to give you an idea of the size of the area and the type of skiing.

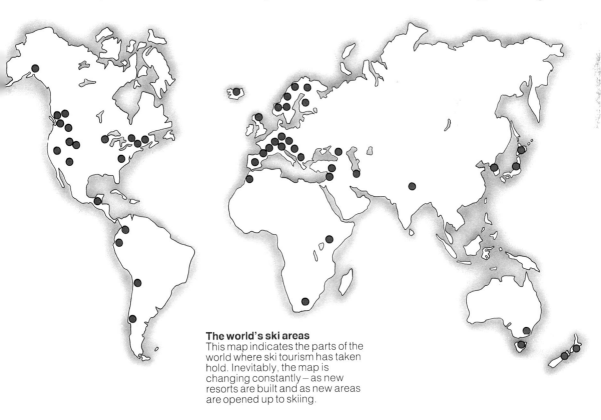

The world's ski areas
This map indicates the parts of the world where ski tourism has taken hold. Inevitably, the map is changing constantly – as new resorts are built and as new areas are opened up to skiing.

Switzerland

Skiing has been popular in Switzerland since its introduction there in the mid-nineteenth century. For many years, the mountains had been visited by summer tourists, and, when skiing began to catch on as a major winter sport, Switzerland quickly established itself as one of the world's leading ski nations. Its mountains proved to be suitable for virtually every kind of skiing: in the younger mountains of southern Switzerland is some of the best and most challenging Alpine skiing; amongst the high peaks on the French and Italian borders are some of the best-known Alpine ski touring and ski mountaineering routes; in the Jura mountains north of Geneva, and in the east, on the Austrian border, there is cross-country touring; and in most of the Alpine resorts, there are special "ski touring" trails.

The largest and best-known Swiss ski resorts are mainly concentrated in the mountainous southern half of the country. They vary in type and include both the international "jet-set" resorts such as St Moritz, Zermatt and Gstaad (which are almost as famous for the people who frequent them as for the skiing) and the smaller "family" resorts such as Saas Fee, Engelberg or Flims and Laax.

There tend to be very few purpose-built resorts in Switzerland; they have mostly grown up gradually – either around existing summer tourist centres or around old farming villages. However, this does not mean that they are poorly organized. The Engadin Valley, for example, which includes St Moritz (the oldest Swiss resort and the first to have winter visitors) has now been developed into a large ski area with interconnecting ski lifts that link up the resorts of St Moritz, Silvaplana and Sils. The same can be said of the Jungfrau region which is now an enormous and very popular ski area incorporating the villages of Mürren (where the British ski pioneer, Sir Arnold Lunn, spent his winters), Wengen, Kleine Scheidegg and Grindelwald.

In many areas of Switzerland, it is possible to ski all year round on the high glaciers where snow lies throughout the summer.

◀ **Verbier**
The town of Verbier, illustrated here, lies at the heart of one of the best-organized ski areas in Switzerland. Sometimes known as *Les Quatres Vallées*, it consists of several main resorts and satellite villages (Thyon 2000, Veysonnaz, Haute-Nendaz, Mayens-de-Riddes, La Tzoumaz, Le Chable and Verbier itself). All four valleys, about 90 lifts in all, are covered by the same lift pass, and new ski areas are being developed all the time.
Verbier: height 1,500m (4,021ft), lowest lift station 821m (2,639ft), top station 3,328m (10,919ft), 49 lifts.
Thyon 2000: height 2,000m (6,562ft), lowest lift station 1,233m (4,045ft), top station 3,328m (10,919ft), 17 lifts.

1 The Bernese Oberland and the Valais

In this, the western half of Switzerland, there are resorts to suit every skier, and all are easily accessible by air, road and rail.

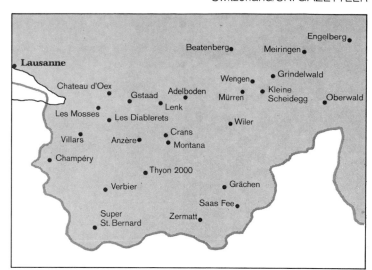

Adelboden/Lenk
All the skiing in this area is covered by the same lift pass. **Adelboden:** height 1,352m (4,438ft), top station 2,330m (7,644ft), 25 lifts. **Lenk:** height 1,068m (3,504ft), top station 2,098m (6,884ft), 11 lifts.

Anzère
Height 1,500m (4,920ft), top station 2,419m (7,937ft), 9 lifts.

Beatenberg
Height 1,300m (4,265ft), top station 1,951m (6,400ft), 5 lifts.

Champéry
Height 1,051m (3,450ft), top station 2,255m (7,400ft), 17 lifts.

Crans/Montana
Although these are two separate villages, they are at the same altitude and they share the same ski area. Height 1,500m (4,920ft), top station 2,999m (9,840ft), 32 lifts.

Engelberg
Height 1,050m (3,444ft), top station 3,019m (9,906ft), 20 lifts.

Gstaad ski area
This very famous resort is linked by road and ski lift to the villages of Chateau d'Oex, Saanenmöser, Saaren and Rougemont. There is a total of 45 lifts in the area and the skiing is excellent. **Chateau d'Oex:** height 1,000m (3,281ft), top station 1,750m (5,741ft), 11 lifts. **Gstaad:** height 1,100m (3,608ft), top station 1,969m (6,461ft), 15 lifts.

Grächen
Height 1,619m (5,312ft), top station 2,620m (8,596ft), 10 lifts.

Jungfrau ski area
It is possible to buy either a lift pass which covers just the area around your own resort or one which extends to all the resorts in the area. The lift systems at Wengen and Grindelwald link up at Kleine Scheidegg. **Grindelwald:** height 1,042m (3,420ft), top station 3,454m (11,333ft), 23 lifts. **Kleine Scheidegg:** height 2,060m (6,762ft), top station 3,454m (11,333ft). **Mürren:** height 1,634m (5,362ft), top station 2,941m (9,652ft), ll lifts. **Wengen:** height 1,288m (4,225ft), top station 3,454m (11,333ft), 25 lifts.

Saas Fee
Height 1,800m (5,905ft), top station 3,250m (10,663ft), 22 lifts.

Villars
Height 1,300m (4,264ft), top station 2,199m (7,216ft), 27 lifts.

Wiler
Height 1,380m (4,527ft), top station 2,700m (8,858ft), 4 lifts.

Zermatt ▶
This internationally famous ski resort lies at the foot of the Matterhorn. The skiing extends over three valleys and it is also possible to ski into Cervinia, Italy. Height 1,619m (5,315ft), top station 3,810m (12,532ft), 30 lifts.

2 Eastern Switzerland

This was the first part of Switzerland to be developed for winter tourism. St Moritz was the first winter-sports resort and Davos was the site of the first T-bar lift.

Andermatt
Height 1,444m (4,738ft), top station 2,961m (9,715ft), 8 lifts.

Arosa
Height 1,829m (6,000ft), top station 2,639m (8,658ft), 15 lifts.

Braunwald
Height 1,298m (4,260ft), top station 1,899m (6,232ft), 7 lifts.

Davos/Klosters
One lift pass covers both these major resorts and also the smaller skiing villages in the valley. **Davos:** height 1,560m (5,118ft), top station 2,844m (9,330ft), 39 lifts. **Klosters:** height 1,191m (3,908ft), top station 2,823m (9,262ft), 20 lifts.

Flims/Laax
These are two fairly small resorts in the same valley with an interconnecting system of lifts. Together, they make an ideal family resort. **Flims:** height 1,150m (3,773ft), top station 3,018m (9,902ft), 18 lifts. **Laax:** height 1,020m (3,346ft), top station 3,018m (9,902ft), 18 lifts.

Lenzerheide
Height 1,470m (4,822ft), top station 2,864m (9,397ft), 32 lifts.

St Moritz ski area
Situated in the Engadin Valley, this area incorporates five ski areas around the main resorts of St Moritz, Pontresina, Silvaplana and Sils. **Pontresina:** height

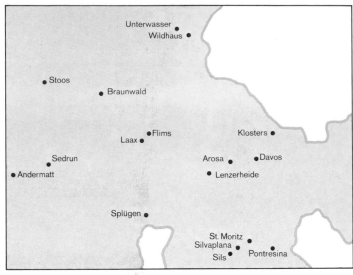

1,820m (5,972ft), top station 3,049m (10,004ft), 14 lifts. **St Moritz:** height 1,822m (5,978ft), top station 3,303m (10,837ft), 33 lifts. **Silvaplana:** height 1,185m (5,978ft), top station 3,303m (10,837ft), 13 lifts.

Sedrun
Height 1,400m (4,593ft), top station 2,840m (9,318ft), 13 lifts.

Stoos
Height 1,300m (4,265ft), top station

1,922m (6,306ft), 7 lifts.

Wildhaus/Unterwasser/St Johann ski area Near the border with Liechtenstein, these resorts lie along the valley floor and are linked by ski lifts across their north-facing slopes. **Unterwasser:** height 910m (2,985ft), top station 2,259m (7,413ft), 5 lifts. **Wildhaus:** height 1,035m (3,395ft), top station 2,259m (7,413ft), 20 lifts.

◀ Andermatt
This attractive, fairly small resort lies just north of the St Gotthard Pass. It offers good skiing conditions and a variety of different runs for intermediate and advanced skiers.

Davos ▲
One of the country's most famous resorts, Davos – together with Klosters, further up the valley – provides one of the most extensive ski areas in Switzerland.

Austria

A great deal of the credit for demonstrating that skiing was a sport which everyone could enjoy – and not something that was restricted to the lone adventurers in the Swiss Alps – must go to Austria. It was here, in the *Arlberg* mountain region, that popular recreational skiing was born. At St Anton, in 1920, the first modern ski school was established under the direction of Hannes Schneider – who is now widely considered to have been one of the pioneers of Alpine skiing.

The skiing in Austria is slightly different to that found elsewhere in western Europe. The mountains are older (so-called "pre-Alpine") and not so high, and because of this much of the skiing is below the tree line. This does not mean, however, that it is any easier. Stuben, for example, is said to have one of the longest and most difficult runs in the world, and most Austrian resorts have at least one trail with a drop of 1,000m (3,281ft) or more. Normally, the skiing conditions are

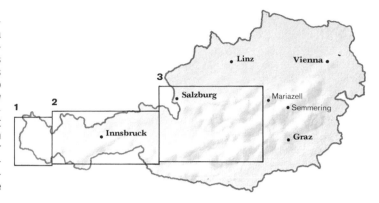

excellent, with good snow cover in spite of the lower altitudes, and a long season, usually from December to April. There are, however, fewer summer skiing areas; the best-known is probably the Dachstein glacier area in Salzburg province.

There are a great many resorts in Austria, and nearly three-quarters of them are in the Tirol. Some, such as Badgastein, started out as summer spas and tourist centers, but the majority

were farming villages before the advent of skiing. Because of an eighteenth-century tax law, most of these villages are at a height of about 1,000m (3,281ft), and most of them have been carefully preserved to maintain the traditional village atmosphere for which Austria became famous. This does mean, however, that – excluding some of the recently developed resorts – there are few large ski areas with interconnecting lift systems.

◀ **Lech am Arlberg**
Situated in one of the most famous skiing regions in Austria (the *Arlberg*), the skiing around the resort of Lech is ideal for beginners and intermediate skiers. More advanced skiers can easily travel over to the slopes of Zürs or Stubens for more challenging runs.

1 The Vorarlberg province

The skiing in this area is very similar to that in eastern Switzerland and it includes the famous *Arlberg* region.

Arlberg ski area

Situated in the Arlberg Pass, Lech, Stuben and Zürs are all linked by road and ski lift. **Lech:** height 1,436m (4,712ft), top station 2,449m (8,038ft), 29 lifts. **Stuben:** height 1,399m (4,592ft), top station 2,399m (7,872ft), 5 lifts. **Zürs:** height 1,703m (5,590ft), top station 2,444m (8,022ft), 11 lifts.

Brand

Height 1,039m (3,142ft), top station 1,919m (6,297ft), 9 lifts.

Galtür

Height 1,583m (5,196ft), top station 2,213m (7,261ft), 10 lifts.

Silvretta Nova ski area

A skiing circuit in the Silvretta Mountains which takes in these three resorts. **Gargellen:** height 1,410m (4,628ft), top station 2,316m (7,600ft), 8 lifts. **Gaschurn:** height 999m (3,280ft), top station 2,249m (7,300ft), 21 lifts. **St Gallenkirchen:** height 850m (2,788ft), top station 2,370m (7,775ft), 11 lifts.

Tschagguns

Height 694m (2,278ft), top station 2,103m (6,903ft), 10 lifts.

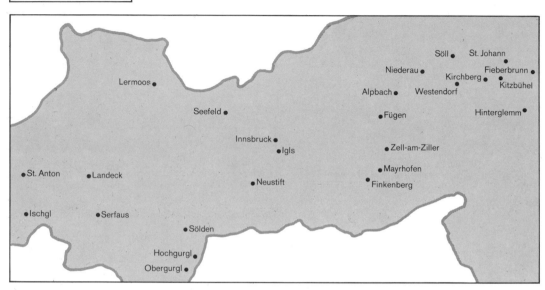

2 The Tirol

This area contains some of the most famous ski resorts in Austria: for example, St Anton, the home of the first ski school and the site of the St Anton-Kandahar race, and Innsbruck, host city for the 1964 and 1976 Winter Olympics.

Alpbach

Height 1,000m (3,281ft), top station 2,126m (6,978ft), 17 lifts.

Igls

Height 893m (2,929ft), top station 2,246m (7,369ft), 6 lifts.

Obergurgl/Hochgurgl

These two resorts are in the highest ski area in Austria and the second highest in Europe. Both resorts share the same skiing facilities. **Hochgurgl** (height 2,419m/7,054ft), **Obergurgl** (height 1,926m/6,322ft), top station for both 3,081m (10,111ft), 21 lifts.

St Anton am Arlberg

Height 1,285m (4,219ft), top station 2,810m (9,222ft), 27 lifts.

St Johann in Tirol

Height 670m (2,198ft), top station 1,600m (5,250ft), 9 lifts.

Seefeld

Height 1,180m (3,872ft), top station 2,099m (6,890ft), 13 lifts.

Ziller Valley ski area

You can either buy a ski pass for each resort or the special *Ski Pass Zillertal* which allows you to ski all ten resorts in this valley. **Finkenburg:** height 843m (2,768ft), top station 2,099m (6,888ft), 7 lifts. **Mayrhofen:** height 629m (2,067ft), top station 2,029m (6,660ft), 15 lifts. **Zell-am-Ziller:** height 579m (1,902ft), top station 2,263m (7,428ft), 9 lifts.

◀ **Kitzbühel**

There are two main resorts in this valley and they both share the same ski area: Kitzbühel itself (height 762m/2,503ft) and Kirchberg (height 862m/2,830ft), top station 1,962m (6,444ft), 56 lifts.

3 Central Austria

Many of the resorts in this region, which includes Salzburg, Upper Austria and Corinthia, have long been established as summer spas. Plans are now being carried out in many areas to extend lift systems and join up the resorts to form larger ski areas.

Bad Goisern
Height 499m (1,640ft), top station 996m (3,280ft), 4 lifts.

Bad Kleinkirchheim
Height 1,073m (3,520ft), top station 2,050m (6,726ft), 14 lifts

Dachstein Mountains ski area Of the several resorts in this area, Filzmoos, Ramsau and Gosau have access to the Dachstein glacier.
Filzmoos: height 1,036m (3,401ft), top station 1,599m (5,248ft), 16 lifts. **Radstadt/Altenmark:** height 862m (2,828ft), top station, 1,768m (5,800ft), 5 lifts. **Wagrain** (height 869m/2,940ft) and **Flachau** (height 927m/3,041ft) share the same top station (2,014m/6,607ft) and 16 lifts.
Gastein Valley ski area
An excellent winter-sports

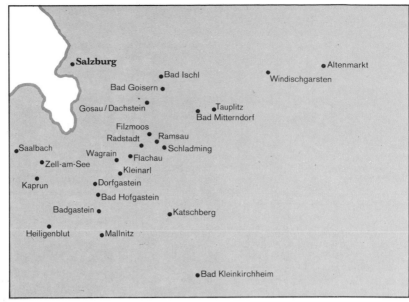

centre, this region caters for all types of skiing, as well as for other sports such as bobsleighing. **Badgastein:** height 1,099m (3,608ft), top station 2,465m (8,809ft), 20 lifts. **Bad Hofgastein:** height 870m (2,853ft), top station 2,299m (7,544ft), 13 lifts.
Dorfgastein: height 865m (2,238ft), top station 2,077m (6,815ft), 9 lifts.
Windischgarsten
Height 600m (1,968ft), top station 859m (2,821ft), 8 lifts.

Sölden ▼
In the Tirol region, the resort of Sölden (height 1,352m/4,436ft, top station 3,056m/10,030ft, 24 lifts) provides good late-season skiing.

France

There are two main ski regions in France: the French Alps and the French Pyrenees. There is also some skiing in the mountains of central France (the Massif Central) and in the mountains north of Geneva (the Vosges and the Jura). These areas, however, are mostly frequented by weekend and day skiers and are better known for their cross-country skiing than for their downhill slopes.

Although France was the host country for the first Winter Olympic Games, held in Chamonix in 1924, the French did not become involved in the winter-sports industry on a large scale until the 1950s. Because of this, they felt that they were in a position to learn from the "mistakes" made in other Alpine countries. Their solution was to establish the purpose-built resorts for which they have become famous. These resorts are mainly found in previously unexploited areas of the Alps and are often connected by ski lifts to resorts in neighboring valleys – thus forming enormous ski areas. The two best known are Les Trois Vallées (where the lift systems of Courchevel, Meribel and Val Thorens are all linked) and the Val d'Isère/Tignes region. The Chamonix Valley ski area spans another very large region, and one lift pass covers thirteen different resorts. Although the lifts do not all interconnect, a bus link is provided between the villages.

The French Alps are divided into two sections: the *Alpes du Nord* (sometimes known as the *Haute Savoie* and the *Savoie* regions) and the *Alpes du*

Sud, the mountains south of Grenoble. Most of the skiing in these areas is above the tree line. There is a good variety, and in some places it is possible to ski all year round.

The French Pyrenees was in fact the birth-place of French skiing, but the area now tends to be little known outside south-western France since it is quite difficult to reach in the winter.

1 The French Pyrenees

Skiing in this area is most suited to beginners and intermediate skiers. Many of the resorts are built around small villages and towns, and most of them cater for large families and weekend visitors. The area is also good for cross-country skiing.

Ax-les-Thermes
Height 720m (2,322ft), top station 2,300m (7,546ft), 13 lifts.
Les Angles
Height 1,600m (5,249ft), top station 2,400m (7,875ft), 17 lifts.
Barèges/Tourmalet/La Mongie
The same ski pass covers both Barèges and La Mongie whose lifts are linked across the Col du Tourmalet. **Barèges:** height 1,250m (4,101ft), top station 2,250m (7,382ft), 20 lifts. **La Mongie:** height 1,800m (5,905ft), top station 2,360m (7,743ft), 21 lifts.

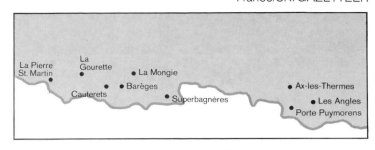

Cauterets
Height 1,850m (6,070ft), top station 2,500m (8,202ft), 15 lifts.
La Gourette
Height 1,400m (4,593ft), top station 2,400m (7,875ft), 21 lifts.
La Pierre St Martin
Height 1,500m (4,921ft), top station 2,200m (7,062ft), 14 lifts.

Porte Puymorens
Height 1,615m (5,298ft), top station 2,520m (8,268ft), 9 lifts.
Superbagnères
Height 1,400m (4,593ft), top station 2,260m (7,415ft), 15 lifts.

2 The French Alps

Resorts in this region are often large and well-organized and there are places to suit every grade of skier The following represents only a selection of the major resorts.

Alpe d'Huez
Height 1,800m (5,905ft), top station 3,550m (10,990ft), 24 lifts.
Avoriaz
Height 1,000m (3,281ft), top station 2,330m (6,070ft), 51 lifts.
Chamonix
Height 1,035m (3,389ft), top station 3,840m (12,599ft), 45 lifts. One ski pass covers the lifts in 13 resorts in the Chamonix Valley.
Flaine
Height 1,600m (5,250ft), top station 2,500m (8,202ft), 26 lifts.
Isola 2000
Height 2,000m (6,562ft), lowest lift station 1,800m (5,095ft), top station 2,601m (8,536ft), 21 lifts.
Les Arcs
Height 1,600m (5,249ft), top station 3,000m (9,843ft), 40 lifts.
Les Trois Vallées
In this region skiers staying in either of the three major resorts or in the satellite villages can buy a lift pass which covers the whole area. **Courchevel:** height 1,850m (6,070ft), lowest lift station 1,300m (4,265ft), top station 2,690m (8,825ft), 58 lifts. **Meribel:** height 1,450m (4,756ft), top station 2,700m (8,856ft), 36 lifts. **Val Thorens:** height 1,850m (6,070ft), top station 3,400m (11,554ft), 50 lifts.
Val d'Isère/Tignes
These two resorts have interconnecting lift systems so that you can ski throughout the whole area. **Val d'Isère:** height 1,850m (6,070ft), top station 3,250m (10,663ft), 56 lifts. **Tignes:** height 2,100m (6,890ft), top station 3,460m (11,352ft), 57 lifts.

◀**La Clusaz**
This is one of the oldest resorts in the French Alps and was established in the 1930s. Height 1,100m (3,609ft), top station 2,600m (8,530ft), 37 lifts.

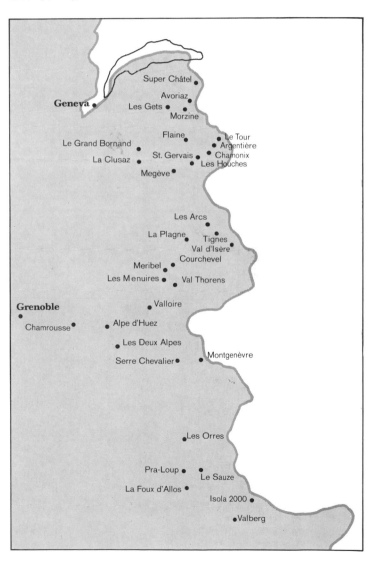

Italy

There are a great many large resorts in Italy, and most of them are concentrated in the Alps in the north of the country. The Alpine region can be divided into two areas. The first is in north-eastern Italy and includes the central Alps, the eastern Alps and the Dolomites. The second consists of the western Alps which extend from Switzerland, through the *Val d'Aosta* on the French border, and down to the *Alpes Maritimes* on the Mediterranean. Resorts in both these areas are easily accessible by air and by road (several of the passes across the Alps are now kept open all winter). Moreover, because they are so close to the international borders, many of the inhabitants and the ski school instructors are fluent in more than one language. In fact, in western parts, French is the first language.

Apart from the Alps, there is also some skiing to be found in the Appennine mountains. The oldest and largest resort is Abetone, near Florence, which has about nineteen ski lifts. Further south, there are ski areas outside Rome and even on Mount Etna on the island of Sicily.

1 The central Alps and the Dolomites
This is an excellent ski area. Most of the resorts are high and well-organized. In the Dolomites, you can buy a special "Dolomiti Super Ski Pass" which you can use at most of the resorts in the region – 390 lifts.

Aprica
Height 1,177m (3,863ft), top station 2,574m (8,448ft), 27 lifts.

Bormio
Height 1,225m (4,018ft), top station 2,772m (9,095ft), 12 lifts.

Chiesa
Height 1,000m (3,281ft), top station 1,900m (6,233ft), 5 lifts.

The Dolomite ski area
These are the most important five resorts covered by the Dolomiti Super Ski Pass.
Colfosco/Corvara: height Colfosco 1,646m (5,401ft), Corvara 1,568m (5,143ft), top station for both resorts 2,200m (7,216ft), 49 lifts.
Cortina d'Ampezzo: height 1,224m (4,018ft), top station 3,213m (10,543ft), 41 lifts.
Canazei: height of resort 1,465m (4,806ft), 20 lifts.
Selva di Val Gardena: height 1,563m (5,128ft), top station 2,520m (8,264ft), 47 lifts.

Foppollo
Height 1,500m (4,920ft), top station 2,164m (7,101ft), 9 lifts.

Forni di Sopra
Height 906m (2,975ft), top station 2,060m (6,761ft), 9 lifts.

Livigno
Height 1,815m (5,958ft), top station 2,799m (9,184ft), 26 lifts.

Monte Bondone
Height 1,300m (4,265ft), top station 1,600m (5,250ft), 10 lifts.

Santa Christina di Val ▶ Gardena
This is a small resort in the Val Gardena region of the Dolomite mountains. The village is at 1,428m (4,685ft) and it has about 11 ski lifts.

294

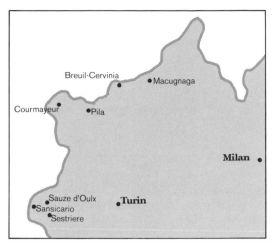

2 The western Alps
The mountains in this area are very high, with many glaciers for summer skiing. Some of the resorts also link up with others in France and Switzerland. You can ski from Cervinia over to Zermatt, from Courmayeur through the *Vallée Blanche* to Chamonix, and from Sestrière over to Montgenèvre.

Breuil-Cervinia
Height 2,060m (6,760ft), top station 3,505m (11,500ft), 24 lifts.
Courmayeur
Height 1,223m (4,015ft), top station 3,000m (9,834ft), 31 lifts.

Macugnaga
Height 1,326m (4,352ft) top station 2,743m (9,000ft), 12 lifts.
Pila
Height 1,371m (4,500ft), top station 2,640m (8,660ft), 11 lifts.
Sauze d'Oulx
Height 1,508m (4,950ft), top station 2,482m (8,145ft), 20 lifts.
Sestrière ski area
A large interconnecting lift system links Sestrière and Sansicario with Montgenèvre in France. It is also possible to ski to Sauze d'Oulx, but you have to get a bus back.
Sestrière: height 2,032m (6,666ft), top station 2,796m (9,175ft), 33 lifts. **Sansicario:** height 1,699m (5,576ft), top station 2,690m (8,826ft), 12 lifts.

Spain

There are two major mountain areas in Spain – the Pyrenees in the north and the Sierra Nevada in the south – and skiing features in both. However, the Pyrenees is by far the most important area. Here, skiing conditions are very similar to those across the border in the French Pyrenees (p.293), and, as in France, the resorts vary in size as well as in age. Moreover, in these mountains lies the principality of Andorra, where skiing is also possible. There are two or three resorts – but the country is probably better known for its duty-free alcohol.

The Sierra Nevada is the home of the most southerly major ski resort in Europe. Called Sol y Nieve, it is large, high (the highest in Spain) and situated just outside Granada, near the Mediterranean. The village is at 1,999m (6,560ft) and the top lift station at 3,469m (11,381ft). There are fourteen ski lifts.

The Spanish Pyrenees and Andorra This region is Spain's major skiing area. La Molina is the oldest resort, but there are also a few new centres, such as El Formigal and Baqueira-Beret. All the resorts have good ski schools.

Baqueira-Beret
Height 1,499m (4,920ft), top station 2,499m (8,200ft), 14 lifts.
Candanchú
Height 1,450m (4,757ft), top station 2,020m (6,627ft), 14 lifts.
Cerler
Height 1,504m (4,936ft), top station 2,363m (7,754ft), 8 lifts.
El Formigal
Height 1,499m (4,920ft), top station 2,413m (7,920ft), 16 lifts.
La Molina
Height 1,440m (7,256ft), top station 2,543m (8,315ft), 17 lifts.
La Tuca
This is the name of the ski area: top

station 2,250m (7,382ft), 6 lifts. The nearest village is Viella: height 1,050m (3,445ft).
Masella
Height 1,600m (5,250ft), top station 2,535m (8,317ft), 5 lifts.
Panticosa
Height 1,164m (4,448ft), top station 1,892m (6,209ft), 5 lifts.

Andorra ski area
There are two or three resorts in this area. Soldeu is the main one, but there are plans to build a cable car to link it with the neighbouring resort of Pas de la Casa. **Soldeu:** height 2,438m (8,000ft), top station 2,630m (8,629ft), 7 lifts. **Pas de la Casa:** height 2,060m (6,758ft), top station 2,800m (9,168ft), 12 lifts.

Great Britain

The British, and Sir Arnold Lunn in particular, have contributed a great deal to modern Alpine skiing. However, because of the unreliable snow cover in Great Britain, there are in fact very few areas where skiing is possible. These are all in central Scotland. There are three main areas: Glencoe in the Western Highlands, and Aviemore and Glenshee in the Cairngorms. Although Glenshee and Glencoe are really only "day ski areas" with limited accommodation, all three areas have uphill transport in the form of chair and drag lifts, and ski schools with registered B.A.S.I. (British Association of Ski Instructors) instructors. Twenty miles (32km) north of Aviemore, there is also a small ski area called Lecht.

The snow conditions in Scotland vary a great deal. Although many areas have snow for much of the winter, the falls are accompanied by strong winds which blow the snow off the main slopes and down into the many small gullies. This, combined with the fact that almost all the skiing is on heather-covered mountain-sides, means that a great deal of snow is required to give good skiing. Perhaps for this reason, Great Britain has a large number of dry ski slopes.

The mountains of Great Britain are very old and, although some are fairly high, most are smooth and gently undulating. Thus, they form ideal terrain for cross-country skiing. This is now becoming a popular sport in many parts of the country.

Scottish ski centers
The map (above right) shows the location of the three ski areas in the Scottish mountains where there is organized downhill skiing. Glencoe is unusual in that groups or ski clubs can rent the entire resort by the day or even by the week.

Aviemore ski area
In the Cairngorm mountains, Aviemore is the town which serves the two ski areas of Coire na Ciste and Coire Cas. These areas lie 13km (8 miles) outside Aviemore and can only be reached by car. **Coire Cas**: height of bottom lift station 655m (2,150ft), top station 1,097m (3,600ft), 9 lifts. **Coire na Ciste**: height of bottom lift station 548m (1,800ft), top station 1,097m (3,600ft), 5 lifts.

Glencoe
Height of bottom lift station 350m (1,150ft), top station 1,106m (3,630ft), 10 lifts. The main ski area can only be reached after 0.8km (½ mile) walk from the top of the chair lift.

Glenshee
Height of bottom lift station 649m (2,130ft), top station 932m (3,060ft), 10 lifts.

Skiing in the Cairngorms ▶
The lift systems in the Cairngorm ski areas of Scotland are modern and well-maintained – although they are often crowded when the snow conditions are good.

Scandinavia

Traditional cross-country (Nordic) skiing originated in Scandinavia. The winter is very long, and much of the country is covered by snow from October to the end of April. Consequently, skis are still an essential means of transport for those who live in remote country districts. In Scandinavia, there is relatively little downhill (Alpine) skiing because the high mountains are largely inaccessible. Most of the terrain consists of gently undulating hills with a very low tree line – around 90-120m (300-400ft) and is therefore better suited to cross-country skiing. Most of the organized ski resorts are found in southern Norway, where some (for example, Voss, Geilo or Norefjell, the site of the 1952 Winter Olympics) have very good skiing. However, many have few prepared runs and their one or two drag lifts are used primarily to take cross-country skiers up to the higher trails.

Cross-country skiing in Scandinavia is extremely popular and very well organized. Many major cities have prepared trails or circuits in the suburbs and parks, some of which are floodlit after dark. In the countryside there are a great many tours which can take anything from a day to two or three weeks to complete. Along the better-known routes, there are often rest huts and hostels. The Telemark area of southern Norway (home of the "Telemark" turn) is one of the most famous ski touring regions and has many long and difficult trails.

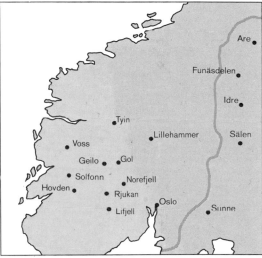

South Norway and south-west Sweden

Scandinavian resorts fall into three categories: those with mainly Alpine skiing; those with Alpine and cross-country skiing; and those that act chiefly as bases for cross-country touring.

Are (Alpine)
Height 400m (1,312ft), top station 1,419m (4,656ft).

◄ **Scandinavian ski touring** Cross-country ski touring is almost a national pastime in Scandinavia. Many of the routes have small huts where skiers can stop for a rest or overnight.

Geilo (Alpine)
Height 760m (2,493ft), top station 1,066m (3,498ft), 10 lifts.
Hovden (Cross-country and Alpine) Height 759m (2,490ft), top station 1,206m (3,956ft), 2 lifts.
Lillehammer (Cross-country and Alpine) Height 199m (656ft), top station 999m (3,280ft), 4 lifts.
Norefjell (Cross-country and Alpine) Height 751m (2,460ft), top station 1,000m (3,281ft), 4 lifts.
Oslo
Ski jumping, cross-country *loipes*, and 5 ski lifts at Nordmarka for Alpine skiing.
Voss (Alpine)
Height 175m (574ft), top station 1,291m (4,235ft), 5 lifts.

West Germany

In Germany, the major ski areas are in the south: Bavaria in the south east, along the Austrian border, and the Black Forest in the south west. Of these two areas, the mountains of Upper Bavaria, in the foothills of the Alps, are the most important for Alpine (downhill) skiing. In the Black Forest, most of the skiing is cross-country – as it is throughout the rest of northern Germany – although there are a few Alpine ski resorts as well. The largest of these is Feldberg (height 950m/ 3,116ft, top station 1,300m/ 4,265ft) and it has about 15 ski lifts. Over the last decade, Ger-

many has really begun to develop its winter-sports industry, and it is now able to compete on a more even footing with most of the other major ski countries. Its resorts are usually built around old farming villages or summer spas, and most of them are easily accessible by road and by rail. Besides skiing, they also offer a wide variety of other winter sports. Bobsledding, in particular, is very popular, and there are international runs at Garmisch Partenkirchen and Konigsee, near Berchtesgaden. Garmisch has now become one of Europe's major winter-sports centers.

Upper Bavaria
The skiing in this region is generally good, and most of the resorts offer a variety of winter sports. However, there are few foreign visitors.

Bergen
Height 560m (1,837ft), top station 700m (2,296ft), 7 lifts.
Garmisch Partenkirchen/Grainau
The site of the 1936 Winter Olympics. There are lifts onto the famous Zugspitze mountain from both resorts. **Garmisch Partenkirchen**: height 720m (2,362ft), top station 2,964m (9,724ft), 48 lifts. **Grainau**: height 750m (2,460ft), top station 2,964m (9,724ft), 12 lifts.
Neuhaus
Height 784m (2,572ft), top station 1,100m (3,609ft), 19 lifts.
Oberammergau
Height 850m (2,788ft), top station 1,700m (5,577ft), II lifts.

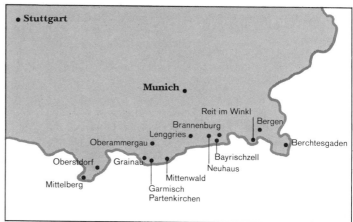

Eastern Europe and the Mediterranean

The high mountain ranges in many Eastern European countries – from Poland in the north down to Greece and Turkey – have excellent snow cover, and many ski areas are now being developed.

Yugoslavia is said to have the oldest skiing tradition, and there are several fairly large resorts. The best known are Kranjskagora (height 809m/ 2,657ft, top station 1,599m/5,248ft, 7 lifts) which hosts rounds of the World Cup championships, and nearby Planica which has an internationally famous ski jumping hill.

Czechoslovakia and *Poland* share the same mountains, the Tatra range, which runs along the border between the two countries and down into

Hungary. There are several resorts in each country, and Czechoslovakia is also well known for its very good cross-country skiing in the south west.

Bulgaria has three or four ski resorts in the Roclopi mountains in the south-western part of the country, near the Yugoslav and Greek borders.

The oldest ski resort in *Greece* is on Mount Vermion in the central Macedonian mountains. The largest resort, however, is on Mount Parnassus in central Greece, near Delphi. There are also many mountains in Greece which have no uphill transport but which are very popular with ski tourers; the most famous is Mount Olympus (2,917m/9,570ft), the highest mountain in Greece.

Japan

The mountains of Japan are very beautiful and have long been popular mountaineering areas. Skiing was first introduced to them early this century by an Austrian, Theodore von Lech. Since then, the sport has flourished, and hundreds of resorts and small ski centers (or *Gelende* as they are called) have now been developed.

The Japanese skiing season normally starts in early November and finishes in March or April. Almost all the skiing is on dormant or extinct volcanoes. The height of the tree line varies slightly but it is normally around 1,500m (4,921ft), and there is very little skiing above 2,000m (6,562ft). The runs are very short by European standards and generally very crowded. Moreover, most of the lifts are not interconnected and serve only one or two trails. The most common lift-type tends to be the chair lift — because it occupies less skiing space than a drag lift.

All the resorts have good ski schools and Japanese ski equipment is excellent. Westerners, however, are advised to take their own equipment rather than rent it: the Japanese are a small race, and it may be difficult to find boots and clothes in large enough sizes.

Japan's ski areas
Information on Japanese ski resorts is hard to obtain in the West. The map (above right) shows the position of the main ski centres. Accommodation in these resorts varies, and you may find that the small resorts only provide Japanese-style "dormitories".

Happo One
Said to have the most difficult skiing in Japan, it boasts one mogul field.
Kusatsu Onsen
Top station 2,100m (6,890ft). This resort is said to have the longest chair lift in Japan: 1.25km (0.8 miles).
Naeba
Top station 1,700m (5,577ft).
Sapporo ski area
Sapporo is the town in the center of the ski area on the island of Hokkaido. It was the site of the 1972 Winter Olympics. Top station 1,000m (3,281ft).
Zao
The newest ski area in Japan. Top station 1,735m (5,692ft), 4 interconnecting lifts.

Snow-encrusted trees ▶
Known as *chouoh*, these are low forest pines which grow at high altitudes in the Japanese mountains. In winter, they become encrusted with windblown snow.

North America

There has been skiing in North America since the middle of the last century, and, in fact, the first American ski club was founded in 1867 at La Porte in California. On the whole, North American ski resorts are well organized. They have carefully planned lift systems, the ski schools are good, and the ski rental equipment, particularly in the large resorts, is very well maintained.

America was responsible for the first "purpose-built" ski resort (p. 281) – constructed in 1934 at Sun Valley, Idaho. Americans were also the first to establish the idea of the "day ski area" – still very popular on the East Coast. These enormous ski centers are often in National Parks where normal resorts cannot be built. Consequently, there are no hotels and, usually, only a large "base lodge" which houses the ski school office, ski rentals, a restaurant, and in most cases, the bottom lift station.

We have divided skiing in North America into three major regions. In the north east, are the American Appalachians and the Canadian Laurentians. They rise to between 1,523m (5,000ft) and 1,828m (6,000ft). The tree line is high and there is very little above-tree-line skiing. Much of the skiing tends to be on steep, narrow, icy runs but when the weather breaks in the spring you can find some of the finest "corn snow" in the world. The terrain is also ideal for ski touring.

In the north west are the mountains of the Canadian Rockies. The peaks are very high indeed (between 2,438m/8,000ft and 3,657m/12,000ft), and the snow is normally good, with conditions similar to those in Europe. Although most of the resorts are fairly small, Canada has recently become one of the world centers for "heli-skiing" (p.238). From special "base lodges" established high in the mountains, skiers are flown by helicopter to different peaks every day.

The third region includes the American Rockies and the Sierra Nevada. These are the highest mountains in North America (between 3,657m/12,000ft and 4,267m/14,000ft). There are many large resorts, and the Rockies in particular are famous for the quality and the quantity of their "powder snow".

Taos, in New Mexico, does not fall into any of these regions. It is one of the older, western resorts: height 2,806m (9,207ft), top station 3,602m (11,819ft), 8 lifts serving 61 prepared trails.

1 The north east

There are numerous ski areas and resorts in these mountains, with many difficult icy slopes. The best known resort is Lake Placid, the site of the 1932 and 1980 Winter Olympic Games.

Hunter Mountain Ski Bowl (New York) Height 487m (1,600ft), top station 975m (3,200ft), 15 lifts.
Killington (Vermont) Height 323m (1,060ft), top station 1,286m (4,220ft), 13 lifts.
Lake Placid (New York) Height 371m (1,220ft), top station (Whiteface mountain) 1,352m (4,436ft), 9 lifts.

Mont Tremblant (Quebec) Height 265m (870ft), top station 914m (3,001ft), 11 lifts.
Mount Snow (Vermont) Height 579m (1,900ft), top station 1,091m (3,580ft), 14 lifts.
Stowe (Vermont) Height 396m (1,300ft), top station 1,338m (4,393ft), 9 lifts.
Sugarloaf (Maine) Height 495m (1,637ft), top station 1,291m (4,237ft), 11 lifts.

Skiing in the Canadian ▶ Rockies "Heli-skiers" can now reach high peaks and off-trail runs which would otherwise be inaccessible.

2 The Canadian Rockies

The resorts in this area, although small by European standards, offer some very good skiing and many also double as bases for heli-skiing.

Banff ski area
There are no ski lifts in Banff village itself, but it is used as a base for heli-skiing and for those who want to ski the nearby Mount Norquay or get to Sunshine Village and Lake Louise. **Lake Louise:** height 1,676m (5,500ft), top station 2,652m (8,700ft), 9 lifts. **Sunshine Village:** height 2,194m (7,200ft), top station 2,727m (8,950ft), 11 lifts.

Big White Ski Village
Height 1,661m (5,450ft), top station 2,225m (7,300ft), 7 lifts.

Grouse Mountain
Height 850m (2,800ft), top station 1,200m (4,000ft), 11 lifts.

Jasper, Marmot Basin
Height 1,731m (5,680ft), top station 2,432m (7,980ft), 5 lifts.

Panorama Village
Height 1,217m (3,700ft), top station 2,103m (6,900ft), 5 lifts, and a heli-skiing base also.

Whistler Mountain
Height 652m (2,140ft), top station 1,956m (6,420ft), 14 lifts and a heli-skiing base also.

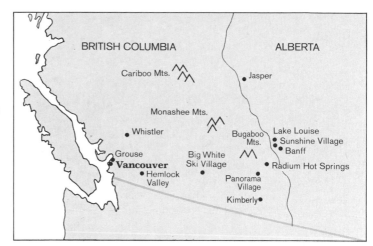

Heli-skiing areas
There are three main mountain ranges in the Rockies where heli-skiing is possible. In each area, there are base lodges (with helicopter landing pads) where you stay throughout the length of your vacation.
Bugaboo Mountains: height of "Bugaboo Lodge" 1,470m (4,823ft), "Bobbie Burns Lodge" 1,370m (4,494ft). **Cariboo Mountains:** height of "Base Lodge" 1,100m (3,609ft). **Monashee Mountains:** height of "Mica Creek" 550m (1,804ft).

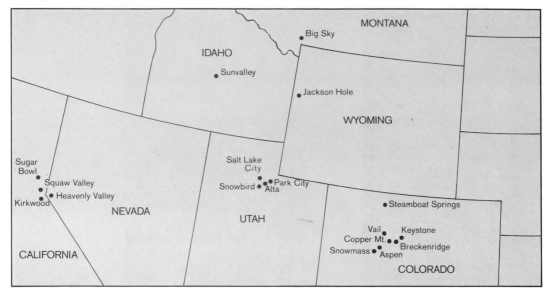

3 The American Rockies and the Sierra Nevada

World-famous for its powder snow, some of the largest ski areas in North America are found in this high, mountain region.

Big Sky (Montana)
Height 2,285m (7,500ft), top station 2,986m (9,800ft), 6 lifts.

Breckenridge (Colorado)
Height 2,935m (9,630ft), top station 3,609m (11,843ft), 15 lifts.

Copper Mountain (Colorado)
Height 2,935m (9,600ft), top station 3,672m (12,048ft), 12 lifts.

Keystone (Colorado)
Height 2,834m (9,300ft), top station 3,791m (12,450ft), 15 lifts.

Lake Tahoe ski area
The three resorts around Lake Tahoe on the Nevada-California state line can all be skied on one lift pass. **Heavenly Valley (Nevada):** height 1,981m (6,550ft), top station 3,099 (10,170ft), 25 lifts. **Kirkwood (California):** height 2,377m (7,800ft), top station 2,743m (9,800ft), 10 lifts. **Squaw Valley (California):** height 1,089m (6,200ft), top station 2,712m (8,900ft), 50 lifts.

Salt Lake City ski area
Alta, Snowbird and Park City are the largest resorts around Salt Lake City, but all fifteen ski areas can be skied using the same lift pass. **Alta (Utah):** height 2,103m (6,900ft), top station 3,215m (10,550ft), 6 lifts. **Park City (Utah):** height 2,103m (6,900ft), top station 3,049m (10,000ft), 11 lifts. **Snowbird (Utah):** height 2,408m (7,900ft), top station 3,352m (11,000ft), 6 lifts.

Steamboat Springs (Colorado)
Height 2,103m (6,900ft), top station 3,200m (10,500ft), 16 lifts.

Sugar Bowl (California)
Height 2,098m (6,883ft), top station 2,555m (8,383ft), 9 lifts.

Sun Valley (Idaho)
Height 1,775m (5,760ft), top station 2,788m (9,150ft), 16 lifts.

Vail (Colorado)
Height 2,499m (8,200ft), top station 3,429m (11,250ft), 18 lifts.

◄Canadian heli-skiing
Accompanied by an experienced guide, a group of heli-skiers track through virgin powder snow on off-trail descents of up to 3,047m (10,000ft).

Aspen (Colorado) ►
The combined ski areas of Aspen village (height 2,416m/7,930ft, top station 3,596m/11,800ft) and Snowmass (height 2,514m/8,208ft) have 47 lifts serving over 200 prepared runs.

Australia

Skiing in Australia started in the mid-nineteenth century when Norwegians emigrated there to join the gold rush. The first Australian ski club, said to be the first ski club in the world, was founded by Norwegian and Australian miners at Kiandra, in the Snowy Mountains of New South Wales, in 1861. The Snowy Mountains are part of the Australian Alps, situated in the south-east corner of the country. They are the highest mountains in Australia and normally have fairly extensive snow cover during the winter; consequently, all of the Alpine skiing in the country is concentrated there.

The Australian ski season officially starts on the Queen's birthday in June, regardless of snow, and finishes at the end of September. The snow conditions are very similar to those found in Scotland, with powder snow and spring snow being quite rare. Many of the resorts are in windy valleys, and so that much of the snow tends to be blown off the main slopes and into the gullies.

Most Australian ski resorts are fairly small. In fact, many of them originally grew up around ski club areas and, even now, there are still a large number of "day ski areas" which are owned by and maintained exclusively for the club members. Consequently, many resorts have limited lift facilities.

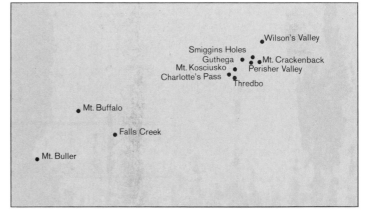

However, ski schools, equipment rental and accommodation are all available.

Besides downhill skiing, Alpine ski touring and cross-country skiing have become increasingly popular in Australia. Mount Buffalo, in Victoria, is one of the best-known cross-country ski areas.

The Australian Alps
The ski resorts in this area are concentrated in two states: New South Wales and Victoria.

In Victoria, there are seven main resorts. Of these, Falls Creek, Mount Buffalo and Mount Buller are the biggest. In fact, Mount Buller is the largest ski resort in the country. All these ski centers are quite easily accessible by road and by air, even though Melbourne, the nearest main city, is about 350km (217 miles) away. Victoria is also becoming a popular area for cross-country (or Nordic) skiing – usually done in the form of off-trail touring.

In New South Wales, most of the ski resorts are situated in the Mount Kosciusko National Park. These are the resorts in the right-hand corner of our map. Mount Kosciusko itself, at 2,230m (7,316ft), is the highest peak in the Snowy Mountains and in the whole country as well. It has good snow throughout the winter and a variety of skiable slopes. These, however, can only be reached by air or on skis from Guthega or Perisher Valley, over Charlotte's Pass. All the resorts in New South Wales are easy to reach by air or road from the main cities of Canberra and Sydney, away to the north east..

Charlotte's Pass
Height 1,750m (5,741ft), 3 lifts. Can only be reached by snowmobile from Perisher Valley in winter.
Falls Creek
14 ski lifts, also a ski touring center.
Guthega
Height 1,402m (4,599ft), 3 lifts. Offers access on foot to Mount Kosciusko.
Mount Buffalo
Top lift station 1,900m (6,233ft), 7 lifts. also a cross-country ski center
Mount Buller
Top lift station 1,807m (5,929ft), 23 lifts.
Perisher Valley ski area
The two resorts in this complex are

connected by road and by ski lift and provide the main access point for ski tourers to get to Charlotte's Pass and Mount Kosciusko. **Perisher Valley:** height 1,718m (5,636ft), top station 2,038m (6,686ft), 16 lifts. **Smiggins Holes:** height 1,675m (5,495ft), top station 1,725m (5,659ft), 5 lifts.
Thredbo
Height 1,370m (4,494ft), top station 1,951m (6,401ft), 9 lifts. Also provides access onto Mount Crackenback (1,990m/6,529ft)

New Zealand

Although there are a large number of snow-covered mountains in New Zealand on which it is possible to ski, many of the peaks can only be reached by air. Most of the organized downhill skiing is found in the Southern Alps on the South Island. But, because of the limited lift facilities, ski touring and heli-skiing similar to that found in Canada are becoming very popular.

The North Island has several volcanic mountains, of which Mount Ruapehu (2,796m/ 9,175ft) in the south is the highest. It has two ski areas: the Wha-

kapapa slopes and a new development at Turoa. The Whakapapa ski area is the largest and has 15 lifts serving a variety of slopes. The top lift station is at 2,194m (7,200ft) and, from there, it is possible to get up onto the glacier (2,560m/8,400ft). The Mount Egmont ski area further west is a ski touring center and is only accessible by air.

The Southern Alps
This map shows the main ski areas on South Island. Many of these slopes are owned by private ski clubs. The details below are for the main "commercial" ski areas.

Coronet Peak
Height 1,158m (3,800ft), top station 1,650m (5,400ft), 5 lifts and a heli-skiing base operated by Mount Cook airlines.
Mount Cook National Park
This is mainly a ski touring area. Mount Cook Airlines have small aeroplanes and helicopters to take skiers onto Mount Cook (3,764m/

2,349ft) and Mount Tasman (3,497m/11,475ft). **Tasman Glacier**: height of base lodges 1,800m (5,905ft), highest air lift (Tasman Saddle) 2,394m (7,851ft).
Mount Hutt
Height 1,300m (4,265ft), top station 2,074m (6,800ft), 8 lifts and a heli-skiing base.
Porter Heights
Height 1,280m (4,200ft), top station 1,981m (6,500ft), limited lift facilities.
Tekapo
3 ski lifts and a heli-skiing base.
Treble Cone
Top station 2,073m (6,800ft), several lifts and a heli-skiing base.

South America

Chile and Argentina were the first two South American countries to establish ski centers in the Andes mountains. Colombia now has one small resort at Ruiz, near Bogota, and small areas are being developed in the mountains of Mexico and Bolivia.

Chile established itself as a "skiing" country when it hosted the World Alpine Championships at Portillo (height 2,890m/9,480ft), near Santiago, in 1966. This resort now also has an annual "flying kilometre" contest (p.157). There are eight other resorts in Chile, including the southernmost resort

in the world, Punta Arenas.

Argentina has about four established ski areas. The best known is San Carlos di Bariloche (2,400m/ 7,874ft). Situated only 20km (12 miles) from the Chilean border, the skiing is very good and there are already eleven lifts, including one cable car.

Ski instruction in most South American resorts tends to be very good because many of the instructors from Europe and North America come down to work in the southern hemisphere during their own northern summer.

Glossary

Note A word in *italics* indicates a cross-reference to another entry in the glossary

A

A.B.S. Acrylobutyl styrene, a hard, strong plastic used as the top surface of most modern skis.

Absorption-extension technique A method of initiating parallel turns by bending the legs (*down-flexion un-weighting*), banking the knees and rotating the legs. Also known as "bending" turning, "compression" turning, *avalement* and "OK technique". It has two variations: *jet turning* and *kangaroo turning*.

Accelerated teaching method Known as A.T.M., this is an instruction method in which beginners are started on 135-150cm (*compact*) skis. It is not a true *short-ski teaching method*.

Acrobatic skiing See *freestyle* skiing.

Action The name given to a *force* to distinguish it from its equal *opposing force*, which is known as the *reaction*.

Active unweighting An *unweighting* of the skis created by the skier himself – the result of an *up-extension* or a *down-flexion*.

Aerials Acrobatic ski jumping involving twists, somersaults, etc., while in mid-air – a *freestyle* discipline performed from specially constructed jumping hills.

Afterbody The rear section of the ski, behind the binding, between the *tail* and the *waist*.

Airplane turn A name sometimes given to a turn made in mid-air following a *terrain jump*.

Alpine skiing The term used to distinguish downhill skiing from its Nordic counterpart, *cross-country skiing*. It is what most people understand by the word "skiing", and it includes the following disciplines: recreational skiing (on or off the specially prepared *trails*), *Alpine ski touring, special slalom, giant slalom* and *downhill racing*, and *freestyle*.

Alpine ski touring *Off-trail* skiing in which skiers walk uphill on skis as well as skiing down. Touring is done on modified Alpine equipment, and *skins* may be attached to the base of the skis to stop them sliding backwards when climbing up moderate slopes.

Altitude sickness Symptoms of breathlessness, nausea, dizziness, headaches, etc., which some people may experience as a result of a sudden increase in altitude – e.g., after a cable car ride.

Angled position A *converging* ski position – tips together and tails apart. Also known as *snowplow, half plow, stem* or "wedge" position.

Angulation A body position in which the knees and hips are pushed into the slope and the head and upper body lean out from the slope. Sometimes called the "comma" or "banana" position because of its shape, it is used to maintain balance while *edging* the skis.

Anticipation A preparatory twisting or "pre-rotation" of the upper body in the direction of an intended turn. The movement creates a pre-tension of the body against the fixed position of the legs and aids the turning of the skis during the *initiation*. It is usually then followed by *counter-rotation*.

Anti-friction pad A smooth plate mounted on the ski (corresponding to a smooth surface at the front of the boot sole) designed to allow the boot to release quickly from the toe-piece of the *binding* in the event of a fall.

Arlberg A mountain region in Austria where *Hannes Schneider* established the first ski school based on the principle of graded ski classes. The term, "Arlberg school", has become synonymous with the techniques he and his followers originated.

Arlberg strap A term sometimes used for a *safety strap*.

Artificial snow Man-made snow, usually produced by a machine which mixes water and compressed air. Most often found in North America and in Japan.

Avalanche A mass of settled snow and ice which for some reason becomes unstable, breaks away and suddenly slides rapidly downhill.

Avalanche cord A length of trailing rope tied around the waist when skiing in potential avalanche areas. The cord floats to the surface if the skier is buried by snow – aiding location by rescuers. It is usually brightly colored and about 10m (33ft) long.

Avalanche dog Dog specially trained to locate buried avalanche victims.

Avalement A French word (meaning "swallowing") used to describe the technique of absorbing terrain bumps by leg and hip flexion. It is sometimes also used for initiating *absorption-extension* turns on bumps or *moguls*.

B

Backscratcher A *freestyle* jumping stance. While the skier is in mid-air, his ski tips point down and his ski tails come up behind his shoulders.

Backward lean Leaning backwards slightly to transfer more weight onto the rear of the skis. The *sit-back* stance is an extreme form of this.

Ballet A *freestyle* discipline rather like figure-skating on skis. A routine of tricks, stunts and acrobatic turns usually performed to music on a smooth, gentle slope.

Banana position See *angulation*.

Banking Leaning into the center of a turn – either with the whole body or chiefly with the hips – in order to keep the skis edged and also to counteract *centrifugal force*. The movement is important when *initiating* and *steering* turns and is rather like banking into a turn on a bicycle.

Base The underside of the ski.

Base wax A special wax preparation applied to the base of a ski so that *running waxes* (which are spread on afterwards) will take a firm hold. Most often used on cross-country skis.

Basic technique In this book, the term "basic technique" refers to each movement in its simplest form. Functional applications – such as how the technique is adapted to different terrain and snow conditions – then follow.

Basic turning/basic swinging A term sometimes used to describe *snowplow turning*. It is the first technique by which beginners learn to make complete *downhill turns*.

Basket The plastic or metal ring on the end of a *ski pole*, which prevents the tip from going too far into the snow.

Bending turning See *absorption-extension technique*.

Biathlon A competitive cross-country discipline, combining racing on skis with rifle shooting. Scores are awarded for both speed and marksmanship.

Bilgeri, Georg One of the pioneers of Alpine skiing, Bilgeri was an Austrian army officer who set up one of the first Arlberg ski schools. He was originally a pupil of *Mathias Zdarsky* and, later, a teacher of *Hannes Schneider*.

Binding The device which attaches the ski to the bottom of the boot.

Bleeper A radio device designed to facilitate the location of buried avalanche victims. Skiers in avalanche-risk areas switch to "transmit"; the search party switches to "receive". Avalanche bleepers are not always compatible and may vary from country to country.

New Zealand

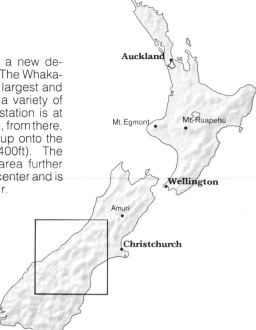

Boiler plate A hard, icy snow surface.

Bump skiing See *mogul skiing*.

Burrs Projecting splinters of metal sometimes left on the ski *edge* after filing.

Button lift A type of ski lift – often called a "Poma" lift after its inventor, Pomagalski. Skiers are pulled uphill by a moving cable. Suspended from the cable are long rods with small disks on the end which skiers tuck between their legs.

C

Cable binding A type of *binding* with a fixed toe-piece from which a metal cable runs around the heel of the boot. Sometimes still used in *cross-country skiing, ski jumping* and *Alpine ski touring*.

Cable car An aerial ski lift, known in France as a "téléférique". Two single cabins, each carrying up to 125 people, travel up and down side-by-side on suspension cables.

Camber The arch built into a ski which means that it curves upwards in the middle when lying flat. It is designed to distribute the skier's weight more evenly over the whole length of the ski. The term "side-camber" is sometimes used to mean *side-cut*.

Canting The insertion of "wedges" or "cant-plates" between the bindings and the skis to compensate for bow-legged or knock-kneed skiers and to guarantee that the skis therefore lie perfectly flat on the snow.

Carving Turning with minimum *skidding* along a groove cut through the snow by the inside edges of the skis. Carved turns are a property of the ski's *side-cut* and *camber*. They can be made only at speed when the ski is in *reverse camber*.

Catching an edge Accidentally allowing the *edge* of one ski to dig into the snow – a common cause of falls.

Center of gravity The single point within a body from which the net force of *gravity* acting on that body can be said to operate. The center of a body's "weight".

Centrifugal force The force produced when a body rotates about the center of its orbit. When turning, a skier will feel centrifugal force throwing him outwards, away from the center of the turn.

Centripetal force The force which must be applied sideways, into the center of the turn, to make a body follow a curved track. When turning on skis, centripetal force is generated by snow resistance. The tighter the turn, the more centripetal force is required. The *opposing force* which it generates is called *centrifugal force*.

Chair lift A type of ski lift whereby skiers are carried uphill in chairs suspended from a moving overhead cable.

Chinook A warm wind occurring in the western United States – the equivalent of the Alpine *föhn*.

Christie/christy An old-fashioned term generally applied to any turn during which the skis skid. The word comes from the Norwegian town "Christiania".

Citizen racing Cross-country ski *marathons* where entry is open to any skier who wishes to take part. A single race often attracts thousands of competitors.

Closed gate Two *slalom* poles set vertically down the *fall line*. Each racer must pass between the poles.

Closed parallel turning Completing a turn from start to finish with the skis in a narrow-track parallel position.

Closed ski stance Both skis in a narrow-track parallel position.

Code of conduct A number of guidelines setting out the principles of safe skiing behavior, drawn up by the International Ski Federation.

Comma position See *angulation*.

Compact ski The shortest and widest ski of the four major categories. Used by beginners and some intermediate skiers, it has little or no *side-cut*. Compact skis are sometimes called "shorts", but they are not as short as the "mini" skis used in *short-ski teaching methods*.

Competition ski The longest ski of the four major categories. It is used by advanced skiers and racers.

Competition stepping Linking two turns by one of the movements collectively known as *stepping techniques*.

Compression The technique of flexing to absorb bumps and dips and to initiate turns on the top of moguls. See *also avalement* and *absorption-extension technique*.

Compression stage A section of a downhill course where the gradient changes suddenly from the steep to the flat, such as when a slope begins to flatten out to form the *out-run* at the end of the course.

Control gate Two flags, each strung from poles, set on a *downhill* course to control the racer's speed and line. Each racer must pass through the gates.

Converging Any ski position in which the tips are closer together than the tails – for example, the *snowplow, half plow* or *stem*. Also known as the *angled* ski position.

Cornice An overhanging crest or ridge of snow.

Corn snow See *spring snow*.

Counter-pressure The upward force which the terrain exerts against the skis when a skier travels up to the crest of a bump or mogul.

Counter-rotation/counter-rotary motion Rotating the legs in one direction and the rest of the body the opposite way. When turning, the legs and feet twist into the turn and the upper body twists out of the turn. All turns are steered and some are initiated with counter-rotation.

Couple See *parallel turning forces*.

Crevasse A deep cleft or fissure in a glacier.

Critical point The point on the landing slope of a *ski jumping* hill where the gradient begins to flatten and the *out-run* starts.

Cross-country skiing Also called "Nordic" skiing because of the Scandinavian origins of the sport, it differs from *Alpine skiing* in that skiers travel not only downhill but also uphill and on the flat. It includes the following disciplines: *ski touring* on or off the specially prepared tracks, *langlauf racing* and *biathlon*.

Crossover A freestyle *ballet* technique in which the skis are lifted and stepped over one another. Also known as a "stepover".

Crud Unpleasant, difficult snow conditions. Usually *crust* which cannot be guaranteed to support the skier's weight.

Crust Soft snow on which a hard, icy top surface has formed due to repeated melting and re-freezing.

Cutting into the traverse A technique used by slalom racers to maintain height and a good line. As they steer out of a turn, they transfer their weight progressively onto their *diverging* inside ski ready to initiate the next turn after a very short *traverse*.

D

Daffy A *freestyle* jumping stance with legs outstretched diagonally – like walking in mid-air.

Descent route An unmarked, unpatrolled, *off-trail* route.

Diagonal side-slipping Skidding sideways downhill – either forwards or backwards across the *fall line*.

Diagonal side-stepping Climbing sideways uphill – but forwards, at an angle to the *fall line*.

Diagonal ski placing Setting the skis at an angle to the *fall line*. When turning, the greater the angle the stronger the braking action.

Diagonal striding See *gliding step*.

D.I.N. The German Industrial Standards Association which, among other things, has established a scale of *release-load settings* for Alpine ski *bindings*.

Direct initiation The *initiation* of a turn in which both skis change from their uphill to their downhill edges at the same time. Also called a "one-phase initiation".

Diverging Any ski position in which the tails are closer together than the tips – for example, the *herringbone* or "scissor" position.

Double-pole push Planting and pushing off from both poles together in order to propel oneself forwards. A technique used in both *Alpine* and *cross-country skiing*.

Down-flexion Sinking down into a low stance by bending the hips, knees and ankles.

Down-flexion unweighting Momentarily removing the pressure from the skis by rapidly flexing the hips, knees and ankles in order to contract the body.

Downhill/downhill racing The fastest of the Alpine ski racing disciplines. It is a timed speed contest over a specially prepared course marked by *control gates*.

Downhill turning Making a turn from a traverse towards the *fall line* – i.e., increasing the angle of descent.

Down initiation Initiating a turn by using *down-flexion unweighting*.

Drag lift A ski lift which pulls skiers uphill while wearing their skis.

Dry slope An artificial surface usually made of plastic brush or bristles and designed to reproduce the skiing characteristics of real snow.

Dual slalom See *parallel slalom*.

E

Edge The metal strip along either side of the ski's *running surface*. It lies flush with the base but slightly proud of the side wall. It protects the ski from wear and bites into the snow when the ski is "edged".

Edge change Rolling one or both skis from one *edge* onto the opposite edge.

Edge-check See *edge-set*.

Edge control Flattening or tilting the skis on the snow to give just the right amount of "edge-grip" or "edge-release" required.

Edge-set Also known as an "edge-check", this involves tilting the skis rapidly onto their uphill *edges*, at an angle across the *fall line*, in order to make them bite and to exert a strong, sharp braking action. An edge-set is sometimes made at the end of one turn in order to create a firm platform from which the skier can spring or "rebound" upwards to initiate the next turn.

Edging Tilting one or both skis onto either *edge*.

Egg A low crouch or "tuck" used to accelerate when *schussing*. Aerodynamically, the body position which generates least air resistance.

End phase The final stage of a turn. *Centripetal force* is withdrawn and the skis stop turning.

Extension Stretching the hip, knee and ankle joints. See *up-extension*.

F

Fall line The steepest, shortest and fastest line down any slope. The line of least resistance.

Fan method A teaching plan in which beginners learn to make parallel turns by varying their angle of approach to the fall line so that the turns become progressively more difficult.

Fanny pack A small bag attached to a belt and worn around the waist, generally at the back.

Finnish step A variation of the cross-country *gliding step* in which the pole-plant is omitted at every second or third step. Also known as the "swinging step" or "triple striding".

First-generation resort A ski resort which has grown up around what was originally a center for summer tourism.

F.I.S. The Fédération Internationale de Ski, the ruling body of international competition skiing.

Flexion Bending the hip, knee and ankle joints. See *down-flexion*.

Flexibility The stiffness of a ski and its resistance to twisting ("torsion"). The "flexibility pattern" measures the distribution of stiffness along the length of the ski.

Flying kilometer A special downhill speed contest where each competitor's speed is measured as he passes through a 100m (328ft) "time-trap". Also known as the "Kilometro Lanciato" or "K.L.".

Flying step turning An exaggerated form of *stepping against the uphill ski* performed with such a strong push-off that, for a moment, during the initiation, both skis are in the air.

Föhn A complex mountain wind. It blows down into the valleys, and it is warm and dry – often causing a sudden thaw. In North America, it is called the "chinook".

Force A simple push or pull which, when applied to a body, will alter its state. "Mechanics" is the study of physical forces.

Forces parallelogram The graphic device used to portray the principle of *resolution of forces*. Also known as a "vector diagram".

Forebody The front section of the ski, in front of the binding, between the *tip* and the *waist*.

Forerunners Non-competitors who ski slalom and downhill courses in order to check conditions and set a track before the racers start. Also called *Vorfahrers* or *Vorläufers*.

Forward lean Leaning forwards slightly to transfer more weight onto the front of the skis.

Forward momentum One of the two component forces into which *gravity* resolves while operating on the skier. It acts parallel to the slope gradient and is the force which propels the skier downhill.

Freestyle Acrobatic or "trick" skiing. It is divided into three disciplines: *ballet, freestyle mogul skiing* and *aerials*.

Friction The force of resistance generated by one object moving against another. In skiing, this is generally caused by resistance between the skis and the snow, although it may also be created by air resistance.

Front pole-flip A freestyle *ballet* trick in which the skier performs a front somersault while supporting himself on both poles. Sometimes called a "Wong-banger" after its originator, Wayne Wong.

Functional skiing Controlled, efficient skiing where technique and speed are constantly adapted to the demands of varying situations.

Funicular A mountain railway in which two carriages travel up and down side-by-side – usually powered by a traction cable.

G

Gaiter A waterproof cuff worn around the bottom of the trouser leg, over the top of the ski boot.

Garland A practice exercise linking *traversing, side-slipping* and *uphill turning*. The *fall line* is not crossed, nor does the downhill ski change edge.

Gate A set of two flags or poles through which slalom and downhill racers must ski on their way down a course.

Geländesprung A German word for a terrain jump – usually made with a push-off from both poles.

Giant slalom An Alpine racing discipline, it is a cross between *special slalom* and *downhill*, and it is a test of high-speed turning ability through specially placed gates. Giant slalom was included in the Olympics only in 1952.

Glide wax A type of *running wax* applied to the base of the ski to make it slide more easily.

Gliding snowplow Using the *snowplow* or "wedge" ski position to control speed of descent in the *fall line*.

Gliding step Also called "diagonal striding", this is the basic technique for *cross-country skiing*. It may be done at a leisurely walking pace or, in its *langlauf* form, at much higher speed (when it is like running on skis).

Glissement A French word describing the *sliding* of flattened skis over the snow.

Gondola A type of ski lift in which small enclosed cabins are suspended from a moving overhead cable. Also called "telecabines".

Graduated length method Known as G.L.M., this is an American *short-ski teaching method*.

Grass skiing Skiing on grass-covered slopes wearing special "caterpillar-track" or "roller" skis.

Gravity The force of attraction which pulls a body towards the earth. Gravity is the force which causes the skier to slide downhill on skis.

Grip wax A type of *running wax* applied to the base of the ski to make it stick to the snow when pushing off from it in order to make a *gliding step* or when walking uphill on cross-country skis.

Gunbarrel A narrow, steep-sided valley or ravine.

H

Half plow A *converging* ski position in which the tail of one ski is pushed out sideways.

Hardpack A compressed, icy snow surface.

Harscheisen A toothed metal plate or blade attached to the ski to give more grip when walking or climbing. It is used in *Alpine ski touring*. Also called a "Firn" or "Harsch" blade.

Haute Route One of the most famous Alpine ski tours, stretching from Argentière in France to Saas Fee in Switzerland.

Head-to-head slalom See *parallel slalom.*

Heel The *tail* or back of the ski – the second widest point.

Heel-and-toe binding An Alpine *safety binding* which has two separate units to hold the boot in place on the ski: a toe-piece and a heel-piece. Sometimes called a "step-in binding" because the heel-piece shuts automatically as the boot goes in.

Helicopter A *freestyle* jumping movement in which the skier stays upright but spins around while in mid-air.

Heli-skiing *Off-trail* skiing where skiers are transported uphill to the top of their run by helicopter. It is particularly popular in the North American and Canadian Rockies.

Herringbone A *diverging* ski position – tails together and tips apart. Also the name of the technique which uses this ski position in order to walk uphill.

Herringbone turning Using the *herringbone* ski position in order to turn around on the spot while standing on a slope. Similar to *star turning* around the ski tails.

Hinge-point The point at which a boot flexes or is angled forwards to facilitate the correct body stance.

Homologation The technical specifications produced by F.I.S. for any international *ski jumping, slalom* or *downhill* competition course. It is usually presented as a graph of the slope gradient.

Hot dog skiing An early term for *freestyle* skiing.

Hotdogging See *mogul skiing.*

Hypothermia A dangerously subnormal body temperature – usually the result of exposure.

I

Indirect initiation The *initiation* of a turn in which one ski changes from its uphill to its downhill edge before the other. Also called a "two-phase initiation".

Inertia Unless some other force is brought into play, inertia means that a body will not move if it is stationary, and it will keep moving in the same direction at the same speed if it is already in motion. This is why, when skiing, you must exert a braking force if you want to stop and a turning force if you want to change your direction of travel.

Initiation When turning, the point at which the skier begins to turn his skis out of their previous line of travel.

Inner boot The soft removable lining which fits inside the rigid outer shell of a modern Alpine ski boot.

In-run The section of a *ski jumping* hill where the jumper gathers speed for his take-off. The point on the in-run at which the jumpers start is varied so that they land on or around the *table point.*

Inside-ski turn A freestyle *ballet* technique in which a turn is made on the inside ski, with the outside ski completely unweighted and often lifted off the snow.

International Ski Federation See *F.I.S.*

Interski An international ski congress, held every four years and organized by the International Association for Ski Instruction. This body has also set up a special commission called "Ski Interterm" to discuss and coordinate international ski terminology.

Inverted aerial Any *freestyle* jump in which a somersault is made in mid-air.

Inward lean See *banking.*

J

J-bar An American version of the T-bar lift – shaped like a "J" instead of a "T"

Jet turning A form of *absorption-extension technique* where the initiation of the turn is aided by propelling both feet rapidly forwards in order to *unweight* the ski tips. An extreme form of jet turning is also used in freestyle *mogul skiing* for turning on the top of bumps.

Jump turning A method of making a parallel turn by jumping both skis off the snow and rotating them directly from one traverse into the next.

K

Kandahar A series of annual international races (including the "Arlberg – Kandahar") founded by the Kandahar Ski Club, named after Lord Roberts of Kandahar.

Kangaroo turning A form of *absorption-extension technique* characterized by an extreme *sit-back* stance during the initiation phase or the turn.

Kicker The arched or *cambered* section in the middle of a cross-country ski – situated beneath the foot. A term also used for the ramp or take-off point on a *freestyle* jumping hill.

Kick turning Turning around on the spot by first lifting one ski and pivoting on its tail through 180 degrees, then swinging around the second ski so that it is parallel with the first and so that the skier ends up facing in the opposite direction.

K.L. (Kilometro Lanciato) See *flying kilometer.*

Kinetic energy The energy of movement. The kinetic energy possessed by a moving body is greater the faster it is travelling and the heavier its mass.

Klister Soft, sticky *running wax* used to help the ski grip the snow and to prevent it from sliding backwards. Used on *cross-country* skis.

Knee-and-thigh technique See *OK technique, absorption-extension technique.*

L

Langlauf The German word for *cross-country skiing* – usually used to distinguish the athletic, competitive form from recreational *ski touring.*

Langläufer A *cross-country* ski racer.

Lilienfeld A village in Austria, near Vienna, where Mathias Zdarsky established his first ski school. Also the source for the title of his book "Lilienfeld Skiing Technique", published in 1896.

LLL The "Langläufers Live Longer" movement, established to promote the sport of *cross-country skiing.*

Loipe A prepared track for *cross-country skiing.* It consists of machine-made parallel tracks in which the skis run.

Loose snow avalanche An avalanche which starts from a single point and is composed of snow that does not slide in blocks or slabs.

Lowlander Skiers who do not live in mountain areas are called "lowlanders" (and, sometimes, "citadins"). Strictly speaking, official lowlander races are open only to skiers from Belgium, Denmark, Holland, Great Britain, Ireland and Luxembourg.

Lunn, Sir Arnold Considered by many to be the father of Alpine ski racing, he drew up the original rules for modern *slalom* and pioneered the acceptance of the *downhill*. He was also one of the first *ski mountaineers* and a leading authority on early Alpine ski technique.

M

Marathon A long-distance *cross-country* ski race. The most famous marathons often have hundreds or even thousands of entrants and begin with a spectacular mass start.

Mashed potato Heavy, wet snow.

Metamorphosis The process by which freshly fallen snow "ages" and the snowflake crystals are slowly degraded. It is largely due to repeated thawing and re-freezing, and it continues until the snow melts away.

Microclimate The climate of a very small area. In mountain regions, where weather conditions are very local, micro-climatology is highly relevant.

Mid-length ski The second shortest ski of the four major categories. It is about 15cm longer than the *compact* ski, with a softer *flexibility* and a deeper *side-cut*.

Mogul A bump or mound in the snow. From the Alpine dialect word, "mugel". Moguls are formed by the repeated turning of skis, following the same tracks and *carving* out ruts in the snow surface.

Mogul field A steep slope covered with large *moguls*.

Mogul skiing This term can mean one of two things: it either describes simple recreational skiing on slopes covered with *moguls* or it refers to one of the three *freestyle* disciplines. In freestyle competitions, participants make a run down a steep *mogul field* and are then judged on the speed, style and technical execution of their descent. This sport is also known as "bump skiing" and, in Europe, as "hot-dogging".

N

Nansen, Fridtjof Norwegian explorer who led a ski expedition across Greenland in 1888.

Nebelmeer See *Wolkenmeer*.

Non-wax ski A *cross-country* ski with a special base that does not require *waxing* to prevent it slipping backwards.

Nordic combined A *cross-country skiing* competition which includes both individual racing and *ski jumping*.

Nordic norm The standardized design of *cross-country* boots and bindings – for use by recreational skiers.

Nordic skiing See *cross-country skiing*.

Norheim, Søndre The Norwegian pioneer of *ski jumping*, the *Telemark* turn, and the parallel stop swing (later called a "Christiania" or *christy*). In 1866, he also revolutionized the design of wooden Nordic skis – by making them shorter, giving them a *side-cut*, and improving the *binding* system.

Norm point The point on the landing slope of a *ski jumping* hill at which the gradient begins to correspond to the flight trajectory of the jumpers. The distance from take-off to norm point is used to classify the jumping hill.

Normal force One of the two component forces into which *gravity* resolves while operating on the skier. It is the force or pressure generated by his weight. It is directed from his *center of gravity* through his feet to the snow, and it acts at right angles to the slope gradient.

Nursery slope A gentle, prepared slope on which beginners can learn to ski away from the main runs.

Nursery slope lift A *drag lift* or rope tow which serves a beginners' *nursery slope*.

O

Off-trail Any slope which is not a marked, groomed, graded and patrolled *trail*.

OK technique A term derived from the German words "Oberschenkel" (thigh) and "Knie" (knee). See *absorption-extension technique*.

One-phase initiation See *direct initiation*.

One-step A variation of the cross-country *gliding step* which leads into a double-pole push. While making a step, the skier misses out the single pole-plant and swings both poles forward.

Open gate Two *slalom* poles set across the slope, more-or-less at right angles to the *fall line*. Each racer must pass between the poles.

Open parallel turning Completing a turn from start to finish with the skis in a wide-track parallel position.

Open ski stance Both skis in a wide-track parallel position – usually about hip-width apart.

Opposing force For every force exerted, an equal force is generated in the opposite direction. This is known as the "opposing force" or "reaction".

Outrigger An *inside-ski* turn, used in *ballet* movements and performed in a low crouch with the inside leg flexed and the outside leg extended sideways.

Out-run The section of a *ski jumping* hill where the landing slope gradually flattens out so that the jumpers can safely slow down and come to a stop.

Overturning Swinging too far into the hill at the end of a turn. Overturning is usually caused by too much *rotation* and insufficient *counter-rotation*, and it often results in loss of balance or a fall.

Packed powder *Powder snow* which has settled under its own weight or been compressed into a firm surface.

Parallel slalom Two identical single-pole slalom courses set side-by-side. Two competitors start simultaneously and race against each other on the separate courses. Also known as "dual" or "head-to-head" slalom.

Parallel turning A change of direction in which the skis are parallel from start to finish.

Parallel turning forces The principle by which two parallel forces acting on different parts of the same body, but in opposite directions, cause it to rotate. Also known as a "couple".

Parallel uphill turning Making a turn away from the *fall line*, into the hill, with the skis parallel from start to finish.

Passive unweighting An *unweighting* of the skis caused by travelling over a natural bump in the terrain.

Pirouette A freestyle *ballet* technique for changing direction by pivoting around the up-ended ski tips or ski tails.

Piste The European term for a prepared ski *trail*.

Plate binding An Alpine *safety binding* consisting of three separate units: a metal "plate" attached to the bottom of the boot, and a toe-piece and heel-piece which hold the plate onto the ski.

Plow See *snowplow*.

Pole-plant The point at which the ski pole is planted in the snow.

Poma lift See *button lift*.

Pony lift The name sometimes given to a *nursery slope lift*.

Powder/powder snow Light, dry, freshly fallen snow which has not yet been compacted.

Powder snow avalanche An avalanche in which the falling snow is thrown up into the air – usually by steep, rocky terrain. The effect of the airborne powder is often "explosive".

Pre-jumping A technique to avoid being thrown up in the air by a terrain bump. The skier jumps his skis off the snow before reaching the bump, just clears the crest, and lands on the other side of it.

Preparation The first phase of a turn – in which the skier makes any movements necessary for the subsequent *initiation* (for example, *pre-rotation*, *anticipation*, opening the skis into a wedge, etc).

Pre-rotation Rotating the body in the direction of an intended turn during the *preparation* phase. It is an aid to the *initiation*. See *anticipation*.

Pre-turning Displacing one ski so that it points in the direction of an intended turn – as in *stem turning*, for example.

Pressure See *weighting*.

Projection circulaire See *rotary motion*.

Pulka A small sledge pulled by *cross-country* skiers. Found in Scandinavia.

Push-off A thrusting movement used to accelerate or to jump into the air. A push-off may be made upwards or sideways with the legs, or from the planted ski poles with the arms.

R

Racing norm The standardized design of *cross-country* boots and bindings – for use by *langläufers*.

Ratrac The name of the Swiss company that made the first trail-maintenance vehicle.

Reaction The *opposing force* generated by the *action* of any force. It is equal to the force itself but operates in the opposite direction.

Rear-entry ski boot An Alpine ski boot which opens at the back.

Rebound A sharp *down-flexion* and *edge-set* from which a skier extends up to initiate a turn.

Release binding See *safety binding*.

Release-load setting An indication of the skiers' weight range for which a particular Alpine *binding* is designed. In Europe, this is a number on a D.I.N. scale of 1 to 10.

Resolution of forces The principle by which two forces acting on a body at the same point but in different directions combine to produce a single, resultant force.

Retaining strap See *safety strap*.

Reuel Dr Fritz Reuel was a pioneer of acrobatic, *freestyle* skiing in the 1920s. The *ballet* turn known as the "Reuel" or "Royal *christie*" is named after him.

Reverse camber When an edged ski is turning at high speed, its normal upward arch or *camber* is reversed so that the ski bows downwards in the center and makes a *carved* turn.

Roberts of Kandahar See *Kandahar*.

Roll A freestyle *ballet* stunt in which the skier rolls over in the snow.

Rollerskis Wooden "skis" which run on wheels. Used for training by *cross-country* skiers during the summer.

Rope tow A simple form of *drag lift*.

Rotary motion/rotation Rotating the whole body into the direction of the turn in order to transfer a turning force to the skis. The movement is usually called "turning motion" in America and "projection circulaire" by the French. As soon as a turn has been initiated, rotary motion is continued only by the legs; the hips and upper body begin to counter-rotate in the opposite direction.

Rotational jump See *twisting aerial*.

Royal christie See *Reuel*.

Running groove A long, narrow channel along the length of the ski's *running surface* which helps to keep the ski stable on the snow.

Running surface The underside or "base" of the ski.

Running wax A special wax preparation applied to the base of a ski. Running waxes come in two types: a "grip" wax, which increases friction with the snow and helps the ski to grip; and a "glide" wax, which reduces friction with the snow and helps the ski to slide more freely.

S

Safety binding/safety-release binding An Alpine ski *binding* which releases the boot automatically so that the ski comes off in the event of a fall.

Safety strap A strap attached to the back of the binding and tied around the skier's leg so that the ski is not lost if the binding releases.

Schneider, Hannes An Austrian who, in 1920, established the *Arlberg* ski school based on the technique of *stem turning* with *rotation*. He is considered to be the father of the modern ski school.

Schussing Skiing straight down the *fall line* with the skis in a parallel stance.

Scissor An alternative name for the *diverging* or *herringbone* ski position.

Scissoring Initiating a turn by angling out the inside ski and pressing the tip into the snow to create an opposing *parallel turning force*.

Second-generation resort A ski resort which has grown up around a mountain village that had no previous tourist industry before the introduction of skiing.

Seelos, Anton The famous Austrian skier and international ski champion who is claimed to have invented *parallel turning* during the 1930s. The "seelos", an arrangement of slalom gates, is named after him.

Shield wiper turn A high exaggerated *freestyle* variation of the *jet turn* – performed on the crest of a mogul

Shell The rigid outer casing of a modern Alpine ski boot.

Short-ski teaching method An instruction program in which beginners learn first on very short (100cm) skis and then move onto progressively longer skis over the next few days. They learn parallel turns from the very beginning. It is taught in America (as the "graduated length method"), in France (as "ski évolutif"), and also in Germany.

Short swinging Tight-radius parallel turning in which the *end phase* of one turn flows directly into the *preparation* for the next.

Shovel The front of the ski – its widest point.

Side-camber See *side-cut*.

Side-cut The "waisted" shape of the ski, sometimes called the "side-camber", which means that it is widest at the front and narrowest in the middle.

Side-slipping Skidding sideways downhill. Side-slipping is initiated by flattening the skis on the snow and stopped by re-setting them on their uphill edges.

Side-stepping Climbing sideways uphill by stepping one ski at a time up the slope.

Single-pole slalom A *slalom* course on which the skier must turn around the outside of each pole.

Sit-back stance A *backward lean* created by flexing the legs and dropping the trunk – used to keep the ski tips up in deep snow.

Skating A technique used mostly for acceleration in which the skier steps from one *diverging* ski to the other and glides forwards diagonally on one ski at a time.

Ski brake A pair of small hinged "arms" which swing down and dig into the snow to stop the ski sliding away when the boot comes out of the binding. Also called "ski stoppers".

Ski deck An artificial ski slope which works on the principle a continuous, moving conveyor belt.

Ski évolutif The French *short-ski teaching method*.

Ski flying *Ski jumping* on specially large hills – where the distance from take-off to *norm point* exceeds 90m (295ft).

Ski jumping A Nordic discipline in which jumps are made on skis from specially constructed "jumping hills". Points are awarded for the length of the jump and for style.

Ski lift A form of transport designed to carry skiers up the mountain.

Ski mechanics The study of the physical forces involved in skiing and in the design of ski equipment.

Ski mountaineering Mountain climbing in winter. As much of the ascent as possible is made on skis – but normal mountaineering techniques and equipment are used where necessary.

Ski patrol The group of specially trained skiers responsible for *trail* and avalanche safety and for mountain rescue.

Ski pole Thin pole with a hand grip on one end and a point on the other. Used for support and balance when skiing.

Ski position The position of the skis in relation to one another (e.g., parallel, *converging*) and to the snow (e.g., flat, edged).

Ski stopper See *ski brake*.

Ski technique The movements, maneuvers and skills which make up the ability to ski.

Ski touring In Europe, "ski touring" means *Alpine ski touring*. However, in North America, the term usually refers to the recreational form of *cross-country skiing*. Like simply walking on skis, this may be done either on specially laid tracks or over fairly long distances, away from the prepared trails.

Skidding The action of a ski skidding or "slipping" sideways over the snow. The word is used to distinguish the movement from *sliding* and *carving*.

Skins Originally seal skin, now more commonly synthetic fiber, these are attached to the *running surface* of the ski to stop it sliding backwards when walking uphill. Used when *Alpine ski touring*.

Slab avalanche An avalanche in which a jagged fracture line forms across the slope and blocks of compacted snow slide downhill.

Slalom Originally a Norwegian word, "slalom" is now used for the Alpine competitive events in which racers ski a course marked out by an arrangement of *gates*. They must pass through each gate with both feet, and the fastest descent time determines the winner. See *giant slalom, special slalom, parallel slalom*.

Stepping against the uphill ski A turn *initiation* in which a *weight-transfer* is made from the downhill to the uphill ski. The uphill ski is on its downhill edge when the step is made.

Stepping onto the uphill ski A turn *preparation* in which a *weight-transfer* is made from the downhill to the uphill ski. The uphill ski is on its uphill edge when the step is made.

Stepping techniques Advanced turning methods in which turns are prepared or initiated by making an early *weight-transfer* to the uphill ski.

Step turning Changing direction while travelling by lifting one ski, angling out the tip or the tail, and stepping onto it. The other ski, now unweighted, is then brought parallel and a second step may then be made.

Stop swinging A swift *parallel uphill turn* – usually out of the *fall line* – which brings the skier to a sudden stop.

Straight running An alternative term for *schussing*.

Swing A *turn*.

Swinging step See *Finnish step*.

Sliding The action of a ski gliding forwards or backwards over the snow – with no sideways *skidding*.

Slipping See *skidding*.

Slope edge A point where there is a marked change in the gradient of a slope – from gentle to steep, or vice versa.

Slush Wet, melting snow.

Snowplow A *converging* ski position also known as the "wedge". It is formed by opening the skis into a V-shape (tips together, tails apart) and rolling them onto their inside edges. Snowplow is the simplest method of controlling speed.

Snowplow turning Initiating a turn by opening the skis into the *snowplow* position and exerting more pressure against the outside (steering) ski. Snowplow turns begin and end in a *traverse*, with the skis parallel. See *turning snowplow*.

Space walk Two or more *daffys* made in mid-air.

Special slalom Often called simply "slalom", this Alpine ski racing discipline was pioneered by *Sir Arnold Lunn*. It is a test of speed and turning agility through a

series of specially placed *gates*. Speed is slower but the turns are tighter and more frequent than in *giant slalom*.

Sport ski The third longest ski of the four major categories. Shorter and usually softer than the *competition* ski, it is for general recreational use by advanced skiers.

Spread eagle A *freestyle* jumping stance. Both legs and arms are outstretched to either side while in mid-air.

Spring snow Also called "corn snow", and typical of spring conditions, this snow type is composed of small ice granules and sometimes has a "honeycomb" structure. It is formed by repeated thawing during the day and re-freezing during the night.

Sprint racing Short distance *cross-country* and *biathlon* races – usually 10km (6.2 miles) or less.

Star turning Turning around on the spot by lifting the skis and stepping them around in a circle – either pivoting them around the tips or the tails.

Steering phase The third phase of a turn – it follows the *initiation*. Turns are steered largely by pressing against the outside ski and by rotating the legs – although, in most cases, *banking, angulation* and *counter-rotation* are also necessary. The radius of a turn is controlled by regulating the *turning force* which is applied during the steering phase.

Stemming Displacing one ski into a *converging* ski position. It may be either the uphill or the downhill ski which is stemmed, and it may be done by either lifting the ski or pushing out the tail. Sometimes also known as the *half plow* position.

Stem turning Initiating turns by *stemming* one ski – either to *pre-turn* it or to aid the *weight-transfer* against the outside (steering) ski. After the initiation, the skis are brought parallel again.

Step-in binding See *heel-and-toe binding*.

Stepover See *crossover*.

Stepping A *weight-transfer* from one ski either onto or against the other. It is sometimes performed with a *push-off*, and it may be done with or without lifting either ski off the snow.

T

Table point The point on the landing slope of a *ski jumping* hill where the jumpers are expected to land. It lies mid-way between the *norm point* and the *critical point*.

Tail The rear end of the ski. It is always slightly upturned.

Tail-hopping An extreme *up-extension unweighting* in which the tails of the skis are "jumped" off the snow.

T-bar A *drag lift* in which T-shaped wooden bars are suspended from a

moving overhead cable. It is designed to carry two skiers on each bar.

Telecabine See *gondola*.

Téléférique See *cable car*.

Telemark The area in south-western Norway where Søndre Norheim lived. It is the name given to the turning technique which he pioneered in the 1850s and 1860s: the skier drops into a kneeling position and advances, displaces sideways and presses against his outside (steering) ski.

Terrain jumping Making a voluntary jump into the air while skiing over a bump or slope edge.

Third-generation resort A purpose-built ski resort created purely for skiing.

Tilting A word sometimes used to mean *banking* and sometimes used for the movement of rolling the skis onto their *edges*.

Tip The front end of the ski. It is always curved and upturned.

Tip roll A freestyle *ballet* stunt in which the skier *pirouettes* around his ski tips.

Touring See *Alpine ski touring* and *ski touring*.

Trail A specially prepared ski run, marked by signposts and patrolled regularly. Trails are graded according to their steepness and difficulty. In Europe, they are called "pistes".

Trail cord See *avalanche cord*.

Trail map A map showing the layout of the *trails* and *ski lifts* in the area surrounding a ski resort.

Traversing Skiing across the slope, at an angle to the *fall line*.

Tree line The altitude above which it is too cold for trees to grow.

Triple striding See *Finnish step*.

Tuck position A low, crouched stance with the upper body bent and the knees tucked up to the chest – either when *schussing* (the *egg*) or while in mid-air during a jump.

Turn/turning Any movement in which the skis change direction.

Turning force/turning pressure The centripetal force required to make skis turn. It is generated by pressing against the edged ski or skis to increase snow resistance and at the same time rotating the legs in the direction of the turn.

Turning motion See *rotary motion*.

Turning push-off A powerful *up-extension* together with a strong *rotary motion*. A turning *initiation*.

Turning snowplow A simple turn made while *snowplow* and initiated by *weighting* one ski (the outside steering ski) more than the other. The skis remain in the snowplow or wedge position throughout.

Turntable A particular heel-piece design for an Alpine *safety binding*. It rotates beneath the foot to give a multi-directional sideways release.

Twisting aerial Any *freestyle* jump involving a spin while in mid-air. Also called "rotational" jumps.

Two-phase initiation See *indirect initiation*.

U

Unweighting The process by which a skier momentarily reduces the pressure that his body weight exerts on his skis. Unweighting reduces the friction between the skis and the snow, and therefore makes turns easier to initiate. It is done either by a rapid *up-extension* or *down-flexion* (active unweighting) or by using natural bumps in the terrain (passive unweighting).

Up-extension Rising up into a high stance by stretching the hips, knees and ankles.

Up-extension unweighting Momentarily removing the pressure from the skis by rapidly extending the hips, knees and ankles. This form of unweighting may be made with a strong push-off from the feet in order to "jump" the skis off the snow.

Uphill turning Making a turn away from the *fall line* – i.e., decreasing the angle of descent.

Up-initiation Initiating a turn by using *up-extension unweighting*.

Upright aerial Any *freestyle* jump in which the skier remains in an upright stance while in mid-air.

V

Vasaloppet The first ski *marathon*. Now held every year, the original race took place in 1922 between Sälen and Mora in Sweden. It was held to commemorate the arrival at Mora in 1520 of the popular leader, Gustav Vasa, and his followers, who were to drive the Danes out of Sweden. It is 85km (53 miles) long.

Vorfahrer/Vorläufer See *forerunners*.

Waist The central section of the ski, where the binding is situated. It is the narrowest but thickest part.

Waltzing A freestyle *ballet* movement in which the skier "spins" around on the snow in a full circle. It is either made on both skis or on just one.

Wand The name used for the arm of a *wishbone* starting gate.

Wax A substance applied to the base of a ski. Wax may be hard or soft, and may be designed to help the ski either "grip" or "glide". Most often used in *cross-country* skiing (both grip and glide) and in Alpine competition skiing (glide only).

Wedel/wedeln Rapid, rhythmic *short swinging* in the fall line with minimum *edge-setting* and minimum *diagonal ski placing*.

Wedge An alternative name for the *snowplow* ski position. A term also used for the wedge-shaped plates used when *canting* boots and bindings.

Weighting The action by which a skier's body weight exerts "pressure" through his skis and onto the snow. Weighting may act chiefly on the front or back of a ski, and either on one or on both skis. See also *unweighting*.

Weight-transfer Shifting body weight or "pressure" from one ski to the other. See *stepping*.

Wellen A German word used for the technique of flexing and extending the legs to absorb bumps and dips or to initiate turns (*absorption-extension*). In France, it is called *avalement*.

White-out Low cloud or fog on the mountain which reduces visibility to nil.

Windblown snow Snow that has been blown into uneven waves by the wind – often with a hard *crust* on the surface. Sometimes called "windslab".

Wind-chill factor The reduction in real temperature by the action of the wind. The stronger the wind, the lower the effective air-temperature.

Windslab See *windblown snow*.

Wishbone The device which forms the starting gate for Alpine ski racing. Kicking aside a horizontal, hinged arm or "wand" at the top of the course triggers the electronic clock.

Wolkenmeer A layer of clouds trapped in the bottom of a valley – caused by temperature inversion. Also called a "cloud ocean" or "Nebelmeer".

XC An abbreviation of *cross-country skiing*.

Z

Zdarsky, Mathias Often considered to be the father of *Alpine skiing*, Zdarsky, in 1896, established the first ever ski school at Lilienfeld, near Vienna. He taught an adapted form of the Nordic *Telemark* turn and invented the ski techniques now known as the *turning snowplow* and *stem turning*.

Index

A

Abetone 294

Absorption-extension
turning 120-29
basic technique 121
in deep powder 227
on moguls 122, 230-33
on slope edges 123
types 120
see also Jet turning,
Kangarooo turning

Accelerated Teaching
Method (A.T.M.) 226

Accidents 248, 249
insurance 284

Acrobatic skiing *see*
Freestyle skiing

Adelboden 287

Aerials 6, 164, 165, 174-7

Afterbody (of ski) 22

Albertelli, Pietro 158

Allais, Emile 13

Allalinhorn 245

Alpbach 290

Alpe d'Huez 293

Alpes Maritimes, Italy 294

Alpes du Nord, France 292

Alpes du Sud, France 292

Alpine ski touring, 8, 236,
241-5
equipment 243
Haute Route 244-5
safety 242

Alps, Australia 304

Alps, Austria 289

Alps, France 292, 293

Alps, Italy 294-5

Alps, Switzerland 286-8

Alta, Utah 302

Altenmark 291

Altitude 218, 281, 283

Altitude sickness 283

American Rockies 300, 302

Amman, Hans 6

Amosova, Zinaida 200

Andermatt 288

Andorra 295

Angled position 179

Angulation 44, 73, 186

Anticipation 38, 103, 183

Anti-friction pad 32, 34

Anzère 287

Appalachians 300

Appennine mountains 294

Aprica 294

Are 297

Argentière 244

Argentina, skiing in 305

Arlberg 13, 281, 289, 290

Arlberg–Kandahar race 144

Arosa 288

Artificial ski slopes 268-71

Artificial snow 214

Aspen, Colorado 302

Australia, skiing and ski
resorts 304

Austria, skiing and ski
resorts 289-91

Avalanches 246-8

Avalanche cord 248

Avalement 120

Aviemore ski area 296

Avoriaz 293

Ax-les-Thermes 293

B

Back somersault 174, 175

Backpacks 21

Backscratcher 176

Backward side-slipping 80,
182

Badgastein 281, 289, 291

Bad Goisern 291

Bad Hofgastein 291

Bad Kleinkirchheim 291

Bags 21

Ballet skiing 164, 165, 166-9

"Banana" position 73

Banff ski area 301

Banking 186

Baqueira-Beret 295

Barèges 293

Base wax 193

Bavaria, skiing and ski
resorts 298

Beatenberg 287

Bergen 298

Bernese Oberland 287

Bernina mountains 241

Biathlon 207, 209

Bierch, General 8

Big White Ski Village 301

Big Sky, Montana 302

Bilgeri, Georg 13

Bindings
Alpine 32-5
adjusting 34
choosing 34
"elasticity" 32
how they work 32
mounting on ski 34
testing 35
types 33
Alpine ski touring 243
cross-country 190-91

Black Forest 298

Blanc, Robert 266

"Bleeper" 242, 247, 248

Bogenlaufen 202

Bogentreten 202

Boots
Alpine 16, 17, 28-31, 269,
272
buckles 29,
choosing 30
getting used to 43
putting on 30-31
types 29
Alpine ski touring 243
cross-country 190-91

Bormio 294

Braking snowplow 66-7

Brand 290

Braunwald 288

Breckenridge, Colorado 302

Breuil-Cervinia 295

British Association of Ski
Instructors (B.A.S.I.) 296

Bugaboo mountains 301

Bulgaria, skiing in 298

Bumps and dips technique
Alpine 62-3, 180, 230-33
cross-country 202-3
freestyle 164, 170-73

Button lift 253

C

Cable binding 160, 190

Cable car 250, 251

Cairngorms 296

Camber 22, 187, 192

Canada, skiing and ski
resorts 300-301

Canadian Rockies 300-301

Canazei 294

Candanchú 295

Canting 31

Cariboo mountains 301

Carving 187

Catching an edge 81

Caulfield, Vivian 13

Cauterets 293

Center of gravity 178, 179,
180

Centrifugal force 180, 181,
186

Centripetal force 180, 181,
182, 186

Cerler 295

Cervinia 159

Chair lifts 250, 251, 256-7,
270

Chamonix 244, 281, 292,
293

Champéry 287

Charlotte's Pass 304

Chateaux d'Oex 287

Chiesa 294

Children 65, 259-60, 261,
262-5
compared to racers 264-5

Chile, skiing in 305

Chinook 209

Chouoh 299

Citizen racing *see* Marathon
racing

Classes *see* Instruction

Climbing techniques
Alpine
herringbone 54, 56-7
side-stepping 54, 55-6
walking uphill 54
Alpine ski touring 242
cross-country
herringbone 196, 197
side-stepping 197
walking uphill 196

Closed gate 148, 149

Clothing
Alpine 16-17, 18-21, 269
downhill racing 156
cross-country 190

Cloud ocean 219

Code of conduct 215

Coire Cas 296

Coire na Ciste 296

Colfosco 294

"Comma" position 73

*Committee Internationale de
Sports Militaires* 206

Compact skis 23, 24

Competition skiing
Alpine 8, 144-59
skis 23, 24
stepping techniques
142-3, 152-5
see also Downhill racing,
Giant slalom, Special
slalom

cross-country 188-202, 206-9
ski jumping 160-63
Competition stepping 142-3, 152
Compression 63, 159
Compression turning 120
Converging position 179
Copper Mountain, Colorado 302
Corcoran, Tom 164
Corn snow 220, 228
Coronet Peak 305
Cortina d'Ampezzo 294
Corvara 294
Counter-rotation 70-71, 103, 183
Couple 178, 181, 187
Courchevel 292, 293
Courmayeur 295
Crans 287
Critical point 161
Cross-country skiing 6, 8, 188-209
  equipment 188, 190-93
  racing 8-10, 188-9, 198-202
  Scandinavia 188-9, 204-5, 297
  techniques 194-201
  trails and touring 10, 188-9, 204-5
Crossover 168
Crust 220
Curran, Jim 250
Czechoslovakia, skiing in 298

D

Dachstein mountains 291
Daffy 168, 176
Davos 280, 281, 288
Day ski areas 300, 304
Deep snow 224-7
  jet turning 127
  jump turning 130-31
  skiing in 226-7
  stem turning 98
Delta 269
Dendix 268, 269
Descent routes 212-13, 236
Diagonal side-slipping 80, 182
Diagonal side-stepping 56
Diagonal stride see Gliding step
Direction of slopes 216-17, 219, 283
Direct parallel teaching 266

Diverging position 179
Dolomites, Italy 294
Dorfgastein 291
Dotta, Giocondo 8
Double camber 192
Double-pole push
  Alpine 49, 95
  cross-country 197, 201
Down-flexion 108, 120, 153, 185
Downhill racing 8, 9, 144, 156-9
  equipment 156
  F.I.S. regulations 8, 157
  homologation 157
Downhill stem 99
Downhill turning 37
Drag lifts 250-55
DriSno 269
Dry ski slopes 268-71
Dual slalom 149

E

Eastern Europe, skiing and ski resorts 298
Eberle, Ingrid 146
Edges 22, 23, 25, 179
Edge control 44, 45, 77, 179
Edge-set
  and parallel turning 111
  and short swinging 116
"Elasticity" (of bindings) 32
El Formigal 295
Emahusen Captain J.H. 8
End phase (in turning) 38, 181
Engadin ski marathon 207
Engelberg 216-17, 287
Epple, Maria 150
Equipment
  Alpine 16-35
    downhill racing 156
    dry slope 269
    hiring 17
  Alpine ski touring 243
  cross-country 188, 190-93
Erikson, Stein 164
European Cup 144
Exercises 274-9
  all-purpose 275
  special skiing 276-7
  warming up 278-9

F

Fall line 37, 39
  skiing down (schussing) 60-63, 179, 261
  turning into 61
Falls 50-51
  getting up 52-3
Falls Creek 304
Fanny pack 21
Fan method 102, 107
Fédération Internationale de Ski (F.I.S.) 8, 144
  Alpine skiing
    code of conduct 215
    downhill regulations 8, 157
    ski jumping regulations 160
    slalom regulations 8, 149
  cross-country skiing 206-7
Feldberg 298
Filing (of edges) 25
Filzmoos 291
Finkenburg 290
Finlandia ski race 207, 209'
Finnish step 200
Firn blade 243
First aid 249
Fitness 274-7
Flachau 291
Flaine 293
Flims 288
Flying kilometre 159, 305
"Flying" step turning 141
Foam-core skis 23
Fog 219
Föhn 219
Foot turn 267
Foppollo 294
Forebody (of ski) 22
Forerunner 149
Forces see Mechanics of skiing
Forces parallelogram 178
Forward crossover 168
Forward momentum 179, 180
Forward side-slipping 80, 182
France, skiing and ski resorts 292-3
Freestyle skiing 164-77
  aerial 164, 165, 174-7
  ballet 164, 165, 166-9
  mogul 164, 170-73
Frommelt, Paul 146
Front somersault 164-5
Frostbite 249
Funicular 250, 251

Funnels 234-5
Furrer, Art 164
Furrer, Otto 8

G

Gaiters 20
Galtür 290
Gargellen 290
Garhammer, Heinz 164
Garmisch Partenkirchen 298
Gaschurn 290
Gastein Valley ski area 291
Gates 148-9, 152
Gazetteer 285-305
Geilo 297
Gelende 299
Getting up from a fall 52-3
Giant slalom
  courses 148, 149
  F.I.S. regulations 149
  racing 144, 148-51
  techniques 142, 152, 153
Glencoe 296
Glenshee 296
Glide wax 193
Gliding snowplow 67
Gliding step 194-5, 196, 198-200, 202-3
Gloves 20
Goellner, Hermann 164
Goggles 21
Gondola 250, 251
Grächen 287
Gradients, measurement of 222
Grading
  of ski school classes 259
  of trails 213
Graduated length method (G.L.M.) 266-7
Grainau 298
Grand Combin 244
Grande Traversée 205
Grass skiing 272
Gravity 178, 179
Great Britain, skiing and ski resorts 296
Greece, skiing in 298
Grindelwald 144, 287
Grip wax 193
Grouse Mountain 301
Grueneberg, Pierre 266
Gstaad 287
Gulmarg 285
Gunbarrels 234-5
Guthega 304

H

Haas, Christl 144
Half plow 68, 75
Hämeenlinna 209
Happo One 299
Hardpack 228
Harscheisen 243
Hats 20
Haute Route 244-5
Head-to-head slalom 149
Heavenly Valley,
    Nevada 302
Heel (of ski) 22
Heel-and-toe binding 32, 33
Helicopter (freestyle
    aerial) 177
Helicopter skiing 238, 300,
    302
    areas 301
    Canadian Rockies 301
    New Zealand 305
Herringbone technique
    Alpine 54, 56-7
    cross-country 196, 197
Herringbone turning 57
Hip turn 267
Hochgurgl 290
Holidays *see* Vacations
Homenkollen 9
Homologation 157
Høting ski 6
Hovden 297
How to Ski (Caulfield) 13
Humidity 218, 219, 220
Hungary, skiing in 298
Hunter Mountain Ski Bowl,
    New York 300
Hypothermia 249

I

Igls 290
Inertia 178, 180, 181
Initiation phase (in
    turning) 38, 181, 182-5
Inner boot 28
Inner sole 31
Inside-ski turning 166, 169
Instruction 10, 13, 15, 36-7,
    258-67
    adults 261, 263
    children 259, 261, 262-5
    classes 259, 260
    dry slope 270, 271
    methodology 13, 15, 37
    private tuition 260
    short-ski methods 266-7
    ski schools 259-60, 261
    terminology 13, 15, 38
Insurance 284
International Freestyle Skiers
    Association (I.F.S.A.) 164
International Ski Instructors
    Association (I.S.I.A.) 15,
    258
Interski 37
Iselin, Christoph 8
Isola 2000 281, 293
Italy, skiing and ski resorts
    294-5

J

Jackets 20, 21
Japan, skiing and ski
    resorts 299
Jasper, Marmot Basin 301
J-bar lift 250
Jet movement 124, 128,
    143, 152, 153
Jet turning 120, 124-7, 172
    basic technique 124-5
    in deep snow 126-7
    basic technique 124-5
    racing 8, 152, 153
Jump construction 160, 161,
    177
Jumping
    pre- 135, 158
    terrain 132-5
    when turning 130-31,
    182
    see also Aerials, Ski
    jumping
Jump turning 130-31
Jungfrau ski area 287

K

Kaiser, Kurt 272
Kandahar 8, 144
Kangaroo turning 120,
    128-9
Keystone, Colorado 302
Kiandra 8, 304
Kicker
    freestyle ski jump 177
    part of ski 192, 193
Kick turning 58-9
    freestyle 168
Killington, Vermont 300
Killy, Jean-Claude 8
Kilometro Lanciato (K.L.) 159
Kilpisjärvi 189
Kinetic energy 182
Kirkwood, California 302
Kitzbühel 290
Klammer, Franz 158
Kleine Schiedegg 287
Klister 193
Klosters 288
Knee turn 267
Konigsee 298
Konstam, Erich 250
Kranjskagora 298
Kristiansand 8
Kusatsu Onsen 299

L

Laax 288
La Clusaz 293
La Gourette 293
Lahti 161, 209
Lake Louise 301
Lake Placid, New York 9,
    214, 300
Lake Tahoe ski area 301
Laminated skis 23
La Molina 295
La Mongie 293
Langlauf 6, 9, 188, 194,
    198-203, 206-9
    see also Cross-country
    skiing
La Pierre St Martin 293
La Plagne 281
La Porte 300
La Tuca 295
Lauberhorn (downhill
    course) 157
Laurentians 300
Lech 281, 289, 290

Lecht 296
Lenk 287
Lenzerheide 288
Les Angles 293
Les Arcs 266, 293
Les Quatres Vallées 286
Les Trois Vallées 292, 293
Lifts 250-57, 270, 272
    tickets and passes 250
Lilienfeld Skiing Technique
    (Zdarsky) 10, 13
Lillehammer 297
"Line" (when turning) 152,
    233
Livigno 294
L.L.L. (*Langläufers Live
    Longer*) movement 6
Local freezing 249
Loose snow avalanche 246
Lowlanders 8, 144, 270
Lundbäck, Sven-Ake 209
Lunn, Sir Arnold 8, 144, 286,
    296

M

Macunaga 295
Mahre, Phil 8, 152, 155, 265
Marathon racing 207, 209
Marchelli, Carla 144
Marcia Lunga 207
Marmolada 144
Masella 295
"Mashed potato" 220
Mayrhofen 290
McKinney, Steve 158
Mechanics of skiing 178-87
    schussing 179
    side-slipping 180
    skiing bumps and
    dips 180
    snowplowing 179
    traversing 180
    turning 182-7
Meribel 292, 293
Mid-length skis 23, 24
"Mini" skis 266-7
Mist 219
Mittermaier, Evi 158
Moebius flip 164
Mogul skiing 130-33
    jumping 132-5, 172, 173
    choosing "line" 233
    turning 122, 231
    see also Freestyle skiing
Mogulslope machine 271
Mogulsno 271
Mohair strips 192
Monashee mountains 301

Montana 8, 287
Monte Bondone 294
Monte Rosa 244, 245
Mont Tremblant,
   Quebec 300
Mora 207
Moser-Proell, Annemarie 9
Mountain railway 250, 251
Mount Buffalo 304
Mount Buller 304
Mount Cook National
   Park 305
Mount Hutt 305
Mount Kosciusko 304
Mount Olympus 298
Mount Parnassus 298
Mount Ruapehu 305
Mount Snow, Vermont 300
Mule kick 173
Müller, Peter 157
Mürren 8, 207

N

Naeba 299
Nansen, Fridtjof 8, 10
Nebelmeer 219
Neuhaus 298
New Possibilities in Skiing
   (Reuel) 164, 166
New Zealand, skiing and ski
   resorts 305
Non-wax skis 192
Norcic, Bogdan 160
Nordic Combined
   event 160, 207
Nordic skiing see
   Cross-country skiing
Nordic norm 190
Norefjell 297
Norheim, Søndre 9
Normal force 179, 180
Norm point 160, 161
North America, skiing and ski
   resorts 300-302
North-facing slopes 217,
   219, 229
Norway, skiing and ski
   resorts 6, 8-10, 144, 188,
   197
Nursery slope 263
Nursery slope lifts 252

O

Oberammergau 298
Obergurgl 290
Oetzal Rundtour 241
Off-trail skiing 223, 236-8
   see also Alpine ski touring
OK technique see
   Absorption-extension
   turning
Olympics see Winter
   Olympics
Open gate 148, 149
One-ski turning 169
One-step 201
Opposing force 178, 181
Outer boot 28
Outrigger 169
Outside-ski turning 169
Overturning 71, 89

P

Package holidays 280, 282,
   283
Pair-jumping 174
Panorama Village 301
Panticosa 295
Parallel slalom 149
Parallel turning 100-111,
   261
   closed 102, 104, 109
   mechanics 178, 181, 183,
      184-5
   open 100, 104-9
   types 104
   unweighting 184-5
   uphill 100-103
   with "down" 108
   with "edge-set" 111
   with "up" 105-7
   with "tail-hopping" 110
Parallel turning forces 178,
   181, 182, 187
Park City, Utah 302
Pas de la Casa 295
Patrol racing 206
Paulcke, Wilhelm 8
Perisher Valley ski area 304
Pfeiffer, Doug 164, 166
Pfeiffer, Karl 266
Pigne d'Arolla 244, 245
Pila 295
Pirouette 168
Pistes see Trails
Pittendrigh, Andy 209
Pivoting (of skis) 122, 185,
   231

Planica 298
Plateau Rosa 159
Plate binding 33
Plow see Snowplow
Poland, skiing in 298
Poles
   Alpine 16, 17, 27
      choosing 27
      grip 42
      planting 87, 185
   Alpine ski touring 243
   cross-country 192
      grip 195
Pomagalski 250
Poma lift 250, 252
Pontresina 288
Pony lift 252
Portillo 305
"Porridge" 220
Porte Puymorens 293
Porter Heights 305
Portillo 305
Powder snow 220-21, 224-7,
   236
   parallel turning 110, 226
   short swinging 119, 227
   stance 227
Powder snow
   avalanche 246
Prager, Walter 8
Preparation phase (in
   turning) 38, 181, 184-5
Pre-jumping 135, 158
Pre-rotation 103, 124, 183
Pre-turning 97, 182
Probing 248
Projection circulaire 183
Puchtler, Martin 266
Pulki 205
Punta Arenas 305
Purpose-built resorts 281,
   292, 300
Pyrenees, France 293
Pyrenees, Spain 295

R

Racing
   Alpine 8, 144-59
      downhill 144, 156-9
      giant slalom 144,
         148-53
      special slalom 144-5,
         146-9, 152-5
      style 264-5
   cross-country 8-10,
      188-9, 198-207
      biathlon 207, 209
      F.I.S. regulations 206-7
      individual 207, 209
      marathon 207, 209
      Nordic Combined 160,
         207
      relays 10-11, 207
   see also Competition
      skiing
Racing norm 190
Radstadt 291
Ratrac 214
Read, Ken 156
Rear-entry boots 29
Release-load settings 34
Resolution of forces 178
Resorts 281-3
   see also Gazetteer
Reuel, Dr Fritz 164, 166
Reverse camber 187
Reverse kick turning 168
Reverse 360° crossover 166
Rickmers, Willi 13
Roberts of Kandahar 8
Rockies
   American 300, 302
   Canadian 300, 301
Roll 169
Rope tow 250
Rotary motion 183
Royal christie 164, 166, 169
Ruiz 305
Running groove 22
Running wax 193

S

Saas Fee 224, 245, 287
Safety
   accidents 249
   avalanches 248
   first aid 249
   off-trail and touring 236,
      242
   on-trail 215, 234
Safety bindings see bindings
Safety straps 26, 25, 40
St Anton 13, 144, 280, 289, 290

St Gallenkirchen 290
St Johann in Tirol 290
St Johann ski area 288
St Moritz 281, 288
Sälen 207
Salt Lake City ski area 302
San Carlos di Bariloche 305
Sansicario 295
Santa Christina di Val
   Gardena 294
Säntis 250
Sapporo ski area 299
Sauze d'Oulx 295
Scandinavia, skiing and ski
   resorts 6, 8, 9, 188, 189,
   204-5, 297
Schneider, Hannes, 13, 280,
   289
Schöbiel glacier 245
School of Exotic Skiing 166
Schussing 60-63, 179, 261
Scissoring 181
Scissor position 179
Scotland, skiing and ski
   resorts 296
Seasons 218, 282, 283
Sedrun 288
Seefeld 290
Seelos, Anton 8, 13
Selva di Val Gardena 294
Sestrière 281, 294
Shawbridge 250
Short-ski teaching
   methods 266-7
Short swinging 112, 119
   basic technique 114-115
   in deep snow 227
   with "edge-set" 116
   "flying" steps 141
   mechanics 183
   in powder snow 119, 227
   on steep slopes 234-5
   wedeln 117, 183
Shoulder (of ski) 22
Shovel 22
Side-camber 22
Side-cut 22, 187, 192
Side-slipping 76-81, 180,
   182
   basic technique 77
   diagonal 80
   mechanics 180, 182
Side-stepping
   Alpine 54-6
      diagonal 54, 56
   cross-country 197
Sierra Nevada 295, 300, 302
Silvaplana 288
Silvretta Nova ski area 290
Single-pole slalom 149
Ski Alpinism see Alpine ski
   touring

Ski brakes 26, 35, 40
Skidding 187
Ski évolutif 266-7
Ski flying 10, 160-61
Skiing, history of 5-13, 144,
   188
Ski instruction see Instruction
Ski Interterm 36, 37
Ski jumping 9-10, 160-63,
   207
   F.I.S. regulations 160
   hills 161
   see also Aerials, Jumping
Ski mountaineering see
   Alpine ski touring
Skins 242, 243, 244
Ski patrol 214, 247
"Ski road" 235
Skis
   Alpine 16-17, 22-7, 266
      carrying 26
      choosing 24
      construction 23, 187
      design 187
      maintenance 25
      putting on 40-41
      short or "mini" 266-7
      taking off 41
      turn mechanics 187
      types 23-4
   cross-country 192-3
      choosing 192
      waxes 193
   grass 272
Ski pants 18, 19
Ski poles see Poles
Ski position 179
Ski schools 10, 13, 158-60
   see also Instruction
Ski straps 26
Ski suit 18, 19
Ski touring 6, 188, 189, 194
Slab avalanche 246
Slalom racing 8, 142-3,
   144-5, 146-55
   on grass skis 272
   see also Giant slalom,
      Special slalom
Slope edges 62-3, 123
   132-5
Smiggins Holes 304
Snow
   and avalanches 246
   artificial 214
   conditions 218-24
   formation of 218, 220
   at resorts 283
   types 220-29
   and waxing 193
   see also Deep snow, Powder
      snow, Spring snow, Corn
      snow
Snowbird, Utah 302
Snow contact stunts 169
Snowplow 64-71, 262-3
   mechanics 179

Snowplow turning
   Alpine 82-9, 182, 186
      advanced 88-9
      elementary 84-5
      intermediate 86-7
   cross-country 202
Snowslope 268
Snowy mountains,
   Australia 304
Socks 20
Söldern 291
Soldeu 295
Sol y Nieve 295
Somersaults 169
South America, skiing in 305
Southampton 268
Southern Alps, New
   Zealand 305
South-facing slopes 217,
   219, 229
Space walk 176
Spain, skiing and ski
   resorts 295
Special slalom
   courses 148, 149
   F.I.S. regulations 149
   racing 144, 146-7
   techniques 143, 152,
      154-5
Sport skis 23, 24
Spread eagle 175, 176
Spring snow 220, 223, 228-9
Sprint racing 207, 209
Squaw Valley, California 302
Stance
   in deep snow 227
   on the flat 42
   in the gliding step 199
   in a schuss 60
   on a slope 44-5
   in a traverse 73
Star turning 46-7
Starting gate 150, 152
Steamboat Springs,
   Colorado 302
Steep slope techniques
   parallel turning 109
   schussing 62-3
   short swinging 234-5
   stem turning 99
   traversing 74
Steering phase (in turning)
   38, 181, 186-7
Stem turning 96-9, 186
Stenmark, Ingemar 8, 146,
   150, 152-4, 265
Step-in binding see
   Heel-and-toe binding
Stepover see Crossover
Stepping
   techniques 136-43, 152-5
   competition stepping
      142-3, 152
   "flying" step turning 141
   and giant slalom 142, 153

and special slalom 143,
   154-5
stepping against the uphill
   ski 136, 139-41, 182
stepping onto the uphill
   ski 136, 137-8, 183
stepping onto/against the
   uphill ski 142, 154-5
Step turning
   Alpine 94-5
   cross-country 202-3
Stoos 288
Stop swinging 103
Stowe, Vermont 300
Stubai 241
Stuben 289, 290
Sugar Bowl, California 302
Sugarloaf, Maine 300
Sunglasses 21
Superbagnères 293
Sunshine Village 301
Sun Valley, Idaho 232, 250,
   281, 300, 302
Sweden, skiing and ski
   resorts 6, 297
Swinging step 200
Swiss Ski School 13, 36, 258
Switzerland, skiing and ski
   resorts 286-8

T

Table point 160, 161
Tail (of ski) 22
Tail-hopping 110, 115
Taos 300
Tasman glacier 305
Taylor, Clif 266
T-bar lift 250-51, 254-5
Teaching see Instruction
Tekapo 305
Telecabine 250, 251
Telemark 297
   stance 160, 161
   turn 10, 202, 297
Terminology (of ski
   techniques) 38
Terrain jumping 132-5
Thredbo 304
Thyon 2000 286
Tignes 292, 293
Tip drag 166, 168
Tip roll 168
Tirol 289, 290
Torsion box skis 23
Tourmalet 293
Touring
   cross-country 188-9,
      204-5
   see also Alpine ski touring

Tour Soleil 241

Trail cord 248

Trail-maintenance
machine 214

Trails
Alpine 212-16
cross-country 188-9,
204-5
difficulties on 234-5
grading 213
maintenance 214
maps 216
markers 213
safety 215, 222-3
see also Off-trail skiing

Travel to ski resorts 284
see also Vacations

Traversing 72-5, 261
and avalanche
hazard 248
basic technique 72
mechanics 180
and stepping uphill 75
and stopping 75

Treeline 218

Treble Cone 305

Triple striding 200

Tromsø 8

Tschagguns 290

"Tuck" position 133
see also Egg position

Turning
Alpine
absorption-extension
120-29
basic 37
bending 120-29
in deep snow 226-7
downhill 37
on the flat 46-7
herringbone 57
initiations 182-5
jet 120, 124-7, 172
jump 130-31
kangaroo 120, 128-9
kick 58-9
mechanics 181, 182-7
moguls 231
on one ski 169
parallel 100-111, 183,
184-5, 261
in powder snow 226-7
short-ski 267
short swinging 112-19
side-slipping 79
on a slope 57, 58-9
snowplow 82-9, 186
star 46-7
steering 186-7
stem 96-7, 186
stepping techniques
136-43, 152-5
step turning 94-5
turning snowplow
68-70, 182
uphill 37, 79, 100-103
cross-country 202-3
snowplow 202
step turning 202-3

Turning snowplow 68-70,
182, 186

Turntable binding 33

U

Unterwasser 288

Unweighting 39, 106, 184-5

Up-extension 105, 106, 107,
184

Uphill turning 37, 79

V

Vacations 280-84
accommodation 282
altitude 283
gazetteer 285-305
insurance 284-5
snow conditions 283
travel 284
resorts 281-3

Vail, Colorado 302

Valais 287

Val d'Aosta 294

Val d'Isère 292, 293

Vallée Blance 295

Val Thorens 292, 293

Vasaloppet 207

Verbier 15, 286

Villars 287

von Lech, Theodore 299

Vorarlberg province 290

Vorfahrer see Forerunner

Voss 297

W

Wagrain 291

Waist (of ski) 22

Walking on skis
Alpine 48-9
uphill 54-7
cross-country 194-5
uphill 196

Waltzing 168

Warming-up
exercises 287-9

Waterville Valley,
Vermont 164

Waxing 25, 193

Weather conditions 218-19,
222-3
and avalanches 246

Wedeln 117, 183

Wedge *see* Snowplow

Wedging 31

Weight-transfer *see* Stepping
techniques

Wengen 157, 287

West Germany, skiing and ski
resorts 298

Whistler Mountain 301

White-out 218, 219

Wilhaus 288

Wiler 287

Wind 219

Windblown snow 220, 221

Windischgarsten 291

Windscreen wiper 173

Winter Olympics 8, 144, 207,
292

Winter sports 280

Wishbone gate 150, 152

Women skiers 65, 261

Wong, Wayne 164, 169

Wongbanger 164, 169

Wolkenmeer 219

World Cup 144

World Ski Championships
144, 207

Y

Yugoslavia, skiing in 299

Z

Zao 299

Zdarsky, Mathias 10

Zell-am-Ziller 290

Zermatt 159, 241, 251, 287

Ziller Valley ski area 290

Zogg, David 8

Zürs 290

Acknowledgments

This book is the result of teamwork. Consequently, I would like to thank the staff of Dorling Kindersley for the help they have given me in its production. In particular, I must express my gratitude to Alan Buckingham who organized the project and, with the help of Jemima Dunne, edited the text, to Denise Brown who designed the book and, with the help of Nick Harris, worked out the many drawings and diagrams, and to Brigitta Haidinger for her research and for her work on the translation.

My special thanks also go to the following: my wife, Alice, and my daughter, Heidi; Walter Stucky and Manfred Russi; the Swiss Ski School Association for giving me the opportunity and for allowing me the time to write this book; and all my colleagues and friends thoughout the world of skiing.

Karl Gamma

Dorling Kindersley would like to thank the following people for their assistance in the production of **The Handbook of Skiing:**

Walter Stucky and Manfred Russi, the two members of the Swiss Ski School demonstration team who patiently and expertly executed hundreds of ski techniques in front of our cameras

Alice and Heidi Gamma for also demonstrating ski techniques and for helping to improve our own skiing

Chris Meehan, David Brown, and Albert Jackson for their design assistance

Simon McCartney and the staff of Alpine Sports Ltd who gave us their technical advice and who very kindly lent us equipment

David and Tessa Brooksbank of Canadian Mountain Holidays for allowing us to use some of their excellent "heli-skiing" photographs

Mr P.A. Judd of Dendix Ski Slopes

Diana Hughes of the Ski Club of Great Britain

The National Ski Federation of Great Britain

Mark Amis

Reg Icke and the staff of Reprocolor Llovet

Mel Hobbs and the staff of Text Filmsetters Ltd

Photography
Over 5,000 photographs were taken specially for this book and were used as reference for the many illustrations of ski technique. A large number of these photographs also appear in the book to supplement the drawings. With the exception of the following, they were all taken by Debbie Mackinnon in Andermatt and Airolo, Switzerland.

Key t=top, c=centre, b=bottom, l=left, r=right

All-sport 146b, 147, 151, 158, 159
Aspect 126, 150b, 196, 204b, 232
Austrian National Tourist Office 281c, 289, 290, 291
Brügger AG, Meiringen 216-17
Canadian Mountain Holidays 4, 6-7, 225, 237, 238, 239, 301, 302
J. Allan Cash 167
Colorsport 146t
Daily Telegraph Colour Library 164-5b, 170-71t
Andrew de Lory 18, 22, 191, 192, 212b, 219, 221br, 275, 276c, 277c, 282, 284l, 294
Finnish Tourist Board 9b, 161, 188, 189t, 197, 205t, b, 206, 207, 209b, 297
French Government Tourist Office 281b, 292
Alice Gamma 15b
Karl Gamma 2-3, 78, 79, 81, 92t, 103, 107, 108, 120br, 128, 129, 131, 149, 153, 154, 155, 183tr, 211, 224b, 229b, 231, 235, 247bl, cr, 265
Len Godfrey/Dendix 268, 270t
Susan Griggs Agency 118, 269, 270b
Image Bank 7tr, 162, 163, 164, 165, 170b, 174, 236b
Japan National Tourist Organization 215, 299
Leo Mason 9t, 10-11, 145, 150t, 189b, 200, 201, 208, 209t
Norwegian Tourist Office 262, 263b
Pictor International 241
Lou-Lou Rendall 273

Danny Rose 195, 204t, 205c, 214, 220t, 251bl, 258, 260
Heini Schneebeli 130, 210, 212t, 220, 224t, 229t, 251tl, br, 283
Scottish Tourist Board 296
Mark Shapiro 10tl, 14, 15t, 221bl, 236t, 240, 280, 284r
Ski Club of Great Britain 144, 264
Spectrum Colour Library 266
Sporting Pictures (UK) Ltd 272
Swiss National Tourist Office (London) 242, 247t, 281t, 286, 287, 288
Swiss National Tourist Office (Zurich) 243, 244, 245
Transworld Feature Syndicate 12, 171r
United Press International 145bl
United States Travel Service 303
Vision International 169, 175
Paul Williams 213t, 251tr, 252, 256, 257, 263t

Main illustrations
Norman Clark
Andrew Farmer
Brian Sayers
Les Smith

Other illustrations
Arka Graphics
David Ashby
Kuo Kang Chen
Dave Etchell
Jeremy Ford
Andrew Popkiewicz
John Ridyard
Jim Robbins

Photographic services
Negs
Ron Bagley

Typesetting
Text Filmsetters Ltd
T.J.B. Photosetters

Reproduction
Reprocolor Llovet, Barcelona, Spain